Capital Gains

HAGLEY PERSPECTIVES ON BUSINESS AND CULTURE

Roger Horowitz, Series Editor

A complete list of books in the series is available from the publisher.

Capital Gains

Business and Politics in Twentieth-Century America

Edited by

Richard R. John and Kim Phillips-Fein

PENN

UNIVERSITY OF PENNSYLVANIA PRESS

PHILADELPHIA

Published by
University of Pennsylvania Press
Philadelphia, Pennsylvania 19104-4112
www.upenn.edu/pennpress

Printed in the United States of America on acid-free paper
10 9 8 7 6 5 4 3 2 1

Library of Congress Cataloging-in-Publication Data
Names: John, Richard R., 1959– editor. | Phillips-Fein, Kim, editor.
Title: Capital gains : business and politics in twentieth-century America / edited by
    Richard R. John and Kim Phillips-Fein.
Other titles: Capital gains (University of Pennsylvania Press) | Hagley perspectives on
    business and culture.
Description: 1st edition. | Philadelphia : University of Pennsylvania Press, [2017] |
    Series: Hagley perspectives | Includes bibliographical references and index.
Identifiers: LCCN 2016026508 | ISBN 9780812248821 (hardcover : alk. paper)
Subjects: LCSH: Business and politics—United States—History—20th century. |
    Industrial policy—United States—History—20th century. | United States—
    Economic policy—History—20th century.
Classification: LCC JK467 .C365 2017 | DDC 322/.309730904—dc23
LC record available at https://lccn.loc.gov/2016026508

Contents

P r e f a c e

Kim Phillips-Fein

In recent years, there has been a remarkable expansion of American historical scholarship on the political engagement, ideologies, and activism of
businesspeople and business organizations. Earlier generations of scholars
explored the politics of working-class people with immense care but left their
business counterparts in the shadows. Now a new literature, one that has
grown in tandem with the developing subfield concerned with the history
of capitalism, considers the various ways that elite economic actors have
sought to exert influence and power over the state.

The essays in this volume embody this new direction. Revisiting longstanding themes and debates about political ideology and the relationship
between business and the state, they have been informed by the idea that
economic life is embedded in political and social relationships. As a result,
they sketch a political tradition in the business world that welcomed certain
kinds of government activity. The businesspeople whose stories are told here
were well aware that government set the terms for the economy, and they
tried to influence and shape the state accordingly, not simply to minimize it.
For much of the twentieth century, many businesspeople and their organizations sought to find ways to actively shape government and expand its
capacities—at the local, state, and federal levels—in ways that they believed
would serve their interests in both the short and the long term.

As Richard R. John suggests in his Introduction, the authors whose work
is collected here build on the insights of both the Progressive school of historical interpretation that thrived in the early years of the twentieth century

and the "corporate liberal" school of the mid-twentieth century. They show how businesspeople might at various points for a range of reasons seek to promote a larger government, while at the same time pressing for the interests of business as a class. These authors are more nuanced in their approach to the politics of business than were the Progressives, but are also more skeptical about the ideological commitments of businesspeople than were the New Left historians of corporate capitalism. They emphasize the role of business in shaping a state devoted to furthering the economic interests and activities of the private sector.

Above all, the scholars whose work is collected here suggest the importance of taking businesspeople seriously as political actors, analyzing the variety of ways that they have sought to shape public life rather than assuming that they automatically wield political power and always do so in the same way. They suggest the difficulties of making generalizations about what businesspeople think, and the coexistence of highly diverse approaches to politics in the business world. They portray businesspeople as possessing a range of political ideas and trying to use their identities as business leaders to advance different political ends. The authors look at struggles inside the business community, and even within organizations, such as the National Association of Manufacturers and the U.S. Chamber of Commerce, which historians have often assumed to speak with a single voice. They suggest the necessity of paying close attention to government at different levels—of looking at local, urban, and state governments alongside the national polity. Finally, they point to the value of looking closely and carefully at what businesspeople actually did, not only at what they said and their explicitly ideological pronouncements. But perhaps most of all, these essays call attention to the unwieldy but often successful efforts of businesspeople to act as a class, and to their various concerted attempts to define and advance their own agendas through political engagement. Even as historians deploy the social history tools developed by specialists in labor, civil rights, and other social movements to study business elites, it is important to remember that the access these elites enjoyed to economic resources and to the halls of political power set them apart from the social movements that often criticized them. Looking at the ways in which businesspeople have mobilized politically, and their attempts to build a state that they could trust and control, helps us to move beyond the partisan rhetoric of electoral politics, and teaches us much about the history of the twentieth century that otherwise remains hard to fully understand.

Adversarial Relations? Business and Politics in Twentieth-Century America

Richard R. John

During the past few years, a growing popular awareness of the large wealth disparity between the many and the few has helped revive enduring questions about the relationship between business and politics in the American past. Some warn that the wealthiest Americans today have more power than ever to rig the game in their favor. Others blame the government for fostering inequality by distorting market forces. Still others deplore the current level of inequality as bad for capitalism. No longer does it seem plausible to echo the hoary platitude that "a rising tide lifts all boats." It is sometimes said that the participants in this debate misunderstand the relationship between capitalism and equality.[1] Yet no thoughtful observer of American public life would deny that the relationship between the business elite and governmental institutions has often been adversarial, and that this relationship can be documented not only in public relations talking points and electioneering sound bites but also in the historical record. Even so, questions remain. How adversarial has this relationship been? Can it be linked to the wider developments in culture, politics, and society? And, if so, how can it best be explained?

This collection of original essays offers a fresh perspective on these and other questions that lie at the intersection of business and politics in twentieth-century America. Just as an earlier generation of historians parsed the politics of working-class people with imagination and insight, so do these historians fix the spotlight on the business leaders who dominated the nation's political economy.

The essays in this collection—all but three of which were first presented at the Hagley Museum and Library, in Wilmington, Delaware, and many of which draw on the Hagley Library's extraordinary archival holdings— explore the engagement of business leaders with governmental institutions from a distinctive angle of vision.[2] In each essay, the relationship of business and politics is a central theme. When our authors refer to business, they are primarily concerned with firms that employ large numbers of people and with business leaders who exert substantial political power. That is, they mostly focus on the business elite. When our authors refer to politics, they are mostly interested in ideology and public policy, which they understand to embrace the enactment and implementation of laws and regulations at all levels of government: federal, state, and municipal. Unlike so much historical writing on recent American history, this collection is sensitive to politics not only in Washington but also in the state house and city hall.

Elections, legislative maneuvering, and campaign finance are, of course, also important to a full understanding of the relationship between business and politics in modern America. Yet they are not a main focus of the essays that follow. Rather, our authors consider some of the more pervasive, though often overlooked, ways in which business leaders—a large and diverse group that includes corporate executives, middle managers, independent proprietors, trade association representatives, and industry lobbyists—have shaped, and have been shaped by, the political-economic rules of the game. Culture matters, but so do institutions—and our authors are mindful not only of the vital, if often elusive, power of ideology and belief, but also of the often hard-edged imperatives of business decisionmaking and political fiat.

The topics that our authors explore build on a venerable tradition of historical writing about business and politics in the American past.[3] More than a century ago, Charles Beard famously proposed, in his *Economic Interpretation of the Constitution* (1913), that powerful seaboard merchants had designed the federal Constitution to limit the influence of popular majorities on economic affairs. Beard's own understanding of the relationship between business and politics is more nuanced than is sometimes assumed. His landmark *Rise of American Civilization* (1927), for example, was suffused with an almost utopian faith in the democratic potential of the modern, high-technology corporation that, at least in his mind, fit comfortably alongside the more mordant critical realism of his *Economic Interpretation*.[4]

Yet it was Beard's people-versus-the-interests dualism, rather than his technological enthusiasm, that would capture the attention of his colleagues in the interwar period. The enormous power wielded by the "captains of industry" was inherently illegitimate, or so Beard's progeny assumed, since it enabled a self-appointed elite to dominate public life in ways that precluded the possibility of a truly democratic politics. The antidemocratic implications of concentrated economic power furnished a leitmotif for Matthew Josephson's *Robber Barons*, a captivating 1934 potboiler written by a popular journalist during the depths of the Great Depression. To document the perversion of democratic politics by the country's late nineteenth-century empire builders, Josephson recycled a half-century of journalistic editorializing that originated not in the rural hinterland, as Josephson disingenuously claimed, but in the big-city press.[5] More muted in tone, yet basically similar in its characterization of the "economic royalists," as Franklin D. Roosevelt termed them, was *The Politics of Upheaval,* an influential overview by the Harvard historian Arthur Schlesinger, Jr., published in 1960, of a critical juncture in the New Deal.[6]

Historians have long faulted Beard, Josephson, and Schlesinger for their almost Manichean, business-versus-democracy essentialism. Yet it should not be forgotten that this genre of historical writing—known today as the "progressive school"—drew its inspiration from a laudable critical realism that in the decades to come would lead a galaxy of talented historians to probe in greater detail—often using archival sources and typically with the benefit of insights derived from social theory—the relationships among politics, democracy, and the business elite.

The progressive historians typically assumed that business leaders were fundamentally opposed to reform, an assumption that was reinforced by their keen awareness of the magnitude of the challenge that Franklin D. Roosevelt's Democratic party confronted in the 1930s, when, in response to the Great Depression, the party backed legislation to create a new kind of "mixed economy" to increase and channel investment, rein in corporate prerogatives, strengthen labor unions, and guarantee prosperity.

The presumption that business and reform were locked in mortal combat would be challenged in the 1950s and 1960s by a constellation of post–New Deal historians that included Lee Benson, Robert H. Wiebe, Gabriel Kolko, James Weinstein, Ellis Hawley, James Livingston, and Martin Sklar.

These historians shared the progressives' fascination with the relationship between business and politics, a commonality that is sometimes overlooked by a later generation of historiographers who drew spurious connections between their rejection of the progressives' people-versus-the-interests duality and the celebration of "consensus" by the cultural historians David Potter and Daniel Boorstin. Unlike Potter and Boorstin, these post–New Deal historians rarely identified themselves as political conservatives: in fact, several would become prominently identified in the 1960s with the antiestablishment New Left. The post–New Deal historians wrote at the high tide of postwar liberalism—an age of wide, though hardly universal, prosperity in which one-third of the nation's labor force paid union dues, and the dominant bloc in each of the major parties endorsed legislation to expand the size and reach of federal power. These historians found it plausible to assume that business leaders might well have supported certain laws and regulations that a former generation would have lauded as "progressive" or "liberal"— making them, in a felicitous catchphrase conventionally attributed to Sklar that would soon do a great deal of historiographical heavy lifting, "corporate liberals."[7]

Historians who specialized in the New Deal and beyond were by no means all of one mind. The presumption that an elite-oriented "corporate liberalism" had successfully stifled dissent troubled historians of labor relations, who could not help but be aware of the continuing opposition toward organized labor in the postwar era of a large and powerful bloc of business leaders. Business opposition to organized labor entered a new phase following the enactment of the Wagner Act (1935), an important New Deal labor law that established a framework for mandatory collective bargaining.[8] Major fissures in the business community were rooted not only or even primarily in party affiliation, but also in regionalism, industry structure, and business strategy. The significance of these fissures remained contested. If, for example, it could be demonstrated that the interests of capital-intensive corporations such as DuPont, General Motors, or AT&T exerted disproportionate political influence, then it might still be plausible to contend that a hegemonic corporate liberalism prevailed.[9] Not everyone, however, was convinced. In the opinion of David Vogel—an influential political scientist who published two landmark studies on the relationship between business and politics in the postwar period—the attitude of business leaders toward the state remained "uneasy," a characterization that he documented by surveying their words and deeds.[10]

Historians who came of age in the 1990s and beyond, or whose assumptions have been shaped by recent events, have also turned their attention to the relationship between business and politics. Troubled by the avowedly anti-regulatory and ostensibly pro-consumerist neoliberal critique of the New Deal, these historians have been impressed by the undeniable power of business leaders in contemporary politics, a predisposition that linked them in spirit, if not in method, to both the corporate liberal historians of the 1960s and the interwar progressives. For these historians, economic inequality is a problem to be explained, and its origins are to be found, in whole or in part, in the baleful and disproportionate influence that the nation's business elite had come to exert in government, journalism, and public life.

Nowhere is this reassessment more evident than in the burgeoning literature on the United States and the world. To consolidate power, improve the terms of trade, and promote economic development—or so these historians contend, building on a long and distinguished tradition of revisionist scholarship in the history of U.S. foreign relations—a coalition of business leaders, diplomats, and lawmakers shaped the relationship of business and politics overseas. Their activities range from William H. Taft's "Dollar Diplomacy" of the 1900s and the creation of the Federal Reserve System in 1913 to the Third World modernization projects of the 1950s, the community development programs of the Kennedy era, and the international supply-chain management strategy of Coca Cola.[11]

The bulk of this still-emerging literature on the relationship of business and politics focuses less on the pre-Second World War era—as had been true, for example, for Wiebe, Hawley, and Sklar—than on the more recent past. In so doing, it often engaged with the ideologically charged critique of the New Deal that has become increasingly influential in American public life since the 1970s. This critique improbably recast the history of American business through a neoliberal lens: It was not until the 1930s, it is worth recalling, that business leaders would launch a publicity campaign to elevate "free enterprise" into a cornerstone of the American political tradition.[12] Prior to this decade, the phrase "free enterprise" had been only sporadically invoked, and almost never with the kind of almost superstitious awe with which it would, at that time, come to be invested. Business leaders had, of course, shaped governmental institutions in many sectors long before the New Deal, as, for example, has been demonstrated in the case of public finance by Stephen Mihm for the nineteenth-century money supply and Julia Ott for the popularization of stock ownership that followed the war-bond campaign of the First World War.[13] Yet the seedbed of neoliberalism would not be laid until the 1930s.

Much of the most thoughtful and ambitious recent literature on the relationship between business and politics in the post–New Deal era echoed, if in new and compelling ways, themes that had earlier been explored by the corporate liberals and the progressives. The launch during the 1930s of a business-led "crusade" to dethrone the New Deal—including, by no means incidentally, its post–Wagner Act administrative protocols—has been probed by David Farber and Kim Phillips-Fein.[14] The influence of a discernibly "corporate liberal" regulatory tradition on the provisioning of health care was canvassed in a similar spirit by Jennifer Klein.[15] The decision of post–Second World War manufacturers to relocate their factories from the industrial heartland in the Northeast to the South and eventually overseas was the result of a sustained effort not only to cut labor costs but also to evade labor unions, in the opinion of Thomas Sugrue, Jefferson Cowie, and Tami J. Friedman.[16] The parallel determination of local boosters to make Phoenix, Arizona, a low-wage, nonunion, business-friendly enclave, was documented by Elizabeth Tandy Shermer.[17] The utter fatuity of early twentieth-century economic forecasting, as well as its dubious political legacy, would find its historian in Walter A. Friedman.[18]

The revival of progressive and corporate-liberal themes and concerns is particularly conspicuous in a shelf of new books on the relationship between business and politics in the 1970s and beyond. The myriad challenges posed by industrial decline would, in the 1970s, spawn a new kind of highly disciplined business lobby, explained Benjamin Waterhouse.[19] The furor of business leaders toward the unprecedented upsurge in environmental regulations in this decade heightened tensions between the federal government and the business elite, concluded Meg Jacobs.[20] The emergence in the 1970s of an anti-regulatory neoliberalism, which would gradually morph from a critique of the New Deal into a totalistic market fundamentalism, would reshape business norms, concluded Kenneth J. Lipartito and his colleagues in an ambitious four-century survey of the history of corporate social responsibility.[21] The adoption of a raft of free-market-oriented political positions—that, as it happens, resonated nicely with the antistatist religious proclivities of its cadre of first-time female workers—would become a central pillar of the business strategy at Walmart, according to Bethany Moreton.[22]

In certain instances, the primary catalyst for neoliberalism originated not in the corporate boardroom but in Congress and the White House. Political choices, rather than market imperatives, best explained the financial deregulation and deindustrialization of the 1970s, according to Greta Krippner and Judith Stein.[23] In the case of consumer credit, the primacy of politics over business could be traced all the way back to the New Deal, in the view of Louis Hyman.[24]

Many of the historians who have considered the rise and fall of postwar liberalism have adopted the lens of political history, a broad and eclectic field that ranges widely from ideology and social movements to legislative behavior and public policy. Much of the best recent work in political history has focused on public policy, which often builds on the burgeoning political science literature known as American Political Development, or APD, a field that stresses the path-dependent trajectory of governmental institutions and civic ideals, a topic of particular relevance to the themes of this book.[25]

Quite different in focus is the rich yet often underappreciated literature on the relationship between business and politics that has been published by specialists in business history. By and large, this literature has contended that this relationship has been shaped less by political ideology than by structural considerations rooted in the interaction of the firm, the industry, and the political economy.

The current upsurge of interest in business history received a major impetus from the publication in 1977 of Alfred D. Chandler, Jr.'s, magisterial *The Visible Hand*. To understand why this one book would prove to be so important for the field, it is useful to provide a brief overview of the field of business history in the preceding fifty years.

Business history—in sharp contrast to political history—would not develop a compelling intellectual agenda until after the Second World War. The self-identity of the field went back to 1927, when Harvard Business School appointed its first professor of business history, the same year Charles Beard published his *Rise of American Civilization*, and fifty years before the publication of Chandler's *Visible Hand*. The early history of the field was closely linked with the professional training of MBAs, and its practitioners were primarily known for their detailed, technically proficient, and rarely controversial primary-source research in business archives. Among the most notable contributions of the early pioneers was their successful campaign to convince business leaders to open their archives for historical research.[26]

Prominent early business historians included New Deal liberals such as Allan Nevins as well as several anti–New Deal conservatives who were highly skeptical of government economic intervention—a consideration that helped keep the latter tightly focused on business decisionmaking and the rise (and, less frequently, the fall) of a firm, industry, or business sector.[27] The books and articles these historians published were richly textured, informative, and well written; many repay careful reading today. Yet they remained very much on the margins of historical inquiry. Little changed until the 1950s, when Chandler began to publish a series of influential articles that combined archival research with insights drawn from social theory. The culmination of this research agenda was *The Visible Hand.*

The explanatory scheme that Chandler laid out in *Visible Hand* grew out of his longstanding frustration with the narrow, uninteresting, and badly posed questions that political historians, journalists, and even specialists in economic history had long asked about businessmen and their world. (The term "businessmen" was apt. The field at this time was almost exclusively focused on men, like much of the rest of the historical profession, even though several influential early business historians were themselves women.[28]) To debate, as historians in the 1940s and 1950s did, whether business leaders had been amoral "robber barons" or visionary "industrial statesmen"—good fellows or bad fellows, as Chandler often put it in conversation—was not only a colossal bore but also a missed opportunity. Did it really matter whether John D. Rockefeller had been a robber baron or an industrial statesman, as the title of a reader aimed at the college history market had asked undergraduates to ponder in 1948?[29] Might he have been neither, or both? And who really cared?

Biographical factors shaped Chandler's outlook as well. Throughout his life, Chandler retained a frank admiration for the innovative potential of large-scale, vertically oriented, manufacturing firms such as the Wilmington, Delaware–based DuPont Chemical Company.[30] Chandler himself was not descended from the du Ponts, his middle name notwithstanding, but he spent part of his childhood in Wilmington, where he met many prominent business leaders, a circumstance that was somewhat unusual for a professional historian and one that prompted in him a strong disinclination to characterize business leaders as either heroes or villains.[31]

For Chandler, innovation and scale were directly related. Like many academics of his generation, and not only in history, but also in institutional economics, he firmly believed that the most disruptive innovations—such as the discovery of a low-cost form of renewable energy that could free the world from fossil fuel—could only originate in large-scale research and development facilities: public, private, or in-between.[32] For Chandler, and for the many historians who followed his lead, whether an organization was public or private mattered less than how it was coordinated, by whom, and toward what end.

Chandlerian business history is sometimes criticized as bloodless and value neutral. Nothing could be further from the truth. Having served as a U.S. Naval officer in the Second World War, Chandler had a profound respect for the enormous organizational capabilities of the country's industrial sector and was firmly convinced that the Nazis would have defeated the Allies had the U.S. military not been able to speedily transform the nation's factories into an "arsenal of democracy." British firms lacked the organizational capabilities of their Nazi counterparts—a recipe for disaster. And a Nazi victory was an outcome from which Chandler, like so many thoughtful and civic-minded men and women of his generation, quite understandably recoiled.[33]

The significance of U.S. military procurement during the Second World War was a theme that Chandler touched on often in his teaching, though only rarely in print. The fullest statement of his position on this topic can be found not in Chandler's own oeuvre, but in a publication by one of his most devoted disciples, Thomas K. McCraw. In his brief, engaging, authoritative, and eminently teachable textbook, *American Business Since 1920: How It Worked*, McCraw devoted half a chapter to the wartime "production miracle." To highlight its significance, McCraw featured on the front cover of its first edition a photograph of the factory floor of a Douglas Aircraft plant in Long Beach, California, that was manufacturing Boeing-designed B-17 bombers for the U.S. military. In the second edition, interestingly, and conceivably in response to a shifting political climate, this photograph had been replaced by a superficially similar, yet, in its ideological import, quite different, image of a factory floor of a Boeing plant that was churning out passenger airplanes.[34]

Like Charles Beard and so many other academics whose mental outlook had been shaped by the optimism of the early twentieth-century progressives, Chandler had a deep and abiding faith in the ability of public administrators and business leaders to work creatively together to promote the

public good. It was in this spirit that he contributed a brief yet incisive essay
to a volume on business and public policy, edited by the labor lawyer and
former labor secretary John T. Dunlop. Why, Chandler asked at the start
of his essay, had government and business so often "appeared as adversaries"? To help frame the question, he quoted a DuPont executive who posed
a question of his own: "Why is it that I and my American colleagues are being constantly taken to court—made to stand trial—for activities that our
counterparts in Britain and other parts of Europe are knighted, given peer-
ages or comparable honors?"[35]

The international comparative lens through which the DuPont executive
viewed the American political economy had much in common with the
intellectual framework that Chandler relied on in *Visible Hand*. *Visible Hand*
was well received in the profession, winning both the Pulitzer and the Ban-
croft prizes. It was and is a theoretically challenging book (though an
absorbing read), which helps explain not only its staying power but also the
presumption that it is less often read than cited. Chandler's theme was not
the role of business in society—nor even the relationship between business
and politics—but rather the evolution of the internal dynamics of the firm.
Chandler's treatment of this topic reached back to the colonial era and forward to the mid-twentieth century. At its core was the arresting contention
that, contrary to what had been a common view, the rise of the large industrial corporation after 1880 was best understood not as a chapter in the
history of economic predation, but instead as the organizational response
to technological imperatives and market incentives of a rising managerial
class.[36]

The emergence in the 1880s of the industrial corporation, in conjunction
with the prior emergence of giant organizations in transportation and communications, was, in Chandler's view, a radically new development with no
real antecedents in the American past. "Big business"—Chandler's conve-
nient and nonthreatening shorthand for these giant organizations—had
become so large so fast that it was hardly surprising that it soon become the
focus of "adversarial" legislation, for example, the Interstate Commerce Act
(1887) and the Sherman Act (1890). Such legislation established an enduring
pattern of challenge and response between "big business" and "big government" that would define the relationship between business and politics in the
United States from the 1880s until the 1970s—if not beyond.[37]

For Chandler and the historians who followed his lead, the sequencing
of the rise of giant organizations in the private and public sector best ex-

plained not only why an adversarial relationship between business and politics emerged in the 1880s but also why it persisted. Only in the United States had big business preceded big government. More than any other single circumstance, this fundamental fact best explained not only why American business executives so often found themselves on trial—or, for that matter, why labor relations would prove so contentious—but also, and more broadly, why the relationship between business and politics in the United States would hereafter remain so much more adversarial than in Europe and Japan.[38]

Chandler's thesis became a cornerstone of the "organizational synthesis" that one-time coauthor Louis Galambos popularized in a series of landmark essays that clarified its implications for political history. If Chandler were right, Galambos contended, then historians have exaggerated the centrality of political ideology in general—and liberalism in particular—as a catalyst for change. Modern America, Galambos famously declared, has embarked on a rendezvous not with liberalism, but with bureaucracy.[39]

Building on Chandler and Galambos, a cohort of historians published richly detailed and analytically sophisticated monographs with titles that often included the words "regulation," "regulating," or "business-government relations." The priority that these titles gave to "business" in "business-government" relations was revealing: Business led, politics (or, more precisely, government) followed, and electoral outcomes (whether liberal or conservative, Democratic or Republican) rarely had more than a marginal influence on the rules of the game.[40] Even in civil rights—or so contended Jennifer Delton, in a boldly revisionist monograph on corporate employment practices in the 1950s and 1960s—big business helped pave the way.[41]

The influence of Chandlerian business history was by no means confined to historians. In addition, it inspired a good deal of attention from social scientists who challenged Chandler on many issues large and small, yet who shared Chandler's interest in the institutional dimensions of economic change. Among them were several who leaned decidedly to the left, including the historical sociologists Neil Fligstein and William G. Roy, the economist William Lazonick, and the political scientist Richard Bensel.[42]

The priority that Chandler accorded business in setting the terms for the relationship between big business and big government has sparked a reaction by several institutionally oriented historians who are impressed by what Colleen Dunlavy called the structuring presence of the state.[43] These historians follow the advice of the historical sociologist Theda Skocpol to "bring the state back in." Unlike Chandler, these historians asked not how the organizational structure of big business had been shaped by business strategy, but instead how business strategy had been shaped by the organizational configuration of the state. By the state, they meant not only individual government agencies but also broader institutional arrangements, such as federalism, common law, and the separation of powers. The influence of an antimonopoly political economy that venerated equal rights and vilified special privilege on the business strategy of post–Civil War railroad and telegraph managers was probed by Richard White and Richard R. John.[44] For each, the political structure not only shaped business strategy but also provided unscrupulous promoters with a rich menu of options on which they readily seized to game the system. Antimonopoly would shape business strategy even after the rise of the industrial corporation, explained political scientist Gerald Berk in an analysis of "regulated competition" in the 1920s, and Shane Hamilton in a monograph on the rise of the post–Second World War trucking industry.[45]

The willingness of historians to combine the firm-specific internalism of the business historian with the comparative institutionalism of the historical sociologist is a welcome sign that the long isolation of business history in American historiography is coming to an end. To be sure, much remains to be done. Political historians too often downplay the operational challenge of meeting a payroll and minimize the limitations that even large and well-known corporations confronted when faced with new technologies, shifting markets, and international competition. By exaggerating the autonomy of business leaders, they discount the structural constraints from which no economic actor is exempt. No business leader could have prevented the collapse of New England's cotton textile industry or the rise of China as a low-cost exporter to the United States of a multitude of goods that had once been manufactured by American workers, under the supervision of American managers, in factories located in the United States.[46]

The neglect by political historians of structural constraints on business behavior is paralleled by the reluctance of business historians to treat economic actors as members of a more-or-less coherent group whose interests diverge from those of workers, investors, and other stakeholders. It is for this reason that, while business historians routinely emphasize the influence on business strategy of technology and markets, they are typically less willing to acknowledge the ability of elite-led social movements to subtly (and not so subtly) revise the political-economic rules of the game. Too infrequently do business historians deploy concepts like "elite" and "class"; following the 2008 economic downturn, even wealth inequality is no longer an issue that they can prudently ignore. The political influence of giant organizations might well be bad for capitalism, a conclusion that business historians sometimes forget, yet one that was self-evident not only to the proprietary capitalists of the 1880s who invented the language and iconography of the modern antimonopoly tradition, but also to the institutional economists of the interwar period.[47]

Notwithstanding these differences of emphasis, political history and business history have much in common. Each recognizes the importance of institutional arrangements, or what is once again being called political economy; each is skeptical of the teleological narratives that once gave shape to their fields; and each is committed, either explicitly or implicitly, to the creation of a "trading zone," in which they share methodological insights drawn from cultural studies, comparative institutionalism, APD, and state-centered social theory, not only with one another but also with kindred spirits working on related topics in political science and historical sociology.

*   *   *

The essays in this collection build not only on political history, business history, political science, and historical sociology but also on the emerging tradition of historical writing that flies under the banner of the history of capitalism.[48] The historian of capitalism aspires, as Louis Hyman has observed, to understand the "agency" not only of the many but also of the "powerful few" who "shaped commerce and industry." To realize this goal, they find it advantageous to focus less on social movements headed up by outsiders and more on the collective behavior of business leaders: "We ask more questions about firms who still have power today, than about movements, who do not. . . . [T]he historians' task is to confront sober reality, not fashion heroic sagas."[49] Their goal, Hyman has declared, is to write history from the "bottom up, all the way to the top."[50] In Hyman's capacious vision, not only workers, social activists, and the downtrodden but also the individuals who occupied the most rarefied heights of society—business leaders, government administrators, policy analysts, even the 1 percent—should be dignified by historians as "real" people—rather than as the one-dimensional stick figures that they so often became in historical writing in the past.[51] No longer are social movements automatically presumed to have been protests of the many against injustices perpetrated by the few; for the historian of capitalism, it is equally important to recognize that the wealthy and powerful have also launched crusades to challenge the prerogatives of the many.

The new history of capitalism is too young to have devised a single overarching problematique. Yet certain themes recur. Among them are the priority of institutions over ideas; the power of material circumstances; the indispensability of long-term credit for economic development; the evolving relationship between finance, business, labor, and the state; and the mutual constitution of the state and the market, an insight that many derive from the historical sociology of Karl Polanyi.[52] In some ways, these themes are new; yet in others, they are venerable indeed. The "language" of ruling and subordinate groups was coeval with the founding of the republic, as the labor historians Steve Fraser and Gary Gerstle observed in 2005 in *Ruling Power: A History of Wealth and Power in a Democracy*, and has informed "one of the grand narratives of American history." In fact, it would not be until after the Second World War that this language would become supplanted by a different vocabulary that stigmatized analytical categories like "class" and "elite" and that reframed American history to downplay the adversarial relationship between social groups. Only then would historians devise explanatory schemes that invested agency in "history," the market, or some "analogous abstractions."[53]

Much was gained in the process, yet something vital was lost. No linguistic legerdemain could conceal the fundamental fact that the "footprint of wealth and power" remained "clearly visible across the whole span of American history." The rising prestige of the market deprived the time-honored critique of wealth and power of its force, until the time was reached when "every overture" to dismantle the apparatus of "public surveillance" over the nation's "business system" was presented by market fundamentalists as a "form of emancipation from the tyrannical hand of bureaucracy."[54]

The essays in this collection were written in a similar spirit. Like historians of capitalism, they paint on a broad canvas, with a particular focus on the business elite. Yet their inspiration is broader still: indeed, in various ways, and with different results, they build not only on the moral vision of the political historian and the comparative institutionalism of the business historian but also on the path-dependent models of the APD political scientist and the state-centered social theory of the historical sociologist. To highlight continuities as well as discontinuities in the relationship between business and politics, we have organized these essays both chronologically and thematically. Part I focuses on the Progressive era and the 1920s; Part II on the New Deal and the Second World War. Parts III and IV focus on the postwar era, which is subdivided into two topics: economic development, and liberalism and its critics.

Part I features essays by Laura Phillips Sawyer and Daniel Amsterdam on the Progressive era and the 1920s; each emphasizes the relationship of business and politics to state building and economic development.

Sawyer shows how corporate executives worked closely with lawmakers in 1912 to establish a new trade association, the U.S. Chamber of Commerce. Their primary rationale was defensive: troubled by the draconian and seemingly arbitrary rulings of the Supreme Court in major cases involving the interpretation of the antimonopoly Sherman Act, business leaders hoped to find a way to better navigate a potentially perilous regulatory environment. To help them move forward, the Chamber worked in tandem with an influential cohort of institutionalist economists to develop for jurists a new, technocratic rationale for interfirm cooperation. In so doing, the trade group helped transform into a working partnership a relationship between the courts and the business sector that had previously been highly adversarial.

Amsterdam reveals how in the 1920s the business elite in Detroit and Atlanta lobbied city officials to float huge bond issues to finance public investments in public works: schools, sewers, libraries, even museums. Eager to transform their hometowns into urban showplaces, business leaders laid the foundations for an expansive "civic welfare state." Notwithstanding what students might once have been taught in their high school history classes, business leaders in the high-flying "roaring twenties" did not reject big-government progressivism in favor of small-government conservatism; on the contrary, they enthusiastically lobbied for the vigorous augmentation of the administrative capacity of city government. In so doing, they built on the well-known achievements of the urban planners of the Progressive era and prefigured the establishment of the federal welfare state that emerged in the New Deal.

Part II features essays on the New Deal and the Second World War by Eric S. Hintz, Mark R. Wilson, and Richard R. John and Jason Scott Smith. In each of these essays, the mid-century business elite confronted powerful adversaries, who obliged them to fashion new, and sometimes disingenuous, narratives about the relationship between business and politics.

In the first essay, Hintz reconstructs a forgotten chapter in the regulatory history of the New Deal: namely, the lobbying campaign organized by the

National Association of Manufacturers (NAM) to block patent reform. High-profile lawsuits involving intellectual property rights often make headlines today, yet few remember that patent reform loomed large on the New Deal reform agenda. By mounting a publicity campaign to lionize independent inventors as "modern pioneers," NAM forestalled a mandatory cross-licensing scheme opposed by both the independent inventor and giant R&D combines like General Electric and Bell Labs.

In the second essay, Wilson demolishes the prevailing stereotype that the management of military procurement in the twentieth century has followed a single trajectory. In fact, and perhaps not surprisingly—as the military has remained throughout American history a very large consumer of government investment—the military's procurement methods have changed markedly over time. The procurement by the military during the Second World War of the celebrated "arsenal of democracy"—a project so consequential that it has long been regarded, and not just by military historians, as indispensable to the Allied victory over the Nazis—represented a midpoint in a multi-decade shift in the military from in-house production to corporate outsourcing. The war itself was a turning point. Confronted with an increasingly adversarial regulatory burden as the military's procurement needs spiked up, corporate executives fought back in a drama of challenge and response that would parallel the neoliberal turn in the postwar political economy, and, conceivably, may have helped to bring it about.

In the third essay, John and Smith trace the intellectual trajectory of historian Thomas McCraw, a "dyed-in-the-wool" New Deal Democrat whose culturally nuanced comparative institutionalist approach to the history of the twentieth-century political economy has already influenced a generation of policy historians, and has much to teach today's practitioners of the "history of capitalism." Historians have much to learn from McCraw's deft interweaving of history and theory; his critical engagement with the often highly ideological discourse of professional economists; and his unabashed admiration for the New Dealers' "mixed economy," a remarkable policy innovation that laid the groundwork for the country's astonishing postwar economic success.

The final two parts of our collection focus on the postwar era. Part III considers the relationship between business and economic development; it features essays by Tami J. Friedman, Brent Cebul, and Elizabeth Tandy Shermer. Part IV shifts the focus to business and liberalism, with essays by Jennifer Delton, Eric R. Smith, and Pamela Walker Laird.

The essays by Friedman and Cebul chart the divergent response of business leaders in different parts of the country to the generous federal funding that lawmakers earmarked for public investment. Friedman documents the sharp divide over economic development that would emerge in the 1950s between NAM and certain business leaders in the Northeast. NAM was a nationally oriented trade lobby, which predisposed it to oppose, on free-market grounds, the earmarking of federal funding for regions that had been adversely affected by plant closings. Northeast manufacturers, in contrast, viewed plant closings from a regional perspective and eagerly courted federal funding to forestall the seemingly inexorable collapse of a once-proud manufacturing sector in a region that had long been a cornerstone of the nation's industrial heartland. In many cities and towns—and in a decade often assumed to have been an economic "golden age"—the deindustrialization often associated with the 1970s had already begun.

Cebul shows how business leaders in rural Georgia vigorously lobbied for federal funding for public works and education, notwithstanding their reputation as reactionary opponents of progressive change. These local business elites mobilized what one might call "supply-side liberalism"—with its characteristic emphasis on technical assistance, research and development, and local infrastructure spending. In so doing, they generated virtually no local business opposition in one of the most conservative corners of the land, even though their program, which was sharply opposed by nationally oriented business organizations such as NAM, would prove to be no less important than the better-known Keynesian "demand-side liberalism" in legitimating midcentury liberal-state building.

In the final essay in Part III, Shermer shifts the focus from the Northeast to the South and West, and to a sector of the economy—public education—that, in marked contrast to manufacturing, enjoyed in the postwar period rapid and sometimes explosive growth. In Arizona, North Carolina, and California, regionally oriented business boosters established a fraught partnership with educational administrators and corporate funders to build up public universities, which, for different reasons, each regarded as essential. Business boosters and corporate funders favored technical and professional education to foster economic development; academic administrators championed the liberal arts to boost their university's prestige. These differences were hardly trivial. Yet in light of recent developments in public education, even more notable was the existence of a broad-based consensus to fund public education and expand the administrative capacity of the state—a consensus that was markedly at variance with the more recent business-backed critique of public education as an onerous fiscal burden.

Part IV of our collection includes three essays on a neglected topic: the relationship between business and postwar liberalism. In the first essay, Delton illuminates an ideological rift in NAM during the 1950s and 1960s that pitted ultraconservatives against moderates. For the ultraconservatives, the only obligation business had was to turn a profit. The moderates, in contrast, endorsed the idea that business had a "social responsibility" to the public good—an idea that looked backward to the reform agenda that the Progressive-era National Civic Federation had championed in the 1910s and forward to the Great Society liberalism of the 1960s. Somewhat surprisingly, given NAM's reputation as a reactionary opponent of the New Deal, the ultraconservatives lost. The fact that such a contest occurred highlights the persistence in the postwar era of a Progressive-era "corporate liberal" mindset in an organization widely regarded as a conservative bellwether.

In the second essay, Smith reconstructs a little-known chapter in the protest movement that emerged in the 1960s to oppose the continued involvement of the U.S. government in the Vietnam War. The opposition of New Left radicals to the war is a textbook perennial, as is the revulsion of antiwar radicals at the complicity with the military of many of the nation's leading corporations. Yet relatively little attention has been paid to the small yet influential cohort of business leaders who led antiwar protest groups such as the Business Executives Move for Peace (BEM). Smith reconstructs the fascinating and little-known history of this protest group, documenting the methods its organizers used to gain public attention, the arguments they advanced, and the contacts their leaders made with antiwar academics. Unlike the decade's better-known protest movements, BEM focused less on the morality of the war than on its deleterious consequences for the American economy. The political influence of business-led protest movements such as the BEM is hard to gauge. Yet it remains suggestive that not only a prominent moderate Republican lawmaker but also the radical activist Noam Chomsky opined in print that the United States would not abandon the war until an organized business opposition emerged.

In the final essay in this collection, Laird traces the emergence of widely accepted ideas and practices concerning equal opportunity for women and underrepresented minorities in the corporate workplace. This development sometimes anticipated, and in others was powerfully amplified by, the sea

change in employment practices that followed the enactment of the landmark Civil Rights Act of 1964. Wary of disgruntled employees, eager to
minimize adverse publicity, and fearful of expensive employment discrimination lawsuits, personnel managers responded to the enforcement provisions in this law by taking a variety of concrete steps to boost minority and
female employment. In so doing, they intensified the entanglement of business
with liberal social reform. By the end of the century, equal opportunity, which
would increasingly come to be associated with the benefits of workplace diversity, would have influential champions not only in the civil rights movement,
the federal government, and many state governments, but also in corporate
America.

*   *   *

Although it would be hazardous to venture grand generalizations about
business and politics on the basis of the essays in this collection, four themes
stand out. The first theme is the relative modernity of the free-market
fundamentalism that has become such a prominent feature of economic
discourse in our own age. Far from being a constant throughout American
history—or, for that matter, a cardinal tenet of public policy during the
nineteenth century, an age that is sometimes mistakenly hailed as the heyday of laissez-faire—the radical rejection of regulatory constraints as incompatible with political liberty was first popularized by a small yet purposeful
group of business leaders opposed on principled grounds to the New Deal.
Indeed, if one compares the ideological pronouncements of business boosters
during the New Deal and Second World War with the ideological pronouncements of their counterparts in the Progressive era and the 1920s, then it
becomes evident, just as specialists in the Progressive era and the 1920s
have long contended, that the dominant ethos of the business elite in the
opening two decades of the twentieth century was most emphatically not
laissez-faire.[55] Even Louis Brandeis upheld in the 1910s a vision of the good
society that had little in common with the doctrinaire antistatism of not only
Herbert Spencer but also Friedrich Hayek. The relative balance between gov-
ernment- and contractor-operated navy yards, to cite one relevant example,
would not shift decisively from the public to the private sector until after the
Second World War.

The second theme is the protean, open-ended, and indeterminate character of the relationship between business and politics in twentieth-century

America. In eleven separate essays, the contributors show how business leaders tried to shape the political-economic rules of the game. Sometimes the relationship between business and politics was adversarial; just as often— indeed, on balance, probably more often—it was not. Some business leaders vigorously opposed legislation to empower certain social groups, a phenomenon particularly evident in labor relations. Others championed laws and regulations to promote economic development, expand the administrative capacity of the state, and even advance a liberal social agenda.[56] Capital *gained* not only from a century of favorable laws and regulations but also from the shift in the 1930s from a "private" economy (in which the primary source of capital for business investment had been the retained earnings of corporations and proprietorships) to a "mixed economy" (in which the federal government had become a major investor).[57] The twentieth-century American political economy has been very good for business, and the essays in this collection attest to this fact.

Had we featured essays on other themes, we might have struck a different balance. In realms as varied as taxation, labor-management relations, product safety, environmental regulation, health care, and social security, business leaders have long crusaded to limit state power. It would similarly be misleading to assume that the relationship between business leaders and politics—the main focus in this collection—paralleled the relationship between ordinary businesspeople and politics. Had we included essays on immigrant entrepreneurs battling city ordinances or self-employed milliners attacking labor laws, the balance might have looked somewhat different. Further complications might have arisen had we featured an essay on Prohibition, a remarkably adversarial chapter in the history of the relationship between a large and powerful business and the state.[58] Even or perhaps especially in the enforcement of the nation's antitrust laws, conflict rather than consensus often prevailed.

One thing seems incontrovertible: among business leaders, the relationship between business and politics has not been invariably adversarial. For much of the twentieth century, much of the nation's business elite lobbied for increased public investment and supported the expansion in the administrative capacity of the state. In some instances, they even backed quintessential liberal causes such as the antiwar movement and civil rights. Notwithstanding the opposition of nationally oriented business organizations such as NAM to many features of the postwar liberal state—including, in particular, its solicitude toward organized labor—large and influential blocs of business leaders proved adept at securing legislation that funneled federal revenue into business coffers and expanded the administrative capacity of the state.

All in all, the range and variety of the realms in which business leaders tried to curry favor from lawmakers was little short of astonishing: from military procurement, public works, and education, to social activism and civil rights. Predictably enough, there were winners and losers. Independent inventors failed to obtain patent reform in the 1930s, having been outgunned by better-connected corporate lobbyists. Certain factory owners lobbied for federal aid to slow economic decline; others did not. The refusal of Arizona business leaders to accept federal funds for education did not preclude them from taking money from the Arizona state government. To conclude that business leaders in Detroit and Atlanta in the 1920s opposed, as they most emphatically did, the creation of a European-style social welfare state did not mean that they also rejected government funding for roads, sewers, museums, or libraries.

The third theme that the essays in this collection underscore is the wide variety of motives that influenced the business elite. It is worth recalling that not all business leaders have been political conservatives, while many political liberals have been staunch supporters of business. Business leaders have been influenced not only or even primarily by the lure for profits or even a determination to retain the upper hand (though that was rarely absent). Rather, they pursued a variety of goals. "Only economists and Marxists ever really believed that capitalism was just about the money," Hyman has waggishly observed.[59] Our contributors concur. Just as historians reject simple-minded generalizations about ordinary people, so too, do our contributors refrain from making ex cathedra pronouncements about what business leaders have said and done. We should be no more surprised that some corporate executives lobbied to end the Vietnam War than that an influential cohort of middle managers continued to champion corporate diversity programs even after civil rights had ceased to be a government priority.

Even on issues on which one might assume consensus prevailed, business leaders were not always of one mind. Sometimes a difference of opinion existed inside a trade group, such as NAM, that historians had often assumed to speak with a single voice. Just because business leaders in upcountry Georgia opposed civil rights legislation does not did not mean that they opposed federal funding for economic development.

The fourth and final theme that these essays underscore is the value of archival research for the ongoing investigation of the relationship between business and politics in the American past. As the essays in this collection reveal, an immersion in the sources remains perhaps the best remedy for the common presumption that the relationship between business and politics followed a single script. If the historians of capitalism have taught us anything, it is that the business elite—no less than lawmakers, social activists, and any other influential social group that has attracted the historian's attention—should not be treated as cardboard cutouts whose behavior can be judged a priori. It is particularly important for today's historians to get this right, since, barring some planetwide environmental cataclysm, the country's business leaders will remain a powerful protagonist not just in the present but also the foreseeable future, wielding vast, though never unlimited, power in the United States and around the world. To hold business leaders accountable for their words and deeds, future historians have an obligation, like the contributors to this collection, to probe the relationship between business and politics with the same analytical depth, imaginative breadth, and critical realism that has long been a defining feature of the historian's craft.

PART I

The Progressive Era and the 1920s

Chapter 1

Trade Associations, State Building, and the Sherman Act: The U.S. Chamber of Commerce, 1912–25

Laura Phillips Sawyer

The U.S. Chamber of Commerce (USCC), an "organization of organizations," was conceived in 1912 in coordination with administrators at the Department of Commerce and Labor to promote the collection of commercially valuable trade information. A critical, though often neglected, aspect of administrative state building has been the information-gathering and dissemination practices spearheaded by the Department of Commerce and later the Federal Trade Commission (FTC) in conjunction with the USCC.[1] Rather than a strictly adversarial relationship, in the early twentieth century business-government relations created mutually constitutive administrative capacities in both private trade associations and public administrative agencies.[2]

An important impetus to the Chamber's formation as a partner to government was the widespread sense of uncertainty regarding the future of U.S. competition policy and its effect on the structure of American capitalism. While the Supreme Court maintained a strict prohibition on overt price-fixing contracts, in 1912, it remained unclear how the Court would interpret the Sherman Antitrust Act against more ambiguous cooperative agreements that affected downstream pricing, such as labor agreements, product standardization, or

information sharing on output, orders, or costs.[3] Chamber documents and litigation records reveal a formidable campaign to extend the more permissive
"rule of reason" antitrust interpretation from the analysis of interfirm agreements to the analysis of trade association rule making as well.[4] Rather than
pursuing "self-regulation" as such, the Chamber endorsed the creation and expansion of government administrative agencies as an alternative to judge-made
law regarding competition policy.[5] The result was an outpouring of trade manuals published by the Department of Commerce and the FTC on standardized
accounting techniques, waste reduction in production methods, and marketing practices for a variety of industries. Ultimately, these practices fostered a
technocratic approach to managing competitive markets, steering American
governance toward a stronger administrative state.[6] In the 1910s and 1920s,
the development of the USCC and the modern administrative state appeared
complementary—not always in opposition to one another and, at least at
times, fostering similar technocratic and administrative visions for economic
development.[7]

*   *   *

On February 12, 1912, representatives from various commercial organizations met to create something new from existing parts. The formation of
the USCC brought together a multitude of organizations—national industry-
specific associations, local and municipal business associations, and state
chambers of commerce.[8] Municipal business leaders, among them Lucius
Wilson (Detroit), W. Mitchell Bunker (San Francisco), and John Fahey and
James McKibbon (Boston), spearheaded discussions with administrators
from the Bureau of Manufacturers of the Department of Commerce, represented by Albertus Baldwin and D. A. Skinner. The Department of Commerce provided stenographic records of the meeting and agreed to contact
hundreds of national trade associations and chambers of commerce to solicit their approval of the new national organization.[9]

What made this organizational effort exceptional was the commitment on
behalf of private business and federal officials to forming a partnership between business and government.[10] Lucius Wilson, one of the most prominent
and most frequent speakers at the inaugural meeting, exemplified the overlapping that came to characterize the Chamber. As the president of the
American Association of Commercial Executives and the secretary of the Detroit chamber of commerce, Wilson urged the Chamber to not only bring to-

gether these private organizations but also to foster collaboration with the federal government. The Chamber, he urged, should be the "official child of the Department of Commerce and Labor" or, put another way, "it ought to exist in such close relationship with the Department that there could never arise any schism between the two."[11] A reciprocal exchange of business information would function through the various overlapping but uncoordinated trade organizations and the Department of Commerce.

The executive summary distributed to potential members and associations made explicit the intention to collaborate with administrative officials in order to rationalize business methods and promote best practices at home and abroad. Similar to the Department of Agriculture in solving the problems of rural America, the USCC founding documents argued, the Department of Commerce and Labor should contribute to the formation of an extra-governmental organization to represent national commercial interests. Herbert Miles, director of the National Association of Manufacturers (NAM), explained that the USCC would act as "a clearing-house for these questions which to-day the separate organizations are very busy on, and [have] no means of communicating with each other."[12]

The nascent Chamber sought public endorsement from President William Howard Taft, solidifying the USCC relationship with executive agencies "to protect and promote their common interests."[13] In an open letter to the president, the delegates emphasized their desire to bolster U.S. competitiveness through strengthened government-business collaboration. The letter read: "It is significant that in each European country, which has made notable advances in commerce and industry, the business organizations of every section work together through a strong central organization, and that there is also, in turn, effective cooperation between this central body and the branches of government."[14]

These voluntary associations would remain autonomous and self-sustaining, unlike in the German system, where the state-coordinated and -funded trade groups through taxes, Wilson explained. The U.S. government, they argued, should collaborate with the Chamber to gather and disseminate business information, much as was being done in Europe. The following month Taft agreed and instructed Charles Nagel, secretary of Commerce and Labor, to issue a call for a national meeting to be held in Washington, D.C.[15] Nagel sent three delegates to the first Chamber meeting and mailed more than 2,000 circulars to various commercial organizations, inviting members to attend the upcoming D.C. conference.

Secretary Nagel played an important role promoting the Chamber as a progressive partner with government regulators to solve current problems in both law and economics. At the Chamber's inaugural meeting he recounted that commerce and industry had undergone "something of a revolution" in their relationship to government. In the early twentieth century, "we abandoned the old laissez-faire doctrine, and began to realize that somehow some system and order must be put into this great development."[16] His address highlighted several current issues in political economy; however, it focused on antitrust reform and administrative law. The Interstate Commerce Commission of 1887, he began, had emerged to limit the monopoly power of railroads and, similarly, the Sherman Antitrust Act of 1890 arose to address the "industrial problems involve[d] in the use of power." Existing antitrust law provided only negative restraints on business actions, he explained. Instead, administrative agencies could be empowered to provide advice and approval for proposed business arrangements, including consolidations, trade association information sharing, as well as employee liability programs, pension plans, and the development of export markets. This partnership could reduce the uncertainty that surrounded antitrust enforcement.[17]

While the Sherman Antitrust Act had empowered the judiciary to determine questions regarding competition policy, the Court lacked a clear legislative mandate and floundered in its early antitrust rulings. The Act provided broad prohibitions of "every contract, combination . . . or conspiracy . . . in restraint of trade" and of any attempt to "monopolize any part" of trade or commerce, which did little more than signal a preference for open competition. Nor had the government created any administrative agency to interpret and enforce the act; thus, litigation arose from the understaffed Department of Justice and private litigants. Early antitrust precedent, what came to be known as the "literalist" interpretation, prohibited any interstate contracts that restrained trade. In an effort to protect "small dealers and worthy men," the Court restricted combinations and trade association practices that affected prices or restricted output; however, these did not affect large-scale, vertically integrated industrial corporations.[18] By 1911, a reconstituted Court emerged and laid down the basic rules that would govern antitrust law.[19] Chief Justice Edward White fostered a political consensus around the "rule of reason," which prohibited only contracts found to be "unreasonable" according to common law, statutory regulations, and the constitutional limitations on the "liberty of contract."[20] Under this governing maxim, the Court could break apart large corporations or combinations if their actions were found to unreasonably restrain trade, such as for the purpose of driving competitors out of business and monopolizing an industry. Nevertheless, it still remained unclear whether these rulings were the final word on antitrust. White had only just been elevated as chief justice, and throughout the previous ten years his position on antitrust had been relegated to dissenting opinions.

The election of 1912 revolved around issues relating to competition policy in addition to tariffs and monetary policy. A divided Republican Party—President Taft and the unexpected contender, former president Theodore Roosevelt—vied against Democratic Party nominee Woodrow Wilson. Eugene V. Debs also ran on the Socialist Party ticket and won nearly 6 percent of the popular vote (although no electoral votes). While Taft won his party's nomination, it was Roosevelt who aggressively campaigned under the Progressive Party banner, dividing Republican voters. He stumped for minimum wages, child labor laws, workplace safety standards, and regulating monopolies through a bureaucratic commission, much as the Interstate Commerce Commission governed railroad rates. Wilson gradually came to endorse a commission to regulate competition and ensure fair practices, though he feared that it might ultimately legitimize big business and promote "big government." Wilson appointed Louis D. Brandeis his economic advisor. Brandeis, a lawyer who in the preceding years had crusaded against "bigness," advocated an expansion of the "rule of reason" doctrine to allow small proprietors to pool their resources in order to protect—if not enhance—their market share. Brandeis lamented that U.S. antitrust law encouraged corporate consolidations, and he hoped that a regulatory commission could protect small proprietors. Although his political rhetoric focused on protecting competitors rather than ensuring market efficiencies, a stance that gained him the denigration of a generation of historians, Brandeis's promotion of what ultimately became the FTC also focused on information-sharing practices as a legitimate form of rationalization and regulation.[21]

At the Chamber's February 1914 meeting, Brandeis explained to the general assembly that the creation of the FTC signified a potential path to "industrial democracy"—"not a program of free and unrestricted competition, but [rather] a program of regulating competition instead of regulating monopoly."[22] Brandeis and others at the Chamber believed that the courts had interpreted antitrust law to the detriment of independent proprietors, the backbone of American liberal democracy. Despite his and Wilson's distrust of big government, their plan embraced a new administrative agency to right the course of that misguided jurisprudence. He believed antitrust reforms could ensure a level playing field among competitors by diminishing the threat of "ruinous competition," where prices chronically did not cover costs. He believed that corporate consolidations resulted from "predatory pricing" during economic downturns when smaller businesses were most vulnerable. Thus, consolidation did not necessarily bring greater efficiencies, but it did threaten to concentrate economic power, which in turn had dire political consequences.

Brandeis gained a following among members who supported regulatory reforms that would facilitate new avenues for managing competitive markets. He proposed revised accounting methods to avoid overproduction and falling retail prices. Widespread uniform cost accounting coupled with information sharing and federal monitoring would ensure that businesses adhered to new standards that prohibited discriminatory pricing and other unfair practices. The "broad question of equality and opportunity" in America required exhaustive study of industrial statistics and business practices, such as the work he pioneered in the discriminatory railroad rates case.[23] He wanted two things. First, he wanted stricter scrutiny of big businesses, which he believed threatened liberal democracy as well as allocative efficiency. Second, he wanted the rule of reason extended to small and medium-sized firms by overturning the per se prohibition on resale price maintenance contracts. These contracts, he argued, provided a contractual vehicle for like-minded producers and retailers to protect against a "race to the bottom."[24] Brandeis saw the FTC as an opportunity to reform the decisionmaking processes of business managers and enact administrative law that would effectively manage the managers. No doubt he hated bigness, but too much attention to that political rhetoric obscures his contributions to constructive policies that empowered proprietary business associations as well as regulators.

University of Wisconsin president and leading Progressive Charles Van Hise provided a foil to Brandeis's optimism on business associations and FTC cooperation. In contrast to the jurist, Van Hise promoted "regulated monopoly." In his role as one of Theodore Roosevelt's key advisors in 1912, Van Hise held that many industries gained efficiencies through economies of scale and scope, and those efficiencies could be passed on to consumers, as in the case of steel production. Such corporations posed a problem only insofar as their market power could be used to the detriment of the public interest or translated into undue political power. Like Roosevelt, Van Hise was a "trust buster" in that he believed that federal regulation and control of certain large-scale industries, such as those involved in telephone and telegraph lines, would benefit the public. Expert commissions could judge whether certain monopolistic industries required greater government oversight—not breaking them apart and ruining the economies they had established, but rather regulating the existing monopolies in the public interest.[25]

That said, Van Hise was not entirely opposed to cooperation of business-people when deemed by government experts to be in the public interest. He advocated relaxing antitrust laws to promote business group cooperation, coupled with greater administrative oversight to safeguard against price fixing, territorial divisions, or other unfair practices that were not in the public interest.[26] In industries such as lumber and coal, greater conservation could result from cooperation on output, pricing, and selling, he argued. While he initially focused on promoting this form of cooperation in natural resource industries, he also advocated its spread to other areas of manufacturing in hopes to curb "cut-throat competition" and waste.[27] Although not an economist by training, Van Hise penned one of the most important books on industrial organization and antitrust policy for the period, *Concentration and Control* (1912).[28] According to Raymond Moley, who was a member of President Franklin Roosevelt's original "brain trust," Van Hise's approach to cooperation ultimately influenced the development of the National Industrial Recovery Act.[29]

The rhetoric of "regulated competition" and "regulated monopoly" captured antitrust debates for the next decades. Brandeis influenced the framing of the FTC and Clayton Acts, which prohibited "unfair competition" and exempted labor unions from antitrust prosecution. But he could not dictate juridical interpretation. The Court continued along a path more akin to the vision espoused by Roosevelt and Van Hise. The Supreme Court limited the FTC's jurisdiction and authority to determine what constituted "unfair practices."[30] Also, it continued to circumscribe attempts at associational management of marketplace competition.[31] Consensus in the Chamber resolved that the Court's stringent antitrust enforcement had encouraged corporate consolidations to the detriment of other business group arrangements.[32] The desired partnership between the Chamber and federal agencies to manage domestic competition appeared increasingly tenuous.

It should be noted that opposition interest groups formed to block Brandeis's proposals for regulated competition—both in the USCC and in Congress. In 1914, for example, R. H. Macy of New York helped form the

National Retail Dry Goods Association, which adamantly opposed the USCC lending approval to the FTC language regarding fair competition.[33] The 1916 FTC report also contained a minority report that rejected the pro-competitive effects of resale price maintenance, a tactic used by independent proprietors to set retail services and prices. Borrowing from classical economics texts, the report stated that "monopoly and competition being the exact opposites, anything tending to destroy competition tends to monopoly."[34] The immutable laws of supply and demand determined market prices, and any previous litigation that allowed resale price fixing, for example, had been superseded by the Supreme Court's prohibition of loose combinations.[35] Nevertheless, the Chamber continued to pass resolutions in favor of legislation to enable various forms of managed competition.

When Brandeis joined the Supreme Court in 1916, it appeared that little headway had been made toward institutionalizing his version of regulated competition. However, this was not altogether true: inroads were being made at the FTC. Edward Hurley, chairman of the FTC, built on Brandeis's notion that fair competition depended on reliable cost information. Hurley, who had been the president of the Illinois Manufacturers' Association, endorsed cost-accounting programs to be taught by trade associations. Although he held the chairmanship for only two years (1914–16), he popularized cost-accounting practices by circulating more than 230,000 cost-accounting manuals through congressional members to their constituents.[36] Hurley and the FTC manual provided important correctives to conventional cost-accounting practices, which had valued volume over other goals. Namely, the report urged producers and retailers to determine costs and revenues of each specific product line and distribute the overhead expenses accordingly (i.e., to actuate product-line expense reports).[37] Hurley continued Brandeis's mission to rationalize independent proprietors' bookkeeping, which he believed would enable smaller concerns to compete with their large-scale competitors and facilitate better FTC oversight to protect against price cutting and destructive competition.

During the First World War, the federal government depended on trade associations in its efforts to regulate wartime production. Rather than create a fully developed institutional order, it left an ambiguous legacy due to the war's exceptional circumstances.[38] The War Industries Board (WIB), established in July 1917, lacked sufficient statutory power to institute compulsory price fixing to keep prices stable and low during the war. As a result, WIB administrators relied on trade associations and industry leaders to administer price stabilization agreements. Through the auspices of the USCC and industry associations, smaller firms led these efforts, despite resistance from larger, mass producers, such as U.S. Steel. Perhaps because President Wilson refused to sanction outright price fixing by WIB administrators, the war's legacy strengthened the appeal of public-private solutions to managing economic competition and stabilizing markets.

From the policymaking perspective, the wartime experiments were inconsistent and contradictory. But from the vantage point of business associations, the wartime experience animated a movement for greater statistical information sharing and coordination. While very few businesspeople endorsed continued intervention in the economy at wartime levels, most did not want a return to so-called free market competition. All were concerned about postwar adjustments, and many believed that managed competition offered a middle ground between the wartime controls and the return of unbridled market competition. The USCC leadership was quick to seek out guidance from public policymakers, administrative regulators, and academic experts. They wanted to know how to navigate new rules of competition and how best to exploit these new opportunities.

It was in this context that Herbert Hoover emerged as the most powerful proponent of public-private cooperation on information-sharing practices. Like Van Hise, he had been an engineer, and he believed in rationalizing industries in the public interest. Like Brandeis, however, he also demonstrated a distrust of "big government" despite his promotion of regulatory agencies. He tempered these conflicting impulses by promoting a public-private regulatory approach.[39] Hoover sought to encourage voluntary trade associations to coordinate industry standards of production, service, and prices first during wartime and later as secretary of commerce. He effectively promoted a new socioeconomic order by advocating a technocratic vision wherein federal administrators played a key role in gathering and disseminating useful business information for the purpose of better management of the competitive economy. What regulatory powers this vision would confer on private associations or public administrators was yet to be fully realized in peacetime.

During the war, Hoover used the USCC to encourage voluntary participation to raise production but maintain stable prices on products vital to the war effort. He warned that shortages during the war could lead to price spikes and cause discontent at home. "We are thus between two fires—to control prices or to readjust the income of the whole community. The verdict of the whole of the world's experience is in favor of price control as the lesser evil."[40] The movement to conserve, stimulate production, and regulate distribution had already begun, Hoover explained, through the organization of 250 volunteer representatives of business and academic experts. By 1917, more than 200 production conferences had been held. That year, the Chamber passed a unanimous resolution in support of President Wilson exercising executive authority to fix prices and control distribution. By 1918, many of the Chamber's members hoped to replicate the wartime success of agricultural combinations. In his 1917 address to the Chamber, Hoover outlined the process by which agricultural cooperatives controlled sales and distribution. Sometimes through a local chamber of commerce or another organization, farmers in remote areas established sales agents in larger eastern cities who monitored prices and supply in their vicinity. Farmer cooperatives collaborated to save on advertising and shipping costs, which gave the groups greater flexibility to guide their products to markets with highest prices and to stabilize distribution.

The following year, George Peek, an agricultural economist for the WIB, explained the role of the Chamber's War Services Committees. With more than three hundred committees, the Chamber helped coordinate government orders for various products with the WIB Requirements Division; it then distributed output and price information to members each day.[41] The purpose of the plan was to handle raw materials and finished products so as to avoid actual or threatened shortages and to control wartime inflation.[42] The Chamber resolved to continue its ongoing study of price fixing and "the conditions relating thereto and [to] provid[e] a formula upon which costs and investments may be ascertained, and reasonable prices fixed."[43] Information sharing on costs, output, and government orders had sufficed to create a coordinated market economy.

When the war ended and President Wilson allowed the WIB to dissolve, the USCC frantically organized an emergency meeting to address fears that deflation would set in as surplus goods reentered the market and consumer goods rebounded in production. In Atlantic City, New Jersey, the leadership of the USCC met to address several potential impending changes—cancellation of wartime government purchasing contracts, rapid deflation caused by overproduction, and a return of antitrust prosecutions. A few days prior to the reconstruction meeting, Bernard Baruch wrote to Harry Wheeler, the Chamber's president, to assuage fears of canceled government contracts or dumping on the American market.[44] The Chamber then redoubled its efforts for greater legal freedom for industrial cooperation. A resolution passed by the group stated their conclusions drawn from the wartime experience:

> The war has demonstrated that through industrial cooperation great economies may be achieved, waste eliminated, and efficiency increased. The nation should not forget, but rather should capitalize [on] these lessons by adapting effective war practices to peace conditions through permitting reasonable cooperation between units of industry under appropriate federal supervision. It is in the public interest that reasonable trade agreements should be entered into, but the failure of the government to either clearly define the dividing line between those agreements which are, and those which are not, in unreasonable restraint of commerce, or to provide an agency to speak for it on application of those proposing to enter into such agreement in effect restricts wholesome cooperation and deprives both industry and the general public of its benefits.[45]

This resolution held that the war had positively affected American capitalism by permitting cooperative combinations of producers and retailers to control output and prices. The role of the government, the Chamber concluded, should be to facilitate such productive arrangements, namely through FTC oversight and congressional codification of "the fair-trade decisions of the American and British courts."[46] A return to pre–First World War antitrust policies, they argued, would be most disastrous.

The Chamber's warnings helped shape postwar policy, which turned toward permitting trade associations a greater role in collecting and sharing information about production. During the 1920s, the USCC received help in this effort from a new group of scholars: the institutional economists. A heterodox group, these economists dissented from neoclassical models of perfect competition. Instead they led efforts at data collection through government agencies (e.g., the WIB) and private groups, ranging from the Brookings Institution (a Washington, D.C., think-tank) to academic centers like Harvard Business School. These economists-cum-regulators envisioned a system of competition that managed production and consumption so as to maintain price stability, facilitate innovation, and ensure fair play among competitors. Finding ways to balance competing interests, or countervailing powers, was a hallmark of the institutionalists.[47] In his first year as secretary of commerce, Hoover headed two major initiatives—coordination of the President's Conference on Unemployment and publication of the *Survey of Current Business*—both of which relied on these new social science research methods as guiding principles for businesspeople and regulators. In the fall of 1921, the Conference on Unemployment produced a new agenda for economic stabilization that embraced institutionalist economics as a guiding paradigm.[48] Similar to the preceding years' USCC deliberations, new social science research on the theory of business cycles influenced proposals to reverse the recession. The conference relied on data compiled by the National Bureau of Economic Research, the social science research agency founded by Wesley Mitchell, who also chaired the conference committee on unemployment statistics. Ultimately, the conference recommended the use of public works projects to accelerate the upturn in the business cycle; public funds, however, were designated for "productive" commercial purposes, such as construction projects and highway work, though not for direct payments for unemployment relief.[49] The recommendations of the conference reflected the ideals espoused by Mitchell, Hoover, and other institutionalists—uncoordinated economic activities could lead to problematic social consequences, like unemployment and waste of natural resources, which required government oversight and coordination of private sector business decisions.

In August 1921, the Department of Commerce began monthly publications of the *Survey*, which provided information regarding changes in wholesale and retail prices, production outputs, and general price trends.[50] Hoover's Advisory Committee on Statistics, a group of academic economists and regulators, compiled tables on current trends from standardized surveys collected from firms across the country.[51] On that committee, Mitchell acted as leading economic advisor to Hoover—both men envisioned a system of disseminating business information to foster rational planning by businesspeople and, therefore, promote macroeconomic stabilization.[52] That Hoover turned to Mitchell was no coincidence. Mitchell's work studying this history of modern business cycles had earned him a reputation as an expert in statistical analysis and business management, which would prove critical in negotiations with businesspeople and regulators.

Still, the legal status of trade associations and the question of whether sharing economic information was a violation of antitrust laws remained ambiguous. Even as the Department of Commerce partnered with trade associations for the collection and dissemination of statistical data regarding production standards and price information, the Department of Justice continued to bring suits against private organizations carrying out these tasks.[53] Attorney General Harry Daugherty maintained an active hostility to information-sharing practices, especially those concerning prices. For Daugherty, any price agreements made by similar competitors constituted an unjust restraint of the free market. Daugherty brought the first criminal prosecution of open price plans against the Cement Manufacturers' Protective Association. This case emerged from an initiative begun by the New York state legislature, in 1920, to investigate prices charged by New York City's building trades. A postwar housing shortage had contributed to rising rents, and political figures sought an explanation.[54] Although the investigation focused on the prosecution of labor leaders, it also encouraged federal prosecutors to take legal action against the construction industry as well. The association coordinated cement manufacturers throughout the mid-Atlantic region, from Pennsylvania to New York. Daugherty, a former Republican Party boss and Harding booster, stepped in with gusto, despite protests from Secretary Hoover.[55]

Daugherty had reason to be confident as he built the government's case against the cement manufacturers. In December 1921, the Court had upheld federal prosecution of the American Column and Lumber Company and the American Hardwood Manufacturers' Association.[56] Although the government did not uncover formal written agreements to restrain trade, the Court's majority held that the circulation of sales reports among members allowed individual firms to effectively raise the price of hardwood products. Justice John Clarke, writing for the majority, inferred that monthly meetings and market letters had been used as tactics to keep prices high and supply low. The prosecution used letters written by association members thanking the statisticians and association leadership for helping eliminate destructive competition as evidence of restraint of trade. Not all of the justices, however, agreed with the majority.

Justices Oliver Wendell Holmes and Louis Brandeis, joined by Joseph McKenna, wrote dissenting opinions—later theirs would become the dominant position on the Court.[57] Both Holmes and Brandeis argued that these kinds of information-sharing practices could in fact help smaller businesses compete on an equal basis with larger manufacturers who already possessed privileged market information and should be legalized as a legitimate business practice. Far from being a restraint of trade, Holmes referred to these practices as "common sense." Brandeis firmly believed that the American

Hardwood Manufacturers' Association had not sought to form a monopoly or control prices but instead had encouraged decentralized competition by avoiding corporate consolidation in that industry. In fact, interbrand competition continued to exist in the industry and among its members.

In response to these Court decisions, trade association efforts to monitor and enforce trade rules that affected prices became more subtle.[58] Instead of written agreements, association members exchanged information "relating to prices actually quoted or charged, terms of payment, manufacturing and selling costs, purchases, stocks, production, orders, shipments, inquiries, bids, contracts, returned goods, cancellations, advertising, and credits."[59] Still, the trend remained toward economic coordination. The open price associations in the cotton textiles coordinated to maintain so-called reasonable profits and market stability through trade information on prices and production levels; the result was to lessen competition.[60]

For Secretary Hoover, governmental oversight and enforcement would help protect against both collective-action problems and antitrust prosecution to "secure more regular production, more regular employment, better wages, the elimination of waste, the maintenance of quality or service, decrease in destructive competition and unfair practice, and oft times to assure prices or profits."[61] The USCC shared this disposition, and its members helped arrange a test case to challenge the Department of Justice prosecution.[62] Colonel George T. Buckingham, a member of the Cement Manufacturers' Association litigation team, explained that the purpose of the trade association had been to balance production and consumption "in order that the results and the evils that follow over-production may not occur."[63] In part, this meant keeping low-quality cement off the market to guard against destructive competition that might bring depressed profits and wages. First, it collected standardized price surveys, called "blank forms," from manufacturers across the country. Next, trade association secretaries prepared, tabulated, and condensed statistics. The result, Buckingham argued, was to "iron out or make flatter the curves" of business cycles.[64] The "chief controversy" arose when statistical information covered "*prices* at which commodities have been sold, and have given out statistical information about the prices at which sales have been made."[65] In thinly veiled terms, he lambasted the attorneys at Justice for enforcing an "archaic" vision of business practices and economic models of unfettered competition—"like a battle royal, in the dark, where every competitor was unintelligent, uninformed."[66] Yet he ended on a positive note, anticipating his team's victory. He predicted that "new economic principles will prevail" and that in fifteen years, the Chamber would wonder "that anybody would have been discussing so elementary a thing" as trade association information sharing on price points.[67]

After years of litigation on behalf of open price associations and collaboration with the Department of Commerce and the FTC, the U.S. Supreme Court finally reversed course in 1925. The appointment of Harlan Fiske Stone to the Court solidified the switch.[68] That year, the Court handed down two important antitrust decisions that changed the trajectory of trade association information sharing. Justice Stone wrote that "the gathering and dissemination of information by trade associations on costs, prices, production and stocks do not necessarily constitute restraint of trade in violation of antitrust laws."[69] The Court upheld the standard sales contracts used by the Cement Manufacturers' Protective Association. The association had standardized cement production methods and contracting and established a monitoring system through producer disclosure rules. Members were required to submit monthly reports detailing all sales contracts, delivery, and cancellations.[70] The association secretary then sent daily reports to members regarding new job contracts, completed jobs, and the freight rates in between.

In the *Maple Flooring* case, the Court found that the sales contracts allowed for the legitimate refusal to deal with disreputable contractors. The association's publication of freight rates, calculated according to a basing point system for standard deliveries, allowed manufacturers to adhere to a "one-price" base rate determined by each mill and to which transportation costs were more easily added.[71] Ultimately, the Court found that the information-sharing practices had the effect of reducing fraudulent contracts and the government had failed to establish a concerted action by the association to fix prices per se.[72] This case significantly advanced the trade-practice rule-making and monitoring procedures developed in conjunction with trade associations and the FTC. Where the *Colgate* case of 1919 had validated individual firm price policies, the *Cement Manufacturers'* and the *Maple Flooring* rulings legitimized association tactics.

Similar to earlier opinions by Holmes and Brandeis, Stone held that the association-guided information sharing merely constituted "intelligent conduct of business."[73] He wrote:

It is the consensus of opinion of economists and of many of the most important agencies of Government that the public interest is served by the gathering and dissemination, in the widest possible manner, of information with respect to the production and distribution, cost and prices in actual sales, of market commodities, because the making available of such information tends to stabilize trade and industry, to produce fairer price levels and to avoid the waste which inevitably attends the unintelligent conduct of economic enterprise.[74]

Greater intelligence in business trades did not disturb free competition, he reasoned. He only cited Leon Marshall, who later joined the National Recovery Administration, and J. A. Hobson's *The Evolution of Modern Capitalism*.[75]

As a complement to Stone's promotion from attorney general to associate justice, William Humphrey joined the FTC, where he instituted significant changes to antitrust investigations. As he explained to the Chamber's general assembly, the FTC would no longer issue public announcements listing companies against which complaints of "unfair trade practices" had been alleged. The FTC instituted this change because of the bad publicity and loss of goodwill created by those public announcements, especially in cases where formal charges were not issued after FTC investigations. Instead, the commission would use its investigatory powers to urge settlements between firms and to guide trade-association rule-making outcomes. All documents and evidence submitted to the FTC would remain confidential.[76] Additionally, Secretary Hoover helped the FTC coordinate trade-practice conferences, whereby trade association members laid out precise by-laws defining the rules of fair competition.

These voluntary meetings of trade associations resulted in both informal and formal rules of conduct internal and external to the firm. Informal rules might dictate conduct or procedures in the distribution system, but they did not carry legal enforcement. In contrast, formal rules enjoyed FTC oversight and enforcement in law. Charged with the responsibility to distinguish between fair and unfair practices, FTC regulators considered whether or not competition had been substantially lessened or whether certain business practices constituted a tendency to monopolize.[77] Otherwise, trade associations enjoyed greater leeway to create industrywide rules regarding standardized production methods, quality standards, accounting methods, and sales practices. Through the late 1920s, FTC regulators, mostly composed of economists and antitrust attorneys, sanctioned some price stabilization efforts, such as prohibitions on price discrimination, secret rebates, and sales below cost; however, the FTC never accepted association attempts to institute price-fixing agreements.[78]

As Hoover put it in 1926, new economic ideas about competition had significantly influenced the administration of antitrust law. The "growth of a cooperative sense" represented a movement toward "more efficient, more ethical business practice and better synchronizing of the parts" of the economy as a whole.[79] "It is a long cry," he continued, "from the conceptions of the old economist."[80] Gradually, the social sciences had become a tool for explaining and implementing trade-practice rules.

Shortly thereafter, Congress approved the creation of a new division of the FTC to oversee trade-practice conferences, where trade associations "presented, and the Commission approved, complete codes of fair practice."[81] Hoover explained that these bureaucratic changes supported constructive information sharing meant to mitigate "destructive competition" and preserve competitive freedom. Where conflict had once existed between the Departments of Commerce and Justice, a new spirit of cooperation and promotion of "self-regulation" emerged, he stated.[82] The following year, the Department of Commerce published *Trade Association Activities* (1927) to clarify the Court's shifting interpretation of trade association information sharing.

*   *   *

It was perhaps no coincidence that the founding of the USCC occurred at the same time as the expansion of federal administrative agencies. In the early twentieth century, the direction of U.S. competition policy was up for grabs. Rather than adopting a strictly adversarial stance toward the growing federal state, USCC records demonstrate that members overwhelmingly supported the creation and expansion of the administrative capacities of the Department of Commerce and later the FTC. This partnership between private business associations and public administrative agencies developed before the First World War and despite the limitations imposed by the judicial branch on the development of administrative law. When the Department of Justice increased its litigation against trade associations in the 1920s, these efforts, though adversarial to be sure, had the effect of encouraging USCC support for public-private collaboration. Similarly, administrators and businesspeople alike appeared undeterred by Supreme Court rulings that circumscribed administrative powers or struck down associations' trade rules.[83] During and after the First World War, the USCC became an embedded intermediary capable of coordinating business practices and regulatory prerogatives. Federal agencies, although still in their infancy relative to their development after the Second World War, held considerable regulatory power when partnered with business organizations. Leaders in these public agencies shifted toward strategies that borrowed from and expanded on trade association procedures in an effort to foster what they believed were public interest goals, such as governing competition, eliminating waste, and stabilizing prices. This public-private governance strategy was less concerned with market efficiencies and lowest consumer prices than it was with promoting an abstract notion of fair competition and administrative capacities. The Great Depression, of course, fundamentally challenged whether any public interest could be surmised from this close relationship between business and government, and the experiment largely broke down by the time of the Second New Deal and Thurmond Arnold's revival of antitrust prosecutions.[84] A new type of adversarial relationship between business and government emerged as both sides worked to develop their own capacities to govern. Nevertheless, the story of American state building requires attention to the early twentieth-century efforts at public-private cooperation, which produced both a robust administrative state and an equally formidable national organization of private businesses.

Chapter 2

Toward a Civic Welfare State: Business and City Building in the 1920s

Daniel Amsterdam

What role did business interests play in the development of American social policy in the early twentieth century, an era when the nation swam in a "sudden abundance" of social policy proposals and debated them with unusual fervor?[1]

Scholars who have grappled with this question head on in recent years have tended to do so in one of three ways. Some have focused on business interests' overarching resistance to the rise of a social welfare state composed of policies like old-age pensions, unemployment insurance, and other government-sponsored benefits and protections for the nation's working class.[2] Others have closely scrutinized employers' experiments with welfare capitalism, or the provision of fringe benefits to workers in the private sector.[3] Finally, a handful of historians have explored the ideas and activism of a small group of moguls who parted ways with the majority of their corporate colleagues during the Great Depression and showed at least modest support for the social welfare state that took shape during the New Deal.[4]

In reality, however, the social politics of American business interests in the early twentieth century were far more extensive than such accounts suggest. Appreciating this fact especially demands scrutinizing how business interests mobilized at the local level—not just in statehouses and in

Washington, the focal points of most recent scholarship examining the intersection of state development and social policy in the early twentieth century. Indeed, even as they resisted many state and federal social programs, commercial and industrial elites in cities across the country—including Detroit and Atlanta, the main examples used in this chapter—turned to municipal government to address a host of social challenges throughout the period, from crime, vice, and political radicalism to the purported need to "Americanize" the foreign born. At the same time, particularly boosterish businessmen in cities like Atlanta championed various local social programs for an additional reason: to attract new firms to their hometown. In fact, despite sharp differences in the economic and political environments of Atlanta and Detroit, business elites in both cities rallied around a strikingly similar vision for government-sponsored social policy in the early twentieth century, especially (but far from exclusively) in the decade following the First World War, a moment when the political activism of business interests in both places helped encourage an unprecedented flurry of social spending.

To paint in broad brushstrokes, Detroit's budget was 340 percent larger in 1929 than it had been just before the United States entered the war, even when inflation is taken into account. All of this growth took place after the armistice. Atlanta's budget grew by 134 percent in the same period, adjusted for inflation. In both cities, spending expanded far faster than the local population, which grew rapidly in both locales. Detroit spent 58 percent more per person in real dollars at the end of the 1920s than it had just before the United States declared war. Atlanta spent 60 percent more per person.[5]

Meanwhile, expenditures in both cities grew more rapidly in the 1920s than they had earlier in the century, a pattern that also held true in New York, Chicago, Philadelphia, Los Angeles, and in many other urban areas. Altogether in the nation's largest cities—those with populations greater than 300,000—per capita spending adjusted for inflation actually decreased by 5 percent between 1904 and 1916. By contrast, in a similar twelve-year increment, between 1916 and 1928, spending per person rose 55 percent, again with all of this growth occurring after the war. These figures belie the notion that the 1920s were an antigovernment moment of retrenchment or a time when government development was limited to Prohibition and the development of a smattering of other initiatives, like the early federal forays into economic planning that Ellis Hawley and others have explored. Rather, in cities like Detroit and Atlanta, the political activism of local business elites helped make the 1920s a moment of extensive government expansion.[6]

Opposed to most forms of social insurance, these businessmen embraced public schooling, the promotion of public health, and the construction of decentralized cities featuring parks, playgrounds, libraries, museums, and single-family homes. Often through a windfall of public spending, they hoped to remake American cities and in many cases the citizens who inhabited them. Largely resistant to a social welfare state, they sought to build what might be called a civic welfare state, a network of government programs that in the minds of elite businessmen promised to further both the goals of urban reform and urban boosterism, to prepare citizens for work and democracy while helping lure new firms to their hometowns.

It was a project that prioritized government-sponsored social policies that urban business leaders believed would bring higher levels of social and political stability as well as economic growth without compromising employers' control over their own firms or their leverage in the labor market, as many social welfare-state programs threatened to do. Still, it was an agenda that hinged on aggressive government action, albeit deployed primarily at the local level. Of course, scholars interested in specific policy areas have emphasized businessmen's support for urban social policies like public schooling, the promotion of public health, or various forms of city planning before. But historians have rarely woven these patterns into broader accounts of corporate social politics per se. The social politics of American business interests in the early twentieth century were a complex amalgam of privatism and antistatism in certain realms with an enthusiastically pro-government approach in others. Moreover, as the case of social policy underscores, businessmen's political activism frequently varied across different levels of the U.S. federalist system. To modify slightly one of Robert Wiebe's characterizations of business attitudes during the period, business interests viewed government action "suspiciously" in certain instances. But above all, they viewed government— whether at the federal, state, or local level—as an instrument to be used "selectively" and in some cases aggressively.[7]

Familiar Stories: Managing Workers and the "Workingman's Risk"

One of the main concerns of recent scholarship focused on corporate social politics in the early twentieth century has been to determine how and to what extent employers attempted to address problems like unemployment or poverty in old age, risks that nearly all working-class employees faced at the time. These were precisely the sorts of hardships that modern social welfare states sought to ameliorate through programs such as old-age pensions, unemployment insurance, workers' compensation, and minimum-wage and maximum-hour laws. Explicit definitions of the social welfare state are difficult to find in many histories, but a tacit understanding tends to run through most of them. When scholars speak of the welfare state, they generally discuss public programs that directly intervene in the labor market and, to borrow from a leading sociologist, to some degree "de-commodify" human labor. In the case of old-age pensions, unemployment insurance, and workers' compensation, these programs lessen, to varying extents, the degree to which eligible participants have to rely solely on the labor market—on the commodification of their labor—to gain a living. In the case of policies like maximum-hour and minimum-wage laws, such measures set limits on the degree and the price at which people can sell or be used as labor commodities on the open market. Through them, governments intervene in labor relations to assert a level of human worth beyond one's value as a labor commodity, and thus they, too, "de-commodify."[8]

Employers in the early twentieth century tended to oppose the implementation of most social welfare-state programs defined along these lines. That said, scholars have noted important exceptions. For instance, in the years leading up to the First World War, business interests generally supported the creation of the nation's first workmen's compensation laws, which many employers preferred to settling disputes related to workplace injuries in the courts. In addition, during a short but sharp economic downturn in the early 1920s, local business leaders in cities across the country helped lead efforts to aid the jobless through a combination of public and private initiatives, from registering the unemployed and pressuring companies to avoid further layoffs to expanding employment on public improvements and creating makeshift work-relief programs. By the late 1920s, a handful of corporate executives had begun flirting with the notion of providing government pensions to the elderly. And during the New Deal, a few especially prominent businessmen took part in deliberations that helped produce the United States' current system of unemployment compensation and old-age pensions through the Social Security Act of 1935. This exceptional few included executives of very large firms, such as Gerard Swope of General Electric, Morris E. Leeds of Leeds and Northrup, and Walter Teagle of Standard Oil of New Jersey. Along with Marion B. Folsom of Kodak and Sam Lewisohn of Miami Copper, these men were tapped by President Franklin D. Roosevelt to serve on an advisory board to the body that was charged with authoring the Social Security Act. Scholars have debated the role that these high-profile executives actually played in the eventual design of the bill. The balance of evidence suggests that their influence was limited at best. Moreover, even if they had extensively influenced the design of the Social Security Act, the fact remains that they did not represent the sentiments of the overwhelming majority of businesspeople at the time. As one of the Roosevelt administration's own handpicked corporate advisers, Marion Folsom, later attested, "only five percent of employers" were supportive of legislation "along the lines" of the Social Security Act. This was indicative of a broader pattern. Whether in the 1930s or earlier, business interests were far more likely to oppose than to support calls for public social policies that threatened to limit employers' control over their own firms or that lessened the degree to which working-class Americans had to rely on the private labor market to get by.[9]

Among a highly visible subgroup of corporate managers and executives, resisting proposals for a social welfare state was linked to another trend: a growing tendency to view issues like economic security in sickness or old age as opportunities that employers, themselves, might be able to leverage. Addressing at least some of workers' economic vulnerabilities through fringe benefits and other initiatives offered a chance to bolster worker loyalty, to limit labor turnover, and to increase productivity, these businessmen believed. In the decades preceding the Great Depression, some companies began to experiment with offering stock options to their workers as well as vacation days, sick pay, pensions, and other so-called welfare capitalist programs.

It was primarily large, highly profitable firms that embraced welfare capitalism in the early twentieth century, although some smaller enterprises did as well. According to one study, only 6.5 percent of companies employing between 500 and 2,000 workers had industrial relations departments at the end of the 1920s—one indicator of a firm's commitment to the welfare capitalist enterprise. By contrast, 50 percent of businesses employing more than 2,000 workers had established one. In 1929, the National Industrial Conference Board (NICB), an employer-sponsored research organization, surveyed more than 4,000 firms with 250 or fewer employees and found that only 4.6 percent of them offered pension programs. By contrast, 26.4 percent of firms with 251 or more employees surveyed by the NICB did so to some degree (a proportion that nonetheless underscores that pensions were far from widespread even among larger corporations). Other programs were more prevalent. The NICB found that more than 70 percent of the firms that it canvassed offered some form of group insurance, while more than 90 percent had implemented initiatives to promote worker safety. Still, these figures mask how greatly welfare capitalist programs could vary from company to company. As much as it is important not to overestimate welfare capitalism's reach, it is just as crucial not to underestimate the shoddiness of the services that some employers actually provided.[10]

Of utmost importance, however, is recognizing that the social politics of American business interests in the early twentieth century encompassed far more than these familiar stories suggest. Famous instances of big-donor philanthropy by themselves speak to this truth, whether Andrew Carnegie's providing funds for library construction across the country or the Rockefellers' funding schools in the South. A close examination of businessmen's political activism in urban America especially drives this point home.

Building a Civic Welfare State in Detroit and Atlanta

Differences in the economies, economic histories, and political environments of Detroit and Atlanta make them useful sites for a comparative examination of business interests' social politics and activism. Detroit emerged as a quintessential boomtown in the early twentieth century. People and capital flooded into the city as the auto industry first took root and flourished. Atlanta's population and economy expanded during the period as well, but not nearly as much as Detroit's, nor as much as Atlanta's boosterish business elite desired. Meanwhile, Detroit was a mass democracy. Its electorate was far more encompassing than Atlanta's, where widespread disfranchisement drastically curtailed the number of eligible voters.

These economic and political trends shaped businessmen's political experience in Detroit and Atlanta in different ways. Yet when it comes to local business leaders' overarching social policy agenda, it is similarities, not differences, that primarily shine through. At various points in the early twentieth century, elite businessmen in both cities mobilized on behalf of local social programs like public schooling, public health, and the construction of parks, playgrounds, and libraries. They also backed forms of city planning that promised to serve certain social political ends, such as alleviating disease, promoting cultural uplift, and eliminating the moral and physical hazards that many businessmen associated with residential congestion. In addition, business leaders' political activism unfolded to a similar rhythm in both locales. Business elites in Atlanta and Detroit championed spending on sundry municipal social programs in the years leading up to the First World War. But it was after the war, in the 1920s, when they turned to public social policy with the greatest fervor and when their attempt to build a civic welfare state bore the most fruit.

The composition of Detroit's business elite was in flux in the opening years of the century. The rise of auto manufacturing produced a new group of tycoons. These men eventually displaced the merchants and manufacturers who had made their fortunes in pre-automotive Detroit as the vanguard of the city's commercial and industrial elite. But this process was more amicable than one might expect. Detroiters who traced their wealth back to the city's old, nineteenth-century economy—rooted in the production of railcars and stoves, in lumber and in mining—were among the first investors in the city's fledgling car shops. Many of them made money on the car boom and quickly realized the importance of building strong social, political, and economic ties to the city's newest moguls. Soon, recently flush automobile executives and the city's old business leaders were comfortably hobnobbing together at Detroit's toniest social clubs and serving alongside one another on various corporate boards. By 1916, the names of a number of the city's new automobile magnates appeared alongside those of Detroit's most established families in Dau's *Blue Book*, essentially a "who's who" of the local upper crust. Despite the almost revolutionary transformation of Detroit's economy, the city's barons, new and old, were coalescing into a relatively coherent business class.[11]

There was one prominent exception to this trend: Henry Ford. Members of Detroit's pre-automotive elite had invested in Ford's early companies as well, but Ford's first venture flopped, and investors quickly pushed him out of his second when he refused to embrace their vision for the company. Even after Ford had become an unparalleled success, he remained at odds with many of his corporate counterparts. His competitors were furious when he announced the five-dollar day in 1914, claiming that it threatened to drive up wages throughout the city. They ridiculed his opposition to U.S. involvement in the First World War. When Ford backed the reelection of Democratic president Woodrow Wilson in 1916, members of Detroit's solidly Republican business elite jeered. Perhaps taking the hint—or maybe out of spite—Henry Ford's involvement in Detroit politics grew increasingly sporadic.[12]

By contrast, other car executives grew all the more involved in local affairs. In the run-up to the First World War, leaders of the automobile industry took charge of the local business community's most prominent civic organizations. Between 1911 and America's entry into the war, the presidents of the Detroit Board of Commerce were all in car manufacturing. Representatives of the auto industry also dominated the board's directorate. Meanwhile, auto executives, like Hugh Chalmers of Chalmers Motor Company, F. F. Beall of Packard, and A. L. McMeans of Dodge, took the helm of the Detroit Employers' Association, the corporate elite's organizational base for waging war on local unions.[13]

Amid these developments, members of Detroit's commercial and industrial elite—primarily auto men, executives at large, older firms, and highly successful downtown merchants—set their sights on achieving a handful of social policy goals. Yet they largely failed to implement them before the end of the war. For instance, when local business leaders called for the construction of a new cultural center—composed of grand, neoclassical homes for the city's public library and art museum—their pleas led to few results. Business leaders wanted local officials to build both buildings along lines inspired by the popular City Beautiful movement, which in part sought to use the power of architecture and urban design to uplift the so-called urban masses. William C. Weber—a Detroit businessman who had made his fortune in timber and real estate—helped lead the charge for the new museum and library. As Weber argued, the cultural center promised to offer everyday Detroiters "high pleasures" as well as "higher ideals," to teach "Detroit residents who could not afford to travel to Europe or New York" that there was "something better" than working-class "nickelodeons," vaudeville theater, and other forms of mass entertainment. When it came to lobbying for the art museum, Weber especially collaborated with the wealthy trustees of that institution, particularly Dexter M. Ferry, a local executive and heir to his father's lucrative seed distribution company. Meanwhile, leaders of the Detroit Board of Commerce were deeply involved in lobbying for the new library building, but to limited avail before the war.[14]

Similarly, when leaders of the Detroit Board of Commerce attempted to prod local legislators to build new playgrounds across the city on the eve of the First World War, their efforts led to a meager $15,000 appropriation from the city even though the board had called for much more. As a representative of the business organization warned, "[T]he caliber of our future citizens depends largely upon the boys of today." Without playgrounds the "animal spirits" of local children were turning toward other "natural outlets," such as "neighborhood gangs, petty thieving" and similar "depredations."[15]

At the time, Detroit was run by a city council made up of thirty-six members elected from wards across the city. The city's school board was also ward based. An enormous, 146-member board of estimates had to approve all city expenditures. Laws placed limits on the amount of funding that the city could appropriate to institutions like the art museum, which at the time was still a private entity. Frustrated with their lack of political influence, members of the city's commercial and industrial elite set out to rewrite the city charter. They succeeded in this task in 1918. Henry Leland, the president of Cadillac Motor Company, spearheaded the effort, working through a business-dominated political organization that he had founded just a few years before: the Detroit Citizens League. Leland was involved in a number of political efforts at the time, including the fight for Prohibition—a reminder that a significant cohort of businessmen viewed banning alcohol as an essential part of their quest to improve the nation's citizenry, and thus as an important facet of the civic welfare state that they sought to build. (Of course, Prohibition was a divisive issue for American business interests, so just as significant a collection of business leaders disagreed.) Joining forces with the Detroit Citizens League, the Detroit Board of Commerce threw its weight behind charter reform, while moguls like John and Horace Dodge, Edsel Ford, and S. S. Kresge (whose name would eventually put the "K" in Kmart) all donated large sums to fund the effort.[16]

Implemented in 1919, Detroit's new charter replaced the existing city council with a much smaller body consisting of nine members selected in citywide contests. As Leland and his corporate brethren well knew, citywide or "at large" elections greatly favored wealthy or well-funded candidates who could afford to wage advertising campaigns in all parts of town. In collaboration with the Detroit Federation of Women's Clubs, Leland and the Citizens League managed to revamp the city's school board along similar lines, an effort that the Detroit Board of Commerce also backed. In addition, the new charter gave the mayor and city council, not a board of estimates, final authority over municipal spending.[17]

With these reforms in place, the city's business leaders and their close political allies would dominate Detroit's government for most of the decade that followed. Except for a brief interval between 1924 and 1926, candidates backed by Henry Leland's Citizens League constituted a supermajority of Detroit's city council in the 1920s. Candidates supported by the league were even more preponderant on the city's school board, and all but three school board members who served during the decade were listed in Detroit's social register. Additionally, the city's mayors, when they were not business executives themselves, made a point of forging close ties to the city's commercial and industrial elite.[18]

With this newfound grip on power, Detroit's business leaders set out to implement a public agenda that grew rapidly during the war and its aftermath. The First World War had triggered a rapid influx of newcomers to the city, straining public services. Reports of crime, vice, and juvenile delinquency had soared. Along with these trends, the strikes, race riots, and bombings that followed the armistice prodded corporate leaders in Detroit to turn to social spending with new urgency.[19] In 1919, the city's newly elected mayor, James Couzens—a multimillionaire and former general manager of Ford—convened what he called a "reconstruction meeting," consisting of "250 bankers, manufacturers" and public officials, to address a host of issues, from a shortage of housing to strains on public services. Frank W. Blair, president of Union Trust, called on the city to spend nearly a quarter of a billion dollars to meet its needs. James Vernor, a local manufacturer and president of the city council, testified that local legislators were "ready to go to the limit as far as construction work is concerned." Wealthy auto-parts distributor and president of the Detroit Board of Commerce Allan A. Templeton pledged his organization's support.[20] Soon thereafter, the Board of Commerce's weekly publication proclaimed, "Instead of a slow and deliberate program of public improvements, it is necessary to do a great number of things all at once.... Immense bond issues must be sold."[21]

In the months that followed, Couzens and members of the city council approved the largest spending program in Detroit's history up to that time, including a multimillion-dollar program to improve the city's water and sewer systems and a similarly robust amount for roads. Much of this construction was geared toward alleviating residential congestion and promoting urban decentralization. As Mayor Couzens explained, "It is the consensus of opinion that there is more immorality being caused by people huddled together in small rooms, who are robbed of normal home life ... than from any other cause." [22] Couzens and the city council also rubberstamped a $10 million program to expand the city's network of playgrounds, a cause that the Detroit Board of Commerce continued to champion. City officials also completed the new central library, a lynchpin of the cultural center that business leaders like William Weber had proposed before the war. In addition, Couzens, the city council, and the city's elite board of education resolved to build schools at an unprecedented pace. Between 1919 and 1921, appropriations to the board of education shot up from $9.8 million to more than $31 million.[23] When the school district's building initiative came under attack in some quarters, leaders of the Board of Commerce quickly rose to the defense. "[T]o say that we must stop building schools is utterly ridiculous." Halting school construction, the businessmen warned, would amount to "civic suicide."[24]

In fact, by 1923, local officials had spent with such abandon that Detroit was on the brink of exceeding its debt limit—a development that precipitated a brief fiscal crisis that temporarily undercut local business leaders' political influence. In elections that fall, Henry Leland's Citizens League was handed its only major defeat of the decade. But business leaders' sojourn in the political wilderness would not last long. In 1924, a new mayor helped put businessmen behind the wheel of the city's policymaking process once again. That mayor, John Smith, was initially elected on a wave of working-class support but in a very tight race. He barely edged out another candidate who was backed by the local Ku Klux Klan, whose ranks swelled for a brief time in the middle of the decade. With the Klan threatening to mobilize again and with Smith's sights on reelection, the new mayor moved to broaden his base, especially by forging ties with the city's business community.[25]

In one of his first speeches after taking office, Mayor Smith appeared before the Detroit Board of Commerce and pledged that his administration would be a business administration. In a move that members of the board of commerce later called "one of the finest steps ever taken by a public official in this city," Smith announced that he would appoint a committee of five of the city's most prominent businessmen to survey the city's financial conditions and make recommendations for a ten-year plan for city expenditures. In the ensuing months, Smith went on to appoint more business-dominated committees to examine municipal affairs. As leaders of the Detroit Federation of Labor complained, Smith gave local unions short shrift despite "plenty of evidence that . . . big business elements received ample recognition."[26]

In June 1925, Smith's business-run finance committee released its ten-year plan. The mayor wholeheartedly endorsed the report, which hewed closely to business leaders' past priorities. The report included an ambitious proposal for infrastructural expansion: $60 million for school construction, the extension and maintenance of playground and park facilities, funding to complete the new art museum building as well as improvements to the city's two public hospitals. All told, the committee recommended the expenditure of nearly $450 million over ten years for public improvement projects alone (the equivalent of more than $6 billion in 2015 dollars).[27]

Local officials pursued many of these projects as the 1920s continued. A new building for the art museum opened in 1927. Spending on recreation and schooling boomed, as did expenditures on sewers, water mains, and roads. After 1925, much of this new construction followed Detroit's first official master plan, which formalized efforts to make Detroit a sprawling, decentralized city of freestanding homes. The Detroit Board of Commerce and the Detroit Real Estate Board both strongly backed the 1925 Master Plan, which was the product of city's Rapid Transit Commission, a body that consisted of five members, four of whom were local executives.[28]

Whether in the 1920s or earlier, elite businessmen in Detroit primarily turned to public social policy to address problems they associated with Detroit's relentless economic and demographic expansion. Their counterparts in Atlanta shared similar concerns and likewise sought to use various government programs to address them. But members of Atlanta's white business elite also turned to government-sponsored social policy to further an additional mission: to attract new firms to their city, an imperative that was far less pressing for Detroit's business leaders amid the Motor City's fast-paced economic growth. As a leading Atlanta booster and former president of the Atlanta Chamber of Commerce proclaimed during a major push to attract new businesses to the city, "When we get ready to advertise [Atlanta], we are going to have to tell what advantages we have in schools, in sewer and water improvements, in civic buildings and general progress. . . . [W]e must first provide these schools and improvements before we can advertise them."[29]

The boosterism that helped fuel the political activism of Atlanta's business elite had important consequences. Not only did Atlanta's business leaders want to expand government programs in certain areas, but they also wanted to keep local taxes low as part of their efforts to attract new enterprises. Thus, Atlanta's business elite put a particularly exclusive emphasis on debt spending as a way of funding major public projects. In Atlanta, however, gaining the right to float bonds was an exceptionally difficult task. By the 1920s, winning a bond referendum not only required the consent of two-thirds of the voters participating in a given election, but that two-thirds also had to constitute 50 percent of the city's registered electorate. In most cities, including Detroit, winning bond elections demanded a mere majority vote no matter the voter turnout.[30]

In part due to these constraints, business leaders in Atlanta managed to win only one major bond referendum prior to the First World War. At the time, Atlanta's business elite primarily consisted of merchants dealing in cotton and other agricultural commodities, bank executives, owners of large downtown stores, and owners and executives in the city's small but growing manufacturing sector. In early 1908, Harry L. Schlesinger, owner of a local candy and cracker factory, published an open letter in the *Atlanta Constitution* calling for a large bond issue to fund a set of initiatives that Schlesinger believed promised to improve Atlanta's "prestige and prosperity" as well as its citizens "mental and moral . . . development." Schlesinger called for new parks, schools, and sewers as well as sidewalks and a new city hall.[31] Many successful businessmen signed onto the plan, including leaders of the Atlanta Chamber of Commerce—the main political organization of the city's white business elite. Chamber leaders denounced "the disgraceful sanitary and hygienic conditions under which 50,000 Atlantans were living" and bemoaned conditions in Atlanta's schools.[32] In 1910, the Atlanta Chamber of Commerce—with the strong backing of the city's mayor (the wealthy banker Robert Maddox)—helped convince voters to approve $3 million in bonds to improve the city's water, sewer, and school systems.[33]

The 1910 bond issue was the largest in Atlanta's history up to that time. But the city's business leaders hoped to accomplish much more. As chamber of commerce president and owner of one of the city's main department stores F. J. Paxon declared, "[W]e need more parks, more playgrounds and breathing spots for the people; we need a museum and an art gallery comparable to the Carnegie library," which the city had constructed in 1902. "We want our city so healthy, so attractive, so wholesome and full of charm in every respect that people will come here because it is the best place to live and to educate their children."[34] By 1912, leading businessmen were already clamoring for another large bond issue, including Paxon, William Blalock (head of Fulton National Bank), and Coca-Cola president Asa Candler. A similar cohort continued to press for debt spending for years to come, but their efforts led to minimal results before the end of the war.[35]

By the 1920s, elite businessmen's commitment to increasing social spending had grown all the stronger in Atlanta, pushing them to launch multiple campaigns on behalf of more bonds and even to forge unexpected alliances to ensure victory. For instance, in both 1921 and 1926, white business leaders made a point of courting the votes of a small group of African Americans who, despite widespread disfranchisement, retained the right to vote in special elections like bond referenda, which were not subject to the restrictions governing all-white Democratic Party primaries. In 1919, African Americans had mobilized to defeat a relatively small, $1 million bond issue that local business leaders strongly backed because none of the funds had been earmarked for the city's African American community. The local branch of the NAACP and the all-female Neighborhood Union—a social service organization founded by Lugenia Burns Hope—galvanized African American efforts. Thus, in 1921, when the city's white business leadership and their close political allies launched a campaign to pass a far larger, $8.85 million bond issue, one of their first moves was to enlist the support of local African Americans, who pledged their votes only after ensuring that some of the funds would be set aside for African American neighborhoods. In the end, the bond proposal won at the polls, funneling $4 million to the city's schools—including funding for the city's first African American public high school—and more than $4 million toward the city's water and sewer systems. A similar interracial alliance threw its weight behind another successful business-backed bond initiative in 1926, which was worth $8 million and went toward a similar array of initiatives.[36]

Of course, Jim Crow still reigned in 1920s Atlanta despite such instances of interracial cooperation. In 1922, Atlanta's white business leaders mobilized on behalf of a citywide zoning ordinance that among other goals promoted residential decentralization in the name of fostering "home ownership and good citizenship," much like Detroit's 1925 Master Plan.[37] Yet Atlanta's zoning ordinance also mandated residential segregation. Members of the Atlanta Chamber of Commerce first proposed the creation of the city planning commission that eventually drew up Atlanta's segregated zoning plan. Business elites also dominated the commission itself. When the zoning ordinance was adopted in 1922, the body consisted of Frank Pittman, the head of a successful construction company; real-estate developer Robert R. Otis; wealthy railroad executive C. A. Wickersham; Joel Hurt, one of Atlanta's preeminent utility owners and real-estate developers; a token representative of organized labor; and U.S. Senator Hoke Smith, a successful lawyer, newspaper publisher, hotel owner, and, as former governor, leader of the 1908 movement to disfranchise black Georgians. The Atlanta Chamber of Commerce and the Atlanta Real Estate Board both endorsed the new zoning plan, which shaped Atlanta's development for years to come.[38]

As the case of segregated zoning in Atlanta suggests, urban business leaders in the early twentieth century championed a host of public social initiatives even as they also embraced and sought to encourage various forms of inequality—racial inequality in Atlanta being just one example. In the city of these businessmen's dreams, the local economy would be robust, immigrants would be "Americanized," crime and disease would be minimal, and working-class children and adults would be pliable in the workplace and shy away from political radicalism in the voting booth. But would these ideal citizen-workers receive adequate wages? Would economic insecurity remain a regular part of working-class life? In businessmen's ideal city, such questions would be for employers, not the government, to decide.

In answering those specific questions, most businessmen continued to embrace largely privatist and antistatist approaches through the 1930s even as the Great Depression dramatically exposed the extent of working-class vulnerability. Indeed, most elite businessmen in Detroit and Atlanta clung to such convictions even as the municipal debt that they had urged local officials to rack up in the 1920s wreaked havoc on local budgets amid the depression. Spiraling loan payments drained potential funding away from public aid to the unemployed and, in Detroit's case, helped to provoke the city's default in 1933. Nonetheless, as the cases of Atlanta and Detroit suggest, businessmen's social politics in the early twentieth century were an opportunistic mixture of antistatism on some fronts and strong support for government action on others. With the right configuration of government programs, these businessmen believed, they could build cities where the upheaval that accompanied urbanization could be tamed. By realizing their vision of a civic welfare state, they could ensure that, in urban America, capital consistently held the upper hand.[39]

PART II

The New Deal and the Second World War

Chapter 3

The "Monopoly" Hearings, Their Critics, and the Limits of Patent Reform in the New Deal

Eric S. Hintz

In April 1938, during the dog days of the Great Depression, President Franklin D. Roosevelt called on Congress to make "a thorough study of the concentration of economic power in American industry" and its impact on the economy. In his so-called monopoly message, Roosevelt warned that collectivism and anticompetitive practices among big businesses had perpetuated the Great Depression, and if left unchecked could even lead to fascism, as witnessed by the "unhappy events abroad" in places like Germany, Italy, and Spain.[1] The resulting Temporary National Economic Committee (or TNEC) spent the next thirty months conducting a comprehensive investigation of the nation's economic ills. By the time the hearings concluded in March 1941, the committee had accumulated a mountain of evidence—more than 20,000 pages of testimony and exhibits from 552 witnesses and forty-three additional monographs commissioned on specific subjects—eighty-two printed volumes in all.[2] The TNEC's thirty-one hearings examined antitrust policies, tax codes, and business practices in various industries, including insurance, oil, and banking. However, the committee did not begin by tackling these core economic issues; instead it began with patents.

In December 1938, the TNEC hearings commenced with two hearings on the use and abuse of patents in the maintenance of corporate monopolies. The committee solicited testimony from witnesses including Patent Commissioner Conway Coe, independent inventors such as television pioneer Philo Farnsworth, and corporate researchers such as Bell Labs director Frank B. Jewett. The hearings also motivated the pro-business National Association of Manufacturers (NAM) to develop the Modern Pioneers program, a sophisticated public relations campaign designed to stifle some of the suggested reforms. Why all the fuss about patents? With so many thorny economic issues complicating the Great Depression, why did the committee and its stakeholders devote so much attention to arcane questions of U.S. patent policy?

The TNEC recognized that the patent system—alongside a common currency, contract law, and other institutions—was one of the fundamental, state-sponsored building blocks of the American economy but feared that it had been corrupted by corporate prerogatives. As Zorina Kahn has shown, the predictable and bureaucratic nature of the American patent system differed substantially from its British and French predecessors, in which patents were precarious privileges granted by monarchs. Article I, Section 8 of the U.S. Constitution granted Congress the power "to promote the Progress of Science and useful Arts, by securing for limited Times to Authors and Inventors the exclusive Right to their respective Writings and Discoveries." The ensuing Patent Act of 1790 duly granted inventors the exclusive rights to their inventions for fourteen (later seventeen) years. In exchange for this temporary monopoly, the inventor was required to publish a full description of the invention (the patent), which became freely available for public use after the term expired. When the Patent Office examined new and useful ideas and granted its imprimatur, the resulting patent became a secure form of intellectual property—a tradable capital asset that inventors could sell, license, or exploit as the basis of new entrepreneurial ventures. Moreover, inventors could turn to the federal courts to defend their exclusive property rights against infringement. Overall, the founders believed the temporary patent monopoly would economically incentivize inventors to create more new technologies, while the eventual free and widespread use of those technologies would benefit the public.[3]

Recently, Petra Moser, Tom Nicholas, and other scholars have questioned this basic trade-off, suggesting that the monopolistic behavior and excessive litigation spurred by patents can actually discourage innovation.[4] These tensions were at the heart of the TNEC's monopoly investigations, because patents constituted one of the few legal, if temporary, monopolies. Patents earned by individual inventors were seen as a legitimate form of monopoly and received a tacit exemption under the Sherman Antitrust Act of 1890. However, contemporary observers had become concerned that large, technology-based corporations were increasingly using patents in ways the founders had not intended. With the emergence of the first industrial laboratories around 1900, teams of scientists at General Electric, AT&T, and DuPont annually earned and assigned hundreds of patents to their employers. In addition, by merging with other firms and buying up useful patents from independent inventors, the biggest firms had acquired massive patent portfolios that could provide monopolistic control over the technologies in certain industries.[5] For example, the appropriation, sharing, and aggressive defense of intellectual property had sustained AT&T's telephone monopoly, and a shared patent pool had helped rivals General Electric and Westinghouse dominate the electrical industry.[6] Collectively, these firms had come to recognize a strong patent portfolio as the "most effective means of controlling competition" in a given market, constituting a "monopoly of monopolies."[7]

In short, the rise of corporate patenting had highlighted an inherent tension between the patent laws and the antitrust statutes, so the TNEC set out to investigate the situation with an eye toward reform. Scholars have devoted considerable attention to the intensification of federal antitrust enforcement beginning in the late 1930s, with frequent references to the TNEC and its findings.[8] Yet to date, there has been little analysis of the TNEC patent hearings or the proposed reforms they inspired.[9] And although several scholars have examined the NAM's general opposition to the New Deal and its specific positions on labor, taxes, and wages, its activities in the realm of patents and intellectual property have been overlooked.[10] Overall, patents—especially in the context of antitrust concerns and fair trade practices—became a key reform issue during the New Deal and a key locus of business-government relations, yet one that has received little scholarly attention.

Accordingly, this chapter examines the TNEC patent hearings of 1938–39, in which independent inventors, industrial researchers, business leaders, and lawmakers debated the political economy of the patent system at a moment when invention was increasingly coming under corporate control. Drawing on the congressional record, contemporary press coverage, and the records

of the NAM, this account demonstrates that patent policy was a central concern during the New Deal and helps move considerations of patent law into
the mainstream of scholarship in the history of capitalism. Finally, this epi-
sode illuminates the NAM's turn toward public relations during the 1930s
and suggests that the association's influence helped block the TNEC's most
liberal reforms, resulting in a patent system that—even today—favors corporate researchers at the expense of independent inventors.

The Political-Economic Impetus for
the TNEC Hearings, 1937–38

When Franklin D. Roosevelt assumed office in 1933, he was faced with a
thorny dilemma. Economically, FDR needed the cooperation of big businesses to jumpstart the recovery, but politically, he needed them to be a
scapegoat. Thus, as Ellis Hawley has argued, Roosevelt's administration
struggled to find a "coherent and logically consistent set of business policies."
Initially, the New Deal turned to business-government cooperation under
the National Industrial Recovery Act of 1933 (NIRA), in which the National
Recovery Administration set prices and wages for various industries via
"codes of fair competition." When the Supreme Court struck down the NIRA
in 1935, the administration engaged in "partial planning" by encouraging
trade associations to self-regulate certain "sick industries" (e.g. coal, oil, and
cotton) and "natural monopolies" (e.g. public utilities, railroads) that were
essential to the economy.[11]

These planning efforts led to a tenuous recovery, and after his 1936 reelection, Roosevelt curbed stimulus spending in an attempt to rebalance the
federal budget; this triggered the "Roosevelt Recession" of 1937. However,
antitrust proponents blamed big businesses for the downturn. They argued
that several industries had enjoyed price gains via the endorsed collusion of
the administration's planning efforts but had pocketed the resulting profits
instead of expanding employment or raising wages. Roosevelt vacillated
among several possible strategies for addressing the recession before settling
on a two-pronged approach combining renewed deficit spending and an invigorated antimonopoly campaign.[12] On April 14, 1938, the president sent his
"spending" message to Congress, encouraging renewal of work relief and
public works programs. Two weeks later, on April 29, FDR sent Congress his
"monopoly" message, calling for the TNEC investigations.[13] The goal of the
forthcoming hearings, a journalist observed, was to gather information and

Table 3.1. Charter members of the Temporary National Economic
Committee, 1938

Chairman: Senator Joseph C. O'Mahoney (D-Wyoming)
Vice chairman: Representative Hatton W. Sumners (D-Texas)
Executive secretary: Leon Henderson, Works Progress Administration

Members of Congress	*Members of the Executive Branch*
Senate	**Department of Justice**
Senator William E. Borah (R-Idaho)	Thurman W. Arnold, assistant attorney general
Senator William H. King (D-Utah)	**Department of the Treasury**
	Herman Oliphant, general counsel
	Department of Commerce
	Richard C. Patterson, Jr., assistant secretary
House of Representatives	**Department of Labor**
Representative Clyde Williams (D-Missouri)	Isador Lubin, commissioner of labor statistics
Representative B. Carroll Reece, (R-Tennessee)	**Securities and Exchange Commission**
	William O. Douglas, chairman
	Federal Trade Commission
	Garland S. Ferguson, chairman

Source: Data are from *Investigation of Concentration of Economic Power: Hearings before the Temporary National Economic Committee* (Washington, D.C.: Government Printing Office, 1939), Part 1, frontispiece, and David Lynch, *Concentration of Economic Power* (New York: Columbia University Press, 1946), 35–50.

"lay the foundation for legislation out of which will emerge a 'modernized capitalism.'"[14]

During the spring and summer of 1938, the thirteen members of the TNEC were drawn from Roosevelt's administration and a mix of congressional Democrats and Republicans (Table 3.1). Like many aspects of the New Deal, the TNEC investigations were highly influenced by disciples of institutional economics, an emerging subfield that rejected laissez-faire principles in favor of government intervention in the economy. For example, Adolf Berle, an expert on corporate governance and a member of FDR's "Brain Trust," prepared a "Memorandum of Suggestions" to guide the committee. Likewise, Isador Lubin, the commissioner of labor statistics, served on the TNEC, and Walton Hamilton authored the TNEC-commissioned monograph, *Patents and Free Enterprise*, which outlined the system's defects and the committee's suggestions for reform.[15]

Reflecting the institutionalists' embrace of empirical data, the first hearing (Part 1), held in November 1938, was an "Economic Prologue," in which TNEC staff members presented a bewildering array of charts and statistics on population, "national income" (i.e., gross domestic product), prices, employment, wages, and other indicators. The next two substantive hearings investigated abuses of the patent system. In Part 2, held December 5–16, 1938, the Department of Justice's Antitrust Division examined the relationship between patents and the antitrust laws by studying their use in two fields, the automotive and glass-container industries. Then, in Part 3, held January 16–20, 1939, the Department of Commerce (with jurisdiction over the U.S. Patent Office) organized hearings on proposals for changes in patent law and procedure.[16]

The First Hearing: Patents in the Automotive and Glass-Container Industries

In the first patent hearing, the committee examined patent practices in the automobile and glass-container industries. Taking the lead was TNEC member Thurman Arnold, a former Yale law professor who now served as the assistant attorney general in charge of the Antitrust Division. Immediately following his appointment in March 1938, Arnold helped Roosevelt draft the April 29 message to Congress calling for the TNEC hearings and began vigorously prosecuting the antitrust laws after years of sporadic enforcement.[17] In justifying his choice of witnesses, Arnold explained that the automobile industry represented a "nonaggressive use of the patent privilege," whereas the glass-container industry represented an "aggressive" abuse of patents.[18]

An automobile is a complex assemblage of hundreds of patented technologies, so it is nearly impossible for an automaker to build a vehicle without infringing on someone else's patented component. Indeed, in its early years, the fledgling industry was vulnerable to the abuses of a so-called patent troll or, more politely, a "nonpracticing entity." In 1879, George Selden filed a patent application covering an internal combustion engine in combination with a four-wheeled car. Selden continuously amended the patent application and succeeded in stalling its issuance for sixteen years, until 1895. By then, several automakers found themselves potentially infringing the Selden patent. Together with William C. Whitney, Selden formed the Association of Licensed Automobile Manufacturers and succeeded in extracting royalties from most automakers, even though Selden had never manufactured an automobile from his own patent. Henry Ford and four other manufacturers contested the Selden patent, and in 1911, after years of litigation, the patent was invalidated, one year before its expiration.[19]

After the Selden affair, the industry had devised various strategies to manage their patents while avoiding expensive lawsuits. As several witnesses explained, thirty-four automakers—basically every key firm except Ford— belonged to the Automobile Manufacturers Association (AMA). Members were granted royalty-free licenses on any of the 1,285 patents in its pool. In contrast, Edsel Ford testified that his firm took out patents to protect its intellectual property but vowed never to join the AMA or any other patent pool. Although Ford aggressively defended itself against infringement charges, the firm granted nonexclusive, royalty-free licenses of its patents to any petitioners. Finally, Packard had joined the AMA to participate in its New York Auto Show, traffic research, and safety campaigns but was not a party to AMA's patent pool. Executives testified that in the past thirty years, Packard had collected $4,099,707 in royalties to license its patents (and recover development costs), while paying $553,401 to license external patents. However, given Packard's $25 million in annual revenues, royalties were a negligible income stream for the firm.[20]

In summary, the automobile industry's firms employed patents mainly to protect themselves from infringement lawsuits, not to control the market or suppress competition. Overall, firms competed on the manufacturing and sale of their automobiles, not through the manipulation of patents. With the exception of Packard, there seemed to be a nearly free exchange of intellectual property in the automobile industry, so why patent? Patents were less essential for the big automakers but were crucial for the independent inventors and small firms that supplied them. Joseph Farley, Ford's patent counsel, explained that "there are a large number of cases where the small company has perfected a very good device" but would be unable to find a buyer or manufacturer of the patent unless the inventor could ensure "some sort of patent protection."[21]

The second set of witnesses provided more fireworks. Through testimony and various exhibits, the Department of Justice revealed how the Hartford-Empire Company and its affiliates used patents and restrictive licensing provisions to gain monopoly control over the glass-container industry.[22] After years of cutthroat competition and several infringement lawsuits, Hartford-Empire and Owens-Illinois called a truce and entered into a patent cross-licensing agreement in 1924. Through this alliance, the firms controlled the two basic patents for the automated manufacturing of glass containers, Hartford-Empire's "gob-fed" method and Owens-Illinois's "suction" process. By 1938, the two firms controlled a pool of more than 700 patents, such that 97 percent of the glassware industry paid royalties and operated under patent licenses held by Hartford-Empire (67.4 percent) and Owens-Illinois (29.2 percent).[23]

Hartford-Empire utterly dominated the glass-container industry by exploiting its impenetrable patent position. The firm did not have a plant. It did not manufacture or sell any bottles. It did not even manufacture its own patented glassmaking machines, which were built and shipped to licensed glass producers by a contract manufacturer. And Hartford-Empire leased these machines, so the firm derived no income from direct sales, only licensing fees and royalties on nearly every glass bottle produced in the United States. But these revenues came to more than $6 million in 1937, and more than $40 million between 1923 and 1937. Hartford-Empire employed dozens of industrial researchers to develop new improvement patents and retained several lawyers to help it maintain its monopolistic grip on the industry. But exactly how did they do it? Asked a different way, what were the defects in the patent system that allowed Hartford-Empire to dominate the industry?[24]

First, the committee found that Hartford-Empire took advantage of the long pendency of certain patent applications to effectively extend the life of their basic patents. By continuously amending their patent applications and purposefully employing dilatory tactics, Hartford-Empire might delay the issuance of their patents for several years, thereby delaying the start of the seventeen-year expiration clock. Later, these "submarine" patents would issue and "surface" years after competitors were already using the process, suddenly placing them in jeopardy of an infringement lawsuit. Then, under the threat of litigation, smaller competitors would typically capitulate and take out a license on the submarine patent on terms favorable to the cartel. This legal extortion was a tactic borrowed directly from George Selden's playbook.[25]

Hartford-Empire also took advantage of ambiguity in the federal appeals process to harass their smaller competitors with nuisance infringement lawsuits. For example, the Obear-Nestor Company was a small glassware maker that commanded about 2 percent of the glass-container market. The firm believed its patented air-feeder method avoided infringement of the Hartford-Empire patents, so they operated outside the cartel. Nevertheless,

Hartford-Empire sued for infringement, but Obear-Nestor was initially successful in defending its patents. However, the plaintiffs merely sued again in different jurisdictions; over the course of twelve years, Hartford-Empire sued Obear-Nestor over the same patents in the third, sixth, and eighth federal circuits. As a further complication, there was a "contrarity of opinion" among the appellate courts, as Hartford's patent claims were held valid in the eighth circuit but invalid in the sixth.[26] Deep-pocketed firms held the advantage in these prolonged and expensive cases, which tended to bankrupt smaller competitors, often forcing them to capitulate.

The real key to Hartford-Empire's monopoly was its highly restrictive licensing agreements. These licenses specified which firms could manufacture milk bottles, beer bottles, or cookware. They also restricted production (i.e., the number of bottles a licensee could manufacture), and even specified the types of customers and geographical territories where containers could be sold. Though none of the licenses contained illegal price restrictions, the effect on prices was indirect; if only one licensee were allowed to produce milk bottles, that manufacturer effectively had a price monopoly. The TNEC members questioned whether a patent holder's exclusive rights to make, use, and sell the items covered in the patent should also extend so forcefully to control over his or her licensees.[27]

In addition, testimony and a damning memorandum revealed that Hartford-Empire used patens to "block" or "fence in" their rivals. As Hartford-Empire's engineers invented several different ways to produce containers, they took out "defensive" patents on these alternative methods. Hartford-Empire then suppressed these patents for seventeen years to block their rivals from using them, while protecting their own favored processes. However, if a competitor did succeed in gaining a basic, alternative patent, Hartford-Empire could "fence them in." By carefully studying the competing art and surrounding it with numerous improvement patents, it became nearly impossible for the owner of the basic patent to exploit the original invention without being subject to infringement. These tactics prevented rivals from "inventing around" Hartford's patent pool, practically forcing glassware manufacturers to take a license on the firm's preferred methods or face an infringement suit.[28]

Finally, if Hartford-Empire caught wind of a rival's new patent application, it might hurriedly submit a specious application on a similar aspect of the art, compelling the Patent Office to declare an interference proceeding to determine which application held priority. For example, testimony revealed how Hartford-Empire laid "a series of traps . . . consisting of new applications" to "stage a delaying fight" with its competitor, Whitall-Tatum. Interferences were bureaucratic proceedings, not lawsuits. However, much like infringement litigation, Hartford-Empire could use its superior legal and financial resources to wear down its competitors, subjecting them to time-consuming depositions, unanticipated legal fees, and time away from technical developments, all while forestalling the ultimate issuance of the competing patent.[29]

Overall, the first patent hearing revealed the nearly free exchange of intellectual property among automakers, and the continuing importance of patents for independent inventors as the best way to reap financial rewards from their inventions. The glass-container hearings also revealed certain legal, but nefarious, practices in which patents were used to obstruct rather than encourage innovation, subverting their original constitutional intent. These abusive practices underscored the inherent tensions between the patents laws (which granted a legal, temporary monopoly), and the antitrust statutes (which outlawed corporate actions in restraint of trade). Moreover, these systemic flaws disproportionately worked to the advantage of wealthier and more powerful firms, a sobering reality for America's independent inventors and small businesses.

The Second Hearing: Proposed Reforms to the Patent Laws

In the second patent hearing, held in January 1939, the TNEC considered several legislative proposals to amend the patent laws. The first witness, patent commissioner Conway Coe, first presented more than a dozen charts and graphs outlining the historical use of the patent system. He showed that in 1938, some 157 large corporations (with assets greater than $50 million) received a total of 6,415 total patents (17.2 percent); meanwhile, individuals (42.9 percent), small corporations (34.5 percent), and a handful of foreign corporations (5.4 percent) accounted for the balance. Coe believed these statistics affirmed that the patent system still offered "hope, encouragement, opportunity and recompense to an individual or a company of small resources. It is as democratic as the Constitution which begot it."[30]

Coe then offered several proposals to remedy the structural defects in the patent system revealed in the earlier hearing. First, several abuses stemmed from applicants' attempts to purposefully prolong the application process. As a remedy, Coe suggested the "twenty-year rule," in which a patent would expire seventeen years from the date of issuance or twenty years from the date of filing, whichever came first. Thus, inventors who diligently prosecuted their applications would enjoy the usual seventeen-year monopoly; however, inventors or firms that employed dilatory tactics would only penalize themselves by diminishing the monopoly term once the patent was issued.[31]

To streamline interference procedures, Coe suggested that the Patent Office should abolish its internal administrative hearings altogether and immediately issue the winning patent following the examiner's determination of priority. Any subsequent disputes over the validity of the issued patent could still be argued in the federal courts, but with the seventeen-year clock already ticking.[32] Coe also proposed the creation of a single court of patent appeals with nationwide jurisdiction. This would discourage well-funded patent holders from suing their competitors in multiple federal districts and would eliminate the ambiguity of contrary opinions across the various appellate circuits.[33]

Coe also proposed simple procedural changes designed to expedite the application process. For example, the current law permitted an inventor to make public use of an invention for two years before filing an application; Coe proposed reducing the term to one year. Similarly, the law allowed an applicant two years after the issuance of another inventor's patent to assert his own priority; again, Coe proposed limiting the challenge period to one year. Finally, applicants were allowed six months to reply to official Patent Office correspondence; Coe asked for more administrative authority to compel dilatory applicants to respond more quickly or face the lapsing of their applications.[34]

Finally, Coe concluded his testimony by describing the patent system's intangible impact on the national psyche. Before making his policy recommendations, Coe had first presented a series of sixteen "classic patents" to remind the committee of the nation's collective "indebtedness" to inventors like Eli Whitney, Cyrus McCormick, and Samuel Morse, but also its indebtedness "to the system which encouraged them."[35] Now in closing, Coe again suggested that, beyond the "evolvement of things purely mechanical," the patent system had instilled in America's citizen-inventors the virtues of "patience, resoluteness, sacrifice—suffering, too, if need be—in the pursuit of an ideal." Coe's romantic appeal to the heritage and traditions of the patent system—invoking its "spiritual influence in our national life and destinies"—would later be adopted by the NAM to oppose various reforms.[36]

Coe was a moderate, and his recommendations were essentially procedural in nature. Although they aimed to correct certain abuses, they did not change the fundamentals of the system.[37] Meanwhile, the government's zealous antitrust czar, Assistant Attorney General Thurman Arnold, proposed more radical reforms. First, Arnold recommended compulsory licensing statutes to mitigate defensive patenting and the suppression of technologies that firms never intended to use. Under a compulsory licensing law, if an allegedly suppressed patent had gone unused for three years, patent holders would be forced to grant licenses to petitioners at a royalty determined by the courts. Second, Arnold sought to ban any restrictions on output, price, use, or geography in patent licenses, which could be used by firms like the Hartford-Empire Company to exert tyrannical control over an entire industry. Third, Arnold proposed a sunshine provision, requiring that all patent sales, licensing agreements, or other patent-related contracts be registered with the Federal Trade Commission. Fourth, he proposed that infringement plaintiffs must first sue the original patent holder before pursuing a licensee, in order to limit excessive litigation as a "tool of business aggression." Finally, Arnold proposed a rule requiring forfeiture of the patent and its reversion to the public domain if patent holders were convicted of engaging in anticompetitive activities. This punitive penalty was designed to discourage abuses altogether.[38]

During the remainder of the hearing, a mix of independent inventors and corporate scientists provided testimony regarding the various recommendations. Nearly everyone approved of Commissioner Coe's procedural reforms to streamline the application process, except for patent attorneys, who stood to lose billable hours.[39] Independent inventors definitely supported Coe's proposals to streamline interference procedures and to create a single court of patent appeals, which together would reduce their exposure to expensive hearings and lawsuits that the bigger firms used as weapons.

However, most independent inventors, like television inventor Philo Farnsworth, joined the bigger firms in opposing Arnold's compulsory licensing proposal, because it effectively shortened their monopoly from seventeen to three years. This severely weakened their patents, the one piece of leverage they claimed against wealthy competitors. After all, what was good for the goose was good for the gander, and a powerful firm like RCA could just as easily petition Farnsworth for a compulsory license to his television patents under such a law. Then with superior capital and marketing resources, RCA would stand to reap most of the sales and profits from Farnsworth's invention, while Farnsworth himself received only a court-approved royalty. Independents also joined the big firms in opposing Arnold's call for unrestricted licenses. For example, with restrictions, a small-scale inventor of an improved internal combustion engine could license the engine to auto and motorcycle firms for use in transportation, but restrict them from use in stationary applications, thereby allowing the inventor to build a business in that sector under patent protection.[40]

Meanwhile, the witnesses from the corporate R&D labs—General Electric's William Coolidge, Bell Labs' Frank Jewett, and Bakelite's George Baekeland—were well coached and generally evasive in their testimony. They described the scale and scope of their sophisticated research operations but denied that their labs and corporate patenting practices constituted an existential threat to individual inventors. Instead, they spoke in platitudes about how their "pioneering" discoveries extended the "frontiers" of knowledge, which in turn opened "new vistas and new avenues" of opportunity for independents. When considering the reform proposals, the corporate witnesses generally agreed with AT&T's Jewett, who would be "very much concerned if anything was contemplated which struck at the roots, the fundamentals, of the system itself."[41]

According to its *Final Report*, the committee acknowledged that patents had become "a device to control whole industries, to suppress competition, to restrict output, to enhance prices, to suppress inventions, and to discourage inventiveness."[42] Thus, as the patent hearings concluded, America's independent inventors, industrial researchers, business leaders, and patent attorneys were anxious to see what Congress might do.

Counterattack: The National Association of Manufacturers

The conservative NAM took a particular interest in the TNEC's proposed reforms, since several of its members—including General Electric, Eastman Kodak, Westinghouse, and RCA—were high-technology firms that were dependent on patents.[43] The association had generally been vocal critics of the Roosevelt administration, especially the NIRA and its attempts to foster government-directed economic planning and unionism. The NAM also disputed the TNEC's overall body of work and even published a polemic titled *Fact and Fancy in the TNEC Monographs*.[44]

Ultimately, the NAM supported some of the TNEC's proposed patent reforms while vehemently opposing others. First, the NAM endorsed Commissioner Coe's procedural recommendations to streamline applications, interference proceedings, and the appeals process. Despite its laissez-faire positions on many issues, the NAM recognized the government's crucial role (via the Patent Office and courts) in securing intellectual property rights, and Coe's procedural recommendations promised to rationalize those aspects of the system. NAM executives even organized a series of town-hall meetings in which Coe discussed various patent issues and then accepted the commissioner's invitation to tour the Patent Office.[45] However, the NAM vigorously opposed Thurman Arnold's more radical reforms. Like the independent inventors, they believed that compulsory licensing statutes would effectively reduce the patent term from seventeen to three years. Likewise, Arnold's proposal to eliminate restrictive licenses was seen as unwarranted government meddling in a firm's absolute right to dictate the terms by which it managed its intellectual property.[46] So the NAM took action.

The leader of NAM's counterattack was Robert Lund, executive vice president of Lambert Pharmaceuticals, former NAM President, and the chair of the NAM's Patent Committee. Much of Lund's response to the TNEC hearings can be characterized as the standard nuts and bolts work of any trade association. For example, Lund probably coached at least four or five NAM members who testified as witnesses before the TNEC hearings.[47] He retained an ace corporate intellectual property attorney, former AT&T patent counsel George E. Folk, to write books and several pamphlets articulating the NAM's position on various patent issues.[48] And he enlisted NAM members to contribute $25,000 to a special patent fund to commission a white paper on the "Contribution of the American Patent System to the American Standard of Living."[49] The study, conducted by the National Industrial Conference Board (NICB) and the American Engineering Council (AEC) would draw on interviews with various business leaders (mostly NAM members) to reach the foregone conclusion that "the patent system deserves to be maintained in its present form . . . instead of being radically reformed because of possible abuses in exceptional cases." This tendentious study would provide the basis for NAM's defense of the patent system as well as the necessary sound bites.[50] Finally, Lund and the NAM's lobbyists conferred frequently with members of the House and Senate Patent Committees, and presented their case for limited, not radical, reform.

The Modern Pioneers Program

Lund also mobilized the NAM's public relations expertise in the fight against patent reform. As Richard Tedlow has shown, Lund spent the early 1930s developing the association's sophisticated approach to public relations in order to combat various aspects of the New Deal.[51] Lund knew that 1940 would mark the 150th anniversary of the original 1790 patent law, and he hoped to take advantage of that observance to defend the institution. Specifically, Lund proposed to honor "the Modern Pioneers on the Frontier of American Industry" by bestowing awards on America's most celebrated inventors and research scientists. These highly publicized awards would bring positive attention to the patent system, giving the NAM a platform for defending it against liberal attacks.[52]

In July 1939, Lund hammered out the essentials of the program. The NAM would solicit nominations of successful inventors and research scientists who might qualify as "Modern Pioneers" and then appoint a committee led by MIT president Karl Compton to evaluate them. Awardees would be honored at regional Modern Pioneers banquets held in thirteen industrial cities in early 1940; these regional banquets would culminate in a national ceremony held in New York City on February 27, designated as Modern Pioneers Day.[53]

By honoring America's Modern Pioneers, Lund drew on the powerful mythology of the American frontier to defend the patent system.[54] In a press release announcing the campaign, Lund wrote: "The pioneer of the geographical frontier of yesterday ventured forth into the wilderness and conquered new territory. . . . The pioneer on the modern frontier of science and technology likewise ventures into the unknown and conquers it."[55] In Lund's reasoning, just as homesteaders were spurred to settle the Old West by the promise of secure property claims, the Modern Pioneers needed the incentive of secure intellectual property claims, upheld by a strong patent system, not one watered down by liberal reforms. This language clearly echoed the appeals to "pioneering" and "the frontier" in the evasive TNEC testimony of the corporate researchers from General Electric, Bell Labs, and the Bakelite Corporation. It is not clear whether Lund had already formulated this rhetorical strategy before coaching these witnesses or if their "pioneering" testimony subsequently inspired the Modern Pioneers campaign.

Lund also marshaled the ideology of self-reliance and rugged individualism, which had been rhetorical hallmarks of NAM's public relations campaigns during the 1930s. In his press release, Lund argued that the patent system had "typified, perhaps better than any other American institution, the American principle of reward for individual initiative."[56] This line of discourse was somewhat ironic, considering that the NAM represented many large firms, whose corporate R&D labs epitomized the value of collective, team-based invention. Indeed, two research directors—GE's William Coolidge and GM's Charles Kettering—and DuPont's eleven-member "nylon group" were named as Modern Pioneers. Yet besides these exceptions, the Modern Pioneers committee bestowed the remainder of its national awards to individual inventors like Edwin Armstrong (radio), Willis Carrier (air conditioning), and Edwin Land (Polaroid film).[57] The TNEC hearings had presented powerful evidence that independent inventors and small businesses had been victimized by aggressive corporate patent practices. However, by emphasizing the achievements of individual inventors, not corporate teams, the Modern Pioneers campaign undermined those critiques.

Here, Lund seemed to borrow from patent commissioner Conway Coe's playbook. Recall that Coe had opened his TNEC testimony by highlighting heroic, individual inventors like Eli Whitney and Cyrus McCormick, while appealing to the heritage, traditions, and "spiritual influence" of the American patent system. For both Coe and Lund, the implicit message to Congress and the American public was that there could hardly be anything fundamentally wrong with a patent system that had inspired the work of these legendary inventors; therefore, Congress should improve the system around the edges but leave it essentially unchanged. Overall, by associating the patent system with "the frontier" and "the individual"—two of America's most treasured cultural touchstones—Lund hoped to put the patent system on a pedestal in order to immunize it from the most radical reforms.

In January and February 1940, the Modern Pioneers program came to fruition. From the 1,026 nominations it received, the selection committee honored 572 Modern Pioneers at banquets that collectively drew nearly 10,000 attendees.[58] On the evening before the final banquet, Lund delivered a speech over NBC's national radio network. He marked the 150th anniversary of the patent laws and described the Modern Pioneers program. Then, using preliminary data from the NICB-AEC study he had commissioned, he described how patents and new inventions had increased productivity and wages while dismissing allegations that valuable inventions had been suppressed. Finally, Lund addressed the TNEC reform proposals. He endorsed Commissioner Coe's procedural recommendations and vehemently rejected Thurman Arnold's proposals for a compulsory licensing statute and an end to restrictive licenses. If Arnold's ideas were enacted, Lund warned, they would "dangerously impair the patent system as an incentive to invention . . . discourage research and invention and hinder business enterprise." Lund concluded by assuring Americans that the NAM stood guard to "protect the institutions essential to the birth of ideas."[59]

The following evening—Modern Pioneers Day, February 27, 1940—more than 1,500 people attended the final, national awards banquet at New York's Waldorf-Astoria hotel. The program, again broadcast over NBC radio, featured actors' dramatizations of the honorees' invention stories and a full slate of speeches from Coe, Lund, Kettering, and others that echoed the NAM's pioneering rhetoric and its call for modest, not radical, reform.[60] It is always difficult to gauge the impact of public relations efforts, but as the Modern Pioneers campaign concluded, Lund believed that "millions of Americans" had become more interested in the patent system through the local dinners and the attendant media coverage.[61]

The Elusiveness of Patent Reform

Ultimately, the TNEC's reform proposals achieved a mixed legislative record. Within months of the hearings, Congress approved five of the seven procedural reforms suggested by Commissioner Coe (and endorsed by the NAM) to streamline operations at the Patent Office. However, Congress was unable to push through any of the major reforms suggested by either Coe or Thurman Arnold: the "twenty-year rule" to reduce the long pendency of applications, a single court of patent appeals to rationalize infringement lawsuits, limitations on restrictive licensing, or a compulsory licensing statute to prevent the suppression of patents.[62]

Overall, the TNEC patent hearings had provided a forum for independent inventors, corporate researchers, business lobbyists, and politicians to debate the changing political economy of invention. In the end, why was meaningful patent reform so elusive?

First, the NAM was extremely adept at influencing the debate in ways that reflected the underlying interests of its members. The NAM coached several TNEC witnesses, lobbied Congress, and aligned itself with patent commissioner Conway Coe, a moderate who hoped to make certain procedural reforms while preserving the fundamentals of the patent system. More importantly, under Robert Lund, the association appealed directly to the American public through its Modern Pioneers program, a sophisticated public relations campaign that celebrated the heritage and traditions of the patent system in order to protect it from Thurman Arnold's more radical reforms. The Modern Pioneers program marshaled the "pioneering" rhetoric and appeals to individual initiative that co-opted the mythology of heroic, independent inventors of the past, even as the association advanced a pro-business agenda more amenable to large, research-oriented firms.

In contrast, independent inventors were utterly disorganized and lacked a comparable professional organization to lobby for their concerns as a counterweight to the NAM. This had not always been the case. For example, in 1910, the Inventors Guild called for several reforms that anticipated the TNEC's proposals, including streamlined interference procedures, limits on depositions, and a special Court of Patent Appeals to expedite infringement trials.[63] As a spokesman told the *New York Times*, the guild objected to "the injustice of 'rich corporations'" competing unfairly with "poor inventors" by bringing specious infringement suits and using legal delay tactics "until the inventors' money gives out and he has to quit."[64] However, the Inventors Guild went belly-up around 1920, joining dozens of short-lived inventors' societies that tried but failed to provide credibility and political support for an increasingly troubled profession. By 1938–39, independent inventors were too disorganized to rally behind reforms they had been championing for nearly twenty years. As a result, independent inventors missed a major opportunity to reform the patent laws in ways that would have curtailed corporate abuses. Instead, huge firms continued to grind down their smaller rivals through delaying tactics, willful infringement, and excessive litigation.[65]

In addition, recall that certain reform proposals were opposed by both independent inventors and corporate researchers. For example, nearly all witnesses testified against Arnold's proposals for compulsory licensing statutes and limitations on licensing restrictions; both Conway Coe and the NAM opposed the measures as well. With nearly unanimous opposition to Arnold's proposals, Congress had no incentive to develop legislation.

Finally, historian Alan Brinkley has argued that the growing demands of mobilization for World War II frustrated American antitrust enforcement and foreclosed the possibility for various domestic reforms.[66] Indeed, by March 1941, when the TNEC submitted its *Final Report*, the United States had become fully engaged in war preparedness efforts, and this probably stalled legislative action on the TNEC's reform proposals. However, mobilization efforts ultimately enabled the Justice Department to expand the scope of its enforcement, as Arnold broke up international patent pools between U.S. firms and foreign (especially German) partners to ensure adequate output and fair prices on key military materials such as aluminum and nitrates. The government's strong enforcement continued after the war, as epitomized by the 1949 antitrust case (and 1956 consent decree) with AT&T, which forced Bell Labs to offer nonexclusive licenses on its patents. In the case of AT&T's transistor, these compulsory licenses enabled both domestic and foreign start-ups such as Texas Instruments and Sony to compete in the consumer electronics industry. In fact, the United States imposed its antitrust traditions on Europe and Japan after the war to prevent business collectivism from sliding again into totalitarianism—the same menace that Roosevelt had referenced in his April 1938 "monopoly" message. Thus, while mobilization may have hindered the passage of new patent laws, it actually broadened the enforcement of the antitrust laws, especially where patents had been abused.[67]

Altogether, New Deal progressives achieved few of the TNEC's proposed patent reforms; in fact, several of the committee's recommendations went unrealized for decades. For example, a single court of patent appeals was not implemented until 1982, and the "twenty-year rule" limiting patent terms was not implemented until 1995.[68] Meanwhile, corporate interests have continued to shape the patent laws in their favor. For example, the "Leahy-Smith America Invents Act," implemented in 2013, changed the Patent Office's determination of patent priority from a "first-to-conceive" system to a "first-to-file" system. This sea change—endorsed by major technology and pharmaceutical firms, and the NAM—clearly favors well-funded corporate labs and patent departments over do-it-yourself independent inventors.[69] Overall, the American patent system has proven remarkably resistant to reform and remains more agreeable to deep-pocketed corporate researchers and less advantageous to independent inventors and small businesses.

Chapter 4

Farewell to Progressivism: The Second World War and the Privatization of the "Military-Industrial Complex"

Mark R. Wilson

In early 1937, Secretary of the Navy Claude A. Swanson sent a note to President Franklin D. Roosevelt concerning the Navy's growing shortage of torpedoes. The only active manufacturer of those weapons was the Naval Torpedo Station at Newport, Rhode Island, a Navy-owned, Navy-operated plant that had been established three decades before. But the Newport facility was already operating at close to full capacity: its 3,100 civilian employees were turning out about two and a half torpedoes each day. This would not be enough to outfit the several dozen new submarines and destroyers then under construction in American shipyards, thanks to the funds provided by Congress in the Vinson-Trammell Act of 1934. In light of the growing demand, how best could the Navy expand capacity?

One option, Swanson noted, would be to contract with the private company that had the most experience with torpedo manufacture, E. W. Bliss Company, of Brooklyn, New York. (During the First World War, Bliss Company had served as the nation's top torpedo producer.) But Swanson recommended against this choice. For one thing, there was no adequate testing range near Brooklyn. But Swanson mentioned another important reason. "The superiority of torpedoes manufactured by the Navy," he told Roosevelt, "has been thoroughly demonstrated by the record of the performance of these torpedoes during the past fifteen years." Given this record, Swanson reasoned, the best course of action would be to spend $2.75 million to renovate a mothballed Navy-run torpedo plant (which had been built in 1918) in Alexandria, Virginia. In other words, Swanson, backed by officers at the Navy's Bureau of Ordnance, favored creating even more government in-house production capacity, instead of using a private contractor.[1]

Swanson eventually got his way. A year after this first request, he and other Navy Department officials again asked the White House to endorse a new Navy-run plant at Alexandria, while raising the recommended investment to $4.5 million. This project did go forward. By July 1941, five months before the Pearl Harbor attacks, the Alexandria Naval Torpedo Station became an independent entity, detached from the nearby Naval Gun Foundry. By then, the Alexandria plant was already producing torpedoes; its output was scheduled to rise over the coming months to eight per day, compared with the twenty per day expected from its older sibling in Newport. After Pearl Harbor, the situation would change: production targets were increased at the Newport and Alexandria plants, but the Navy also started to engage for-profit firms, including Westinghouse and Ameritorp (a subsidiary of American Can), to make torpedoes. However, this turn to contractors came late: until 1942, the Navy relied on in-house production capacity, Swanson's preferred method.[2]

This bit of the record of twentieth-century military-industrial relations may seem too small to deserve much attention. However, it suggests some interesting puzzles. What are we to make of Swanson's choice to avoid contracting, which seems to violate common assumptions about the normal workings of the U.S. defense sector? As the young economist Michael Reich put it in the early 1970s, in an angry critique of the Vietnam War–era military-industrial apparatus, "it has always been presumed that as much as possible and ideally all armaments production should be carried on [sic] by private profit-seeking corporations."[3] In the case of torpedoes in the late 1930s, this rule seems to have been broken. Was this just a trivial exception, perhaps attributable merely to the fact that Swanson, a Virginian, wanted to steer resources to his home state? If so, must we dismiss his comments about the superiority of Navy-made weapons as deceitful? Or, alternatively, can we understand Swanson's actions as somehow related to the broader trends in the long-run history of American business and politics?

Connecting developments in the defense sector to those in the broader political economy might seem to be an obvious task for historians of

American business and politics, if only because defense has been the biggest single consumer of national government expenditures for most of American history. However, over the past several decades, historians have fallen down on this job. As they have focused on a variety of other important subjects, our understanding of the development of the military dimensions of the American political economy has stagnated.

This essay has two aims. First, by offering a new overview of a rich but often overlooked secondary literature, it invites historians of business and politics to do more, in their future work, to consider the military-industrial sphere. Second, it offers a somewhat unconventional interpretation of the long-run history of the so-called military-industrial complex. This essay claims that the defense sector has been less unique—less isolated from broader political developments—than much of the scholarly literature and popular accounts have suggested. Early in the twentieth century, the military-industrial field, like so many other parts of the U.S. economy, was affected by Progressive and New Deal reforms. A progressive approach to military economy shaped the nation's giant military-industrial mobilizations for the First and Second World Wars, when state enterprise and intense regulation were far more prevalent than we have usually remembered. However, during the later twentieth century, the nation's military economy was transformed again by antistatist, deregulatory initiatives that also affected many other industries. Over the long run, the dynamics of U.S. military-industrial relations have changed repeatedly, often in a nonlinear fashion. More than we have imagined, developments in the so-called military-industrial complex have been entangled with broader reconstructions of American politics and capitalism.

Among all the many important pieces of the broader subject of modern American business and politics, the military-industrial sphere has been and remains one of the most misunderstood. Today's historians mostly ignore it. Influential critics of the military-industrial complex, including economists on the political left, such as John Kenneth Galbraith and Seymour Melman, failed to appreciate its dynamism. Many of those Vietnam War–era critics claimed that the military-industrial sphere had evolved into a thoroughly noncapitalist, no-risk arena of government-business "fusion," state planning, bureaucratic management, administered prices, and corporate welfare.[4] In fact, during the second half of the twentieth century, the Cold War–era military-industrial complex, like the broader American economy, was experiencing continuing, significant structural transformations, which trended in the direction of a rising importance of capitalist markets and competition. Contemporary critics and historians may be forgiven for failing to fully appreciate this shift, which is easier to see in retrospect. However, whereas historians have used their observations of recent trends to help them steer away from teleological narratives that emphasize the triumph of the modern large industrial corporation, they seem to be willing to cling to comparable narratives about the development of the military side of the political economy.[5] This essay suggests that it is time to reassess such stale assumptions.

This record of misunderstanding, fueled by inattention and ignorance, may help explain why this essay may seem to diverge from many of the other contributions to this volume. On the whole, this collection encourages us, rightly, to do more to consider the ways in which business leaders—even as they sometimes denigrated the public sector—found creative ways to use an expanding governmental apparatus to promote their own interests. In the case of the military-industrial sphere, however, conventional wisdom has long emphasized the theme of government-business entanglement. This essay suggests that in this important case, we have understated, rather than exaggerated, the capacity of antistatist politics to transform economic structures. In this sense, the long-run record of the military-industrial complex reminds us to be mindful of nonlinear historical transformations, including the remarkable rise and fall of national state enterprise and regulation over the course of the twentieth century.

A View from the Early Twenty-First Century

Today, more than half a century after President Dwight D. Eisenhower issued his 1961 warning about the potential dangers of a "military-industrial complex," there does not seem to be a great deal of interest among academics in its history. Among the most talented historians of the past couple of generations, few have concerned themselves with the defense sector. This is understandable. For many of the new social and economic historians, as for scholars reconsidering the past in light of feminist theory and the "cultural turn," many other historical subjects seem more interesting, and more deserving of attention, than the business and political elites who evidently dominated the defense sector. However, we should acknowledge that one of the costs of this tendency has been a growing ignorance about the military side of American political and economic development.

Once upon a time, the situation was somewhat different. The short period between 1964 and 1969 saw the completion of at least half a dozen of the best doctoral dissertations ever written about the business and politics of military-industrial relations in U.S. history. Covering the era from the late nineteenth century through the Second World War, these works, by scholars such as B. F. Cooling, Robert Cuff, and Paul Koistinen, offered rich histories of America's efforts to mobilize and demobilize economically for modern war.[6]

What inspired this brief golden age of military-industrial histories? Although the Vietnam War would certainly shape the reception of these studies, most of them were launched before 1965, in the context of earlier Cold War developments. These included not just Eisenhower's 1961 address, but the specter of nuclear war, the Korean War, and unprecedented peacetime levels of American defense spending and intervention abroad. In the 1960s, the New Left, condemning what it regarded as an imperialistic Cold War foreign policy, described American democracy as having been hijacked by a cabal of corporate, political, and military elites. One of the most obvious manifestations of this corruption was in the defense sector, which, as the Students for a Democratic Society put it in their "Port Huron Statement" (1962), had become overtaken by "the intermingling of Big Military and Big Industry." Here the New Left was inspired by C. Wright Mills, the radical American sociologist and author of *The Power Elite* (1956). Since 1945, Mills, among others, had been warning of the dangers of a "permanent war economy" and a turn to "militarized capitalism."[7] Such concerns only intensified during the Vietnam War, when many critics of the defense sector, including Galbraith and Melman, described it as a unique political-economic wonderland, in which the boundaries between big business and the national state were virtually nonexistent, but military contractors, who took on zero risk, were still allowed to reap big profits.[8]

Although these Cold War–era critiques suggested that the degree of government-business entanglement in the defense sector may have been exceptional, their description of the military-industrial sphere was part of broader portrait of the long-run decline of American democracy and competitive capitalism. In the defense sector, as elsewhere in the economy, business was corrupting American politics in the usual ways: via lobbying and capture. That is, the defense industry, like other industries, gained undue influence by using its outsized financial and organizational resources to sway not only members of Congress but also would-be regulators in executive agencies. It was really the latter problem of regulatory or government capture, more than lobbying per se, that tended to be emphasized in the New Left critiques. Mills and his followers decried the revolving-door-style flow of personnel back and forth between the Pentagon and military contractors, whose interests and priorities converged.

Although Mills and his followers were often more focused on the highest circles of military and executive leadership than with traditional lobbying and congressional pork-barrel politics, the latter subject was also at least implicitly raised by many critics of the military-industrial complex.[9] By 1970, many critics emphasized that one of the main reasons for what they regarded as wasteful overspending on weapons was a dysfunctional political dynamic, in which members of Congress played a leading role by approving virtually any outlays that would bring money and jobs to their constituencies.[10]

Following the U.S. withdrawal from Vietnam, the military-industrial complex became less of a pressing concern for scholars and the general public. Given that after the Vietnam War, there was a significant decline in the defense sector's relative economic importance, perhaps this shift was to be expected. Perhaps scholars and the public had simply become weary of talk of the military-industrial complex. Perhaps, as the nation's political center of gravity appeared to shift to the right, and as the nation's economy and its big corporations looked more vulnerable, harsh characterizations of the defense sector became less viable. As Cooling has pointed out in a valuable recent essay on the military-industrial complex, this was an era in which more people began to refer to it with a far less politically charged label: the "defense industrial base." Whatever the causes, it was evident that in the aftermath of the Vietnam War, fewer historians and other scholars, and fewer Americans more broadly, chose to focus on the workings of the defense sector.[11]

Despite these trends, valuable new work continued to appear, long after 1970. Many of the richest contributions came from scholars connected, in one way or another, to the subfield of the history of science and technology. Thanks to their work, we now know a great deal about the long-run development (starting in the early nineteenth century) of the relations among military organizations, high-tech manufacturers, and, eventually, universities and think tanks.[12]

This valuable work by historians of science and technology diverged from the foundational studies of the business and politics of war mobilization, written in the 1960s, in two important ways. First, the historians of technology pointed to a different kind of political history by offering more stories in which the national state and its military organizations, instead of being fully captured by business, retained more autonomy and agency, and—in some cases, at least—deserved some credit, for promoting technological innovation and economic growth. Second, the works of the historians of technology also exposed their predecessors' tendency to overstate the influence of civilians in the military-industrial arena while underplaying the importance of military officers and organizations.[13] The reasons for this systemic weakness in the standard academic and popular understandings of the subject remain unclear, although it may have had something to do with the difficulties of accessing records of twentieth-century military organizations and contractors.[14] Perhaps it was also fueled by naïve assumptions about how things must have worked, even at the micro level, in a nation with a constitution and political tradition that ostensibly demanded full civilian control over the military.[15]

In any case, it should be understood as a serious deficiency, which will require a good deal of new work to correct. Many historians of business and politics, even those without any particular interest or expertise in the defense sector, are familiar with how America's past military-industrial mobilizations for war have been managed by emergency civilian agencies dominated by business leaders, such as the War Industries Board in the First World War and the War Production Board in the Second World War. But what if these civilian agencies were considerably less influential than we have imagined, especially in comparison to actors on the military side of the state? This question is raised by some of the most thorough, recent studies of the U.S. mobilizations for the world wars, which emphasize the domestic economic powers of military organizations.[16] Given such findings, many historians of business and politics should be uneasy about the adequacy of their assumptions about how war mobilizations and peacetime military-industrial interactions have worked.

One reason that academic histories in this area often say too little about the military may be that, since 1945, many of the richest available accounts of the work of military organizations have been commissioned and published by the military establishment itself. Needless to say, such in-house studies can contain major oversights and weaknesses. But many of them are of high quality, offering essential, well-documented accounts of important subjects.[17] Until they do more to familiarize themselves with this literature, historians of business and politics have little hope of understanding the military-industrial complex.

We also need to engage with the work of political scientists, who have done at least as much as historians, since the 1970s, to add to our knowledge about the past and present of the defense sector. Certainly this is true when it comes to the subject of lobbying, capture, and regulation. Historians of business and politics, in their own recent studies of these matters, have tended to focus on subjects such as price and wage controls, environmental regulation, consumer protection, and tax policy; they have studied a variety of industries, including banking, insurance, transportation, energy, pharmaceuticals, and health care.[18] They have said little, however, about the defense sector. But in the field of political science, there remains at least a small circle of scholars who continue to investigate questions about defense-sector lobbying and capture, and the organization of defense industries. Any historian aspiring to make new contributions in the field needs to engage with this valuable work.[19]

After 2001, the military-industrial sphere grew once more, this time in support of the hugely expensive military operations in Afghanistan and Iraq. Recent years have seen the appearance of some valuable new scholarship. A growing body of studies considers the social and environmental history of the Cold War era at the regional and local levels; some of this work deals with the political history of the business of defense.[20] Some attention has been paid, at least by social scientists, to the recent globalization (or reglobalization) of military procurement and the arms trade.[21] Meanwhile, leading journals in the fields of business history and political history seem to have been publishing more pieces dealing with the defense sector.[22] These are complemented by what seems to be an upswing in the number of more journalistic, sometimes sensationalist, popular or radical academic works on the military-industrial complex, many of which reiterate the New Left's complaints about corporate capture of the Pentagon and U.S. foreign policy.[23]

Despite this most recent outpouring of work, it is probably not accurate to see the subfield of the history of the defense sector, if it exists at all, as particularly vibrant. Even the best recent academic contributions, in comparison to the studies written in the 1960s, do relatively little to make ambitious claims about the relationship between the military-industrial sphere and national politics. Things might be at least slightly different, if students and scholars were not hamstrung by conventional narratives about the rise of the military-industrial complex. The second section of this essay offers a different kind of overview, which raises new questions and may serve to encourage new work.

Rethinking the History of the Military-Industrial Complex

For all its richness, the historical literature on the business of war and defense that has appeared over the past half century has tended to mislead us. On one hand, some accounts describe the rather sudden emergence of the national security state in the 1940s and 1950s, which created an enormous new defense sector, with immense and unique political influence that ensures its stability, enduring more or less unchanged to the present day. On the other hand, some historians have reached farther back in time, to the nineteenth and early twentieth centuries, where they have discovered the origins of the military-industrial complex. This literature has tended to describe an inexorable, and rather linear, rise of the sort of business-government relations that would be identified in the 1960s as the military-industrial complex.

To be sure, these are crude generalizations about a complex historiography. But they can be applied, without too much unfairness, to some of the most influential work in the field. For example, the tendency to describe the military-industrial complex as snowballing over many decades can be seen in the work of Paul Koistinen, who recently completed a heroic, five-volume history of the American defense sector, from the colonial era through the twenty-first century. According to Koistinen, an "institutional interdependence" between the state and private industry was evident even before the Great War and increased in 1917–18; a full-blown, politically conservative "industry-military alliance" emerged during the Second World War. The development of the military-industrial complex, Koistinen suggested, was an "evolutionary process," starting in the late nineteenth century, if not before.[24] This account seems to be consistent with the findings of other master historians of the defense sector in the Progressive Era, such as Cooling, and, more recently, Katherine Epstein.[25]

Such accounts of the military industrial complex's long-run evolution appear difficult to refute, especially when they come from our greatest historians of the subject. However, they should be challenged. In fact, the record of the defense sector's twentieth-century development is rather more interesting than they suggest. Certainly, the arms industry became much larger during the Second World War and the early Cold War; certainly, we can see something like a miniature military-industrial complex in operation at the end of the nineteenth century. But these generalizations fail to describe important shifts in the political economy of the defense sector, including a rather dramatic rise and fall of the national state's in-house capacity for weapons design and production, which appears to have roughly coincided with a rise and fall of the intensity of state regulation of defense-sector output and profits.

Table 4.1. Number of major U.S. combatant vessels constructed, by type of yard, 1880s–2010s

| Period | Type of yard | | | |
	Navy-operated	Contractor-operated	Total	Percentage built in public yards
1880s–1900s	5	130	135	4
1910s (including the First World War)	42	438	480	9
1920s–1930s	91	95	186	49
1940s (including the Second World War)	171	600	771	22
1950s–1960s	53	162	215	25
1970s–2010s	0	229	229	0

Source: http://www.shipbuildinghistory.com (accessed July 2014). For comparable data in print form, see books by Paul H. Silverstone, including *The New Navy, 1883–1922* (New York: Routledge, 2006); *The Navy and World War II, 1922–1947* (New York: Routledge, 2008); and *The Navy of the Nuclear Age, 1947–2007* (New York: Routledge, 2009).

Notes: The dates indicate the fiscal year of appropriation of funds. Only ships actually launched are counted. Major combatant vessels include battleships, monitors and cruisers, destroyers, submarines, and aircraft carriers.

One problem with the many histories that emphasize a growing business-government entanglement, starting in the later nineteenth century, is that they tend to obscure the extent to which the defense sector, like other parts of the American economy, was transformed during the first half of the twentieth century by Progressive and New Deal reforms. Here we return to the puzzle of Navy Secretary Swanson's recommendations, in the late 1930s, about torpedo procurement.[26] This short essay cannot provide much evidence about the vulnerability of the military-industrial sphere to broader political trends. However, it may be suggestive to consider some data about American warship construction since the emergence of modern steel ships in the late nineteenth century (see Table 4.1).

What is this simple table telling us? For one thing, it appears that Swanson's effort to have the Navy make all its own torpedoes in the late 1930s was not inconsistent with broader trends in the naval-industrial complex during that era, when half of the Navy's warships were built in its own shipyards.[27] The table also suggests that there may be serious problems with extrapolating from observations about the military-industrial sphere around 1900 to observations of conditions at the end of the twentieth century. At both of those moments, private contractors reigned supreme. However, in between those two points in time, the table suggests, there may have been some very significant shifts in the balance of public and private capacities. Moreover, despite its obvious limitations, the table also might inspire questions about whether the historical development of the defense sector may in fact track more closely with broader trends in the long-run history of American government-business relations. Was there a rise and fall of the Progressive and New Deal order in the military-industrial sphere, as well as in the broader political economy? The warship construction data may at least encourage us to do more to ask and answer such questions. It supports the notion that the Progressive and New Deal eras saw growth in the capacities of the military institutions of the national state, not just its civilian agencies.[28]

This essay's invitation to rethink the grand narrative of the history of the military-industrial complex is related to what I have found in my own recent research in business and military archives from the era of the Second World War. In a book about the business and politics of the nation's giant industrial mobilization in 1940–45, I concluded that we need to do more to remember the ways in which that effort involved huge amounts of state enterprise and unprecedented levels of state regulation of business, not least in the defense sector. My story diverges from the one developed half a century ago by Koistinen and Barton Bernstein, not least in its treatment of the question of wartime corporate capture of the national state. In my telling, the average corporate executive during the Second World War, far from being delighted at how much the war emergency was allowing him to recapture political power and reap big profits, was more inclined to support an essentially antistatist politics, designed to ensure that government would never again hold such sway over the private sector. Business leaders, I argue, developed and broadcast a simple but potent interpretive frame for understanding the workings of the war mobilization, a frame that boldly erased any positive contributions public actors may have made to the giant effort while highlighting the many contributions of for-profit firms. This frame proved remarkably influential, not just in the business community but also among moderate and liberal officials and politicians. Its influence was especially important in the medium and longer runs, as the nation demobilized from the Second World War and reshaped its defense sector.[29]

Since 1945, the national state has become a less enterprising, less intrusive overseer of the defense sector. Certainly this is suggested by the warship construction data, which show that the Navy, which for much of American history made a significant fraction of its own warships, no longer has comparable in-house capacities for weapons production.[30] On one level, this shift in the direction of increased reliance on for-profit contractors may seem to do nothing more than confirm traditional accounts of the emergence, during the Cold War, of a permanent military-industrial complex. But here again, we should be wary of embracing linear or teleological narratives that leave little room for contingency and ignore the ways in which even apparently stable political and social fields are continually being reproduced and reshaped.[31]

President Eisenhower's military-industrial complex of 1960 was actually far less privatized than the one desired by many pro-business conservatives, including former president Herbert Hoover, who during the Cold War led high-profile commissions that called on the Pentagon to shed in-house capacities.[32] The most dramatic examples of this shedding, which occurred on the Army side as well as the Navy side, did not happen until the tenure of Secretary of Defense Robert S. McNamara, before and during the Vietnam War.[33] Over the past half century, the balance has continued to shift, for the most part, in the direction of less public capacity and control. Probably the best-known example of this comes not from the military-industrial sphere but rather from the case of soldiering itself. In the era of the Iraq War, many Americans became familiar with Blackwater (which has several descendants and cousins), a for-profit provider of soldiers in overseas theaters of war.[34] The rise of mercenaries in the last years of the twentieth century was consistent with the somewhat longer-run trends already underway on the military-economic home front. As the historian Jennifer Mittelstadt has shown in an important recent work, the movement in the direction of privatization occurred not only in the cases of soldiers and weapons systems but also in the military's provision of services and welfare.[35]

This outline of the history of the military-industrial complex points to important structural transformations over the course of more than a century, first in the direction of heightened regulation and even nationalization, and then swinging strongly toward deregulation and privatization. (In fact, if the clock were started in the early nineteenth century, we might describe an additional, initial shift, in the direction of privatization, as the nation made more use of contractors, and less of the Navy's own shipyards, in the building of the first steel navy in the 1880s and 1890s.[36]) Again, this could well be interpreted as suggesting that the defense sector's political history, far from being unique, may have been rather tightly bound up with what we understand as the broader history of U.S. political economy.

If we are willing to endorse this account, what difference might it make for historians and for policymakers? One way to understand it is as a positive story, in which the military economy was transformed in ways that made it less wasteful, even less dangerous. Such is the argument of one of the finest studies of the Cold War military-industrial sphere, written by the political scientist Aaron Friedberg.[37] Some historians, including Michael Sherry, have argued that Friedberg exaggerated the extent to which political antistatism affected the military-industrial complex, which seemed at the end of the century to continue to be characterized by wholesale government-business entanglement.[38] But Sherry, like so many of his predecessors, underestimated the dynamism of the military-industrial sphere at its height. In fact, we need to take Friedberg's story of antistatism and privatization more seriously; but we also need to ask whether that story may be less of a happy one than he implied. It seems quite possible, for example, that privatization in some cases may have degraded (or will degrade) military effectiveness by sacrificing long-time-horizon approaches to weapons development to concerns for short-term profitability. Not surprisingly, as the financial performance of U.S. military contractors in recent years demonstrates, privatization and deregulation have failed to reduce defense-sector profits. Equally important, it seems likely that privatization has tended to promote arms proliferation by creating larger for-profit investments, which are more likely to seek out foreign markets, especially in times of slack domestic demand. Here, historians may benefit from following the lead of social scientists like Ann Markusen, Harvey Sapolsky, Eugene Gholz, Thomas McNaugher, and Daniel Wirls, who have provided some of the best available accounts of developments in the military-industrial complex over the past half century. Even without using the longer chronological frame this essay provides, they have pointed out that the defense sector has seen substantial privatization in recent decades; much of their work suggests that this has probably gone too far. Long-run cost savings often turn out to be lower than advertised, and the government has lost knowledge and capacity in some areas that require substantial public oversight.[39]

The recent structural transformations of the defense sector have been affected not simply by objective measurements of optimal efficiencies but also as the result of decades of self-interested lobbying on the part of for-profit contractors and by a broader ideological push for deregulation.[40] Certainly from the point of view of some of those familiar with the military's shrinking in-house weapons research and design agencies, such as the Naval Research Laboratory, the changes seemed to be driven more by political decisions and the private sector's ability to pay higher salaries more than any objective consideration of the quality of work.[41] As Markusen has argued, it seems clear that the reforms in the direction of further privatization, carried out in the 1990s and 2000s during the Clinton and George W. Bush administrations, were pushed by private business interests, including expert lobbying groups such as the Defense Science Board and Business Executives for National Security.[42]

These concerns may seem even more compelling if we adopt the long-run historical frame presented in this essay. With that in mind, the shift in the direction of privatization over the past half century looks like a rather radical break from the long run of American history. For the better part of two centuries, the military maintained important in-house weapons design and manufacturing capacities. In more recent years, this important aspect of state capacity has degraded, along with other measures of state regulatory power over military and nonmilitary industries.

Conclusion

Before and during the Second World War, the U.S. Navy chose to rely heavily on its in-house manufacturing facilities at Newport and Alexandria for its torpedoes. But in the past half century, those facilities have been transformed into far more peaceable places: Goat Island, site of the Newport Torpedo Station, is now home to private condominiums and hotels; in Alexandria, the former weapons facility became the "Torpedo Factory Art Center," home to dozens of artists. This swords-into-plowshares story is in some ways a positive one. But it should also be understood as part of an important broader development in the dynamics of military-industrial relations in the United States. The Navy still requires torpedoes, but for the past several decades, they have all been supplied by for-profit firms instead of its own facilities. This is just one example of a more general shift in the direction of the demilitarization, or privatization, of the so-called military-industrial complex.

This essay encourages historians of business and politics to re-engage with the defense sector, which since the 1970s has not attracted much of their attention. It has suggested that such a move might bring some exciting opportunities, not least of which might be the chance to enrich our understanding of the more general history of American economic and political development. Perhaps scholars will conclude that important shifts in the organization of the civilian side of the national political economy have been mirrored by changes on the military side. But it also seems possible that historians might find that developments in the defense sector may have figured in some instances as leading indicators, or even driving forces, of broader developments. For example, historians might do more to explore how the steps taken toward the privatization of the military-industrial complex in the 1950s and 1960s might have related to other aspects of the transformation of the so-called New Deal order. They might even consider whether those developments in the defense sector may have prefigured, and contributed to, changes in the broader political economy, including the moves toward deregulation and neoliberalism that are often described as flowering in the 1970s.[43]

This essay may also serve to suggest how revisiting the past may liberate us to consider a wider range of viable policies in the present day. It may well be that even after looking harder at the longer-run history of the military-industrial complex, policymakers will still conclude that the military should continue to get most of what it needs from for-profit contractors. But at least that policy choice would be better informed by an awareness that many intelligent policymakers in the past favored different arrangements, in part because of their concerns about equity and the balance of power between public and private actors.

For today's historians of business and politics, the opportunities for doing important new work in this area seem substantial, in part because their predecessors, over the past couple of generations, have let the ground lie mostly fallow. A new generation of scholars, by doing more to comprehend the defense sector, should be able to write fuller, richer histories of business and politics in America.

Chapter 5

Beyond the New Deal: Thomas K. McCraw
and the Political Economy of Capitalism

Richard R. John and Jason Scott Smith

Political economy is back. Following a long hiatus, the relationship between business and politics has reemerged in recent years as a compelling concern for historians of the United States. Writing in 2014, historian Beth Bailey put it well. American history, she observed, was currently in the midst of "what appears to be a major historiographical transition," bringing to a close the "long dominance of social and then cultural history" while lifting up "new studies of politics and institutions, political economy, and transnational history."[1] One testament to this sea change is the frequency with which the contributors to *American History Now*, an influential survey of recent trends in the field, invoked the phrase "political economy" in their essays. As recently as the 1980s, the frequency with which the phrase is now popping up would have been inconceivable: instead of putting political economy front and center, it would have been would have been more likely for a senior scholar to dismiss the topic as a dry-as-dust relic of an outdated mode of institutional-economic analysis. Now it is all the rage.[2]

If such a transition is indeed under way, and we believe that it is, then historians will naturally raise questions about its lineage. Might there be visionary forebears who can furnish the current generation with guidance as they navigate a new and perilous terrain? All historians stand on the shoulders of giants. This essay contends that the Harvard historian Thomas K. McCraw anticipated—and, if carefully read, can help inspire—the legion of historians who are turning their attention to topics that lie at the intersection of business and politics (understood broadly to include public policy, public administration, and the state), including those who have enlisted under the banner of the history of capitalism.

This essay has four sections and a brief conclusion. The first section showcases affinities between McCraw's oeuvre and the history of capitalism, a field that would not acquire a widely recognized collective identity until 2011, one year before McCraw's death.[3] McCraw, in our view, was a historian of capitalism *avant la lettre*, a distinction that has been echoed by McCraw's longtime Harvard colleague Sven Beckert, a leading light in the field.[4]

The second section surveys the first phase of McCraw's career, during which he was primarily concerned with the relationship of individuals and ideas. During this phase of his career, McCraw relied on an actor-oriented contextualism to demonstrate how a small number of business managers, government administrators, and lawmakers used institutional economics to influence public policy during the New Deal, inventing an innovative array of new institutional arrangements that he called the "mixed economy." The third section shows how McCraw shifted from contextualizing institutional economics to using institutional economics as an explanatory scheme. No longer did McCraw merely historicize theory; now he used theory to write history. It was in this phase of his career that McCraw published what probably remains today his best-known book, the Pulitzer-Prize winning *Prophets of Regulation*.[5] The fourth section, which is followed by a brief conclusion, shifts attention to what we regard as the major phase in McCraw's career, during which he expanded his range beyond the United States to compare and contrast the evolution of institutional arrangements in the United States with those in other parts of the world. It was during this phase that McCraw published what we regard as his two most enduring single-author books—both of which, interestingly, appeared following his retirement: *Prophet of Innovation: Joseph Schumpeter and Creative Destruction* (2007) and *Founders and Finance: How Hamilton, Gallatin, and Other Immigrants Forged a New Economy* (2012).[6] Since the focus of this book is the twentieth century, we will focus on *Prophet of Innovation*. Readers interested in *Founders and Finance* can learn more about its relationship to

McCraw's oeuvre in an already-published essay by one of this essay's coauthors.[7]

Prophet of Capitalism

Although McCraw taught business history for many years at the Harvard Business School, he was never only a business historian. Instead, he drew on several disciplinary traditions to explore a wide array of topics that ranged from biography, entrepreneurship, and regulation, to public policy, innovation, and economic thought. In Joseph Schumpeter's seminal *Capitalism, Socialism, and Democracy*, McCraw observed, the Austrian economist "freely crosses traditional boundaries of economics, history, political science, sociology, philosophy, law, and business."[8] Much the same could be said of McCraw himself.

McCraw's death in 2012 (he was 72) deprived the rising generation of historians of capitalism of an inspirational, eloquent, and influential ally. Though McCraw grew up in a very different world from the historians who currently dominate this field, he shared many of their aspirations and concerns. Like today's historians of capitalism, McCraw was impressed by credit creation as an engine of innovation; admiring toward the New Deal and its legacy; skeptical of what we today call the neoliberal turn in politics and economics; hostile toward market fundamentalism; sympathetic to institutional economics; committed to locating American cultural norms and institutional forms in a cross-national setting; dedicated to depicting key figures in politics, business, and economics as fully rounded protagonists rather than one-dimensional stick figures; and convinced that the relationship of business and politics (or what McCraw preferred to call "business-government relations," or "regulation") should be studied as a single, ever-evolving process.

Historians of capitalism presuppose, as Beckert has observed, that "states and markets, politics and business, cannot be understood separately from one another."[9] McCraw could not have put it any better. Beginning in the early 1970s, McCraw turned his attention to the relationship of business and politics in the American past, a theme that he would explore not only for the twentieth century, his own specialty, but also for the early republic.

McCraw's understanding of capitalism built not only on the social and cultural themes that have proven so influential for historians of capitalism but also, and even more directly, on the celebrated insight of Joseph

Schumpeter that, at its core, capitalism is a "perennial gale of creative destruction."[10] For McCraw, as for Schumpeter, capitalism was protean, unpredictable, disruptive, and surprisingly fragile. Nothing about its past was inevitable, and nothing about its future could be taken for granted. In all these ways, McCraw and Schumpeter differed profoundly from the law-and-economics orthodoxy of the Chicago School of economics, with its equilibrium models and self-regulating price mechanisms. Underscoring this distinction, McCraw explained that Schumpeter was perhaps the "most insightful" of "all critics of perfect competition." This was because the "creative destruction" that Schumpeter had in mind was driven not by price competition but instead by innovation, or what Schumpeter called the competition from the "new commodity, the new technology, the new source of supply, the new type of organization." By commanding a "decisive cost or quality advantage," this kind of highly disruptive, non–price-based competition struck "not at the margins of the profits and the outputs of the existing firms" but, instead "at their foundations and their very lives."[11]

McCraw's understanding of capitalism became increasingly sophisticated as his career evolved. In his first two books—each of which he researched in graduate school, and each of which focused on the Tennessee Valley Authority (TVA), a vast public works project that helped define Franklin D. Roosevelt's New Deal—McCraw deployed an actor-oriented contextualism to understand his protagonists. In his next major publication, *Prophets of Regulation* (1984), McCraw combined actor-oriented contextualism with the conceptual apparatus of institutional economics to chart the evolution of the independent regulatory commission. In the years between 1984 and his death in 2012, McCraw expanded his ambit still further in a series of publications that compared and contrasted the relationship of business and politics in the United States, Britain, Germany, and Japan. His most important single-author books from this period were *Prophet of Innovation*, a sweeping, evocative, and penetrating biography of Joseph Schumpeter, and *Founders and Finance*, a perceptive and persuasive history of the origins of American public finance.

McCraw never wavered in his deep admiration for Franklin D. Roosevelt's New Deal—and, in particular, for its embrace of the "mixed economy," a public-private hybrid in which private corporations remained the primary engine of wealth creation, while public agencies assumed an unprecedented measure of responsibility for regulating business and labor, monitoring financial speculation, increasing business investment, and promoting economic prosperity. The preponderance in the 1950s and 1960s of a rapidly expanding middle class could best be explained not by demographic expansion but instead by "government actions instituted during Roosevelt's presidency" to safeguard the elderly by instituting Social Security, protect the jobless through unemployment insurance, establish a living minimum wage, manage aggregate demand through deficit spending, and strengthen the labor movement by mandating collective bargaining with the Wagner Act. On certain topics, such as the most likely locus of innovation, McCraw would shift his views over time. Yet he never abandoned his bedrock conviction that, as an engine of wealth generation, the "mixed economy" had been a stunning success. The United States could be faulted for many things, but not for its failure to expand output in ways that earlier generations would have found utterly astonishing.[12]

In his later publications, McCraw would move beyond the New Deal in a dual sense. Most obviously, McCraw would shift his attention to other topics. Instead of doubling down on the history of regulation, he expanded his range to capitalism, innovation, and the history of economic thought. The second way in which McCraw altered his perspective was by adopting a chronologically expansive understanding of the New Deal's legacy. McCraw's New Deal did not end in 1939 or, as it would for Columbia University historian Alan Brinkley, with Roosevelt's death in 1945. Rather, it became the indispensable modus vivendi for the historically unprecedented upsurge in economic growth that the United States would enjoy between the Second World War and the economic downturn of 1973.[13]

Historians of capitalism might prefer to call the "mixed economy" a "political economy" rather than an economy, and some skeptics will certainly raise questions about McCraw's enthusiasm for economic growth.[14] Even so, if American historiography is indeed taking a political-economic turn, then we would be well advised to reflect on the economic ideas and institutional arrangements that undergirded the postwar boom. And these ideas and institutions were emphatically not the free-market fundamentalism that is so fashionable today. On the contrary, economic growth was stimulated not only by the private sector, which McCraw always regarded as the single most powerful wealth creator, but also by governmental institutions that operated not only as an engine of innovation but also as an agent of liberal reform. At his most ambitious, McCraw probed the relationship of institutions and ideas, as Schumpeter had before him, on five different layers: the firm, markets, institutions, cultural values, and leadership.[15] All in all, this was a hugely ambitious agenda that, if it were to be embraced by today's historians of capitalism, would have the potential to complete the epochal "historiographical transition" to which Bailey alluded in the passage that was quoted at the beginning of this essay.

Actor-Oriented Contextualism

It is one thing to recognize the merits of a multilayered explanatory scheme to explore the relationship of ideas and institutions and quite another to devise a suitable method to facilitate its study. The first method McCraw hit upon was, like so much of his best writing, biographical. For McCraw, biography was a means rather than an end. In particular, it provided him with a highly flexible tool to reconstruct the character and significance of the decisions of identifiable historical actors. The primary unit of analysis was never the individual or even the group, but instead the context in which historical actors lived, worked, and thought. Toward the end of an essay on the legacy of early twentieth-century progressivism, McCraw paused to "indulge" in what he termed the "ahistorical and risky enterprise" of identifying the most important generation of reformers in the American past. In this exercise, McCraw awarded first place to the late eighteenth-century founders of the republic; second place to the New Dealers of the 1930s; and third place to the progressives. This exercise in "rankings and reputations," McCraw freely conceded, was nothing more than a parlor game, since the historians' primary unit of analysis was neither the individual nor the group but the process through which individuals and groups interacted.[16]

McCraw's fascination with process had its origins in his graduate training in the 1960s at the University of Wisconsin in Madison. The Madison history department in McCraw's day was a petri dish brimming with new and sometimes radical ideas. A distinguished galaxy of left-leaning historians that included Merle Curti, George Mosse, and William Appleman Williams was creatively reworking the half-century-old progressive canon of Charles Beard, Vernon Parrington, and Frederick Jackson Turner. Warren Susman, who had studied history at Wisconsin in the 1950s, summed it up this way: "There are three parts of the god-head here at Wisconsin—the Father, the Son, and the Holy Ghost—Beard, Parrington, and Turner."[17] The persistence of the progressive tradition in a department that was receptive to the radical currents of the 1960s would shape the influential interpretative tradition known as the "Wisconsin School" and would help make the department-sponsored journal *Studies on the Left* (founded in 1959) what intellectual historian Peter Novick would call the "first, and in many ways the most important organized vehicle of the new historiographical left."[18]

Madison exposed McCraw to both the familiar, and sometimes ossified, political-economic radicalism of the Progressive era and the New Deal, as well as to the emerging New Left critique of American power that had been energized by the Civil Rights movement and the growing furor over the Vietnam War.

McCraw shared the Wisconsin School's interest in the relationship of business and politics and in 1989 would publish a thoughtful review of one of the foundational monographs to come out of the New Left–inspired "corporate liberal" tradition.[19] Yet his intellectual orientation had already been fixed by the time he arrived in Madison. The son of a TVA engineer, McCraw obtained his B.A. at the University of Mississippi, which he had funded by winning a scholarship from the Navy ROTC. Following his college graduation and prior to his arrival at Wisconsin, McCraw would serve an obligatory four-year stint as a naval officer—a venture that would give him first-hand exposure to a giant organization that he would repeatedly draw on in his scholarship, and that would set him apart from the vast majority of his graduate-school peers.

The TVA was a signal achievement of Franklin D. Roosevelt's presidency, and McCraw proudly described himself as "a dyed-in-the-wool New Deal Democrat."[20] McCraw's dissertation on the TVA, a topic suggested to him by his TVA-engineer father, was, as he initially conceived of it, a study of individuals and ideas. Only later, he would observe, would he come to see that its actual subject was the "the seductive power of organization."[21]

McCraw's mentors in graduate school included the intellectual historian Paul Conkin and the legal historian James Willard Hurst.[22] McCraw's dissertation advisor was Paul W. Glad, a political historian who had published a sympathetic biography of Populist firebrand William Jennings Bryan. Glad joined the Madison faculty in 1966, the same year McCraw began graduate school. McCraw obtained his Ph.D. in 1970, just four years after he had arrived in Wisconsin. By the end of the following year, he would have two books in print. Although Glad would not exert an enduring influence on McCraw's career, he was, McCraw reminisced, a "wonderful adviser" who helped set McCraw on his future path by constantly pushing him to make "more rigorous connections between ideas and policies."[23]

Two books grew out of McCraw's years at Wisconsin: *Morgan vs. Lilienthal: The Feud Within the TVA* (1970) and *TVA and the Power Fight, 1933–1939* (1971). The first was McCraw's master's thesis, which was published as a book after winning a prize administered by the history department of Loyola University in Chicago. Like many of McCraw's subsequent publications, its primary focus was biographical. In particular, it traced the bureaucratic infighting between TVA directors Arthur E. Morgan and David E. Lilienthal. Lilienthal proved to be the savvier operator, and he succeeded brilliantly in "identifying himself with a progressive program and portraying Morgan as an ally or dupe of the utilities."[24]

McCraw's dissertation, which became *TVA and the Power Fight*, focused less on the interplay of individuals and ideas than on the process by which ideas became transformed into public policy. Its principal protagonists were the empire-building Chicago utilities magnate Samuel Insull and the progressive Nebraska Senator George Norris. Each became a stand-in for "mutually hostile" traditions of electric power management: a "private tradition" promoted by Insull, which "started it and built most of its network of generators and high-tension lines," and a "public tradition" defended by Norris that "tried to curb private financial and political excesses, sometimes by going into the business itself."[25]

Among the most notable features of *TVA and the Power Fight* was the close attention McCraw paid to contemporary issues in institutional economics. Institutional economics was a venerable tradition of academic inquiry that in the 1960s was rapidly being eclipsed by a new neoclassical orthodoxy that substituted abstraction, quantification, and mathematical theory for the industry-specific empiricism that the institutionalists prized. By imaginatively glossing 1930s accounts of public utilities, McCraw reconstructed a forgotten debate over the allegedly "inherently monopolistic" cast of electric power generation. The construction of an electric power plant entailed huge fixed costs that were most easily recouped by operating at high volume. Electricity—in contrast to, say, automobiles or steel—could not be stored but rather "must be generated, transmitted, delivered, and consumed in virtually the same instant."[26] To cover their costs, power companies organized themselves as holding companies, a legal instrument that, although prone to corruption, facilitated access to capital markets, simplified the

transportation of electric power, and streamlined the recruitment of technical and managerial personnel.[27]

History and Theory

McCraw's performance in graduate school won him an assistant professorship at the University of Texas at Austin, where he moved with his family
in 1970. In other circumstances, he might have settled down to a long and
productive career at one of the nation's premier public research universities. Within three years, however, he received an unusual opportunity: a
one-year postdoctoral fellowship at the Harvard Business School. McCraw
moved his family to Cambridge, Massachusetts, for his fellowship in
1973–74. It would be, for him, a turning point in his career. McCraw's
teaching and research impressed his business school colleagues—including,
in particular, the senior business historian Alfred D. Chandler, Jr.—and, in
1976, McCraw was offered a two-year visiting professorship. Two years later,
McCraw obtained tenure. He would remain at Harvard until his retirement in 2006.

McCraw found the intellectual environment at Harvard to be challenging and demanding, and he rose to the occasion. Prior to his arrival in Cambridge, his research had focused on a single government agency. Now at
Harvard, he expanded his range to include the firm. McCraw's next major
project reflected this more expansive agenda. Chandler had analyzed the
firm's internal dynamics; McCraw set out to analyze the regulatory context
in which the firm operated. In so doing, McCraw built on the sturdy foundation of Chandler's magisterial history of the managerial corporation, *The
Visible Hand* (1977), which had appeared in print during McCraw's stint as a
visiting assistant professor at Harvard, one year before he received tenure in
1978.[28]

To analyze the relationship between government regulation and the firm,
McCraw drew for the first time on the vocabulary and methods of social science. No longer content to rely on the actor-oriented contextualism that had
served him so well in his first two books, he now turned his attention to
deploying social science, rather than merely to studying it. In making this
theoretical turn, as in so much else, McCraw's built on Chandler as well
as on the institutionalist tradition that he had first encountered when writing about the TVA. From Chandler McCraw drew the social scientific

distinction between vertical and horizontal integration, and from institutional economics, the contrast between "center" and "periphery" firms.

The first fruits of McCraw's new project, "Regulation in America," appeared in 1975 in the *Business History Review*. A culmination of McCraw's fellowship year, this essay analyzed two "widely known but troublesome" concepts that haunted both academic and journalistic accounts of economic regulation: "public interest" and "capture."[29] McCraw found both of these concepts unduly simplistic. The relationship of business and politics, in his view, was far too complex to be encapsulated in a single explanatory scheme.[30] Building on the literary skills he had honed as an undergraduate English major, he noted the startling rhetorical symbiosis between the critical evaluation of Progressive-era economic legislation popularized by the New Left historian Gabriel Kolko—who characterized the period's most important regulatory laws as a "triumph for conservatism" engineered by big business lobbyists terrified of competition—and the highly disparaging assessment of federal regulatory policy proffered by the Chicago School economist George Stigler. For both Kolko and Stigler, the government had been "captured" by the interests it was ostensibly regulating—and the "public interest" was nowhere to be found. Kolko's embrace of the "capture" thesis was unequivocal. "Federal economic regulation," Kolko concluded in his *Triumph of Conservatism* (1963), a revisionist history of progressivism from which McCraw quoted in his review essay—was "generally designed by the regulated interest to meet its own end, and not those of the public or the commonweal."[31]

Stigler was no friend of the New Left. Even so, his assessment of the Interstate Commerce Commission (ICC) bore a remarkable similarity to arguments that Kolko had advanced in *Triumph of Conservatism*. Inspired by what McCraw sardonically termed Stigler's "near-worship of the market as allocator of resources," the Chicago School economist had added a "measure of ideology" to the "cold logic of price theory." And in particular, McCraw faulted Stigler for transforming his burning resentment at the "interference" of lawmakers with market forces into a full-blown market fundamentalism that—surprisingly enough, given their markedly different political orientations—had refashioned the "Kolko model" to fit his ideological agenda.[32] Stigler vented his wrath on ICC administrative rulings—rather than, like Kolko, on the political maneuvering that had culminated in regulatory legislation. Yet the "capture" that Stigler lamented found its consummate expression not in anything the ICC did, but, rather, in the "prior political power" that had called forth its original establishment as a "regulatory mechanism."[33] Stigler, as McCraw would acerbically note several years later in a review of a collection of Stigler's essays on economic regulation, had ventured sweeping claims about the origins and operations of early twentieth-century regulatory commissions without consulting either historians or the "available evidence" and had theorized about their politics while "ignoring political scientists": "And why? Because for him, price theory is sufficient unto all things. It is not just another tool, but the philosopher's stone, The Answer. It is a religion, and he is a true believer."[34]

The most impressive feature of McCraw's 1975 essay is to be found not in the perceptiveness with which he glossed the large and sprawling academic literature on regulation—though this is, by itself, a major achievement—but, rather, in its method.[35] For the first time, McCraw moved beyond the actor-oriented contextualism of his two books on the TVA to deploy, rather than merely to describe, the explanatory scheme of institutional economics. The country's principal independent regulatory commissions, McCraw observed—including, in particular, the ICC and the Securities and Exchange Commission (SEC)—had embarked on a multifunctional project of diverse and sometimes even contradictory economic, political, and cultural agendas.

Historians, and here McCraw included himself, had painstakingly chronicled these agendas by recovering the protagonists' own language. It was time to do more. To fully contextualize the regulatory process, historians had to transcend the actors' own conceptual categories and investigate the structure, conduct, and performance of the industries that the regulatory commissions had been established to regulate. "If, as seems likely"— McCraw cagily observed, in venturing an educated guess that would soon transmogrify into an article of faith—"the inherent nature of an industry is the most important single context in which regulators must operate, then the range of policies open to them has been narrower than many observers have hitherto believed."[36] McCraw framed his industry-centrism as a hypothesis; it would quickly become a cri de coeur. By positing that the "inherent nature" of an industry was the "most important" context for regulatory decisionmaking, he presumed that industries did in fact have an inherent structure that rendered them impervious to political fiat in some fundamental, though ill-defined, way—a presumption that would shape everything he wrote about business and government for the next twenty years.

McCraw's creative juxtaposition of history and theory informed a two-day interdisciplinary conference on the history of regulation that he organized in 1980.[37] The attendees discussed precirculated essays by four historians (McCraw, Morton Keller, Ellis Hawley, and Samuel P. Hays) and one political scientist (David Vogel), all of which would be collected shortly thereafter by McCraw in *Regulation in Perspective* (1981).

Among the most wide-ranging and provocative of the essays to come out of this conference was McCraw's own "Rethinking the Trust Question."[38] In its ambitiously titled opening section—"Elements of a Fresh Analysis"— McCraw borrowed from institutional economics to better understand the operational challenge that overcapacity posed for the large-scale industrial firms that had once been called "trusts" and that were now popularly known as "big business." Certain reformers, McCraw contended, had conspicuously failed to understand this operational challenge, with disastrous results. Historians should do better. In particular, they should gird themselves against the profoundly mistaken "central assumption" that had been endorsed by so many big-business critics: namely, that the trusts were "unnatural," the "bastard offspring of unscrupulous promoters."[39]

Among the critics that McCraw had in mind was Louis Brandeis. Hailed as the "people's lawyer," Brandeis had represented several defendants in antitrust lawsuits before he obtained a seat on the U.S. Supreme Court. Yet in his assault on economic consolidation, or what he was wont to call "bigness," Brandeis had, or so McCraw contended, conspicuously failed to comprehend even the most rudimentary facts about the nature of the firm.

To make his point, McCraw analyzed a set of unpublished lectures that Brandeis had prepared in the 1890s for a course on business law that he taught at the Massachusetts Institute of Technology. These lectures, in McCraw's view, provided a key to Brandeis's jurisprudence as both an advocate and a jurist. In his explication of the law, McCraw observed, Brandeis had displayed an inability to "grasp the distinction" between vertical and horizontal integration and between center and periphery firms. As a consequence, Brandeis was fundamentally confused about how and why big businesses evolved, which business practices "would or would not help consumers," and which types of organizations "were or were not efficient."[40]

Perhaps the most startling feature of Brandeis's lectures was the surprising cast of characters for whom he served as a "mouthpiece." They were, most emphatically not "the people"—Brandeis's earnest protestations to the contrary—but instead a motley group of retail druggists, small shoe manufacturers, and other members of the "petite bourgeoisie."[41] By failing to locate the "inherent nature" of the industries in which they operated,

Brandeis had demonstrated one of the "characteristic shortcomings of the American regulatory tradition"; namely, a "powerful disinclination" to persist in hard economic analysis that might "lead away from strong ideological preference."[42]

McCraw's indictment of Brandeis's economic literacy would eventually occasion a vigorous rebuttal from McCraw's former student Gerald Berk. McCraw, in Berk's view, had exaggerated Brandeis's naïveté and ignored his political critique of the potentially deleterious consequences of concentrated economic power.[43] Even so, McCraw's indictment quickly gained adherents, at least in part because it echoed, and very possibly drew inspiration from, the markedly similar critique of the progressives as backward-looking, economically naïve denizens of a status-anxious middle class that the political historian Richard Hofstadter had famously mounted several decades earlier in his *Age of Reform*.[44] Further support for McCraw's position came from one of McCraw's graduate school mentors, Willard Hurst. Hurst, as it happens, had once served as a law clerk for Brandeis, and when queried by McCraw about Brandeis's economic literacy, proved to be "enormously helpful" in reassuring him that "I was right in my heretical interpretation of Brandeis's thinking about economic matters."[45]

The theoretical position McCraw staked out in his "Trust Question" would inform much of what he would write in the next few years on the independent regulatory commission. The "great achievement" of the SEC during the Great Depression, McCraw concluded, in a thoughtful analysis of its early years that he published in 1982, "was to restore legitimacy to an essential element of the capitalist framework."[46] The key to this achievement lay in the process SEC regulators hit upon to restore public confidence in the nation's capital markets. By recruiting brokers, bankers, accountants, and lawyers to police corruption, the agency mobilized the talents of interested parties, a strategy that the economist Charles Schultze would famously term the "public use of private interest."[47]

Gifted regulators sometimes changed their minds. A case in point was SEC chairman James M. Landis. Though Landis had relied on institutional economics to defend commission regulation in his 1938 book, *The Administrative Process*, he would later undertake a "merciless dissection of regulatory failure" in a 1960 report for the incoming John F. Kennedy administration.[48] The evolution of Landis's thinking, McCraw concluded, paralleled the wider arc of American liberalism from the New Deal to the Great Society.[49]

McCraw's research on the regulatory commission culminated with the 1984 publication of *Prophets of Regulation: Charles Francis Adams, Louis D. Brandeis, James M. Landis, and Alfred E. Kahn*.[50] Here, as in his essay on the SEC and his books on the TVA, McCraw relied on biography to carry his narrative. To a greater extent than had been possible in his first two books, McCraw located his dramatis personae in a theoretically informed explanatory scheme. "This book is about people," McCraw would later explain, "but more importantly it's about the strategy of regulatory agencies."[51] McCraw's goal as author, as he would later elaborate, was to place a "very intelligent person inside a regulatory agency," confront that person with a "series of problems that demanded innovative polices," and "see what outcomes followed."[52] To reconstruct such a complex sequence of events demanded far more than a fluid expository style. In addition, it presupposed a robust theoretical framework that McCraw gleaned from Chandlerian business history and institutional economics.

Although *Prophets of Regulation* was widely regarded as an intellectual history, McCraw took care to emphasize the interplay of ideas and institutions: "Despite the power of thought in the history of regulation, ideas in themselves could not determine concrete outcomes."[53] From the vantage point of the 1980s, neoclassical economics had triumphed: the economist (Alfred E. Kahn) supplanting not only the lawyer (James M. Landis) but also the jurist (Louis D. Brandeis) and the advocate (Charles Francis Adams). Yet the future remained open. "What I have called in this book the 'economist's hour' of the 1970s and 1980s," McCraw cautioned, "represents a phenomenon of unpredictable duration."[54]

The thinly veiled skepticism with which McCraw regarded the "economist's hour"—the vindication, as it were, of the law-and-economics orthodoxy about which he had long harbored such misgivings—was balanced by his unabashed confidence in his method. What had remained in 1975 a promising hypothesis about the "inherent nature" of the firm had now acquired the status of an iron law of social science: "Every industry, whether regulated or not, does possess a certain underlying economic structure: characteristics that make it different from other industries and that help to shape the internal conditions for regulatory opportunities and constraints. *More than any other single factor, this underlying structure of the particular industry being regulated has defined the context in which regulatory agencies have operated.*"[55]

Prophets of Regulation was well received both inside the academy and among the general public. In addition to garnering the 1985 Pulitzer Prize for history, it received the *Business History Review*'s triennial Thomas Newcomen award for the best book in business history. Sympathetic reviewers played down its industry-centric essentialism and focused on its mastery of biographical detail. "By centering his analysis around biography," observed Barry Karl in the *Business History Review*, "McCraw might be making "his most important historical assertion," yet he had done it "so subliminally that its significance could get lost": "Economic and political ideas, he implies, are neither pure abstractions nor fixed realities. They are conceptions held by men who seek to give them effect in the world they see in front of them."[56]

More skeptical was the economic historian Gavin Wright. Writing in *Reviews in American History*, Wright raised penetrating questions about McCraw's essentialism while praising *Prophets of Regulation* as a "landmark" in the "modern resuscitation of 'the market' to intellectual and political respectability"—a backhanded compliment, given McCraw's misgivings about neoclassical economics.[57] The hard-and-fast distinction that McCraw made between center and periphery firms, Wright observed, was "not matched by a rigorous body of research documenting the economic basis for survival-power on the part of large, vertically-integrated corporations." As a case in point, Wright cited an innovative monograph on the great merger movement (by Naomi Lamoreaux, then a recently minted Johns Hopkins PhD) that had pointedly questioned the economic rationale for late nineteenth-century economic consolidation.[58] Even McCraw had conceded, Wright elaborated, that the center-periphery duality would become "somewhat less useful" as a conceptual tool after the Second World War, given corporate diversification, the rise of the conglomerate, and the growing allure of franchising.[59] Each of these developments revealed the contingent character of the supposedly "natural" technological imperatives that McCraw, following Chander, had so admired: "Since the corporate structure of modern business enterprise only stabilized in the 1920s, and began to escape its bounds in these ways in the 1960s, this means that the window in historical time during which these alleged deep technological imperatives were at work was in fact rather brief."[60]

Wright's critique highlighted a limitation of McCraw's method that, by the end of his career, even sympathetic students of McCraw would concede. From the standpoint of hindsight, and notwithstanding its enviable renown, *Prophets of Regulation* remains an artifact of a post–New Deal debate in institutional economics over the intellectual merits of the technologically driven explanatory scheme that lay at the heart of Chandlerian business history.

The United States and the World

Looking back on *Prophets of Regulation*, McCraw reflected that he had taken inspiration not only from Chandler but also from the interdisciplinary hothouse of the Harvard Business School.[61] This school had a marked influence not only on McCraw's scholarship but also on his teaching. Unlike most history professors, McCraw's primary classroom audience consisted neither of impressionable undergraduates nor would-be history professors. Rather, they were ambitious and assertive MBA students, of whom roughly one-third hailed from outside the United States. In keeping with the Harvard Business School tradition, McCraw abandoned formal lectures (a pedagogical style at which he had excelled at Texas) in favor of the Socratic question-and-answer "case method." It was not always easy. On more than one occasion, McCraw repeated the observation of his predecessor N. S. B. Gras—the first professor to hold the chair in business history that McCraw inherited following Chander's retirement—that it could be an "exceedingly difficult task" to persuade MBA students of the relevance of history in the months just before they embarked on careers in "practical affairs": "I am not sure that I will succeed, but I do sympathize with the motive behind the experiment, that is, to give the students a cultural background for their work and a perspective to their training."[62]

The challenges of teaching such a diverse and demanding group of students helped prod McCraw to expand his intellectual horizons beyond the United States. Cross-national comparisons were an integral component of a required first-year MBA course on business, government, and the international economy that McCraw taught for many years. These comparisons furnished the rationale for an innovative second-year elective course on "the coming of managerial capitalism" that McCraw helped design. By focusing on what McCraw termed *"the relentlessness of change"* in myriad realms—including managerial prerogatives, firm and industry structure, technology, and the external environment—McCraw's courses surveyed the evolution of economic institutions in four countries—the United States, Great Britain, Germany, and Japan.[63]

The internationalization of McCraw's outlook on the relationship of business and politics received a boost from Chandler's own example. In the late 1970s, Chandler began research on a cross-national history of industrial capitalism in the United States, Great Britain, and Germany. Following Chandler's lead, McCraw published in 1984 a cross-national essay that compared the sequencing of the rise of big government and big business in the United States, Europe, and Japan.[64] Only in the United States, McCraw concluded, had big business emerged before big government, a circumstance that he believed went far toward explaining the persistence of what he called—following Chandler, who had floated a similar argument several years earlier—the uniquely "adversarial" relationship between government and business in the post-1880 United States.

The cross-national contrast that McCraw found most intriguing involved the United States and Japan. In the United States, McCraw hypothesized, the relationship between business and politics was far more conflict-ridden than in Japan, a distinction that helped explain the rapid rise of Japan as an industrial power. To find out what Americans might learn from the Japanese, McCraw spent a few weeks in Japan for several summers in the 1980s, gaining insights into Japanese business history that he would draw on in an ambitious cross-national research project on the relationship between business and politics in the United States and Japan. This project culminated in the publication of a multiauthor collection of essays titled *America versus Japan* that compared and contrasted the relationship of business and politics in the United States and Japan, to the decided advantage of the latter.[65] The adversarial nature of the relationship between business and politics in the United States—and, in particular, the constant threat of antitrust prosecution—made the United States a much less business-friendly place. In Japan, in contrast, a benign and paternalistic Ministry of International Trade and Industry promoted harmony and economic growth by matching production to demand while fostering technological innovation.

American versus Japan was McCraw's least successful scholarly project. Few of its contributors were East Asianists, and none had conducted extensive primary research in Japanese-language primary sources. Even so, it provided McCraw with a glimpse of the possibilities of cross-national institutional comparisons. "As the great historian Macaulay once wrote," McCraw observed in a summary essay, "'He knows not England who only England knows'; and our experience in writing the book has confirmed the wisdom of Macaulay's comment."[66] The "basic point is well made," as one not entirely sympathetic East Asianist observed, in a review of the collection: there was "not simply one form of competition, one best way to organize, one effective way to manage. . . . Instead, every economy is really a *political economy* and the structures that emerge in the course of history and of political and economic maneuver lead to differences in national and corporate strategy, policy, and action."[67]

Decidedly more successful was McCraw's next major venture in cross-national comparative history, a multiauthor textbook—designed for the business school market, and for many years required reading for first-year MBA students at Harvard Business School—that analyzed the evolution of economic institutions in both the private and public sectors in the United States, Great Britain, Germany, and Japan.[68] Titled *Creating Modern Capitalism: How Entrepreneurs, Companies, and Countries Triumphed in Three Industrial Revolutions*, edited by McCraw and published by Harvard University Press in 1997, this surprisingly coherent and eminently readable overview included sparkling essays on all four countries by leading specialists in their fields that were complemented by highly informative synthetic chapters by McCraw. Almost twenty years after its publication, it remains one of the best, if not the best, single-volume institutionally oriented histories of capitalism in print.

Creating Modern Capitalism's largest theoretical debt was to Schumpeter, who remained almost a half century after this death (or so McCraw proclaimed in his introduction), "one of the most astute of all analysts of capitalism."[69] From a Schumpeterian perspective, McCraw reflected, any "worthwhile analysis" of economic phenomena had to contain "elements of history, theory, and statistics." The contributors to *Creating Modern Capitalism* took Schumpeter's advice.[70] So too would McCraw himself in his hugely successful U.S. business history textbook, *American Business since 1920: How It Worked*, which he published three years later.[71]

McCraw would not publish his biography of Schumpeter until 2007. Yet he had had the economist on his radar ever since he had first arrived at Harvard in 1973. Schumpeter's presence loomed large at Harvard, where he had taught from 1932 until his death in 1950. Though Schumpeter's primary appointment was in economics, he would furnish the inspiration for a short-lived Center for the Study of Entrepreneurship, funded by the Rockefeller Foundation, that would help advance the careers of a highly distinguished cohort of specialists in economic history. The center's fellows, McCraw later quipped, were a veritable "Who's Who of economic historians from the 1950s to the 1980s." Among them were Chandler, Hugh Aitken, Bernard Bailyn, David Landes, Douglass North, and Henry Rosovsky.[72]

McCraw's first major publication on Schumpeter dates from 1991. It took the form of a capsule summary of Schumpeter's life and work, intended for a general audience, that McCraw had been commissioned to write for a semi-popular magazine, *The American Scholar*.[73] In it, McCraw affirmed what would become known as the "Schumpeter hypothesis"—that is, the presumption that the most fundamental economic innovations originated not in the dingy garret of a mad-genius inventor—or, to update the metaphor, in the Silicon Valley garage of a teenaged boy-wonder—but in a well-established institution such as Bell Labs or General Electric.[74]

Giant organizations, of course, could sometimes become sclerotic, and it was entirely conceivable for innovation to originate on the periphery rather than at the center. In 1991, however, these were possibilities that McCraw did not see fit to entertain. McCraw had a longstanding fascination with giant organizations of all kinds—from Alfred Sloan's General Motors and David Lilienthal's TVA to James Landis's SEC—and simply assumed that sites like these had spawned the most fundamental innovations of the age. McCraw's bigger-is-better bias derived partly from his personal familiarity with the TVA and the Navy; partly from his deep skepticism toward the market fundamentalism that by 1991 had become firmly entrenched in the economics profession; and partly from his embrace of certain theoretical insights derived from Chandlerian business history—including, in particular, its valorization of "organizational capabilities" and "economies of scope."

McCraw's bigger-is-better bias received further validation from his reading of Schumpeter. The "creative destruction" wrought by innovations originating inside giant organizations, McCraw believed, was one of the main themes of *Capitalism, Socialism, and Democracy*. McCraw elaborated on this characterization in his 1991 essay, in which Schumpeter became a crypto–New Dealer, who combined a pragmatic understanding of institutional economics with a Chandlerian faith in the power of organizational capabilities to spawn technological innovation.[75] It was a remarkable interpretation, not the least because of the extent to which McCraw would back off from its implications when he came to write his Schumpeter biography.

McCraw's interpretation of Schumpeter sparked a pointed rebuttal from Louis Galambos, a history professor closely associated with Chandler who had assumed Chandler's teaching responsibilities at Johns Hopkins when

Chandler moved to Harvard. The occasion for Galambos's rejoinder was a wide-ranging U.S. Federal Trade Commission–sponsored seminar on the history of antitrust that McCraw had helped organize in 1981. In one of the most revealing moments in this seminar, Galambos conceded that, at present, there existed a consensus among historians of innovation (and here Galambos lumped together McCraw and Chandler) that linked an organization's size with its capacity for innovation. To make his point, Galambos proposed a thought experiment. If Schumpeter were alive, Galambos hypothesized, who would he pick as the more disruptive innovator: the maverick General Motors president Billy Durant or Durant's successor, the organizational genius Alfred Sloan? Most of his colleagues, Galambos predicted, would pick Sloan over Durant. Galambos demurred. In his view, Schumpeter would pick Durant over Sloan, since, as a believer in the power of "creative destruction," he favored disruption over stability and chaos over calm.[76]

Galambos's reading of Schumpeter would eventually gain widespread traction in the academy, and, beginning with *Creating Modern Capitalism*, would be endorsed even by McCraw. Among Schumpeter's intellectual gifts, McCraw wrote in his introduction, was his encouragement of a "dynamic, flexible, and future-oriented way of thinking" that "injected a pattern of ceaseless and merciless competition into nearly every aspect of life."[77] Not until the publication of *Prophet of Innovation*, however, would McCraw fully back off from the implications of the bigger-is-better argument that he had advanced in 1991.

Prophet of Innovation was in many ways McCraw's most impressive book. Beautifully written, well researched, and consistently illuminating about matters large and small, it offers its readers a superb introduction to an economist whom McCraw and many others have come to hail as the world's preeminent theorist of capitalism. In its opening chapters, McCraw dutifully recounted the economist's Austrian upbringing and German education. Yet it was not until Schumpeter relocated in midcareer across the Atlantic to take a professorship at Harvard that McCraw really hit his stride. For it was at Harvard that Schumpeter would nurture a generation of economists who would rise to the front ranks of their profession after the Second World War, while writing three of his most impressive books—*Business Cycles* (1939), *Capitalism, Socialism, and Democracy* (1942), and the posthumously published *History of Economic Analysis* (1954). The second and third of these books—*Capitalism, Socialism, and Democracy* and *The History of Economic Analysis*—were hailed from the moment of their publication as masterpieces;

the first, *Business Cycles*, made reviewers' heads spin. Sprawling, pretentious, and overlong, it discouraged even sympathetic readers—which was highly unfortunate, in McCraw's opinion, since it included enough trenchant insights into business behavior to make it a foundational history of capitalism in the United States if only a creative editor had reorganized it to make its central argument more compelling.[78]

The Schumpeter of McCraw's *Prophet of Innovation* was no longer the proto–New Dealer of his 1991 *American Scholar* essay. Yet he was also not the Roosevelt-phobic anti–New Deal covert Nazi sympathizer that McCraw might have made him out to be had he been so inclined.[79] More importantly, McCraw's 2007 Schumpeter had become, rather like McCraw himself, much more sympathetic than McCraw's 1991 Schumpeter had been toward the innovative potential of insurgent start-up firms and adversarial regulatory regimes. The "Schumpeter hypothesis" linking bigness and innovation had ceased to be an article of faith among historians and social scientists, and McCraw embraced the new consensus. "Innovation," McCraw now conceded, in a revealing footnote, was simply "not as automatic in large enterprises as Schumpeter makes it out to be in *Capitalism, Socialism, and Democracy*."[80] Had McCraw lived, he might well have published yet another masterwork. Following the publication of *Founders and Finance*, McCraw embarked on a new research project on the history of immigrant entrepreneurship that built on his newfound appreciation for the innovative potential of individuals who worked not at the center but on the periphery.[81]

Conclusion

McCraw's major publications in twentieth-century U.S. history—*TVA and the Power Fight, Prophets of Regulation,* and *Prophet of Innovation*—offer up a heady mix of insights for historians interested in the relationship of business and politics in the American past. When McCraw began to publish on what historians today call "political economy" (a term McCraw rarely used), institutional history remained marginalized in the historical profession.[82] To hasten its revival, he combined an actor-oriented contextualism with theoretical insights drawn from Chandlerian business history and institutional economics to craft compelling analytical narratives about key developments in the making of the modern world.

The defining events that shaped McCraw's historical imagination were the Great Depression, the New Deal, the Second World War, and the postwar economic boom. Unlike today's historians of capitalism, McCraw remembered how business and politics had interacted in the period preceding the post-1973 economic downturn, the dot-com bubble of 2000, and the Great Recession of 2008. This reservoir of personal knowledge gave McCraw a sense of optimism about creative statecraft that is often missing today.

At the heart of McCraw's achievement lay an enviable gift for combining lucid prose and theoretical rigor to explore the character and significance of five different kinds of phenomena: business, markets, institutions, culture, and leadership. He was, in short, an exemplary historian of capitalism who helped lay the foundations for a field that would take as its primary subject a nexus of relationships that, as one of its most penetrating practitioners has observed, are perhaps best characterized not as capitalism but as political economy.[83]

To understand the relationship between business and politics in the twentieth century—or what McCraw would call at different times the "mixed economy" or "modern capitalism"—historians would do well not to forget the legacy of the New Deal, a legacy that extended well beyond the 1930s and would lay the foundation for the unprecedented prosperity that the American people would enjoy in the postwar era. To understood how this all came about, it is incumbent on the historian to look not only to contingency, luck, and the momentous transformations wrought by the Second World War, but also to statesmen, business leaders, and social scientists.[84] To be sure, McCraw's faith in the collective wisdom of lawmakers would be sorely challenged by the regulatory failures that contributed to the 2008 financial crisis. Yet McCraw remained to the end, as he had been throughout his career, a principled champion of liberal reform and a pointed critic of the market fundamentalism that he feared would imperil not only the economic foundations of capitalism, but also the humanistic, theoretically informed, and morally grounded exploration of modernity that McCraw's scholarship exemplified, and that remains a resource, a challenge, and an inspiration for historians today.[85]

PART III

The Postwar Era:
Economic Development

Chapter 6

"Free Enterprise" or Federal Aid? The Business Response to Economic Restructuring in the Long 1950s

Tami J. Friedman

Between the late 1940s and the early 1960s (the long 1950s), U.S. business leaders fought hard to regain their preeminence as drivers of the nation's economy—a status that had been severely undercut by the union gains and federal intervention unleashed during the Great Depression and the Second World War. To that end, employers pursued a host of workplace, legislative, and public relations strategies designed to hinder organized labor. Some engaged in such techniques as capital migration, plant consolidation, and automation, which weakened unions while also reducing labor costs. At the same time, many businessmen—particularly those promoting business interests at the national level—sought to prevent what they perceived as intrusive economic planning by the federal state. These postwar goals have much in common with conditions achieved in recent decades: deregulation, declining job quality, a decimated labor movement, unchecked capital mobility, and other "free-market" markers of what historian Judith Stein has called an "age of inequality." Although we tend to associate such private sector victories with the Reagan era and its aftermath, an earlier generation of business conservatives made considerable headway in accomplishing similar aims.[1]

Reaching these objectives, however, was no easy task. Although the long 1950s is widely heralded as a golden age of industrial peace and prosperity that moved U.S. workers into the middle class, many workers and their communities faced serious hardship as the result of multiple recessions, fluctuating consumer demand, and corporate cost-cutting measures that diminished the availability of well-paying unionized jobs. These conditions produced intense conflict between unionists and employers not only at the point of production but also in the federal arena: while laborites (still wielding a measure of influence in this period) sought the use of federal power and resources to cope with the harsh effects of economic dislocation, business leaders typically insisted on private initiative and local aid. But the fight over federal involvement also exposed tensions and contradictions within the business community, for some businessmen in struggling areas found an antistatist agenda incompatible with local needs. In recent years, scholars have produced important studies of postwar efforts by business to influence the federal state. This essay, by exploring how such efforts intersected with the local impact of economic restructuring, suggests that national business groups sometimes faced serious challenges from within their own ranks. These developments remind us that, at particular historical moments, the business community—particularly in its relationship to federal authority—has been more complex and less monolithic than is often believed.[2]

In broad terms, the long 1950s was marked by sustained economic growth. Between 1945 and 1960, the nation's gross national product increased by 250 percent, while per capita income rose by 35 percent. Much of the postwar prosperity accrued to middle-class Americans, who enjoyed greatly expanded access to suburban lifestyles, homeownership, and consumer goods such as televisions and automobiles. Many working-class people were also able to enjoy these advantages; between 1949 and 1959, real pretax weekly earnings for production employees in manufacturing grew by nearly 31 percent, and real disposable income for a typical industrial worker supporting a family of four rose by nearly 18 percent. Although federal programs (e.g., housing and educational aid for veterans and investment in scientific research) were pivotal in driving postwar economic advancement, organized labor's efforts played a key role in winning wage and benefit gains. "For the industrial worker of this era," historian David Brody has observed, "the union contract was becoming a passport to a better life."[3]

And yet, during this period, many working-class Americans experienced economic strain. As industrialists decentralized manufacturing operations, installed labor-saving machinery, and adopted other techniques to increase efficiency and productivity, employment declined not only in long-troubled industries such as coal and textiles but also in stronger sectors such as auto, electrical, and steel. In the summer of 1949 (during the 1948–49 recession, when unemployment peaked nationally at 7.9 percent), the U.S. Department of Labor reported that ten major labor-market areas (of about a hundred that were regularly surveyed) had jobless rates of 12 percent or more. The areas included Muskegon, Michigan (parts for durable-goods manufacturers, including automakers); Lawrence, Massachusetts (textiles); and Wilkes-Barre, Pennsylvania (coal). (There were also twenty-two smaller areas in this category; for these, employment data were gathered on request.) Such conditions did not simply coincide with significant troughs in the business cycle. In mid-1955, a full year after the post–Korean War slump ended, thirty-one major areas (of a total of 149, including several in Puerto Rico) and 101 smaller areas showed unemployment rates of at least 6 percent; of the major areas, five had jobless rates of 9–12 percent, while seven others reported rates of 12 percent or more. During the 1957–58 downturn, U.S. unemployment reached 7.5 percent. By the spring of 1961, as yet another recession wound down, major media outlets such as the *New York Times* were treating "hard-core unemployment" as a national concern. Among those documenting the problem was Michael Harrington, whose stirring investigation of poverty, *The Other America*, published in 1962, explicitly addressed the crisis facing miners, packinghouse workers, auto workers, and others in mass-production industries who had been idled as the result of mechanization and other causes of economic decline.[4]

Federal authorities pursued a range of responses to economic distress. In January 1947, President Harry S Truman issued the first *Economic Report of the President*, as mandated by the Employment Act of 1946. In it, he noted the presence of "a few chronically depressed areas, and some areas left stranded by the end of the war." Because the "interplay of Nation-wide forces" had created these conditions, he asserted, it was the government's responsibility to offer help. In July 1949, the president expressed concern about "acute unemployment problems" in "many localities and even some States." In response to these conditions, he urged federal agencies to modify their procurement, construction, and lending policies in order to direct resources to hard-hit areas, with the goal of treating "pools of heavy unemployment . . . before they spread." Truman appointed special assistant John R. Steelman to coordinate this effort; among other activities, Steelman ensured the distribution of information about forthcoming government contracts for which firms in "critical labor market areas" could bid. During the Korean War mobilization, the Truman administration promoted military procurement policies designed to channel war work to areas of labor surplus; under President Dwight D. Eisenhower, companies receiving accelerated tax write-offs for building or expanding defense plants (a policy adopted during Truman's tenure) enjoyed a larger share of benefits if they located projects in economically troubled sites.[5]

By the mid-1950s, labor unions and some congressional Democrats—led by Illinois senator (and economist) Paul H. Douglas—were proposing new strategies to relieve economic distress at the local level. They advocated direct federal aid to struggling communities, in the form of loans, grants, and technical assistance designed to facilitate industrial revitalization. President Eisenhower opposed these efforts on the grounds that, as he insisted in January 1955, federal programs "can make only a limited contribution to relieving spot unemployment"; for the most part, he argued, the work of helping hard-hit areas to adjust to changing conditions "can and should be carried out by the local citizens themselves." Nonetheless, the "developing clamor for action," as Council of Economic Advisors chair Arthur F. Burns put it, compelled the Eisenhower administration to propose its own (watered-down) version of depressed-areas aid. In both 1958 and 1960, the president vetoed Democrat-initiated versions of such legislation when they reached his desk. In May 1961, President John F. Kennedy signed the Area Redevelopment Act, which established an agency in the U.S. Department of Commerce to coordinate and distribute nearly $400 million in aid over the next four years.[6]

The nation's leading business organizations—the U.S. Chamber of Commerce and the National Association of Manufacturers (NAM)—articulated powerful ideological arguments against federal intervention to assist suffering communities or regions. In 1956, the NAM's board of directors adopted an official policy emphasizing the need for "community initiative and resourcefulness" to address the problem. Federal depressed-areas aid, the NAM contended, "undermines community responsibility, perpetuates local economic dislocation and impedes economic growth" and indeed "is contrary to the principles on which the growth of our American system has been based." Similarly, Chamber leader Robert P. Lee, addressing a Senate subcommittee a year later, championed "locally conceived and executed industrial development programs, supplemented by statewide activities." "Dynamic change requires inevitable adjustment," he argued. "We can try to shelter everyone from the effects of change only at the expense of growth and progress. If we encourage individual and community adaptability to change, we will be maintaining the climate which has made possible our tremendous advances of the past." A 1960 Chamber report, citing economist Joseph A. Schumpeter's notion of "creative destruction," argued that declining employment in certain areas, industries, and occupations flowed naturally from the twists and turns of economic progress. While acknowledging that plant shutdowns and relocations caused hardship for those immediately affected, the best solution, these groups insisted, was to allow America's free-enterprise system to work. These views reflected a commitment to "limited government, individual initiative and freedom, a competitive market economy, and economic growth with reasonable stability," as the Chamber put it in 1961.[7]

This critique of federal intervention reflected, to a great extent, business leaders' concerns about organized labor's postwar campaign to expand social welfare programs and increase the government's role in economic affairs. In response to the economic uncertainty that characterized much of the long 1950s, unionists urged federal authorities to restore growth and prosperity not only by aiding distressed areas (the Textile Workers Union of America was especially active in this effort) but also by providing greater financial security for workers—through, for example, federal standards for unemployment insurance and a higher federal minimum wage. Laborites also sought broader measures to combat depression. In the spring of 1950, for example, the Congress of Industrial Organizations (CIO) called for the creation of a special Labor Department bureau to coordinate the federal response to severe unemployment. In addition, the CIO advocated advance preparations for public-works projects (including those that would help white-collar workers in such fields as health, education, and the arts) and supported Democrat-sponsored proposals to establish an emergency relief fund and revive the New Deal–era Civilian Conservation Corps. Such actions threatened to undermine businessmen's influence over the nation's economic arrangements by shifting power to unions and the federal state.[8]

National business groups' opposition was also motivated by their interest in protecting employers' advantages at local sites. If communities hoped to "stem the tide of industrial migration and attract good employers," the monthly Chamber publication *Economic Intelligence* proclaimed in September 1955, it was their responsibility to eliminate conditions that created "a social climate unfavorable to business." These included "unfair taxes" and zoning problems along with "restrictive state labor legislation, slow-downs, resistance to technology, an 'advanced' concept of the welfare state on the state and local level and a general suspicion of business." Many firms, unable to "carry on business at a profit" under such circumstances, were "forced to move." "The goose that lays the golden eggs rarely asks for special favors from its constituents," the publication observed. "But when instead the ax is brandished, the goose cannot be blamed if it has an urge to fly." In 1960, the NAM's board adopted a formal policy asserting that "a favorable business climate" was "essential" for new product development, job creation, economic expansion, and national prosperity. That top leaders within the NAM and the Chamber included high-ranking executives of corporations with a strong commitment to decentralizing production—General Electric, Ford Motor Company, Radio Corporation of America, Borg-Warner, E. I. du Pont de Nemours, Armstrong Cork, and others—likely strengthened these groups' desire to block national pro-labor policies that threatened to reduce employers' leverage in particular locales.[9]

These concerns generated multiple resistance techniques. One tactic was to tie the depressed-areas problem to inflexible, artificially high wage rates imposed by unions or labor legislation; in response to the Truman administration's Korean War–era efforts to channel procurement to hard-hit places, the Chamber's monthly *Labor Relations Letter* asked: "Why can't a surplus labor area readjust its wage structure realistically enough to compete successfully with other areas for the almost limitless amount of government contracts?" Chamber officials also minimized the gravity of the post-Korea recession, because serious downturns were likely to boost support for federal policies with which they disagreed. In August 1955, the Chamber's weekly *Washington Report* (formerly the *National Chamber Washington Report*, or *NCWR*) crowed that new reports of increased labor-market participation were silencing last year's "doom and gloom prophets" and "further confounding those who were demanding all kinds of drastic federal action and intervention 12 months ago to halt the 'recession.'"[10]

Domestic anticommunism helped strengthen the business case for a diminished federal role. The CIO's appeals for federal action, the *NCWR* reported in December 1953, raised the specter of the New Deal, whose "hastily-conceived, ill-advised" policies had "thwarted recovery" during the Great Depression by handicapping free-market forces and job creation. The publication likened this approach to "the alien philosophy that an all powerful central government should solve our economic problems," which contrasted sharply with its own emphasis on "the self-reliance of communities and individual businesses." "The alternative to independent constructive action by private industry and private citizens," the Chamber warned elsewhere, "is obvious: government action, restrictions and red tape. This is the pathway to economic slavery and totalitarianism." These views sounded strikingly similar to the ideas of Friedrich von Hayek, who argued in his 1944 book *The Road to Serfdom* that "state interference" to protect people from economic insecurity would destroy liberty; planning, he declared, when substituted for market competition, "leads to dictatorship." The Eisenhower administration, too, sought to downplay federal involvement. In the fall of 1955, the president unveiled his own depressed-areas proposal, which called for a new federal agency to coordinate existing relief efforts and provide technical and financial support. Council of Economic Advisors chair Arthur Burns, highlighting the program's "very definite accent on private enterprise," denied that it "smacked of the New Deal." "The essence of this plan," he insisted, "really is to help communities to help themselves. I wouldn't call that New Deal-ism."[11]

Of course, national business groups were quite comfortable with certain forms of federal support. As Chamber director (and chair of General Mills) Harry A. Bullis told the organization's spring 1949 annual meeting, "What we need is positive action by government that will nourish our free economy" by "encourag[ing] the flow of capital into business, and a release from the mounting pressure of taxation." The Cold War strengthened this approach. The Chamber did not oppose Korean War–era enhanced tax write-offs for firms building plants in distressed areas. The group actively promoted industry's efforts to "'do business' with the Air Force," and lobbied for federal funds to strengthen "the nation's sagging shipbuilding industry" on the grounds that it was essential for national defense. The point was not to eliminate federal authority but rather, as the Chamber put it in the early 1950s, to ensure "that governmental operations, which are the essence of public policy, be properly attuned to our free market economy." It was noteworthy that, in all of these cases, federal resources went directly to businessmen themselves.[12]

When it came to rehabilitating distressed areas, however, the NAM and the Chamber were staunchly opposed. In congressional testimony, policy reports, and elsewhere, they argued that the depressed-areas problem was local, not national, and thus did not warrant direct federal aid. In the spring

of 1957, Union Bag-Camp Paper executive Donald J. Hardenbrook—
testifying before a Senate subcommittee as vice chair of the NAM's Industrial Problems Committee—contended that depressed areas were a "truly
minute" problem, because unemployment in the thirteen major areas with
jobless rates of at least 6 percent (the federal government's definition of
"substantial labor surplus") continuously for the past four years accounted
for "less than one-fifth of 1 percent of the total national labor force." In early
1959, NAM chair (and chair of Singer Manufacturing) Milton C. Lightner—
citing "all the inherent evils attached to Federal Government loans and
grants"—asserted that such a program either "would be proven to be a
wrong approach and quite ineffectual" or "will be so expanded by future appropriations as to become a far more serious threat to the fiscal solvency of
the country" than was currently foreseen. Moreover, it could place the federal government in the "intolerable" position of "pulling enterprises from
one State to another," thus benefiting some regions at others' expense. Urging Eisenhower to veto depressed-areas legislation passed by both houses of
Congress, Lightner warned that it would create a "whole new program of
Federal expenditure which would be contrary to Administration policy of
narrowing the scope of Federal operations." By 1960, as pressure for federal
action mounted, the Chamber was insisting that "aggressive privately sponsored programs fostered by local industrial development organizations, together with such new techniques as privately financed state-wide credit
corporations," were the most effective and equitable ways to correct "prolonged and substantial localized unemployment."[13]

The battle over whether and how to help struggling communities was
waged in the local as well as national realms. Encouraged by President Truman's July 1949 message, unionists pressed for relief for local areas. In the
fall of that year, for example, the United Mine Workers of America urged
John Steelman to preserve jobs by helping facilitate a federal Reconstruction
Finance Corporation loan to a coal mining operation in northeastern Pennsylvania. The following spring, a United Steelworkers of America local, representing iron workers in nearby Luzerne County (the Wilkes-Barre area), urged
politicians to address the "impending economic recession" there. Textile
unionists in Utica, New York, even lobbied their city to purchase a local plant.
In late 1949, Truman's Labor Department secretary, Maurice J. Tobin, called
for the creation of "community employment program committees" across the
country, to include labor representatives alongside business, civic, and political
leaders; such groups, he suggested, not only could address short-term emer-

gencies but also could function as "planning agencies" to consider "new ways to expand economic activity and employment" in the long run. National media coverage of economic hardship invariably featured poignant personal stories of unemployed workers and their families in particular communities, such as the saga of George Wilson, a 32-year-old father of four who was laid off from a Celanese plant outside Cumberland, Maryland (Allegany County). The *New York Herald Tribune* interviewed Wilson in the spring of 1950 at his Textile Workers Union of America local union hall. More than a decade later, a *New York Times* series on the unemployment crisis brought to life for readers the tribulations of, among others, jobless coal miners in West Virginia, steelworkers in Pittsburgh, and auto workers in Detroit.[14]

These circumstances compelled the national business organizations to mobilize their own local base. In the spring of 1953, shortly after Eisenhower took office, the national Chamber advised its more than 3,100 affiliates of the need for a "permanent program" to "prevent [economic] emergencies" and thereby "lessen trouble ahead." Action to "meet economic changes," the Chamber observed, was best undertaken by "the business interests of the community" at the local level, because "it is at the local level where prosperity, or a lack of it, will be felt." To that end, the group launched a major initiative to achieve "the maintenance and expansion of Jobs, Markets and Production," exhorting affiliates to conduct community surveys of economic conditions, identify policy objectives based on the resulting data, and develop an "action program" involving consultation with "*all* economic interests in the community"—a process that, incidentally, would provide new opportunities to "interest all business" in the local chamber's work. The national body provided sample survey materials and other resources to facilitate these goals.[15]

Claiming the mantle of a "grass-roots organization," the Chamber not only guided but also publicized the activities of local groups. In January 1952, Chamber president (and head of the Dallas-based Lone Star Gas Company) D. A. Hulcy asked local affiliates to pledge their intention to refrain from seeking federal appropriations for local projects and to "actively oppose any proposals for increased spending" except for emergencies. (At the time, conservative business leaders were exhibiting considerable anxiety about President Truman's efforts to mobilize the domestic economy for the Korean War.) The *NCWR* then showcased instances in which local communities were eschewing such assistance and lobbying elected officials for federal spending cuts. In June 1952, for example, it covered a group of businessmen from Fitchburg, Massachusetts, who—armed with "3,000 voluntarily signed statements and 2½ miles of tape recordings of man-in-the-street interviews"— visited their congressional delegation in Washington to "protest the extravagant spending and perilous taxation of the federal government." Meanwhile, the more informal monthly *Chamber of Commerce Newsletter* ran upbeat stories about local industrial promotion campaigns. In the summer of 1953, it lauded the Canandaigua, New York, chamber's leadership in coordinating, on short notice, a citywide labor-market survey required by an industrial prospect—a massive undertaking involving a thousand volunteers. Such accounts reinforced the notion that private-sector actors were the principal drivers of economic growth.[16]

The NAM, while lacking the Chamber's local branch structure, also found opportunities to celebrate economic progress achieved locally without federal aid. The NAM's Donald Hardenbrook, in his 1957 testimony, praised the "initiative and resourcefulness" (traits he called "inherently American") with which New Bedford, Massachusetts, and Utica—two hard-hit textile towns—had overcome economic distress. In New Bedford, he reported, civic leaders had formed a local industrial development commission and "turned to diversification"; as a result of their efforts, several types of manufacturing and a "revived fishing industry" were now "meeting the job requirements of the local citizens." As for Utica, thanks to "aggressive community action" spearheaded by local businessmen, "the city is building a new economy, more stable and prosperous than in the past." (New Bedford and Utica had indeed attracted new industries, with Utica proving particularly successful at luring electronics and metal-fabricating firms that paid better than its departing textile mills. During the late 1950s and early 1960s, however, both cities remained firmly in the federal "substantial labor surplus" category, with jobless rates periodically rising to at least 9 percent.) In 1960, the NAM distributed its new publication *Favorable Business Climate* to 1,800 community-based industrial development groups.[17]

Local businessmen often moved in lockstep with the national groups. In the summer and fall of 1949, Commerce Department secretary Charles Sawyer and his staff toured the United States to "explore with responsible business and civic leaders practical plans for maintaining industrial production and employment at high levels." In the Southwest, they reported, businessmen decried John Steelman's program to channel government procurement to distressed areas as "both unnecessary and ineffective." "Too much welfare and too much coddling," the business leaders argued, "may create problems far worse than those intended to be solved." Although many chambers signed on as local contacts for Steelman's plan to notify prospective bidders of federal contracts, within a few months several of them had angrily withdrawn on the grounds that the effort was netting no results. The executive secretary of the Greensburg, Pennsylvania, chamber of commerce, for example, found that distributing the information was "useless and very expensive," while the head of the industrial development group Southern Illinois, Inc., complained that the program "was of little value and holds little promise." Their actions may have been part of a larger campaign of noncooperation with a Democratic administration; Republicans in the Cumberland, Maryland, area—whose party, according to leading Democrats, "is in favor of no Federal action to alleviate economic ills in hardship localities"—nonetheless were reportedly "criticizing the Federal government for Allegany County's plight."[18]

In some instances, local resistance to federal help reflected public relations concerns. In March 1950, Greater Lawrence (Massachusetts) chamber of commerce president Ralph B. Wilkinson disputed claims that more than 12 percent of Lawrence's workforce was jobless and that local manufacturers had received federal contracts through the Steelman plan. When asking his Democratic congressional representative to explain the discrepancies, a frustrated Wilkinson wanted to know "what benefits to this community, if any, have been received to compensate for the adverse publicity that is being constantly given to Lawrence" as the result of its designation as a "so called 'distress area.'"[19]

Meanwhile, numerous Chamber affiliates took the federal-aid abstinence pledge. By March 1952, more than 250 local bodies—from Denver and Salt Lake City to Minneapolis and Twin Falls, Idaho—had signed on. Other communities on board to "fight federal handouts" included Dayton, Ohio, whose chamber was promoting a campaign to conserve water in a seven-county area by building dams and reservoirs without federal funds. The city's diminishing supply of clean water seemed "the perfect opportunity for the federal government to spend millions," but "the good citizens of Dayton aren't going to let that happen"; instead, they planned to fix the problem with local levies designed to ensure that "only people benefiting will be taxed." In tiny Wythe County, Virginia—which, as the result of massive drought-induced crop losses, was "on the verge of being declared a disaster area by the U.S. Department of Agriculture"—business and farm leaders decided to reject federal loans in favor of borrowing from local banks, which promised interest rates no higher than the government would charge. The plucky county, according to the *NCWR*, had already "earned the respect of the nation in 1950 by whipping a polio epidemic without federal aid." In Jonesboro, Arkansas, where hungry farm families were experiencing seasonal unemployment, a "citizen's committee" found the problem less dire than initially reported. After "delivering a firmly polite 'no thank you' to Uncle Sam's surplus commodity division," the committee arranged for "those unable to work and actually destitute" to be "helped by the chamber and a civic club."[20]

Some local business leaders, however, exhibited a more complicated and even contradictory relationship to the national groups. In the summer of 1949, for example, chamber leaders in Buffalo appealed to John Steelman for federal assistance even though their city's jobless rate was below the priority minimum of 12 percent (Buffalo was in the 7–12 percent range). The Muskegon, Michigan, chamber sought the "critical area" designation in hopes of improving opportunities for area industries to obtain federal contracts, and its counterpart in the Wilkes-Barre, Pennsylvania, area (the Wyoming Valley chamber) set up a Federal Procurement Information Center that was very active in helping industries submit bids. In the early 1950s the national Chamber was hailing its local affiliates' abstention from federal assistance— but a few months after the campaign launch, more than 2,300 had not signed on. In 1961, just after the Area Redevelopment Act became law, the president of Pennsylvania Power & Light, addressing industrial boosters in still-struggling Wilkes-Barre, criticized "this sour phrase, 'distressed area,' which betokens weakness and defeat." He also emphasized that "the future hinges on self-help." And yet, he looked forward to "new federal legislation which will expand the availability of government assistance." "Unquestionably," he added, the aid "will be helpful and can be usefully applied here and in other Pennsylvania communities."[21]

How do we explain these divergent views? In some cases, they reflected local businessmen's own economic relationships to the places where they lived. Some worked for large national corporations whose stake in any particular place was beyond local managers' ability—or desire—to control. In the fall of 1949, Commerce Department officials visiting the southern Maine cities of Biddeford and Sanford found that leading employers—including some major textile firms—were "strongly opposed to [federal contract] bids being awarded on any but a competitive basis." Such orders, these men argued, "should not be channeled to localities on any artificial set of standards."

In Lawrence, local representatives of several large corporations—probably textile giants American Woolen and J. P. Stevens—attended but could not participate in discussions, as "policy matters and procurement details are handled in New York"; indeed, even Commerce's survey questionnaire "would have to go through their New York offices." Similarly, in the case of Bates Manufacturing, another large textile producer that operated a plant near Biddeford, bid requests went directly to New York. Not surprisingly, these big national companies—whose commitment to New England was waning as the industry shifted southward—preferred policies that favored corporate interests, not the interests of particular locales. This type of thinking was reinforced at the community level when national firms made the strategic move to integrate executives into local business networks, as when, in the spring of 1954, Pitney-Bowes "ordered all its 86 branch and sales offices" to immediately join the chambers in their local sites.[22]

In contrast, business leaders who advocated federal assistance were often more deeply attached to local places and more dependent for their livelihoods on local communities' economic health. In the summer of 1949, at a Commerce Department meeting in New Bedford, Fred Steele—a former textile mill executive now heading the New Bedford Cotton Manufacturers Association—argued that government orders should go to distressed areas "regardless of [the] level of bids." He and his colleagues even suggested that contract allocations should "take into consideration the higher wages paid in Northern plants." In early 1956, Karl M. Kempf, former president of the Amsterdam (New York) chamber of commerce and head of Industries for Amsterdam, Inc. (a group formed to recruit new employers to the small upstate city, a declining center of carpet manufacturing), weighed in on proposed depressed-areas legislation spearheaded by Senator Douglas (S. 2663). Kempf wanted federal aid limited to loans of risk capital to solid industrial prospects that could not meet the borrowing requirements of local banks or other government agencies, and he insisted that "no community should be helped that will not help itself." At the same time, he felt that the baseline for federal-aid eligibility should be an unemployment rate of 5 percent (lower than in the proposal), and he wanted financing available not only to build new industrial facilities but also to renovate existing plants. Kempf owned a Buick dealership in Amsterdam. William F. Wright, Jr., president of the Sanford-Springvale (Maine) chamber, compared S. 2663 with an alternative (and more limited) Republican-sponsored bill. While "going along with the 'do-it-yourself' philosophy," he favored the former measure, in part because its long-term lending program allowed federal funds to cover two-thirds of the cost of plant construction, whereas the latter restricted the federal portion to 25 percent. He also advocated a public-works provision and a much shorter waiting period for declaring communities eligible for assistance (the Douglas proposal stipulated eighteen months). Wright was publisher of the *Sanford Tribune*. All these men had a direct stake in the economic revival of the places they called home.[23]

The local balance of class forces also influenced whether the national business agenda prevailed. Some of the New Bedford leaders' 1949 federal aid proposals—which included eliminating legislative provisions that allowed a North-South minimum wage differential in federal contracts—probably reflected that several union representatives participated in the talks. In Lawrence in 1950, concerned citizens formed a Greater Lawrence Committee for Industrial Development that included representatives from government, large and small industry, retail, banking, the American Federation of Labor, and the CIO. That the city's mayor, James P. Meehan, was a union leader who supported establishing a federal agency modeled on the Works Progress Administration—"unless more adequate arrangements could be made for unemployment compensation and public assistance"—may help explain the creation of this apparent counterweight to the Greater Lawrence chamber; although the chamber president had a seat on the new committee, his voice was one among many that composed the group. In Cumberland, Maryland, attorney David Kauffman—who chaired the Steering Committee on Economic Development for Allegany County—expressed frustration and disappointment that, despite a long litany of "pledges, promises, directives, and law," President Truman's commitment to aiding distressed areas was going unfulfilled. Instead of attacking federal programs, however, the group called for greater coordination of federal efforts to deliver information about available public services and facilities, conduct economic surveys, provide advisers, offer financing for industrial development purposes, and establish an accelerated program of public works. This approach no doubt reflected that, as Commerce Department staff reported, the steering committee "is over-weighted on the labor side and the Chamber of Commerce and management are at best mildly cooperative." Indeed, the committee worked closely with the Western Maryland Labor Unity Conference and the Western Maryland Full-Employment Committee, both of them union led.[24]

The scale and scope of economic hardship, too, helped determine whether local business leaders felt they could manage on their own. In the spring of

1956, participants in a meeting of the New England Council—a group of business and industry organizations dedicated to the region's economic development—weighed in on the two competing depressed-areas bills. Several clearly articulated the agenda of national business groups. Harold M. Gruener, vice president and general manager of the Greater Burlington (Vermont) Industrial Corporation, opposed both measures, fearing "a danger of 'breathing life into communities' which haven't the initiative to do it themselves." "Profit is the only motive for relocating industry," he argued, "and communities must provide conditions under which this can be accomplished." As an alternative, he suggested allowing manufacturers "to deduct rental payments on a building put up by community groups as a tax expense." Similarly, a Mr. Lee of the Connecticut Development Commission insisted that "people can do it themselves without government assistance" and came out "strongly against the philosophy of government agency activity in this field"; like the NAM and the national Chamber, he supported privately financed credit corporations instead. When a vote was taken, delegates rejected both legislative proposals by a margin of three to one. (A few attendees may have voted "No" because they felt neither proposal went far enough.) At the time, unemployment in Burlington (classified as a smaller labor-market area) was in the 6–9 percent range. In Connecticut, only one smaller area, Danielson, appeared in the 6–9 percent category, and all six major areas showed jobless rates of just 1.5–3 percent. (Mr. Lee, moreover, was almost certainly Robert Lee of Connecticut Light & Power, a member of the national Chamber's Economic Policy Committee, who officially represented the Chamber's views on depressed-areas aid.)[25]

In contrast, advocates of such measures faced much higher levels of economic strain. At the New England Council meeting, William J. Farrell, executive director of the Industrial Development Foundation of Greater Woonsocket (Rhode Island), expressed concern about, among other issues, "too much federal authority" in the Douglas proposal's handling of public works. Still, he "saw real value in the urban redevelopment and technical assistance features" of such legislation and was "all for New England getting its share." He and Sanford-Springvale's William Wright reminded their fellow delegates that "there are differences in degree of need and that in the needier situations the bills could be very helpful." As Wright told a Senate subcommittee when urging that loans allow a larger share of federal dollars than the Republican bill called for: "We still have a long way to go toward full recovery . . . I think many times the experts who do not live with this problem have perhaps too light a knowledge of the problem in the effect of how much money a community can raise." When Wright pleaded for a shorter waiting period for eligibility, he had in mind "communities suddenly receiving a large unemployment load with the closing of a major, and perhaps only industry"—that is, communities like his own, where textile giant Burlington had recently acquired a factory and then began moving out within a week of announcing plans to close the plant. Karl Kempf of Amsterdam told the senators, "There are a lot of places in this Nation that need this help the same as we need it." These men's views reflected desperate conditions: Woonsocket's jobless rate stood at 15–16 percent (between 4,000 and 5,000 employees), while in Sanford—with a population of about 15,600—some 3,000 people were out of work. Amsterdam had just lost a leading carpet manufacturer (the company was consolidating production in Connecticut), and as of the fall of 1955, 3,150 workers (18 percent of the labor force) were unemployed.[26]

At times, businessmen in the same community disagreed about how to proceed. In the spring of 1957, Kurtz M. Hanson of Lawrence (where a new mayor had replaced trade unionist Meehan several years earlier) assured U.S. senators that his area was "generat[ing] its own renaissance" without federal or even state aid. In a stirring tribute to self-reliance delivered before the Advertising Club of Boston, Hanson—president of Champion International (coated-paper goods)—praised the work of the Greater Lawrence Citizens' Committee for Industrial Development under the new mayor's leadership while ignoring Meehan's previous role. At first some had wanted help from Washington, Hanson admitted, but instead, "true to the New England tradition, we took off our coats, rolled up our sleeves, and met the situation ourselves." Among their actions, these "modern pioneers of progress" borrowed money from the privately owned Massachusetts Business Development Corporation and launched a bold advertising campaign. As a result, Hanson asserted elsewhere, Lawrence was "today a labor shortage area"—at a time when the city's jobless rate stood at 10.6 percent (down from 21.4 percent in 1954). In its new incarnation, the citizens' committee opposed depressed-areas assistance, suggesting that Hanson's was now the dominant view. Some businessmen, however, decried the committee's courtship of labor-intensive, low-wage industries and criticized inaccurate claims about the labor supply that could thwart recruitment of additional firms. Hanson's strategy may have reflected that, as historian William F. Hartford has noted, "certain employers in declining areas welcomed increased joblessness as a salutary form of labor discipline." That Hanson was president of Associated Industries of Massachusetts, representing employers' interests well beyond the local level, may have informed his approach as well.[27]

Alongside these distinctions between and even within localities, the depressed-areas dilemma heightened intrabusiness tensions in other ways. Some smaller companies found themselves at odds with big employers; in their 1949 meetings with federal Commerce officials, businessmen in Port Huron, Michigan (auto parts and metal industries), and Worcester, Massachusetts (metalworking), reported that they could not compete successfully with large manufacturers for federal contracts—even when, as in Port Huron's case, they themselves submitted the lowest bids. Others experienced conflict with counterparts in other regions; in Lowell, Massachusetts, textile employers considered it "a waste of time" to bid for contracts, because they could not "compete with southern mills" that benefited from lower wages and higher workloads. The disparate impact of tariff policies also undermined business solidarity. The Naugatuck Valley (Connecticut) Industrial Council opposed a move by U.S. senators from Arizona to reinstate import duties on copper—as a means of protecting the southwestern state's mining interests—on the grounds that the added cost would handicap efforts to preserve jobs in Waterbury, a leading center for production of brass and brass goods.[28]

Tariff and trade issues posed a particularly uncomfortable challenge for national business groups. In the context of the Cold War, the federal government actively sought to lower barriers to international trade in order to consolidate the United States' dominant position in the global economic order and prevent overseas allies from succumbing to communist or nationalist appeals. The leading business organizations found this strategy attractive, because, in theory, it promoted unfettered competition, thus helping drive down domestic wages while strengthening America's status as leader of the "free world." At the local level, however, many employers worried about the impact of lower-cost foreign imports. During the 1949 Commerce Department meetings, businessmen expressed concern about a variety of imported products, including textiles (Providence, Rhode Island), Swiss clocks and watches (Bristol, Connecticut), and British-made safety pins (Danielson). In 1955, the Amsterdam chamber of commerce gathered more than 16,000 signatures on a petition pleading with federal authorities not to reduce import duties on machine-made carpets and rugs, on the grounds that further reduction "will in all probability destroy our only industry" in a city already classified as a "critical labor area." Such actions led the NAM to acknowledge, in 1953, that "it is impracticable for the Association to generalize in the national interest on a matter such as tariffs which is so specific to divergent points of view of its some 20,000 members and their employees." Similarly, the national Chamber—while arguing that the nation's "economic health" required "a large volume of imports as well as exports" and that trade barriers reduced competition and increased costs to consumers—recognized that "basic conflicts between domestic and foreign economic policies" militated against the wholesale elimination of tariff protection for various industries at home.[29]

As a result, when the national Chamber tried to assert its preferences on the tariff and trade question, many affiliates rebelled. In 1956, the national group's leaders sought approval for Eisenhower-driven legislation allowing U.S. participation in the Organization for Trade Cooperation, an agency that would administer the General Agreement on Tariffs and Trade and thus help eliminate obstacles to foreign trade. The proposal touched off a firestorm of protest within the organization, culminating in a "floor fight" that "erupted" on the last day of the national convention, held in Washington, D.C., in May. The Chamber subsequently held a referendum on the issue, which failed to garner the two-thirds vote required for approval by affiliates (it received 53 percent). Even staunch allies, such as the Ohio chamber, opposed the measure on the grounds that chambers—because they represented "widely diversified interests and competitive industries and business enterprises"—should not "pronounce upon a policy which some members believe to be potentially capable of their own destruction." In the wake of the controversy, Chamber leaders were careful to support safeguards attached to international trade agreements legislation "which permit modification or withdrawal of concessions in instances of serious injury to American industry, judged in the light of the national interest."[30]

The depressed-areas problem of the long 1950s, then, brought divisions within the business community—and, in particular, conflicts between national and local business interests—into sharp relief. By resisting federal action on behalf of struggling areas, national business organizations hoped to stimulate greater competition for industry between communities and states. Not surprisingly, they did not make a point of openly congratulating local businessmen who managed to lure employers from elsewhere. But when the Chamber's *Newsletter* publicized General Electric's decision to locate a guided-missile research laboratory in Norristown, Pennsylvania—"after a study was made of more than 20 areas in the United States"—its readers understood that the Norristown chamber's triumph came at the expense of chambers and communities elsewhere. In some of those other places, economic conditions were so dire that local businessmen—despite their rhetorical commitment to "self-help" strategies—simply could not follow the national line. "When we discuss depressed areas, we are not talking about bricks and mortar," William Wright reminded senators in 1956. "We are talking about human beings." "You cannot indict a corporation for not having a heart," he added, referring to outside firms that took over and "wiped out" local industries, "but you can indict it for giving the people such a tremendous blow and practically breaking their hearts."[31]

Although Wright and his allies won the battle over depressed-areas assistance, the NAM and the Chamber won the war. The Area Redevelopment Act established the Area Redevelopment Administration (ARA), housed in the Commerce Department and charged with distributing $394 million in federal funds. Most of the money was earmarked for loans to cover the cost of land, buildings, and equipment for industrial and commercial enterprises ($200 million) and for loans ($100 million) and grants ($75 million) to support public infrastructure intended to enhance prospects for establishing or expanding such enterprises. The rest was designated for technical assistance and the retraining of displaced employees. The program's proponents had envisioned it as a way to help a limited number of declining industrial areas. In its final form—as a condition of support from southerners in Congress—it included rural and very small urban areas; Indian reservations were added as well. By May 1963 nearly 1,100 separate areas, covering about 20 percent of the U.S. population (including overseas territories), were deemed eligible for aid. Given its vastly expanded scope, the ARA's resources were stretched far too thin. Much of the aid went to the rural and very small urban areas, especially in the South (and Appalachia), where ARA projects helped support labor-intensive, low-wage industries and prepare workers for low-wage, unskilled employment. Despite language meant to guard against the use of federal funds to facilitate plant relocation, the program probably helped shift jobs away from older industrial strongholds—an outcome that its detractors had both predicted and, by dramatically broadening its jurisdiction, virtually ensured. In the spring of 1963, President Kennedy sought another $455.5 million in ARA funding, but strong opposition in the House thwarted the request. In 1965 the ARA was supplanted by the Economic Development Administration, structured to support public-works projects at the community level through a multicounty development approach. By the end of its life, the ARA had spent about $320 million and was responsible for creating, directly and indirectly, perhaps 117,000 jobs.[32]

That a war was waged at all, however, was an important step. By opposing federal aid to depressed areas, national business leaders hoped to compel hard-hit communities and regions to compete more aggressively for industry by reinventing themselves as favorable investment sites. They proved powerful enough, with support from political allies, to ensure that the ARA did not undermine their goals. With its emphasis on local initiative, the ARA, as historian Gregory S. Wilson has observed, "was not truly planning"; nor, he adds, did it constitute industrial policy directed at specific sectors—an approach some advocates would have preferred. And yet the impact of economic restructuring drove some local businessmen to press hard for federal action, pushing the NAM and the national Chamber to mobilize their forces and mount wide-ranging antistatist campaigns. That these national groups faced pressure from among their own constituencies revealed the extent to which, in certain places, "free enterprise" itself was a key source of economic strain. The competing voices of the long 1950s serve as a useful reminder that—in apparent contrast to present-day conditions—some business interests saw federal intervention as an acceptable and appropriate way to relieve domestic economic distress.[33]

Chapter 7

"They Were the Moving Spirits": Business and Supply-Side Liberalism in the Postwar South

Brent Cebul

"My Dear Mister Santa Claus," began a peculiar 1937 Christmas wish list: "let's get down to business—the business of giving." No child had written this list. Rather, John L. Morris, the editor of the *Southern Secretary*, had compiled wishes submitted by his magazine's readers: chamber of commerce members from across the southeastern United States. In all, seventy-six chamber secretaries submitted Christmas wishes. Roanoke, Virginia's Ben Moomaw hoped for "a fine new municipal airport." Hod Lewis, "over in Little Rock," wrote Morris, "wants a new auditorium ready for business." In Ocala, Florida, Horace Smith needed "an athletic field, an air mail passenger line, a municipal auditorium, and a five-year agricultural program—a whale of an order, I'll grant." Morris appealed especially for Bill Blanton in Houston, who "gave us such a wonderful convention . . . that he deserves a whole flock of gifts, so how about . . . a flood prevention program, finishing up the airport, a street improvement plan, four-lane highways, more conventions and industries?" "I hope I haven't been piggish, Nick," but these businessmen "really . . . are deserving."[1] Tongue in cheek to be sure, Morris's list nevertheless reflected businesspeople's expanding developmental dreams in cities and towns across the United States. But as these businessmen knew, there was no Santa Claus. American taxpayers would foot the bill to grant these wishes through New Deal works programs.

Considering the New Deal's subsidized labor programs, particularly the Works Progress Administration (WPA), from the perspective of local business and civic elites offers fresh perspectives on twentieth-century business history and politics.[2] As the *Southern Secretary*'s wish list suggests, New Deal works programs offered local businesspeople inducements for industrial, business, and community development.[3] Far from deploring these inducements as perversions of free markets, chamber members viewed federally subsidized, locally administered works programs as unprecedented well-springs of economic stimulus. Yet by focusing scholarly attention on elite, national business associations that organized against New Deal spending—and by presuming these organizations spoke for smaller, local interests—historians have missed the vast locus of consensus and partnership between the liberal state and key actors in the private sector. This bond persisted well after New Deal works programs ended and defies pat distinctions between the public and private sectors as well as overly ideological readings the relationship of business and the state.[4]

This perspective on Depression-era public works also reminds us of the often decentralized and associational nature of the New Deal state.[5] Historians have construed localism as a barrier to state building, but in this case, preferences for local control helped build and legitimize national state capacity by bringing local business interests into the administration of the state's growing infrastructural power.[6] For New Dealers, partnership with local elites offered pragmatic and politically expedient solutions to the crisis of state capacity that the Depression had so dramatically exposed. New Dealers sought auxiliary state capacity in a variety of places, but the most significant—in terms of number and ability—were local governments, which, since the nineteenth century, had led the way in expanding the nation's infrastructural endowments, generally at the behest of local business boosters.[7] As the WPA's Harry Hopkins put it, "We would have been awful damned fools if we thought for a minute that we have either the power or the ability to go out and set up 100,000 work projects as we are going to have to do, probably 200,000 before the year is over, without the complete cooperation of local and state officials. We couldn't do it if we wanted to."[8] By marrying national revenue-raising authority with public and private administrative capacities, New Dealers forged a nimble and potent intergovernmental apparatus capable of meeting many of the Depression's challenges.[9] As Franklin D. Roosevelt early and often maintained, the pragmatic association of public and private, local and national, did not auger "Government control" but offered "rather a partnership."[10]

As local elites organized to manage favorable aspects of New Deal, wartime, and postwar spending (and blunt those they found less desirable), they formed an institutional and civic bedrock on which liberal policymakers built subsequent local-national, public-private development partnerships.[11] As they did so, the burgeoning service economy generated a set of business actors—retailers, lawyers, utility officers, bankers, and real estate developers—particularly attuned to the health of their regional economies.[12] With bottom lines rooted in local soil, business and civic associations flourished during these decades: Rotary, Lions, Kiwanis, and local chambers of commerce all saw membership spike.[13] Charles E. Merriam, director of the New Deal's National Resources Planning Board, applauded the emerging partnerships among the public, private, and voluntary sectors. They had the power to carry out the "common good."[14] By the late 1930s, New Dealers like Merriam envisioned a decentralized system of public subsidies underwriting far more than periodic unemployment relief or infrastructure projects. Locally administered federal spending might stimulate economic growth that would generate social progress without politically onerous redistribution or regulation.

The synergies between local boosters and liberal policymakers in Washington only deepened in the 1940s. As New Dealers' ambitions for vigorous social democratic reform faded, they embraced a new version of liberalism that made bold claims toward ameliorating poverty and delivering social goods such as jobs or housing by shaping market developments and patterns of consumption.[15] Liberals increasingly construed properly managed economic growth as sufficient to generate progress. As a result, they sought a new and expanded role for the federal government in financing and subsidizing infrastructure that seemed likely to result in economic growth. While "supply side" today connotes a conservative policy regime—cutting taxes to stimulate private capital formation—New Dealers' vision of supply-side policymaking emphasized a range of direct and indirect public subsidies designed to foster market creation. Initially, these chiefly included targeted infrastructure expenditures, public-to-private transfer of intellectual expertise and technical knowledge, or incentivizing private capital accumulation by structuring markets of affordable consumer or mortgage debt. As the twentieth century unfolded, however, these expanded to include direct forms of finance, such as public venture-capital pools that sometimes even made local or state governments equity partners in start-ups in emerging sectors.[16] Critically, however, this liberal vision of supply-side investment often relied on state and local administration, avoiding pitched ideological battles over national, centralized industrial policy, which has often served as the third rail of domestic development policy debates.[17]

Within this emerging ethos, New Deal economists Seymour Harris and Alvin Hansen saw that businesspeople like the *Southern Secretary*'s readers were using New Deal programs to pursue "structural approaches" to growth. Harris considered structural economic policies to be those that addressed "specific weak spots in the economy" by "encouraging movements of the factors of production, improving technical methods, finding markets, and so on."[18] These fundamentally supply-side interventions could perform a complementary role to national, consumer-oriented, Keynesian, demand-based policies. As Hansen maintained in 1938, "We are . . . rapidly entering a world in which we must fall back upon a more rapid advance of technology than in the past if we are to find private investment opportunities adequate to maintain full employment." But, he cautioned, rehearsing a characteristic concern about secular stagnation and a "mature economy," "private investment needed for growth and progress may not be adequate," in which case "it will become necessary" to deliver to the supply side "public investment partly or wholly loan financed."[19] In other words, demand-side Keynesianism alone might not deliver capital and planning sufficient for economic and social progress. It would be necessary for the federal government to focus on the supply side as well.

As the United States emerged from the war, some New Dealers contributed to a volume, *Saving American Capitalism,* which laid out a vision for a second New Deal. Harris advocated national subsidization of regional planning bodies that could facilitate "the transfer of resources to growing industries"—a national system of regionally administered industrial policies.[20] To staff these planning bodies, Merriam encouraged formalizing New Deal–era "standing advisory council[s]" of local public and private, "lay representatives." Merle Fainsod explained, "A mixed economy . . . means that responsibility for the economic welfare of the nation is decentralized. Over most of the economy we look to businessmen to make the important decisions determining output, prices, and profits." The postwar challenge was to use "government creatively, not as a threat to private enterprise, but as a positive guiding force to strengthen the economy and to adjust it to the needs of the basic economic groups—consumers, farmers, laborers, and businessmen—to whom it is directly responsible."[21] As Alvin Hansen put it, a "postwar plan" would feature a "compensatory and developmental fiscal program." This approach, he wrote in the *Nation*, would "enlarge the sphere for private investment" by supporting "large-scale and small-scale development projects, public investment, federal, state, and local, in areas that will increase our productive power."[22] Based on their reading of the local, real-world ends of New Deal stimulus, these liberals called for the creation of decentralized supply-side policies to complement macroeconomic, demand-oriented Keynesianism.

Once the war was over, congressional conservatives killed the National Resources Planning Board, the vehicle through which liberals like Merriam had hoped to foster decentralized planning and public investments. Yet local business and political interest in such cooperative, regional approaches to economic growth persisted. More than a decade's worth of enthusiastic experience with public works, planning, and wartime defense contracts had concretized a local developmental politics that looked first to Washington rather than state capitals for market-creating subsidies.

Nowhere was this local policy feedback more entrenched than in the capital-poor, rural South. WPA projects and the Tennessee Valley Authority played important roles in expanding boosters' developmental horizons and teaching the value of coordinated planning. Most enduring was New Dealers' response to the sociologist Haward Odum's *Southern Regions of the United States*, the 1936 treatise demarcating the South not by its culture or history but for how its exceptional poverty prefigured its social and racial pathologies. Franklin Roosevelt's 1938 declaration that the South was the "nation's number one economic problem" built on Odum's logic.[23] As a result, for decades the federal government would send unprecedented and disproportionate funds Southward, further entrenching a local booster politics that happily conflated social progress with economic growth.[24] This political ethos, which historians often term "Sunbelt conservatism," was underwritten by supply-side liberalism. Ironically, these developments would bind local elites more tightly to the very state they attacked for its redistributive welfare or regulatory labor policies.[25]

The chamber of commerce in Rome, a small city of thirty thousand in Georgia's northwestern corner, was among those that submitted wishes for the *Southern Secretary's* Christmas wish list. Boosters there drank deeply from the well of New Deal funds, which nourished a business regionalism that dated back to at least to Henry Grady's heyday in the late nineteenth century. By the 1960s, Rome businesspeople's New Deal–inspired public-private growth partnership would shape the supply-side liberalism of the Great Society. Indeed, the seeds of Kennedy and Johnson's billion-dollar antipoverty Appalachian Regional Commission were planted by Georgian businesspeople immediately following the Second World War.

Partnering for Growth

While Southern politicians resented Roosevelt's characterization of their region as the nation's number one economic problem, they nevertheless lined up to win federal funds., The number of Georgians employed by the WPA grew rapidly. In December 1937, just 24,272 Georgians worked on WPA projects. One year later, the total nearly tripled to 67,203, while the national total had not doubled.[26] By 1942, Georgia's WPA administrator put a fine point on the role WPA funding played in developing the state's air infrastructure: "Cancel out the work of the WPA in the past six years and, I assure you, it would seem that Hitler's *Luftwaffe* had suddenly visited us in the night."[27]

By January 1945, however, with the end of the Second World War looming, local businesspeople across the country worried that federal aid would come to an end, and many began organizing local planning commissions.[28] In northwestern Georgia's Coosa River Valley, businesspeople and civic leaders explored novel strategies for stimulating regional growth. Their unique emphasis on multicounty, cooperative, regional planning sprang from their efforts to win improved river and transportation infrastructure from the New Deal state. The Coosa Alabama River Improvement Association linked chambers of commerce from northwestern Alabama, northwestern Georgia, and southern Tennessee to lobby Washington for millions in subsidies. Ultimately, they won a $60 million grant for levies and canals, improvements boosters had dreamed of since Reconstruction. A Rome merchant recalled, "49 years ago the main topic of discussion was the Coosa river development, and now, almost half a century later," the project was real. An Alabama retailer called it "one of the grandest achievements . . . in the history of [his] city."[29]

New Deal–inspired regionalism shaped their postwar strategies when a Georgia Power Company official convened sixty businesspeople to formulate a "program of development of Northwest Georgia."[30] The Northwest Georgia Trade Potentialities Committee would educate the public on the value of public spending for growth: "What these people must be taught," one report urged, "is that" public investments are "but a means to an end": economic progress.[31] Fred F. Starr, a young Georgia Power employee, was Dalton, Georgia's chamber secretary. His efforts pursuing Coosa River improvements, for which he traveled to Washington on lobbying missions, convinced him of the value of federal-local partnerships. Starr became the committee's vice chairman, and Georgia Power soon promoted him to the larger Rome Area Development office, where he oversaw "community development" initiatives—recruiting businesses and promoting appliance sales to spur electricity usage.[32] Over the next decade, Starr grew the Potentialities Committee into a multistate initiative of towns in southern Tennessee, northwestern Georgia, and western North Carolina. By 1955, Starr won state support, forging partnerships among the Highway Department, Parks Commission, and local chambers to develop local "potentialities."[33] These partnerships would be neither Starr's last nor his most significant.

A parallel set of New Deal–inspired developments soon transformed rural businesspeople's developmental vision from one primarily focused on public works and infrastructure to one that echoed Alvin Hansen's interest in subsidizing technological progress and market developments through industrial policy, economic planning, and research and development (R&D). Georgia's wartime governor, Ellis Arnall, was an enthusiastic "little New Dealer," who embraced the optimism of supply-side liberalism, linking social progress to economic growth. "There is no problem in the South," he maintained, "that does not have its origin in the poverty and exploitation of this region." "Injustices, instances of racial friction . . . and lack of economic advancement are all attributable to the low income of the people of our section." "Wipe out poverty and the friction will become negligible."[34] Arnall established the Agricultural and Industrial Development Board in 1943, a decentralized body comprising nine statewide districts to "plan [the] ordered and comprehensive development of the state and its resources."[35] Though he failed to secure adequate funding, Arnall envisioned the board becoming a state version of the Reconstruction Finance Corporation, a "little RFC," authorizing up to $100 million in state loans to new, relocating, or expanding businesses and to support infrastructure development. Georgia Power, perhaps the most influential company in the state, was a great advocate, and its development experts like Fred Starr encouraged local chamber members' attendance at regional board meetings. During 1944, some two hundred communities across Georgia held "mass meetings for the purpose of organizing permanent committees on industrial development."[36]

Mobilized businesspeople looked as well to the state's public technical university, Georgia Tech, for planning and development support. Though it was established in 1919, Tech's Engineering Experiment Station was not funded by the legislature until 1934. That year, the station took its first steps toward aiding "in the promotion of engineering and industrial research." It sought the "complete development and utilization of the natural resources" and "encouragement of industries and commerce."[37] Georgia Power helped form Tech's Industrial Development Council, a board of business and industrial interests that guided the station's research contracting.[38] While Northern states such as Massachusetts considered but resisted creating such New Deal–style public-private development authorities, Georgia's council got to work.[39] In 1943, the year Congress defunded the National Resources Planning Board—eight years before the national Council of Economic Advisers (CEA) began its version of regional studies—Tech's Engineering Experiment Station partnered with a local chamber, conducting an economic planning survey of Macon's twenty-six-county trade area.[40]

Dr. Kenneth Wagner directed the Engineering Experiment Station, which despite Arnall's support, struggled under meager budgets. As the Cold War dawned, however, increasing federal R&D spending was routed to Tech. In 1943–44, the station's budget was a modest $240,000. By 1951, its budget surpassed $1.3 million. Eighty percent came from federal military-industrial grants that disproportionately favored the South.[41] Wagner aimed to broadly distribute Tech's influence and expertise to boost the state's private, civilian economy. In 1955, he secured a $50,000 state grant to develop a decentralized "Industrial Development Branch" in the Experiment Station that could act on Chambers' requests for economic base analyses and public-to-private technology transfers. Between 1956 and 1960, Wagner's research team grew to a professional staff of thirty-three. By 1959, the year North Carolina opened Research Triangle Park, Governor Ernest Vandiver commissioned from the station a comprehensive plan for the state's long-term industrial development. Wagner seized his opportunity, proposing "industrial extension" satellite offices to "supply needed technical assistance to local development groups, to expedite the collection of resource data, and to provide technical assistance to established business and industry."[42] Vandiver wrote Wagner's recommendations into legislation funding Tech's Industrial Development Branch offices.

The timing and emphasis on "local development groups" was no coincidence. Rome's chamber was among Wagner's most frequent correspondents. Since at least 1957, Starr and Wagner had imagined establishing a new public-private regional development organization focused on stimulating modern industry. Starr's confederate in Rome, T. Harley Harper, reflected the growing ranks of civically engaged local service-sector elites. Harper owned a Rome furniture store, was an active chamber member, and chaired the city Planning Commission. In 1957, Harper hired Sidney Thomas, a graduate of Tech's masters in planning program, as the Planning Commission's first professional planner.[43] To court the growing liberal state, northwestern Georgia's business leaders also modernized local government.

Harper, Starr, and Wagner traveled the twelve-county region, evangelizing for a new public-private development body comprised of representatives from business and government. The organization would commission strategic plans, land use studies, and conduct natural resource and technology R&D, all to improve the region's infrastructure and industry. As Harper's wife Mary Ruth recalled, even "when we'd go to the market," Harley would "talk planning, planning, planning."[44] Wagner encouraged businessmen at the Calhoun Elks Country Club to "make a complete audit of resources and assets, locally and on a region-wide basis, and to draft a program for development of these potentials." "Pin down your local specific problems and assets, analyze . . . your resources and develop a long-range comprehensive program."[45] Northwestern Georgia's elites worked to forge a regional industrial policy.

Despite growing enthusiasm for regional planning, the men understood that local taxes or state subsidies would never offer adequate funding.[46] As the New Deal had taught them, they looked past the state capital to Washington. While much of President Truman's Fair Deal failed, one key piece of legislation, conceived of by Alvin Hansen in the late New Deal, succeeded. The Housing Act of 1949 set aside considerable federal funds for public housing, urban renewal, and development planning. Often overlooked in discussions of the Housing Act and its 1954 amendments was its creation of two-thirds matching grants for planning commissions in communities with populations of up to 25,000, which targeted once-rural communities being pulled into metropolitan regions and facing new demands for service and infrastructure (the population threshold was subsequently raised to 50,000). With federal funds, planning commissions emerged across the country to develop infrastructure, shepherd growth, and encourage the rational development of business, industry, and housing. By 1964, the section 701

Planning Grant Program, as it was known, had distributed $79 million to 4,462 local governments.[47]

To secure 701 funding, however, Harper and Starr had to win changes to state law. Well into the 1950s, Georgia's state legislature resisted granting local governments the power to raise local revenue or set zoning standards.[48] Wagner, northwestern Georgia's boosters, and Georgia Power Company officials pressed Governor Vandiver to pass legislation enabling adjacent communities to create regional Planning and Development Commissions that could win 701 funding. Like 701 grants, the legislation included a "self-help" provision: local funds were to be raised to receive state or federal matching funds. The law also stipulated that the commissions bore no responsibility to state officials, ceding to local governments and private interests the power to invite a stronger federal presence in regional development. To raise local seed money, Harley Harper's "Quarters for Prosperity" campaign secured a special $0.25 county tax assessment for each of the 249,193 residents of the Coosa River Valley's twelve counties.[49] Harper and Starr's organization was christened the Coosa Valley Area Planning and Development Commission (CVAPDC). Sidney Thomas moved from the public Planning Commission to become the executive director of the publicly funded and privately inspired CVAPDC. The federal government delivered $109,000 in 701 funds, and by 1963, the CVAPDC enjoyed a $248,998 budget comprised of just $62,000 in local revenue.[50] Said one state official, the CVAPDC would "attract needed private investments, and maintain or achieve viability for each substate district—to the ultimate benefit of the State as a whole."[51]

In an era characterized by acrimony over the *Brown v. Board of Education* decision, emphasis on the "American Way," and suspicion of centralized planning, Georgia's businesspeople's embrace of federally backed planning and cooperative regionalism is striking.[52] "What affects Cartersville affects the rest of the region," explained Charles Cowan, the mayor of Cartersville, Georgia. The *Rome News Tribune* extolled the Coosa Commission's vision for "the fullest development of Northwest Georgia—business-wise, economically, industrially, culturally and educationally." The paper crowed, "What is good for Rome, or Dalton, or Cartersville, Rockmart, Cedartown, Calhoun, Dallas, Summerville, LaFayette, Ringgold, Chatsworth, Trenton, Buchanan, Bremen, Tallapoosa and other towns is good for the entire area. . . . Selfish motives in seeking industry, in which one town or one county vied with the others, have disappeared."[53]

The predominantly service-sector elites—bankers, retailers, and distributors—who composed the Coosa Commission were civic leaders, embodiments of the mid-century participatory spirit. But their sense that they represented northwestern Georgia's broader interests—textile workers, African American farm and industrial laborers, and women who worked part time in mills—suggested a profoundly myopic reading of the "community."[54] Col. Douglas E. "Froggy" Morrison was a founding commissioner, representing Dade County. Froggy served thirty years in the U.S. Army. A Mason, a Lion, and former commander of Dade's Foreign Legion Post, Morrison served on the Board of Directors of the Bank of Dade and was president of the County Farm Bureau and the Soil and Water Conservation District.[55] R. D. Barton, Jr., served as the CVAPDC's vice chairman and owned a furniture store. His other business, the Barton Funeral Home, inspired his nickname, "The Friendly Undertaker." Barton was a deacon in his Baptist Church, the vice moderator of the Middle Cherokee Baptist Association, a charter member of the Adairsville Lion's Club, and a Mason and Shriner.[56] John D. Bankson was vice president and general manager of the Summerville-Trion Ice and Coal Company and was the Pure Oil Company's primary distributor. He served as president of the Southeastern Retail Coal Association and of the Summerville Retail Merchants Association, and was the director of the National Coal Dealers Association. Bankson was a charter commissioner, serving as chairman in 1964 and 1965. He was a Baptist deacon, a Lion, and was unexceptional among his peers on the Coosa Commission.[57]

Not since the New Dealers touted the possibilities of economic planning had planners been so vaunted. Commissioners were simply referred to as "The Planners," and planning became a ubiquitous feature of northwestern Georgia's boosterism. As one front-page article glowed:

planners will meet regularly . . . The planners will also be working with local officials and agencies on related programs that influence the development of the community. This will involve coordinating the various Federal programs in order to most effectively serve the needs of the Community.

"FUTURE PLANNING IS BEING STRESSED," boomed the headline.[58]

In July 1960, the CVAPDC hosted its second annual meeting under a massive tent dubbed "Starr Hall," a toast to Georgia Power's Fred Starr. The event culminated more than a decade of hard work. Some 1,000 business-people and politicians attended.[59] They "lustily cheered" Kenneth Wagner when he announced Tech's first Industrial Development Branch would be established in Rome. Georgia Power's president, Jack McDonough, a Rome native, had led the New Deal–era Coosa River improvement lobbying effort, the lessons of which had inspired the Coosa Commission's founding. McDonough celebrated economic planning: "High sounding phrases and long lists of objectives won't do the job. What will do it is down-to-earth, everyday planning and working in the individual cities, towns and communities."[60] So long as it was shepherded by local elites, economic planning was wholly legitimate—and necessary.

Tech's Rome Branch officially opened in June 1961. Reflecting the inter-twined public and private interests, the Coosa Commission, the public Planning Commission, and Tech's Rome branch all shared the second floor of Rome's Chamber building, rent free.[61] Tech's decentralized network of experts set to work helping less-sophisticated industries identify weaknesses and capitalize on new practices. Explained Kenneth Wagner, "The preventative aspects of this program are one of its most important contributions." Businesses "may succumb for lack of guidance with distribution and sales problems. Still others urgently need information on new market opportunities, on machine design problems, and other production difficulties."[62] The partnership went far beyond regional economic analyses, touching practically every aspect of industry. During 1962 alone, planners undertook 103 separate "technical assistance" projects, a bland term that obscured how involved publicly funded expertise was becoming in regional industry. Thirty-eight "assistance" contracts spurred Tech engineers' work on "product design, product packaging, product line design . . . production contracts, public relations, materials procurement, patent application, export opportunities and many others." Another fifty-one projects supported industrial recruitment efforts through analyzing labor markets, planning industrial zoning, arranging finance, and generating data on transportation and infrastructure. The Branch even conducted mineral research that generated a new product for a tile manufacturer. In another instance of "technical assistance," the Rome branch developed a more efficient production method for a quarry.[63]

As Rome's chamber put it in a 1962 newsletter, the partnership was "of much value" in underwriting efforts to "locate prospective industries to the Rome-Floyd County area."[64] In 1962 alone, twenty-five new manufacturing operations opened in the Coosa Valley, and thirty existing plants underwent

Tech-supported expansions. Federal spending for defense, development, and University-led R&D had moved far beyond Atlanta and was shaping Georgia's rural economy. Far from a top-down story of Washington pork or of big government crowding out voluntary initiative, the prospect of federal funding had inspired vigorous voluntary action.

The state partnered with Georgia Power to publicize the benefits of "Planning for an Area Development Program."[65] For many businessmen, the CVAPDC model was a revelation. Plains, Georgia, peanut farmer Jimmy Carter was particularly inspired, and he traveled to Rome to attend a Coosa Commission meeting.[66] For Carter—who relished his background in Naval scientific expertise, who touted his identity as a businessman, who shared liberals' enduring faith in social reform and progress through economic growth, and whose instincts engendered skepticism toward centralization— the CVAPDC was a wonder. Decentralized, rooted in expertise, organized through public-private partnerships, and geared toward a localist vision of community and economic progress, such commissions seemed an ideal form of government economic action. Carter soon formed the eight-county West Central Georgia Area Planning and Development Commission, which won state and federal funding. He was not alone. By 1965, fourteen multicounty commissions had mobilized, and by 1970, every county in Georgia had joined a federally backed, privately led, regional planning and development commission.[67] Most took trips to Rome, Sidney Thomas recalled. "We were observed by people from everywhere." He went on: "Even the folks in Washington came down to see how we were doing."[68]

The Commissions Go National: Supply-Side Liberalism Confronts "Depressed Areas"

During the 1950s, debates over stimulating economic growth versus stabilizing the business cycle (by perhaps raising interest rates to slow growth) became an increasingly partisan issue. President Eisenhower's CEA emphasized curbing inflation and pursued stability rather than growth. When the economy slowed during his second term, Eisenhower excused the downturn as a lesser evil in the service of maintaining stable wages and prices. By privileging stability over growth, however, Eisenhower created a wedge issue.

Leon Keyserling, the Southern-born New Dealer, acolyte of Rexford Tugwell, and former chairman of Truman's CEA, proclaimed the regnant consensus among liberals: "there is not meaningful stability except *a stable rate of constant growth.*"[69] Yet "pockets of poverty" persisted in cities and isolated rural regions. Democrats formed the Democratic Advisory Council to develop policies that might highlight growth as both a partisan and a social issue. A believer in the New Deal's emphasis on regional approaches to Southern social and economic development, Keyserling became the council's strongest voice, where he forcefully rearticulated the New Deal's vision of supply side–based economic-qua-social progress.[70]

Drawing on the experiences of the South, liberals from across the ideological spectrum began developing stimulative, growth-based policies that targeted the supply side of the economy. Senator Paul Douglas—a leader of the left-liberal coalition—sponsored the 1950s' Depressed Areas Bill. The $251 million legislation aimed to spur employment by stimulating business and industry with infrastructure improvements and federal loans to attract or keep industries in impoverished or deindustrializing regions (like Douglas's southern Illinois). Advocates frequently cited New Deal economists such as Alvin Hansen to make their case.[71] Eisenhower, however, twice vetoed the bill, and the National Association of Manufacturers and the U.S. Chamber of Commerce fought the legislation as a threat to free markets.[72] The 1960 Democratic presidential hopefuls in the Senate—Lyndon Johnson, John F. Kennedy, and Stuart Symington—all voted to override the president. After a visit to Appalachia exposed him to abject rural, white poverty, Kennedy especially emphasized the potential antipoverty benefits of enabling local elites to tailor federal spending programs to stimulate regional industrial assets.

Once in office, the Kennedy administration sought workable models for economic and social policy formation while simultaneously seeking political carrots to entice the Democratic South. While Douglas' initial Depressed Areas bill targeted the struggling Midwest, Kennedy's 1961 Area Redevelopment bill pivoted away from that emphasis. His campaign overtures to Southern and Appalachian governors meant he had promises to keep.[73] In eastern Kentucky, a growing business-led development body akin to the Coosa Commission had an aggressive advocate in Kentucky's Governor Bert Combs, and Combs joined Governor Vandiver (then scaling up Georgia's commission system) in relating to Kennedy officials the promise of public-private commissions.[74] The federal government could use planning grant money and loans to get similar commissions off the ground in depressed areas.[75] Kennedy's Area Redevelopment Administration (ARA) advanced the principle that local businesspeople and politicians would voluntarily unite to plan regional development and administer federal stimulus. The ARA would encourage Coosa Commissions in "depressed areas" across the country.

Like Franklin Roosevelt three decades earlier, ARA staffers emphasized the program's localism, "self-help," and ostensibly market-based nature, arguing their agency represented a "New Partnership" between federal agencies, state and local governments, and the private sector. Indeed, they felt compelled to downplay the federal role. The onus was on local communities, "for unless [they] take the initiative there is little that State or Federal Governments can do for them."[76] As one administrator explained, "the ARA believes in solving the unemployment problem by the free, private enterprise system."[77] Local market actors who demonstrated "self-help" were once again the engines a new generation of supply-side liberals primed to grow the nation out of poverty and unemployment.

In practice, the ARA suffered difficulties that led to its speedy demise. The legislation offered no seed funding for local planning, which meant depressed regions were forced to develop leadership, matching funds, and plans prior to seeking federal subsidies. As a result, several well-mobilized counties won the bulk of support.[78] Most vexing, local elites eagerly trying to boost local economies bristled at being branded leaders of "depressed areas." Senator John Tower (R-TX) complained, "They rightfully resent being held up before the nation as a static underdeveloped area in need of a Federal handout."[79] A Virginia businessman "deplore[d] the 'distressed area' tag."[80] At bottom, however, the ARA was slow, prompting Kennedy to personally demand that officials "process these projects at an even faster rate."[81]

Unsatisfied by the ARA, in 1961, the region's governors approached the White House for a new program. Bemused by their demands for federal aid amidst simultaneous desegregation-related states-rights ranting, ARA administrator William Batt quipped, "I never thought the day would come when I'd be arguing with Southern governors in favor of states' rights, states' responsibilities."[82] Nevertheless, by the spring of 1963, with the ARA floundering, a series of disastrous storms in Kentucky raising anew the specter of rural poverty, and the elections of 1964 looming amidst intensifying Civil Rights mobilization, Kennedy believed a vigorous "Appalachian program" would be politically expedient and, perhaps, effective. Like Franklin Roosevelt's advisors a generation earlier, Kennedy's team explicitly tied federal support for Southern development to party building and faith that economic growth would spur social progress and more a moderate South.[83]

Kennedy commissioned the President's Appalachian Regional Commission to generate "a comprehensive program for the economic development of the Appalachian Region," shifting the rhetorical emphasis from the ARA's "depressed areas" to "economic development," a more palatable framing for local elites. In a decision local leaders hoped signaled a return to New Deal–scale spending, Kennedy appointed Franklin Roosevelt, Jr., to chair the planning body tasked with developing the program. The Coosa Commission again was the model for what became, after his assassination, Kennedy's "Appalachian program": the Appalachian Regional Commission (ARC). As Roosevelt, Jr., put it in Rome, the Coosa Commission would "be our guide in setting up the poverty program for the entire Appalachian area." Rome and northwestern Georgia, he said, were "fortunate in having such a group which I consider a step ahead in solving the many problems that confront us."[84] The Coosa Commission became the prototype for Local Development Districts—the multicounty units that were the primary building blocks of the Appalachian Regional Commission's effort to fight rural poverty. In contrast to the ARA, which relied on local leaders to be primary movers, the ARC sent funds to governors who created a system of development districts and dispersed federal funds.[85]

The ARC's mandate would have been familiar to supporters of the Coosa Commission or the New Deal's National Resources Planning Board or the WPA. The ARC emphasized infrastructural solutions for generating growth and fighting poverty. Congress authorized nearly $1.1 billion, of which $840 million went to a six-year bonanza of highway construction meant to spur the "individual initiative" to overcome poverty.[86] The ARC, read one report, "will formulate continuing comprehensive, coordinated plans and programs for the overall development of the region. It will help to provide the basic facilities essential to the region's growth, will help to develop its human resources, [and] will seek to encourage individual initiative and private investments."[87]

The astronomical budget appropriations made manifest the converging priorities of local businesspeople and supply-side liberals. Appalachian governors, boosters, and planners viewed highways as necessary steps toward economic growth, while federal poverty planners saw new transportation networks as critical social, antipoverty programming.[88] As one ARC chairman put it, the "regional highway system" would "break down . . . the psychological isolation" of Appalachia's poor: "I've always billed this highway system not only in economic terms, but in social terms . . . because it provides a way for linking people with contemporary America, quite literally."[89] Regional boosters received a massive infusion of federal development spending and, as in the New Deal, were assured their efforts would benefit the poor and the unemployed.

In striking contrast to their many local affiliates, however, the National Association of Manufacturers and the U.S. Chamber of Commerce "were passionately opposed" to the programs. As ARA and ARC official William Batt recalled, the conservative magazine *Human Events* made the liberal programs its "whipping boy."[90] While national business associations led an antistatist charge against federal overreach, the specter of centralized planning, and wasteful spending, local affiliates advanced a pro-growth agenda that was essential to developing new forms of state capacity. Said Batt, "in depressed areas we worked with local Chambers hand in glove. They were the moving spirits."[91]

Georgia's commissions gained a reputation for winning ARC funds. "Keep your Confederate money," staffers joked, "because the South will rise again."[92] In 1965 and 1966, the ARC delivered more than $7 million to Coosa Commission counties for new sewage plants, access roads to industrial sites, and improvements to a vocational school.[93] Commissioners reported that between 1961 and 1972, the percentage of local budget contributions shrank from 67 to 19 percent. "This is not to minimize the importance of local financial contribution," they cautioned, "but rather to emphasize the fact that cities and counties in the" Coosa region "have gotten an increase in services at no increase in costs."[94] By 1970, commissioners teamed with Tech's engineers on more than 300 studies and worked with more than 220 new industries, which, during the 1960s, brought some 11,000 manufacturing jobs to the region. With ARC funds, the CVAPDC's work underwrote a remarkable inventory of business-backed, public-sector projects that read like a WPA report from three decades earlier: thirty-seven water and sewer projects, six airports, eight golf courses, and eight hospitals.[95] These developments augured improved fortunes for the regions' skilled workers, too. Between 1960 and 1967, Georgia saw a slight (1 percent) uptick in manufacturing as a percentage of total employment; in contrast, in most of the CVAPDC's counties the percentage leapt upward. Bartow County saw a 9.4 percent increase; Dade 7.7 percent, and Gordon 8.1. (Rome's Floyd, with a larger population and growth in the service sector, declined a bit, by one percent, though its total manufacturing employment increased by 6.7%).[96] Between 1960 and 1967, family income in the CVAPDC's twelve counties experienced astonishing growth. While the state of Georgia generally tracked national trends (48 percent growth in family income), the Coosa region enjoyed an average increase of 58.75 percent. Its per capita income increase outpaced the state, too, 75.7 to 53.2 percent.[97]

The CVAPDC accomplished a great deal, though poverty alleviation and racially equitable development were never priorities. By 1973, for instance, acceding to some pressure for token inclusion, across Georgia's eighteen Area Planning and Development Commissions, just twenty-one of 367 board seats were held by African Americans.[98] Much of the region's income growth was concentrated among skilled and unionized workers, barely touching the rural poor, open shop workers, or economically disfranchised black Georgians.

Nevertheless, liberals were eager to tout their supply-side "antipoverty" spending. They considered the Coosa Commission a showpiece, and in 1966, the ARC's director sent representatives from developing nations to visit the CVAPDC. In the junket were members of the Turkish Promotion and Information Center and the Nepal Industrial Development Corporation. The ARC also steered a Filipino community development officer to Rome.[99] The *News Tribune* reported, "the primary reason for his trip to the United States was to see how the U.S. is tackling some of the problems of poverty and raising the standard of living for those who need it." For many liberals, the CVAPDC signified antipoverty spending put to most effective use.[100]

As Georgia's commissions matured, between 1968 and 1973, the proportion of funding they received from local, state, and federal sources shifted considerably. Local revenue dropped from 26 percent to a mere 14.5 percent; state support fell from 31 to 18.8 percent; and the federal share soared from 43 to 66.7 percent. A study found one commission in which "each local dollar invested in the APDC program" generated $113 for "members." This "demonstrate[s] the importance of local dues in the APDC budget," the study concluded.[101]

It also demonstrated the generosity of supply-side spending at the high tide of mid-century liberal state building and the degree to which businesspeople had become essential administrators—and guardians—of that state. Reflecting on the degree to which New Deal–style spending directed at local industry had come full circle, the economist James Tobin noted that Alvin Hansen "must have found irony in the 'new economics label' attached to the 1961–65 revival of his central ideas, but he certainly rejoiced in the substance."[102] Although historians have generally looked to the Sunbelt to explain the attenuation of New Deal liberalism, Georgia's businesspeople carried the torch of New Deal supply-side spending until a new generation of liberals again touted the fantastic social possibilities of economic growth. The careers of Presidents Bill Clinton and Barack Obama suggest they were hardly the last.

A Fraught Partnership: Business and the Public University Since the Second World War

Elizabeth Tandy Shermer

"By far the best thing about America is its universities," the late historian Tony Judt warned in the face of mounting budget cuts, tuition increases, business donations, and student debt levels. He was not concerned about the millennial fate of private Harvard, Yale, or Princeton but of the country's state schools: "Even the smallest of these land grant universities—the University of Vermont at Burlington, or Wyoming's isolated campus at Laramie—can boast collections, resources, facilities, and ambitions that most ancient European establishments can only envy." He, like so many others fearing privatization, warned that "Nowhere else in the world . . . can boast such *public* universities."[1]

Yet the mid-century birth of American public university systems had depended on outside capital. Nationwide, state policymakers and school administrators relied on local businesses and large corporations for political and financial support. Such coalitions were especially important in the South and West, which had far fewer and less well-developed private or public schools. In these states, state university presidents struggled to convince legislatures that schools needed to offer more than agricultural research and mechanical training. They also had little direct federal funding. Washington policymakers were divided over whether any postsecondary school should or could receive robust federal aid. As a result, throughout the 1940s and 1950s, Congress only offered support for departments important to defense or public health. Congress also offered small short-term loans to students, whose tuition money was vital to collegiate bottom lines. Neither revenue stream was enough to underwrite mass higher education, especially in the South and West, where underdeveloped university systems struggled to compete for grants and students. Only private money and political capital enabled teachers' colleges, like Arizona State Teachers' College, to turn into universities; existing institutions, such as the University of North Carolina, Chapel Hill (UNC), to expand; and entirely new universities, including the University of California, San Diego (UCSD), to be built.

Administrators found the most help from nationally ranked industrialists and local boosters eager to shift manufacturing out of the better-unionized, well-regulated, and higher-taxed Steelbelt. Small-town retailers, bankers, and professionals could not attract this era's leading wealth-producing industries, aerospace and electronics, without universities capable of supporting these manufacturers' research, development, and workforce needs. Capital flight was not just about profit. Business interests most intent on fleeing the Steelbelt were conservatives hostile to mid-century liberalism and eager to gain control of governance and redirect public policy toward entrepreneurial ends in the Southern and Western states being turned into veritable bastions against modern liberalism and unionization. Executives expected universities to be paragons of their conservative, free-enterprise values and oriented toward much-needed training, research, and testing. Their demands subsequently and importantly differed from educators' and liberal politicians' desires for universities whose primary services were to the citizenry and the state. Such overlapping contradictory goals created short, fractious partnerships, which initially increased opportunities for higher learning but did not guarantee public postsecondary schools would remain affordable or high quality.

Education for Industry

Strident disagreements over higher education, social welfare, and governance lay below the surface of the seemingly benign industrial exodus from the Northeast, Midwest, and coastal California. Postwar capital flight and its emphasis on education started during the Depression, when many Southern

and Western small-town retailers, bankers, lawyers, and professionals des-
perately searched for outside investment to alleviate their communities' reliance on extractive industries, such as agriculture, mining, and ranching. Such
entrepreneurs, like future Arizona senator Barry Goldwater, eagerly sought
to boost their municipalities' manufacturing potential in order to relieve unemployment and encourage economic growth. Many also wanted to prove
New Deal relief programs unnecessary. Some of the most energetic promoters, like the Atlanta chamber of commerce, opposed liberal reforms that
increased regulations, taxes, and labor rights. Yet these entrepreneurs also
made use of loan programs, construction projects, and federal guarantees.
For example, the 1941 executive order dictating that war production take
place in the interior gave Southerners and Westerners a chance to lobby
major defense contractors, military officials, and federal authorities for war-
production plants and military installations, as well as the schools needed to
train workers and soldiers.[2]

Contracts yielded the job opportunities, infrastructure improvements,
and school options to lift struggling towns, like Marietta, Georgia, and Phoenix,
Arizona, out of poverty. Agreements also introduced small-town businessmen
to leading executives. Defense needs forced the War Department to depend
on major manufacturers, like General Electric and Alcoa. Historians have
shown that many leading businessmen in the 1940s were already skeptical
or even hostile to liberal reforms. More than a few actively resisted Depression
and wartime regulations, protections, and social welfare programs, either
through law suits, refusals to comply, or donations to Roosevelt's political
opponents. Such executives found common cause with the small-town
boosters, who boasted that their communities would put business needs
first. Local tax breaks, land giveaways, and anti-union ordinances not only
clinched war contracts but became a part of a general business insistence
that "free enterprise" needed to be defended at home and abroad. Yet this
nascent business right's disdain for the New Deal was not stridently antistatist. Rather, boosters and executives sought to ensure public policy benefited
the private sector, whether through generous cost-plus defense contracts,
outsized tax write-offs, or fire sales of factories and military installations
after the war ended.[3]

Local business owners and top manufacturers continued to collaborate
for politics and profit after 1945. Their allegiance to preserving "free enterprise" became integral to the postwar conservative movement but also

foundational to the business climates that they sought to build in the interior. At the local level, business associations (e.g., local chambers of commerce and Rotary International chapters) increasingly directed their energies toward local politics. As boosters, like Goldwater, made their way into local and state politics, they repealed industrial regulations, passed restrictions on unionization, and cut taxes on manufacturers. Out-of-state executives, for their part, publicly proclaimed their investment contingent on such policies. Chief executive officers (CEOs) also demanded that business climates be much more than just a refuge from the redistributive labor-liberalism governing the Steelbelt and coastal California. Favorable investment environments also had to include state and local spending on the kind of infrastructure manufacturers needed.[4]

Schools were of the utmost importance to any town that wished to attract and retain the most lucrative postwar industries, aerospace and light electronics. Those sectors' companies needed universities nearby with science and engineering programs that supported firms' research, development, and workforce training. Northeastern and Midwestern postsecondary schools, usually private institutions, had already grown tremendously by defraying such business expenses in the late nineteenth and early twentieth centuries. The South and West generally lacked the kind of universities that such manufacturers needed, a fact that concerned the Roosevelt Administration by the early 1940s. National Resources Planning Board officials stated in 1942 reports that more schooling options would improve the long-term economic health of these interior states. Education would encourage investment but also improve personal fulfillment, career advancement, and social progress. "A region is dependent in no small way upon the products of its colleges and universities," planners declared. The South had only 14 percent of the nation's colleges, and the majority of these 252 institutions were private. The arid states also lacked educational opportunities. Progress necessitated schools with far better science courses but also "scholarships to State universities, sufficient to cover minimum living expenses, so that qualified young people, remote from proper educational opportunities, can obtain a higher education."[5]

The Roosevelt administration never offered colleges a comprehensive New Deal, which inaugurated a postwar tradition of targeted or indirect aid. In the 1930s and 1940s, leading educators in the National Education Association and Ivy League rejected direct assistance. University presidents, like Columbia University's Nicholas Murray Butler and Harvard's James Conant, feared relief would come at the expense of local control or, in the case of higher education, institutional autonomy. Many top leaders, Roosevelt included, initially thought that underwriting the nation's patchwork system of schools was wasteful, even though many depended on tuition and teetered on the brink of collapse in the 1930s. Citizen demand for more opportunity convinced leading New Dealers, such as Harry Hopkins and David Lilienthal, that schooling had to be integrated into relief, to teach not only vocational skills but also the New Deal's merits. There was never enough support to adequately expand education. State schools could only take advantage of federal programs to make repairs, construct new buildings, or offer continuing-education courses if surrounding communities applied for such assistance. The National Youth Administration's work-study program only helped applicants find a job and a college willing to accept them. Paychecks from the federal government covered living expenses and tuition, an intentionally circuitous federal lifeline to amenable schools, which often put enrollees to work maintaining, improving, or expanding campuses.[6]

Work-study did not survive the Second World War. A conservative congressional coalition managed to abruptly defund key New Deal agencies in 1943. The National Youth Administration's demise halted the educational programs that Roosevelt officials, school administrators, manufacturers, and students had increasingly considered vital to industrial development, individual advancement, and civic prosperity. Only patriotism enabled New Dealers to pass the 1944 GI Bill of Rights, whose scholastic provisions Ivy League academics, like Harvard's Conant, publicly attacked. By then, he and other elite university presidents had made their peace with federal support for their science departments but not for working-class veterans. The rest of the citizenry received no such opportunity after their service at home and would have had difficulty finding a seat in the oversubscribed public colleges and universities. These schools struggled to fulfill the educational obligations outlined in the Servicemen's Readjustment Act. It did not directly fund campus enlargements but, like work-study, circuitously aided small expansions through tuition payments. That tradition remained in place throughout the 1950s, when Congress remained bitterly divided over federal support for colleges and universities. The federal government provided research grants for science programs vital to defense and public health. Congress also agreed on a small loan program for students studying subjects of national importance. But targeted or indirect aid could not underwrite mass higher education.[7]

Engineers, Not Teachers

Public-private partnerships instead financed educational expansion, which ceded institutional autonomy to private interests, not the federal officials Conant had feared. Boosters and outside executives, for example, had enormous power in the evolution of Arizona State Teachers' College into Arizona State University (ASU), even though educator Grady Gammage first realized this school's potential. This Arkansas farmer's son had immersed himself in books before becoming a grammar school teacher and principal after high school. Tuberculosis prompted the liberal Democrat's move to Tucson, where he joined the University of Arizona's maintenance crew and took classes, first for his bachelor's and then his master's degrees in education (he finished his New York University doctorate while dissertating in Arizona). His politics and dedication impressed state officials, who lobbied the governor to place Gammage at the helm of Flagstaff's teacher's college in 1926 and then to send him to Tempe's failing Arizona State Teachers' College in 1933.[8]

Few cared about Arizona State Teachers' College. Only nine of fifty-two faculty had a doctorate, several buildings had leaky roofs and peeling paint, and enrollment had stagnated. Gammage met with the Phoenix chamber of commerce in 1934 but found boosters (most of whom had advanced degrees from the University of Arizona or out-of-state universities) uninterested in the nearby school. State Board of Education officials only reluctantly permitted him to apply to New Deal programs. He championed improvements in the name of employment, recovery, and opportunity, which convinced liberal Senator Carl Hayden, governor Sid Osborn, and the legislature. New Dealers allocated just $445,000 in 1935, which enabled Gammage to construct a woman's dorm, add a heating plant, acquire 10 acres of land, underwrite a sports stadium, and erect a new student center. Enrollment subsequently surged past 1,000 by 1938.[9]

Mining and agricultural interests proved protective of University of Arizona research stations but opposed to Gammage's ambitions. A 1938 survey revealed that undergraduates wanted arts and sciences baccalaureate degrees and had only matriculated because they "couldn't afford to go anywhere else." Coed complaints enabled him to expand wartime offerings, especially in business, biological sciences, industrial arts, and agriculture. He could not persuade the legislature to allow either the Flagstaff or Tempe schools to grant BAs in nonteaching fields. He convinced an *Arizona Republic* editor (also a state representative) to sponsor such a bill, but Tucson delegates (protective of the University of Arizona) buried the proposal. Representatives of agriculture- and mining-dependent areas helped, because extractive-industry constituents bristled at expenditures unrelated to their trades. "I personally favor your bill," a legislator confided, "I was elected by Phelps Dodge (Mining Co.) and if I vote for it, my political career is finished."[10]

The GI Bill of Rights' education provisions and the first wave of returning servicemen enabled Gammage to prevail. He drew public attention to Arizona's "extremely deficient" opportunities and, in the process, convinced business groups, service clubs, veterans' organizations, and newspaper editors to support a Phoenix-backed bill to meet postwar educational needs and veterans' demands. Tucson senators watered down legislation that ended Tempe and Flagstaff schools' teacher designation and created a new Board of Regents for all three schools. The interim board's composition better reflected population figures: five seats went to Tempe's Maricopa County, three to Tucson's Pima County, and two represented other parts of Arizona. The body's inaugural 1945 meeting also ended with an agreement to hire outside consultants, who recommended both colleges expand degree and course offerings. The regents approved the recommendations, permitting the just-renamed Arizona State College (ASC) at Tempe to award education, liberal arts, and science degrees.[11]

Booster support grew steadily. Phoenix businessmen were among the South and West's most aggressive promoters. They publicly attacked the New Deal and, in turn, fostered the area's formidable business climate. Initially chamber members only embraced college athletics to supplement their tourism initiative. At a fall 1949 breakfast meeting, Gammage tried to sell them on the college's importance to economic development, individual opportunity, and social welfare. "You need a great educational institution to make Phoenix great," he proclaimed, "you have the makings of it right here at your doorstep." One financier recalled, "this breakfast at Tempe was a pitiful little affair—some eggs and toast and juice served at tables in the old gymnasium," but "he did the best he could. It worked."[12]

Gammage, for example, partially convinced Walter Bimson, a conservative financier influential in local and national business circles. This Coloradan had learned bookkeeping in his father's bank but went on to study at Harvard's School of Business Administration before joining Chicago's premier Harris Trust and Savings Bank. His superiors' willingness to work with New Dealers prompted his 1933 decision to take over Phoenix's struggling Valley National Bank, which he used to run experiments for private solutions to the financial crisis (some of which openly flouted new banking rules). Success made him famous among anti–New Deal businessmen, who helped Phoenix chamber members recruit industry before, during, and after the war. Bimson also concerned himself with higher education, serving on the Regents' Executive Committee for the State College at Tempe and the Finance and Educational Relations Committees. He never shared Gammage's politics and plans. "I should not want to see established at Tempe a Law School, an Engineering School or a scientific, technical School of Agriculture," Bimson explained to Gammage in 1952. The banker had more practical desires for a free-enterprise Phoenix. This metropolis did not require the full-fledged public university that Gammage imagined. Industrialization required "expansion of the [college's] Business School, the Trade Schools covering machine shop practice, mechanical methods and practical building and architecture procedure."[13]

Bimson and his contemporaries embraced ASC's evolution into ASU, because manufacturers increasingly demanded the kind of engineering and science departments to be found in universities, not colleges. The chamber had initial success drawing high-tech outsiders to the Valley without such resources but, by the mid-1950s, unmet requirements and favorable business climates elsewhere yielded executive complaints about Phoenix's pool of trained engineers, scientists, and skilled laborers. One manager, for example, demanded "education and campus laboratory facilities to better support the over-all requirements of industry." Recently transplanted Motorola executives bemoaned "the availability of engineers and scientists," which "failed to keep pace with the expanding demands of industry." Just before Sputnik's 1957 launch, executive Daniel Noble emphasized, "this brainpower shortage endangers the economic health, as well as the national security of our country." Yet cost calculations often trumped defense assurances. "We must have a truly high quality of graduate school in engineering and the physical sciences," Noble warned, "The industries can bring the brainpower to Phoenix, but they cannot keep them here in an intellectual vacuum."[14]

Neither outside investors nor local boosters embraced Gammage's capacious plans. They shared liberal educators' and policymakers' interest in economic development and increased educational opportunities but only in the departments and services that directly benefited their firms' immediate needs. Hence business pursuit of "brainpower" was generally limited to the sciences and grounded in the conservative, free-enterprise values endemic to business climates. Businessmen sought to help capital retreat from liberal strongholds, not to fulfill working-class demand for the liberal arts or to use education to put liberal democracy on a march through the South and West, as New Dealers had once hoped.

Executive pressure to guarantee better science departments nevertheless aided Gammage. By the mid-1950s, the Board of Regents' eight members included Bimson and another chamber member, which improved Gammage's odds when he presented a four-year plan to transform ASC into ASU. Unlike his industry-minded collaborators, he cast the undertaking as part of a national movement to ensure increased access, more opportunity, and democratic advancement. His 1954 proposal divided the university into four colleges. ASC already offered training in general education, liberal arts, and science education, but the university would include applied sciences as well as business and public administration. The chamber's support was critical. Phoenix and Flagstaff representatives favored the scheme that Tucson regents rejected. Governor Howard Pyle broke the tie in Gammage's favor, because this Republican had deep connections to the chamber, which considered Pyle's 1950 election essential to securing the political power needed for the free-enterprise policymaking that now included improving postsecondary education.[15]

Chamber members and manufacturing executives expedited the establishment of ASU's highly regarded engineering program through the private ASU Foundation. This association united education-dependent high-tech manufacturers, who proclaimed support for a general research university but nonetheless dedicated most private contributions to science and engineering. Early achievements included raising $15,000 for a solar furnace as well as additional contributions from relocated firms to underwrite the equipment, lab space, and faculty hires needed for an engineering department devoted to aerospace and electrical fields. The ASU Foundation also enabled business leaders to covertly circumvent state wage scales, reluctant legislators, and skeptical voters so the school could pay the "highest possible base salaries" with foundation monies "supplement[ing] the base." "Every dollar spent would come back to the community, not only in cash," Noble promised, "but in pride in the college accomplishment and standing, pride in the constructive community achievement, and pride in the sound growth not only of industry but of educational opportunities." Money also provided scholarships and purchased land for the proposed engineering program, for which General Electric provided equipment.[16]

Private interests also had an important, behind-the-scenes role in ASC's 1958 "name change" to ASU. Official histories attributed this rechristening to a grassroots movement of students, alumni, and Phoenicians, who supported two recent graduates in putting the issue before voters (not regents and legislators). This successful crusade was more top-down than bottom-up. Both spokesmen for the referendum belonged to the junior chamber of commerce. Moreover, the events of 1958 just put in writing what had already happened in practice during the fifteen-year initiative to turn a teacher's college into a research university. The real milestone had occurred in 1956, when representatives from the chamber and the manufacturing community persuaded the regents to allow a new bachelor of science in engineering degree, which all but guaranteed ASC's eventual ability to grant masters and doctorates in the applied sciences. This essential step had only been possible because earlier private and public investment had provided the college with the foundational infrastructure for scientific and engineering research. The much-heralded "name change" was only necessary because regents and legislators still refused to designate the school a university.[17]

The nominal upgrade hardly lessened business's targeted enthusiasm for advanced learning. Chamber higher-up Lew Haas, for example, urged administrators to radically improve the engineering program in "a simple decade," not the proposed twenty years. "We can enlist the most powerful influences in the community to help you in any problems you might encounter," Haas promised in 1961. Motorola also offered vital help. Executives headed the ASU Foundation and its Industrial Advisory Committee, which included science faculty, who often appeared on the payrolls of area branch plants. These men collaborated to recruit academics, improve the library, develop the College of Business Administration's "Engineers in management" curriculum, and integrate the humanities and social sciences "into a program in which industry would be interested."[18]

ASU also depended on boosters in elected offices, especially Phoenix propane magnate Paul Fannin. He had headed the chamber's industrialization effort before Republicans drafted him to run for governor in 1958, when he famously called the just-passed National Defense Education Act "blind determination to reduce local government and individual initiative to dependence and ultimate subservience to a supercentralized [sic] Federal power." Arizona famously rejected this post-Sputnik funding. But Fannin only opposed national, not state, education spending. Advanced study appeared high on his agenda to bolster ASU and start a state system of vocational schools and community colleges. The conservative wanted, for example, "funds for the salaries and services of scientific minds as teachers in our institutions of higher learning and the expanded facilities and equipment in which they must work."[19]

Educational expansion fulfilled boosters' and manufacturers' narrow expectations, not Gammage's desire for a sprawling, multifaceted university. Despite the name change, the private money directed at science and engineering made "technical institute" a more accurate descriptor for ASU, whose liberal arts programs remained, especially in comparison to other universities, underdeveloped. Science programs also grew according to industrial demand. An affiliated faculty plan brought area specialists into classrooms in order to tailor graduate offerings to manufacturers' needs. Motorola and General Electric employed more than two-thirds of these advanced students, who often participated in a work-study program that ensured employment, a salary, and time to attend classes and study. Students nonetheless bore a substantial portion of advanced learning's overall bill. They paid tuition but also higher personal taxes in an area whose business climate dictated that manufacturers contribute significantly less to state revenues than in the Northeast, Midwest, and coastal California, where pay scales for engineers easily eclipsed rates in central Arizona.[20]

Technology, Not Textiles

ASU's industry-attuned metamorphosis represented but one variation in postsecondary schooling's broader transformation. Local politics and institutional histories mattered, even though the basic, corrosive disagreements among policymakers, educators, and donors remained remarkably similar across the industrializing South and West. The free-enterprise business climate ideal, for example, directly reshaped the public flagship university that eventually anchored North Carolina's storied Research Triangle Park. As at teacher's colleges, limited, indirect New Deal aid made local promoters and outside executives pivotal to developing existing universities, like UNC. Power, moreover, determined who had the most say in transforming these schools and deciding their primary postwar uses.

For example, self-identified "businessman in the statehouse" Luther Hodges played an outsized role in UNC's maturation, even though the governor had not immediately ascertained UNC's potential. He instead considered UNC threatening to free enterprise. Historian Frank Porter Graham had placed this long-established school at the disposal of the Roosevelt administration when he headed it in the 1930s and 1940s. Graham's alliance with liberal Democrats reflected his personal politics but also served as a means to keep money coming into cash-strapped UNC, which the General Assembly starved during the Depression. New Dealers hardly shackled Graham in the manner Conant had feared. Governor Hodges decried educational autonomy when he took office in 1954. He, like elite university presidents a decade before, opposed the kind of institutional expansion that could fulfill grassroots demand and liberal desire for mass higher education. Hodges also decried the autonomy that educators like Conant cherished. Public university administrators "were presenting new programs for courses and degrees," Hodges fumed, "without consulting anyone but their own trustees, who could not be expected to judge the worthiness of such programs objectively." "Unregulated proliferation," he warned, "could result in a duplication of expensive teaching skills, libraries, laboratories, and other facilities that would wreck the entire system of state-supported higher education."[21]

Hodges, however, was not innately hostile to learning. Like Gammage, destitution and schooling defined Hodges's childhood. The mill boy graduated from UNC in 1919. He, like Bimson, worked his way up in business circles. Hodges soon oversaw the textile plant in his hometown, which he left in 1929 to become a New York–based Marshall Field and Company vice president. He spent the 1930s in executive circles colluding against the New Deal but, like many other CEOs, had the opportunity during the war and just after to oversee policymaking, because his employer loaned him to federal wartime bureaucracies. Hodges brought his free-enterprise principles home with him when he retired to North Carolina in 1950. He had the opportunity to practice what he preached once voters elected him lieutenant governor in 1952, over the objections of agriculturalists threatened by Hodges' ambitions. The governor's sudden death in 1954 gave Hodges the pulpit to do something for Southern working-class whites, whose per capita income ranked forty-fourth nationwide. Hodges, having been reared in poverty but trained for management, genuinely considered inadequate pay indicative of meager individual opportunity and outside investment. As a result, new tax codes, industrial recruitment offices, and budgetary overhauls (similar to those used in the larger civil war for investment) defined his early gubernatorial boosterism.[22]

The business-climate ideal shaped his later higher-education initiatives. "[N]ew or expanding industries . . . asked about the quality as well as the quantity of the labor supply," Hodges recounted. "The answer we had to give was not satisfactory." He, like Pyle, used the governor's mansion to bolster public higher education. His policies (like Pyle's and Fannin's prescriptions) were not designed to generously underwrite higher education but to specifically serve lucrative industries in search of a cheaper workforce, less regulation, and less taxation.[23]

Hodge's emphasis on manufacturing initially frustrated his plans. As in Arizona, commodity-based enterprises (like North Carolina's tobacco and textile concerns) relied on the cheap, low-skill workforce into which Hodges had been born and then escaped through higher learning. In 1955, Hodges could only persuade assembly members to approve modest outlays for the state's four community colleges. He contended that adult education and technical training were cheap options that would relieve oversubscribed senior colleges (like UNC) that were intended to train white-collar workers and professionals. Two years later, Hodges' growing popularity helped him push the General Assembly to approve an unprecedented $1 billion budget for the 1957–59 biennium, with more than a third earmarked for K–12 and higher education. His 1957 Community College Act also included bonds and taxes to fund new schools and also incorporate existing small, private colleges into a state system.[24]

Hodges then collaborated with the State Board of Education in 1958 to enable interested municipalities and local education boards to submit funding requests for the equipment and instruction needed for so-called Industrial Education Centers. The inaugural $2.3 million increased opportunities for more than 8,000 residents by enabling communities to bypass hostile legislators. The program also kept the federal government out of educational improvements for industrialization, an important clause when whites across the South often seemed more eager to close schools than to abide by Supreme Court desegregation decrees. This training program also did not offer the broad liberal arts education that many students demanded before and after the war. Instead these courses, Hodges enthused, trained "machine operators, craftsmen, technicians, and supervisors" through "courses in electrical code work, heat treating, precision measurement, and color television servicing." By 1960, more than 20,000 Tar Heels had matriculated. Enrollment requirements still dictated that these opportunities were largely for whites, who had more access to the obligatory K–12 schooling and had money for textbooks.[25]

Hodges' scholastic about-face was most apparent in his enthusiasm for North Carolina State College and UNC, the Research Triangle's public corners. Ideas for a pastoral research park situated between Raleigh, Durham, and Chapel Hill circulated among faculty and boosters throughout the mid-1950s. The governor welcomed the plan as a shared venture among state officials, school administrators, and industrialists, which he united under the Governor's Research Triangle Committee. It advocated, as at ASU, state funds and private investments but also included public shareholders. Hodges considered the endeavor far from wasteful or redundant. "Education is the chief business of the State of North Carolina," he crowed. Policymakers had taken "a step further than most" to actively promote "greater interest in research in all areas of business, industry, and applied science." Those fields would define the "towers of colleges and universities" for this "enlightened land."[26]

A Grand Adventure in Social Engineering

Business interests also dictated that those lucrative disciplines would be important to entirely new postwar universities. Discord among policymakers, faculty members, and business interests likewise remained important to these institutions' establishment. For example, conservative boosters and executives had significant say in UCSD's establishment, even though they enjoyed far less power in 1950s and 1960s California, where coastal areas had far more industrial investment and educational facilities than piedmont North Carolina and central Arizona. The Golden State's legislature was nonetheless as malapportioned as were the North Carolina and Arizona assemblies. But a majority of voters supported liberal politicians and policies over the objections of conservatives concerned about free enterprise as well as commodity barons uninterested in educational advancements that did not help agriculture or mining.[27]

The dynamic initially differed among educators, politicians, boosters, and investors collaborating to determine the size, shape, and principal use of UCSD. For example, state politics had yielded not scattershot improvements to a few institutions but a broad initiative for a veritable revolution in West Coast postsecondary schooling: the 1960 Master Plan for Higher Education. The act established a three-tiered system of research universities, state colleges (now universities), and community colleges to ensure a tuition-free education for every resident who wished to enroll. Noted labor economist and University of California (UC) president Clark Kerr covertly infused this legislation with the promise of meritorious, democratic advancement, a desire that grew out of his Depression-era observations of the violence and poverty in California agriculture and his experiences serving on Roosevelt's War Labor Board. By the mid-1950s, he foresaw a newly postindustrial America needing "multiversities" with "operations in more than a hundred locations, counting campuses, experiment stations, agricultural and urban extension centers, and projects abroad involving more than fifty countries." Kerr intended the postwar UC to be centuries removed from the European "academic cloister . . . with its intellectual oligarchy." The system would instead serve and absorb undergraduates, graduates, humanists, social scientists, engineers, professionals, administrators, farmers, industrialists, and politicians. This vision dictated a rapid, unprecedented educational explosion, which included enlarging the Santa Barbara campus and starting branches in Irvine, Santa Cruz, and San Diego.[28]

Speed hinged on support from the sort of business interests that envied business climates elsewhere (including neighboring Arizona's). San Diego chamber of commerce members studied Phoenix rivals, whose postwar success threatened to eclipse the Crescent City's place in the top tier of wealth-producing Western cities. San Diego seemed a stalled military-industrial juggernaut in the 1950s. Chamber membership had declined substantially. The aerospace industry was also slowly leaving. Chamber leaders still resisted " 'give-away' concessions" even in the late 1950s but found themselves "continually pressed for increased promotional effort, more positive community support and businesslike handling of the needs of new industry."[29]

Promoters had already expressed some interest in schooling. Their decades-old education committee had assessed nursery, elementary, secondary, vocational, and postsecondary options. In the late 1940s, members had even advocated that the entire chamber publicize existing public and private higher education facilities to attract newcomers. Boosters also had a working relationship with San Diego State College's leadership, who oversaw 5,000 students studying business administration, nursing, education, art, music, and the liberal arts or pursuing pre-med or pre-law programs. Yet local businessmen ignored the San Diego State College administrators, who begged local businessmen to back legislative proposals to allow the school to award an MA, affiliate with the American Association of Universities and Colleges, and offer nonvocational courses in the liberal arts.

As in Arizona and North Carolina, investor demand forced boosters to put a premium on postsecondary science and engineering. Outsiders first pressured San Diego State College deans to set up extension classes for employees, who had to choose from a prescribed set of courses that their managers considered necessary.[30] Executives then demanded that the chamber lobby for a second Southern California campus, which had been discussed among UC officials well before the Master Plan's legislative fiat for mass education. The chamber subsequently created a University of California subcommittee in 1955, which brought bankers, newsmen, CEOs, and Naval Electronics Laboratory officials together to monitor relations with legislators and UC administrators, debate potential sites and transportation improvements, and negotiate gift agreements between industrialists and university officials to quicken the campus's development. General Dynamics gave $1 million in 1956 to develop the physics, chemistry, mathematics, and engineering departments. As in Phoenix, this money raised salaries, supplied research funds, and equipped labs. CEOs and local promoters also formally proposed a small university with the equipment and faculty to train the graduate students needed to fill predicted openings in area firms. Only 1,000 undergraduates would matriculate, receiving a thorough grounding in the natural sciences with "sufficient courses in the humanities and social sciences to insure . . . a well-rounded education experience."[31]

UC officials had much grander ambitions than technical schools focused on the immediate needs of private enterprises. Kerr considered the branch in the state's third-largest city foundational to his larger vision of offering every Californian advanced study, whereas scientist Roger Revelle envisioned an educational acropolis, "the center to which all men turn to find the meaning of their lives and from which emanates . . . the light of understanding." The head of the UC's Scripps Institution of Oceanography, as one journalist asserted, stood at "the forefront, arguing, explaining, bulldozing, pleading, and finally winning approval for . . . a university made up of twelve independent colleges." Revelle built UCSD on land surrounding Scripps "from the top down and not from the bottom up—from the inside out, not from the outside in." Unlike ASU's early reliance on locally-employed engineers, Revelle headhunted at top schools with full professorships and (privately supplemented) above-scale wages. Revelle welcomed radical scientists, who had hidden their politics during the early Cold War. He promised such recruits a science-focused university fully attendant on the liberal arts in order to support an adventure in modern science and progressive education, not free enterprise. His eagerness to experiment would be reflected in the kind of radical campus politics found at UCSD and elsewhere, which increasingly alarmed liberal policymakers, tax-paying parents, and conservative businessmen. This controversial zeitgeist hardly hindered UCSD. By 1966, the faculty included two Nobel Prize winners and fifteen National Academy of Sciences members. Staff also supervised 500 PhD and 900 undergraduate students.[32]

Boosters and industrialists were thrilled. The chamber's president lauded UCSD's 1960 founding as "probably the most important development in some time." "We'll be able to attract the kind of industry we need to broaden our industrial base," he enthused. "It's exactly what we wanted, a scientific and technical graduate school," a Convair executive celebrated, "it will encourage light industry to locate here."[33]

Business interests embraced UCSD because it, like ASU, initially seemed more like a technical school than a university. Despite the desires of the liberal and left-leaning scientists whom Revelle recruited, the arts, humanities, and social sciences languished until the University of California, Los Angeles, historian John Galbraith became chancellor in 1965. The administrator was not related to Keynesian economist John Kenneth Galbraith but nonetheless personified the liberal faith in broad-based mass higher education. The chancellor, for example, wanted to "build the most exciting intellectual environment in the States" through a great library and high-caliber hiring (most notably radical philosopher Herbert Marcuse). Galbraith still needed businessmen to support the library and theater, warning: "the big question confronting us is whether the University of California will have two great campuses or three." "We must see to it that the Legislature does not cut us off at the knees," he asserted, "we must . . . promote contributions from private sources." He needed entrepreneurial help, because Kerr would not budget for additional books. Galbraith publicly denounced Kerr for keeping UCSD "one of the lesser campuses, or a science institute with a humanities tail" and threatened to delay his inauguration, leaving the campus rudderless.[34]

Kerr hesitated, because politicians and voters seemed less enthused with California liberals' mid-century policymaking, including the Master Plan. He had found himself unable to boost faculty salaries in 1964 and feared requesting library acquisitions in 1965. Kerr was rightly afraid. Ronald Reagan condemned Kerr throughout his 1966 gubernatorial campaign. The candidate called Kerr too lenient on the campus left, who attacked Kerr as part of a hegemonic Establishment of executives, educators, and liberals who, students mistakenly surmised, colluded to suppress academic integrity and personal freedom in the interest of capitalism. Such students frightened suburbanites, an important constituency. Reagan also wooed businessmen, whose cooperation with liberals and educators belied the fundamental ideological differences between these factions. Kerr had relied on conservative boosters and executives to expand UC but later maintained that he knew that many had never made peace with his politics. Reagan offered them free-enterprise educational policies that increased state funds for science and engineering but also reduced overall spending, increased student costs, raised teaching loads, and limited academic freedom. Entrepreneurial support and suburban votes enabled him to win, and he immediately pressured the regents to fire Kerr. After Kerr's 1967 departure, the governor proposed a yearly $250 fee to attend a UC ($180 for a state college). Campuses would keep this money and then divide funds among scholarships and student loan guarantees, capital projects such as classrooms and laboratories, and resources to improve teaching. California businessmen publicly defended Reagan's ideas. "We don't believe," an Los Angeles–based CBS Radio vice president explained, "that tuition would result in wholesale dropouts as some opponents charge."[35]

Galbraith struggled to keep San Diego industrialists' and chamber members' allegiances. In 1967, he presented them with a detailed explanation of UCSD's benefits, which now prioritized (as his Arizona and North Carolina predecessors had done) how the school furthered free enterprise. "The growth of distinguished public institutions of higher learning in San Diego will result in substantial economic benefits with only modest investments of taxpayers' funds," he promised. He made this argument when the thriving campus seemed unconcerned with industrial needs. Executives complained, for example, that employees could not pursue advanced degrees, because administrators refused to force faculty to offer evening classes. In response, San Diego boosters, especially those serving on the chamber's higher education and UCSD committees, circulated editorials in favor of tuition increases, limiting campus autonomy, and stopping state colleges from duplicating costly UC graduate programs "at the expense of the taxpayers." Promoters even reconsidered their unequivocal support for mass higher education. Board members first adopted a stance, passed by a majority vote, that opposed undermining the "philosophy of the Master Plan" and the UC's competitiveness in regards to education quality and faculty retention. They still supported "any future increase in funds raised from students" as long as "adequate provision is made for scholarships or grants in aid" and "a precedent is not established so that each time a budget is tight that student contribution is increased."[36]

Free Enterprise Epilogue

Tuition rates nonetheless rose dramatically in the years following Kerr's exodus, both in California and across the country. His departure symbolized a sea change in the complicated, fractious politics responsible for building the public, research-intensive universities supporting mass higher education. Manufacturers across the country (not just in California, Arizona, or North Carolina) increasingly proved themselves in favor of higher tuition, decreased public funding, and less academic freedom. They remained willing to make targeted contributions to schools, but their donations lessened as manufacturers moved operations overseas and service-based industries became increasingly important domestically. They left behind schools, which often struggled to build the departments and programs of interest to the financial, medical, and communication sectors. Voters were partially to blame. They proved less eager to fund public universities, whose multifaceted offerings, particularly in the liberal arts, seemed unable to guarantee undergraduates the well-paying work needed to pay off student loans. Legislatures could thus more easily slash state support, which coincided with a steady decline in federal research money. Tighter budgets forced schools to cut costs, including for teaching. During the Great Recession, for example, many administrators embraced online courses to provide cheap, flexible instruction. Digital classrooms often appealed to working students, whose enrollment greatly benefited institutions that increasingly found themselves once again dependent on tuition.[37]

UCSD, ASU, and UNC remain emblematic of the promise and peril embedded in the fraught public-private partnerships. Science and engineering structured ASU, UC, and UNC, but Kerr, Revelle, and Galbraith had nonetheless maintained that the social sciences and humanities were vital to the academy and the citizenry. Galbraith's mid-1960s library expansions transformed UCSD into a true, not titular, multiversity. Just twenty years later, the repository served students and faculty, whose ranks included eight Nobel laureates, sixty-four National Academy of Sciences members, two Pulitzer Prize winners, six National Medals of Science awardees, six MacArthur

Foundation fellows, and more than one hundred Guggenheim recipients. Multifaceted UCSD hence had the kind of programs and departments that served Californians well once the aerospace industry's withdrawal accelerated and this and other manufacturing sectors ceased to be as lucrative in an increasingly service-oriented America. 2010s UC President Janet Napolitano also preserved the essence of the Master Plan, when she rebuked online instruction advocates. This "tool for the toolbox" was not a cheap option for undeserved students, who "need the teacher in the classroom working with them."[38]

UNC also had an online arm but reaped much more from its century-old pharmacy school. Its millennial importance underscores how unprepared Research Triangle Park and UNC were in the 1950s for the knowledge-based economy that Kerr had already seen coming. Initial industrial recruitment had disappointed boosters, who had speculated on Research Triangle Park's competitive potential. Before 1960, major investors included Astra, a Connecticut consulting firm specializing in nuclear power; the Atomic Energy Commission; and the Chemstrand Corporation. Dissatisfaction invigorated Hodges, whose gubernatorial success had made him Kennedy's pick for Commerce Secretary. Hodges moved to Washington in 1961 but still funneled Triangle higher-ups insider information, including assessments of impending amendments to the 1935 Social Security Act that he predicted would make medical research and technology an important sector in the coming years. Boosters, in turn, lobbied for the bill's passage. Medicare and Medicaid not only reshaped America's health system and larger political economy but also Research Triangle Park, whose value increased with the late twentieth-century expansion of the medical and pharmaceutical schools atop UNC's "Pill Hill." These programs' profitability had not been clear when retired textile executive Hodges had hedged state funds on attracting mobile manufacturers. Drugs were a safe investment in 2014, when a former regent and pharmaceutical executive donated $100 million. UNC's chancellor called this gift an example of "collaborative public-private investments . . . [to] drive the future of innovation at Carolina."[39]

Aerospace and light electronics had seemed a similar economic engine when Gammage colluded with boosters and just-relocated executives. He died shortly after the name change and just before the risks of his reliance on conservative business interests became clear. His replacement soon discovered that an unwritten gentlemen's agreement gave General Electric empty lab space for personnel and equipment in exchange for the use of the firm's computer. This deal left faculty and staff without guaranteed access to vital equipment. Complaints prompted General Electric's dramatic 1962 departure, which forced campus heads to rent a prohibitively expensive computer from another firm that benefited from this extra income. This manufacturer and others still ensured that specific ASU programs grew. But light electronics and aerospace businesses began leaving Phoenix for more inviting business climates in the 1970s and 1980s, Motorola included. Executives left behind a university whose faculty had not kept pace with undergraduate enrollment: millennial ASU had the largest student body in the United States but far fewer faculty than other enormous schools, like Ohio State University. Moreover, ASU remained strong in the science and engineering fields that were of less use to millennial America's largest employers and wealth-producing enterprises. So President Michael Crow arrived in 2002 with energetic plans to transform ASU into a "New American University" that served researchers, students, and surrounding communities. His ambitious plans crashed along with the housing market in 2008, because the business-climate ideal had made real estate a major source of state revenue.[40]

The Great Recession necessitated Crow finding a benefactor, even if collaboration came at the expense of his original, progressive plans. In June 2014, he and Starbucks CEO Howard Schultz announced the Starbucks College Achieve Plan, a "pioneering collaboration" for a "unique opportunity for a first class education" that set a precedent for "the responsibility and role of a public company" to provide "access to education." This employee benefit paid tuition for any eligible baristas wishing to enroll in ASU Online's forty wide-ranging programs, even if history, engineering, and nursing would not help workers operate registers, pour drinks, or wipe counters. Education experts quickly labeled this perk a farce, which promised "'free college' to employees" but only offered "the chance to pursue a degree at one specific university, only online, only if you enroll full time and work at least 20 hours a week." Starbucks also capped refunds at $75,000, which, given fees, could only help staff complete already-started degrees if they were able to cover upfront costs and afford supplies. The plan also assumed enrollees would take out federal loans, which further reduced Starbucks' expenses. Plus, as specialists pointed out, low-income students usually struggled to complete online courses, a prerequisite for reimbursement. These critics unabashedly labeled ASU Online "a profit venture . . . geared to pushing more students through the system." The portal was predicted to generate one-fourteenth of

ASU's operating budget ($200 million) by 2020. The need to underwrite the brick-and-mortar campus did not concern naysayers, who insisted that this deal represented nothing more than "two businesses . . . [getting] together and creat[ing] a monopoly on college ventures for Starbucks employees."[41]

ASU was just one of many state schools then attacked as commercial. Yet public universities, especially in the South and West, have always been businesslike. Educational entrepreneurship had been needed when state funding was scarce and after fraught public-private partnerships collapsed. Those coalitions left a decidedly mixed legacy. They created the physical foundation for the American system of mass, public, higher education. Nevertheless, the power struggle among educators, policymakers, and business interests created policies that ensured postsecondary schooling would become increasingly dependent on tuition and fundraising even as education remained a civic need and a corporate concern.

PART IV

The Postwar Era:
Liberalism and Its Critics

Chapter 9

The Triumph of Social Responsibility in the National Association of Manufacturers in the 1950s

Jennifer Delton

One of the major themes in twentieth-century U.S. history is how business groups facilitated the growth of the state in ways that are at odds with today's antistatist free-market conservatism. In the twentieth century, a group of enlightened business leaders known as corporate liberals believed that business and government could cooperate in ways that promoted both economic growth and social progress. One way to gauge the influence of this belief is to examine its triumph in perhaps the most ideologically conservative business group of the post–Second World War era, the National Association of Manufacturers (NAM).

Founded in 1895 for the purpose of expanding foreign trade, the NAM became best known for its fierce opposition to the labor movement and the New Deal. Standing athwart history, it defended "individualism" and warned of "creeping socialism." During the 1950s, NAM leaders held close ties to rightist organizations such as the Foundation for Economic Education, the American Enterprise Institute, the Manion Forum, and the Freedom School in Colorado Springs. No less than three NAM presidents were founding members of the John Birch Society, which gained notoriety after one of its leaders accused President Eisenhower of being a communist. Armed with the writings of Friedrich Hayek and Ludwig von Mises, the group's leadership excoriated the corporate liberal ethos of "social responsibility" and government-business cooperation. For a time, the NAM represented a conservative alternative to the then-dominant corporate liberal philosophy. And then it capitulated. Its members revolted against the conservatives and brought in a new president who espoused the socially responsible rhetoric of corporate liberalism. An examination of the conservatives' fall in a major trade association can give us a greater appreciation for just how strong the so-called liberal consensus was in the mid-twentieth century.

Corporate Liberalism, Social Responsibility, and the Liberal Consensus

The term "corporate liberalism" was first used to describe the ideology that emerged during the Progressive era as businessmen such as Edward Filene, Owen D. Young, and members of the National Civic Federation tried to adjust to and shape a new stage of American capitalism characterized by large, integrated, professionally managed corporations.[1] Corporate capitalism required the abandonment of the principles of competition on which the old proprietary capitalism had rested and the adoption of ideas more conducive to the new world of economic cooperation, administered markets, and government regulation. "Corporate liberals" were the actors (in both business and politics) at the forefront of the movement to reconcile old traditions with new conditions. They sought above all "good government," a government that could create a predictable, favorable investment environment and maintain and encourage social stability. Both of these endeavors expanded the government's power to intervene in the economy. The trick was to make this intervention compatible with America's liberal political tradition.

In his analysis of the Progressive era, historian Martin Sklar argues that of all the corporate liberal possibilities, Woodrow Wilson's struck just the right balance between government activism and restraint. That is, Wilson's version of corporate liberalism, which relied heavily on business associations to regulate and standardize business behavior, was "liberal" in both senses of the word. By not giving government "a statist command over society," Wilson preserved the supremacy of society over the state, in much the way Louis Hartz accused him of doing.[2] As Sklar put it, Wilson's policies "assigned to the market, in the form of the corporation, banking, and trade associations, the primary task of regulating the market, and to the state the secondary task of regulating the corporations."[3] At the same time, however, Wilson embraced "positive government action" to ensure equality and redistributive justice, hallmarks of modern liberalism, which saw a role for government in bettering the condition of its citizens. Wilson's achievements— the Federal Reserve System, the Federal Trade Commission, the reduction of tariff rates, a federal income tax—contributed to the stabilization and expansion of the emergent corporate capitalist order, while at the same time preserving the viability of small, proprietary capitalism, that is, "the little guy." They also laid the legal and institutional groundwork for a more comprehensive regulatory welfare state.

During the Depression and New Deal era, questions about political economy that had been settled with Wilson were reopened and re-argued in circumstances far more conducive to statist approaches. But in the end, statist and European style solutions were rejected; the private sector retained primary responsibility for the economy, while the state took on additional regulatory and social-welfare responsibilities.[4] In the Second World War, the U.S. government expanded its control over the economy, but it largely retreated after the war, selling the plants it had built and dismantling price and wage controls. But even as control of the economy ostensibly remained in the private sector after the war, the U.S. government vastly increased its power (and spending) in fiscal policy, economic regulation, social welfare, infrastructure, and Cold War military commitments. This expansion of government power contributed to economic stabilization and growth in ways that strengthened corporate capitalism and illustrate what Sklar identified as the great achievement of corporate liberal activism: "the mix of the public and private sectors as seats of authority and initiative in shaping, planning, regulating, and containing development," wherein "development" meant economic growth.[5]

Regardless of whether one agrees with the entirety of Sklar's argument, it does provide a theoretical and historical background for understanding post–Second World War corporate liberalism, which, like its Progressive era counterpart, was an ideology that eschewed "rugged individualism," encouraged a more cooperative relationship between industry and government, and urged businesses to be more socially responsible. It was articulated and popularized after the Second World War by management experts and business journalists such as Peter Drucker, James Worthy, Stuart Chase, and *Fortune* magazine's Russell Davenport and Henry Luce, who sought to convince businesspeople and the public that the United States had outgrown its traditional commitment to laissez-faire economics and rugged individual-ism. According to these advocates, things had changed since the nineteenth century. Corporations were no longer run by individual owners, for one, but by professional managers, who, as *Fortune* editor Russell Davenport wrote, "have a responsibility to society as a whole."[6] This did not mean that profit wasn't the goal—it was—but managers had long-term profits in mind, not short term. To make money in the long term, according to Frank Abrams, chairman of the Standard Oil Company of New Jersey, managers had to "conduct the affairs of the enterprise in such a way as to maintain an equi-table and working balance among the claims of the various directly inter-ested groups—stockholders, employees, customers, and the public at large."[7]

Abrams's statement was a basic, oft-repeated statement of the doctrine of "social responsibility," which emphasized the long-term economic advan-tages of "doing the right thing." More than simply improving business's rep-utation, social responsibility was rooted in (and a vehicle for) the corporate liberal agenda. In an economic system no longer based on competition and short-term profits but, rather, on cooperation and long-term economic sta-bility, it was in corporations' best interest to treat their employees humanely, to respect the communities in which they put their factories, and to sell safe, affordable, quality products. It didn't mean that corporate heads had to become "do-gooders." It meant that they had to make responsible decisions that took into account the long-term economic consequences of, say, low wages, pollution, urban blight, and poor educational opportunities. It meant that they had to see themselves and their organizations as part of the whole.[8] The expansive corporate structure facilitated and demanded this. As James Worthy, a Sears & Roebuck public relations executive, explained: "The cir-cumstances of the large corporation necessarily emphasize the concepts and sentiments of trusteeship, service, and long range planning and at the same time minimize personal acquisition and self-aggrandizement."[9]

A key component of social responsibility and corporate liberalism was an emphasis on groups, which connoted cooperation, over the individual, which suggested competition. This emphasis on groups was the basis not only of mid-century social science but also of a management trend called "human relations," which dominated management schools and industrial re-lations departments in the 1950s.[10] Proponents of human relations saw the workplace as a web of interconnected, dynamic groups constantly seeking equilibrium. A manager's task was to integrate the different groups into an efficient, productive system. This philosophy tended to diminish the individual as the basic economic unit. According to management expert Peter Drucker, in modern industrial society, the individual was obsolete. Individuals no longer produced anything. The producer, wrote Drucker, "is actually the organization of large groups of men standing in definite relationship to each other. . . . By himself, the human being, whether worker or manager, is incapable of producing."[11] The key to good management, then, which was also the key to production and profits, was to harmonize and integrate these groups (as opposed to incentivizing or browbeating individuals). While not every chief executive officer embraced the human relations approach, the heads of their industrial relations departments usually did (because it was taught in management schools), and its ideas and jargon dominated the workplace.

The group-oriented framework of human relations gave managers a way to deal with the unpleasant reality of labor unions, which was to accept them as one of many groups that had to be integrated and harmonized (if one's company had the misfortune to be unionized). In their celebratory exposition of American capitalism, *U.S.A.—The Permanent Revolution*, the editors of *Fortune* depicted "Big Labor" as just one of the political realities of the day, the same as "Big Business" and "Big Agriculture," just another group of self-interested individuals who have realized that organization is the best way to protect one's interests and livelihood in a modern democratic society.[12] The authors assured readers that unions in the United States had matured, they were not like the ones in Europe, they were not interested in class consciousness or socialism. Here we see *Fortune* magazine endorsing unions as a legitimate economic group in a democratic society. Not all corporate heads gave up their anti-union activities, but a significant number adopted these evolving, increasingly sophisticated views about unions.

Finally, the ideology of corporate liberalism had a more open, even welcoming, view of government intervention. Business organizations like the Business Advisory Council and its offshoot, the Committee for Economic Development, both composed of the heads of major corporations, believed that government spending and strategic fiscal policies could stave off recession and smooth economic cycles.[13] Drucker called for "positive state action" to prevent unemployment. If it were true that the individual could produce nothing by himself, then the state had a responsibility to ensure full employment. Government should use its power to influence what we now call the macroeconomy, something he claimed was unprecedented outside times of war but absolutely necessary in the new industrial order. In addition to looking to the government to smooth economic cycles, corporate heads also viewed the government as a major customer. By 1954, 70 percent of the federal budget went to defense-related areas.[14] Given that most of the major corporations were government contractors in an age of military-industrial expansion, this openness to government-industry cooperation is unsurprising.

In the 1950s and 1960s, corporate liberalism gained a significant foothold in corporate America. The heads of General Motors, U.S. Steel, Proctor and Gamble, Eastman Kodak, RCA, and other major corporations accepted and welcomed government policies that created a good economic environment for their investments while at the same time leaving primary control of economic decisions in the private sector. Indeed, many of them, including General Motors' Charles E. Wilson, Eastman Kodak's Marion Folsom, and Proctor and Gamble's Neil McElroy, served in Eisenhower's cabinet, enacting a personal version of social responsibility. Some corporate leaders embraced social responsibility explicitly and publicly, speaking against racial prejudice and "rugged individualism," for instance. These included IBM's Thomas Watson, Jr., Inland Steel's William Caples, Pitney-Bowes' Walter Wheeler, Henry Luce of Time-Life, Inc., and Frank Abrams, chairman of the Standard Oil Company of New Jersey. But most, as represented by the leadership of the Committee for Economic Development and Business Council (formerly the Business Advisory Council), went along with it as part of their efforts to be influential actors in government circles. A small group of executives, active in the NAM and including Howard Pew of Sunoco and various Du Ponts, eschewed it, critical of the expansion of government power and what they saw as the loss of individualism (although their own companies benefited from these trends).[15]

Despite the ways in which corporate liberalism celebrated "free enterprise," its precepts were very much in line with the political liberalism of the day. Like liberals in both the Republican and Democratic parties, corporate liberals believed that government could be a positive force in society, promoting economic growth at home and containing communism abroad. Like liberals, they believed that the key to managing society lay in integrating and harmonizing various groups into an efficient whole rather than pitting them against one another. Like liberals, they saw progressive reform as the best way to circumvent unrest. Facing an ideological Cold War, they sought to make capitalism work for the masses.

This was the era of liberal consensus, in which, it was thought, the big questions about economic organization had finally been settled. Communism was obviously not the answer, but neither was laissez-faire capitalism. Instead, mid-century liberals espoused a middle way that preserved property rights and avoided state command of the economy, but greatly expanded the role of government in growth-oriented economic activity and social welfare issues. This arrangement rested on and encouraged economic growth as the answer to class struggle, poverty, racial discrimination, and inequality.[16] For liberals, such an arrangement promised to end the conflict that had historically accompanied those maladies. The role of the state expanded after the war, but not in a threatening, totalitarian way. Industry stood to benefit from government policies designed to produce growth, encourage social harmony, and create consumers. Thus, it largely cooperated.

There are historians who question whether the liberal consensus was really liberal (in the modern, progressive sense) or even a consensus. Although there was widespread support for civil rights legislation in polls, for instance, whites fought integration in their own neighborhoods, schools, and workplaces, even in the North.[17] There was little consensus between the Democratic Party's white working class and its African American constituency. And although corporations may have mouthed acceptance of labor unions, their actions indicated that they were trying to escape their influence, often by moving factories to "right-to-work" states in the South and eventually out of the country altogether.[18] Moreover, there was widespread conservative activism at the grassroots during this era, which would eventually give rise to an ascendant Right in the 1980s.[19] In retrospect, these historians say, whatever "consensus" there was seems shallow and fragile, given the enduring racial, class, and ideological divisions in the political and economic structures of the nation. Fair enough. But from the perspective of NAM conservatives in the 1950s and 1960s, the liberal consensus was real and inescapable, penetrating even the most reliably conservative organization in America.

The Struggle in the NAM

Throughout its history, the NAM has teetered back and forth between an ideological conservatism widely seen as extremist and a more pragmatic flexibility that could better represent the actual interests of its members. In the 1930s, a group of particularly conservative leaders launched a propaganda campaign against New Deal "socialism" and opposed almost all New Deal legislation, thereby gaining a reputation as an ineffective, reactionary organization. *Fortune* magazine wrote of these years: "all industry has suffered from N.A.M.'s maladroit presentation of industry's case."[20] After the war, NAM moderates took control and tacitly supported labor-management cooperation, international trade expansion, and economic productivity. In 1951, the organization's leadership reverted back to a small group of ideologically conservative men from mostly privately-held companies in the Midwest who had ties to rightist organizations.

Prominent in this conservative group were William J. Grede, president of the Milwaukee-based Grede Foundries from 1920 to 1973, and later president of J. I. Case, a large farm and heavy-equipment manufacturer, from 1953 to 1967; Cola Parker, president of Kimberly-Clark Corporation, a large Wisconsin lumber and paper company, from 1942 to 1955; and Ernie Swigert, who from 1929 to 1971 was director and board chairman of the Hyster Company, a heavy equipment manufacturer based in Portland, Oregon.[21] These men and their close allies controlled the NAM's Executive Committee and finances. They would also become founders of the John Birch Society in 1958.

Despite their leadership positions, however, they felt like they had little control over the pronouncements and direction of the NAM, which depended on the dues of its fluctuating membership of 16,000–20,000 and funding from a few idiosyncratic businessmen. A decentralized committee system made it difficult to maintain any kind of ideological or principled consistency on specific issues, and there was constant bickering over the positions endorsed by different committees. In 1956, for instance, the NAM's Industrial Relations Committee passed a resolution supporting unemployment compensation, much to the consternation of the Executive Committee. Worse, members of the NAM staff, which wrote its publications and conducted its research, supported the Marshall Plan, the United Nations, foreign aid, and the latest human relations management techniques, which endorsed social responsibility and antidiscrimination policies.[22] NAM members were from different regions, different industries, and had conflicting economic interests, which meant that the NAM avoided taking positions on controversial issues such as civil rights legislation or the tariff, issues that obviously affected manufacturers, albeit in different ways. This neutrality policy pleased no one. As one member complained, "the NAM will never take a clear-cut position on any issue when it stands to lose members."[23]

Despite these organizational issues, NAM conservatives blamed their problems on the doctrine of "social responsibility." Conservatives like Grede believed "social responsibility" was part and parcel of a larger socialistic sensibility that denigrated the individual, justified government activism, and endorsed unionism. While *Fortune* magazine could portray "social responsibility" as the natural culmination of modern industrial development, conservatives experienced it as an ideological attack on the laissez-faire ideas they sought to conserve (which it was). NAM conservatives thus always referred to "social responsibility" in quotes, scoffingly, impatiently. Here is NAM member Robert Gaylord of the Ingersoll Milling Machine Company in a letter to William Grede complaining about the NAM report endorsing unemployment compensation: "If the real purpose of the report is to embrace compulsory unemployment compensation as a 'social responsibility' so the self-labeled 'liberals' will not consider the NAM a reactionary, hidebound organization refusing to recognize the realities of present day life, it is 'too little, too late,' nor will a public profession of something we do not actually believe in effectively serve even that purpose."[24]

Gaylord refused to accept that some NAM members might actually see unemployment compensation as a useful policy in its own right. Like many historians, he could only see it as "window-dressing," a ploy on the part of reformer types who wanted to make the NAM "relevant." Grede concurred. He too saw "social responsibility" as an ill-advised public relations gambit, generated by public relations departments not on the basis of sound economics "but rather on the basis of what is popular with the public." Large corporations were particularly guilty of this practice, he noted, suggesting that their broad ownership or their dominance of industry led them to "develop a sense that they are a public corporation and therefore, must be responsive to the popular public opinion." Grede was right; this was exactly how corporate liberals saw large corporations.[25]

An active philanthropist, Grede didn't have anything against social responsibility per se; it was the corporate liberal version of it that he hated. What guaranteed real social responsibility, according to Grede, were not regulations or compromise or negotiation, but each man's individual moral sense, combined with his own self-interest. Corporate liberalism's social scientific emphasis on groups was the problem. Groups did not have an innate moral sense. Groups acted according to group decisions, which as Leonard Read, founder of the Foundation for Economic Education, pointed out, were inevitably amoral compromises between opposing positions—watered-down, piecemeal versions of a once whole and coherent position. Agreements between groups rather than individuals, such as the collective agreements between employers and unions, were "mongrel," distorted contracts even if they favored management.[26] Liberals saw the back and forth that occurred in committees, in union negotiations, or in pluralist politics, as democratic, because it involved the participation and reconciliation of different interests and groups, all voices heard. It was the process that mattered in a democracy, not the outcome per se. In contrast, conservatives saw this forced consensus as tyrannical and leading to mediocrity. Sometimes, often, the correct position is the one held by the minority, or the sole individual who marches to the beat of a different drummer.[27]

By 1960, the conservatives' stock in the NAM was fading. After NAM member Robert Welch accused President Eisenhower of being a communist, the NAM board met and informally censured Welch, Grede, Swigert, and Parker for their activities in the John Birch Society, adopting a resolution that the NAM fully believed in the loyalty and integrity of President Eisenhower and was not associated with any group that believed otherwise.[28] Then the board hired a management consultant firm to survey its operations and make recommendations. The Heller report came out in late 1961 and recommended a reorganization of NAM governance, including the appointment of a full-time, paid president from outside the organization (previously presidents had been unpaid and chosen from the board).[29] The changes were meant to address dwindling membership and were aimed at lessening the influence of the conservative old guard in the organization. Grede and his friends on the Executive Committee opposed the move.[30] Nonetheless, in testimony to their dwindling influence, the new structure was adopted and a new president elected.

It is unclear exactly who on the 150-member board instigated the reorganization. Historian Jonathan Soffer argues that it reflected the growing militarization of business conservatism, as evidenced by large corporations with government contracts taking control of the NAM from the small capitalists who retained the principles of a bygone proprietary capitalism.[31] His argument is in accordance with the general scholarly consensus that large, publically traded corporations supported corporate liberalism, while small or mid-sized family-owned firms held on to the old (conservative, parochial) ideals of competitive capitalism. Large corporations obviously had a stake in the military-industrial complex and the Cold War, but so too did many smaller, conservative firms. Moreover, conservatives in general were in transition about military spending during these years. It isn't clear that this was the major factor leading to the NAM's reorganization. Historians have assumed that the ideological views of NAM board members correlated with the size of the company they represented. But the most active and "ultra" conservatives in the NAM—Grede, Howard Pew, Lammot du Pont—headed large corporations with government contracts. What does seem clear is that there was a decline in membership, and many board members, regardless of the size of their companies or their ideological inclinations, blamed the small group of ultraconservatives that had managed to commandeer the Executive Committee and garner bad press.[32] As NAM members, they were generally conservative in their outlook, but they were ready for a change.

Werner P. "Gully" Gullander of General Dynamics became the first paid, permanent head of the NAM on November 1, 1962.[33] What Gullander offered was an allegedly conservative version of "social responsibility," one that called on industry to step up and develop "private solutions" to social problems. The argument was that private industry could find more efficient and creative solutions to the problems of poverty, urban blight, and minority unemployment than could government bureaucracies. He called this a conservative version of social responsibility, but it is worth noting that James Worthy, the corporate executive most associated with the "social responsibility in business" movement, also argued that businesses (i.e., the private sector) had always been more efficient and flexible in solving social problems than the government had been. Worthy made this argument to persuade businessmen to get involved in solving social problems, lest government get further involved, which would cost businesses even more in taxes. He wrote: "Even under a federal system, government tends toward the monolithic. Private efforts are more efficient, more flexible, and more responsive to changing needs and circumstances, more experimental, more inclined to explore alternatives."[34] Worthy's adherence to the idea of a private sector (society) that was separate from and more influential than the public sector (the state) marks him as a true corporate liberal as theorized by Martin Sklar. The fact that Gullander and other businessmen were claiming that this was a "conservative version" of social responsibility in 1962 shows not only how pervasive corporate liberalism was, but also that (modern) liberals were pushing it leftward, calling for a more active role for the state in solving social problems.[35]

In 1963, the NAM launched what was loosely referred to as the "minority program," the objective of which was "to provide free market solutions to the current Negro employment problem."[36] Gullander also instituted new programs like MIND (Methods of Intellectual Development) to train inner-city youth for white collar jobs, and STEP (Solutions to Employment Problems), which helped companies begin minority employment programs.[37] To liberals who were trying to solidify the legitimacy of the welfare state, this type of activity and rhetoric was deeply conservative, even dangerous, because it discredited government programs and revived animosities about "Big Government." But to conservatives like Grede, Gullander may as well have been Lyndon Baines Johnson himself. Gullander purged the Birchers from leadership positions and urged industry to take seriously businesses' social responsibility.[38] He asked New York governor Nelson Rockefeller—conservative Republicans' bête noire—to give the keynote address at his inaugural Annual Meeting in December 1962, while Eisenhower, another liberal Republican, spoke at the closing luncheon.[39] NAM speakers began to urge industry leaders to try working with the government, not against it (i.e., to practice social responsibility), and in December 1963, the NAM pledged to cooperate with the new Johnson administration.[40] While conservatives, including Grede, opposed the 1964 Civil Rights Act, Gullander's NAM began a nationwide series of seminars to help business owners and managers adjust to what it called "the new era in industrial relations." These seminars endorsed Title VII and instructed NAM members on how to comply.[41]

Gullander kept NAM members informed of the NAM's many activities under his leadership. This was a time of increasing government regulation. He and his staff were working on issues of overtime and taxation; they were monitoring proposed packaging and pollution requirements; they were meeting with representatives on the National Labor Relations Board and other government agencies. Gullander took care to tailor his reports to show conservatives that he upheld a conservative, "free-enterprise" position. This did not involve any fiery anti-labor rhetoric but rather wry comments about how the NAM "stepped on a sensitive Big Labor nerve," or how Walter Reuther's radio spokesman, Guy Nunn, nominated Gullander "for a major niche in his mythical 'Hall of Shame.'"[42]

Such anecdotes were hardly enough to stanch the anger of conservatives at the NAM's new direction. They wrote to Gullander and Grede (whom they regarded as their leader) with their complaints. A Georgia businessman wrote to Grede, "I never thought I'd see the day when a conservative point of view is unwelcome in a business oriented organization like the NAM." The Hussman Refrigeration Company in St. Louis reduced its annual donation.[43]

Gullander insisted that he was upholding free-market principles. He listed the ways that the NAM was opposing new packaging regulations ("if these don't sound like opposition, I'll eat them"), overtime, minimum wages, and Medicare, concluding: "It simply isn't true that we have ceased being against socialism. What we have done is become more aggressively for private solutions to social and public problems." Then to Grede: "Bill, believe me we have not forgotten principle. We have forsaken the discredited technique of attack, attack, and attack."[44] As Gullander explained, he was trying to make NAM effective; the old NAM had lost its audience, it had veered too far to the right. To recapture that audience and reestablish believability, he wanted to put the NAM in a leadership position, encouraging members to assist in solving the nation's problems. "Our approach is different from the NAM as you knew it in the past, but our objective of maximum freedom is still identically the same."[45] In another letter, he wrote, "My burning desire is to influence the decisions made by government to the maximum extent possible and this can only be accomplished if you have two way communication."[46] He insisted that communication was not cooperation.

Grede defended the old NAM, scolding Gullander for presuming to judge it on the basis of hearsay and its enemy's accusations. The good publicity the "new" NAM was receiving because of the changes only meant that the NAM was less of a threat to its enemies and more easily controlled by them—and hence less effective. Grede mocked the "social responsibility" focus of that year's annual meeting, suggesting that it was a distraction from the real work that the NAM needed to be doing: "When we spend a whole morning listening to how somebody raised 16 million dollars for a Music Hall or some other great guy tells us we ought to plant trees in our parking lot, and you have the cream of the crop of American industry in the audience it seems to me, as I remarked at the time, 'while Rome burns, the NAM fiddles.'"[47]

In a letter that went to eleven other NAM leaders, Grede conceded that Gullander might be sincere in his techniques, but that it wasn't enough to oppose individual bills if one didn't offer as well a strong ideological critique: "It is true you oppose the packaging bill, but we don't vigorously oppose the government's interference in the free market. We oppose a shorter work week, but we don't oppose the interference by the government with the establishment of a minimum work week in itself. We oppose raising minimum wages, but we don't vigorously oppose the establishment of the minimum wage as a principle."[48]

This statement gets to the crux of their disagreement. Gullander was focused on business's interests and explicitly wanted to avoid ideological disagreement. He accepted the premise of the liberal consensus and in that framework maneuvered to get manufacturers the best deal on specific legislation. For Grede, the whole point was to reject the premises and institutions of the liberal consensus—that was the great struggle. If you joined the government in its attempts to end poverty, say, as the NAM did when it cooperated with the Office of Economic Opportunity in 1967, you may get a couple of favors for specific businesses and maybe some favorable press from *Time* magazine, but you have declared defeat in the greater struggle, or as Grede put it: "When you live too close to the web you are apt to get caught."[49]

Gullander never did convince Grede that his method of social responsibility and private solutions would stop the trend toward socialism in America. He did, however, maneuver the NAM into a position where it had influence in government agencies. Thus, for instance, NAM representatives worked closely with officials in the Office of Federal Contract Compliance (OFCC) in the late 1960s to hone affirmative action guidelines. In November 1969, the OFCC announced that it would require all government contractors to hire minority applicants at a rate approximating the ratio of minorities to the applicant population in each location. In discussions with the OFCC, the NAM fought against hard quotas. The final version made targets (not quotas) mandatory, and the NAM succeeded in getting some leeway for companies that failed to reach their targets if they could show a good-faith effort. In contrast, the NAM was unable to amend the requirement that companies dedicate resources to training programs; population surveys; and in some cases, recalculating where black workers would be in seniority had they been white when they were hired. Responding to one disgruntled small business owner, the NAM defended its influence in the process, writing that the NAM had actually forced the OFCC to take a "much modified and softer approach" than it had originally started with.[50] But for anyone who felt that affirmative action requirements were an extreme example of government interference in business's decisions, the NAM had not only capitulated to the corporate liberals, it was doing their job for them.

*   *   *

One doesn't have to agree with Grede's politics to appreciate his assessment of Gullander's policies. Gullander's strategy represented the NAM's taming, its acquiescence in a dominant liberal world view. Journalists and historians have been distracted by Gullander's rhetorical attempts to convince NAM members that his positions were in fact conservative. Yes, he took a combative approach in congressional testimony against specific liberal positions but, as Grede pointed out, he never questioned the underlying premise that government had a role to play in the economy. "Private solutions for public problems" seemed like a conservative idea in 1968 as businessmen sought to respond to the social disruption of the late 1960s by discrediting the Great Society. But in effect it meant that the NAM would urge industry to fight its own war on poverty by replicating the techniques and assumptions of government agencies. Nowhere was this more apparent than in the NAM's cooperation with the Equal Employment Opportunity Commission and the OFCC, wherein the NAM performed the valuable service of helping its members put their firms in compliance and urging them to adopt what became known as affirmative action.[51]

Ultimately, as the election of Ronald Reagan in 1980 showed, it was not corporate liberalism that triumphed, but rather the ideas of Grede and his friends. Corporations downsized, shedding social programs and benefits along with now-cumbersome divisions. The Cold War ended, and with it the need to show that capitalism was humane and democratic. The old values of individualism and competition emerged anew in what was labeled "neoliberalism." Corporate liberalism turned out not to be an ideologically neutral next step in the natural evolution of society but rather the ideologically charged philosophy of a corporate liberal elite. The New Left was the first to point this out. But Grede's complaints previewed the Left's critique. That is, both the New Left and Grede understood that corporate liberalism was deeply ideological and hegemonic in its influence. Both understood how it marginalized those who did not accept its premises. The difference was the New Left saw it as a conservative ideology, while Grede saw it as socialism.[52] The New Left believed business had co-opted liberals and unions, whereas Grede believed liberals and unions had co-opted business.

Some historians have seen the dominance of the Right and neoliberalism since the 1980s as evidence of the weakness of the liberal consensus. In a review article about books on conservatism, Kim Phillips-Fein suggests that "the entire postwar period was one of struggle and that the liberal order was always more fragile than its victories suggested."[53] Indeed, its victories were accompanied by backlash that ultimately subverted them. The work of historians like Thomas Sugrue, Lisa McGirr, Jefferson Cowie, and many others have shown that conservative ideas were stronger and more pervasive than previously assumed, able to water down liberal legislation in every area from civil rights to pollution control. Scoffing at the way prosperous conservatives like Grede portrayed themselves as "aggrieved victims," these historians challenge the alleged hegemony of the liberal consensus.[54]

The triumph of social responsibility in the NAM, however, illustrates how pervasive the consensus was. It may have been short-lived, but it had the power to get generally conservative businessmen and business organizations to overcome their commitment to laissez-faire ideas and to accept the prevailing standards of the 1950s and 1960s. It had the power to get them to embrace an ethos of social responsibility that was at odds with traditional conservative ideas. When the tide turned, when the mixed economy of modern liberalism proved unable to address the economic downturn of the 1970s, when ideologues of Grede's ilk, people like William Rusher, Richard Viguerie, and others, managed to capture control of political discourse and power, businesspeople and their organizations turned back. They made adjustments. That is what major business organizations like the NAM do if they want to remain relevant. They follow and adjust to the prevailing political winds. That the NAM was forced to adjust to the corporate liberalism of the 1950s and 1960s is testimony to the strength of the liberal consensus.

Chapter 10

"What Would Peace in Vietnam Mean for You as an Investor?" Business Executives and the Antiwar Movement, 1967–75

Eric R. Smith

On May 21, 1968, while the warring parties in Vietnam held peace talks in Paris, twenty-four business executives engaged in a heated exchange with Republican Illinois senator Everett Dirksen in his Washington, D.C., office. As described by the *Chicago Daily News* reporter Betty Flynn, the fifteen-minute meeting began with a plea by the business delegation to a "Republican candidate not persisting in hawkish attitudes" to push for a military withdrawal from Vietnam. The delegation misjudged Dirksen's outlook. Although he was arguably a press favorite, Dirksen was also critical of congressional doves. Insisting that "whether we like it or not, this is a military operation," Dirksen then added, "I can't betray the people back home." One of the businessmen retorted, "We are the people back home" before trying to explain that "Twenty minutes after we leave Saigon, that government would fall apart. We are laying waste to a country without just cause." Dirksen snapped: "You don't have the facts. . . . I know my history. I know my geography. We're not going to get anywhere arguing like we do." Recovering his composure at the end of the meeting, Dirksen thanked the men for their visit.[1]

The delegation could be forgiven for misjudging Dirksen, who had questioned overall military strategy and as early as 1966 cited war expenditures and Great Society programs as inflationary. "Every housewife who shops in a grocery store knows this. [Higher prices] are the living, breathing, signs of this destructive burglarizing force."[2] On the matter of military expenditures, the businessmen had arrived at a similar realization and only the year before their meeting with Dirksen had organized into the Business Executives Move for Vietnam Peace and New National Priorities (BEM). The group served as a new voice in the growing chorus of opposition to American involvement in Southeast Asia.

The businessmen involved in the BEM had been shaped by the Second World War and Roosevelt's New Deal, and they tended to accept postwar liberalism's assumptions, including the continuation of the New Deal with Lyndon Johnson's Great Society programs.[3] These were also men and women of privilege whose well-being relied on a healthy economy where American consumers could buy their products and services and where monetary policies ensured low borrowing rates. Moreover, these were parents and citizens who could not but be affected by the events of the period. Their collective critique of the Vietnam conflict was unified by a concern for what former president Eisenhower called the "military-industrial complex" and the wisdom of the market, which, according to their data, had been negatively affected by the war.[4] The decade of the sixties was a "drama acted out on many stages," and the BEM occupied one of them.[5] The men and women of the BEM are often recognized in the standard script of the period for their role in the Moratorium, when millions of Americans took part in the largest political demonstration in American history on October 16, 1969.[6] Much of the BEM's work has remained obscured by the more overt protests of the period and what is at present limited archival material, but extant manuscripts offer insights into the importance of a segment of the business community's involvement in the antiwar movement. As will be made apparent, these business executives recognized that their titles and their social status could be used to shape the political debate about the war and domestic policies. This essay offers a first step toward the inclusion of these significant antiwar activities into the future histories of the Vietnam War and is an attempt to account for the economic critique that was a chief motivation for these businessmen's activities. Conservative economic attitudes among business leaders of this period—at the National Association of Manufacturers, the Business Roundtable, and the U.S. Chamber of Commerce—have been well documented, but the history of the BEM suggests another, much less studied, aspect of business activism in the late 1960s and early 1970s.[7]

In early 1968, Paine, Webber, Jackson & Curtis ran a full page ad in the *New York Times* asking, "What would peace in Vietnam Mean for You as an Investor?" At the end of April that year, BEM activists Erwin Salk and John Tittle testified before the House Committee on Veterans Affairs, where they left, in addition to a prepared statement, a copy of this ad. Salk, the main spokesman, was active in founding the BEM, and in his testimony to Congress proceeded to answer the question: "Peace in Vietnam would be the most constructive—and the most bullish thing that could happen to the stock market." The Paine, Webber analysis concluded that defense demands had "stretched the nation's production facilities to the point where there was virtually no remaining reserve of economic resources. Result: a substantial increase in inflationary pressures." An end to the war, the analysts reported, would bring an end to these inflationary pressures as "the threat of demand/pull inflation would subside."[8] Even the *Wall Street Journal* took notice: "On the increasingly rare occasions that rumors of Vietnam peace negotiations circulate, stock prices go up sharply—and that's about the only time they do go up. Whenever the fighting intensified or threatens to intensify, inventory sell shares in enough volume to produce a sharp price break."[9] However, this trend of buying when escalation began and selling on word of peace began to fade as "the war also adds to the drain of dollars out of the U.S., which both Wall Street and the White House see as reaching crisis proportions. In the fourth quarter, the balance-of-payments deficit hit a seasonally adjusted $1.8 billion, the worst in any quarter since 1950."[10] In short, the material cost of the war was becoming increasingly evident, so that even conservatives like Phyllis Schlafly questioned the war and its demand for resources that could be better utilized elsewhere.[11]

The BEM entered into these robust foreign policy discussions when it was created in 1966. The origins of the group lay in the protracted correspondence of Chicago-based mortgage broker Erwin "Bud" Salk with Seymour Melman of Columbia University, a professor of industrial engineering and operations research. Melman was a co-chair of the Committee for a Sane Nuclear Policy that opposed the Cold War arms race. His academic work focused on analyses of the military-industrial complex—what Melman refers to as the "Cold War Institutional Machine"—and the country's commitment to Cold War Keynesianism, which he argued helped pull the United States into the Vietnam conflict. In his 1965 book *Our Depleted Society*, Melman described his research as "an economic audit of the price that America has paid for twenty years of Cold War." Melman observed how a "process of technical, industrial, and human deterioration has been set in motion within American society. . . . The wealthiest nation on earth has been unable to rally the resources necessary to raise one fifth of its own people from poverty." This was a result, he argued, of "an unprecedented concentration of America's talent and fresh capital on military production." Melman then proceeded to lay out the variety of ways in which these resources were being squandered on firms and projects that ultimately siphoned off public revenues but contributed no growth to the economy.[12] In his correspondence to Salk, Melman connected what he observed to be a "new, viable strategy for the new condition of the civil rights movement" that emphasized economic opportunity with these other underlying assumptions. The "start of a debate on guns vs. butter" could now be had, with the result that the "civil rights and the peace movements will move in mutually supporting, parallel action."[13]

Melman included a prescient observation on the outflow of gold from the U.S. economy and its implication for the country's prosperity and world standing. By 1949, having become the world's creditor, he found, the United States had accumulated a gold stock worth $24.4 billion. By 1964, that reserve had been depleted by 35 percent to $15 billion. As Melman recognized, "the foreign commitments have been growing and by the middle of 1964 the total short-term claims against the United States amounted to $20.5 billion." This threatened the value of the American dollar. The debts were the result, Melman observed, of a $3 billion annual cost of foreign military presence (apart from the domestic cost of paying for troops and equipment). Indeed, quoting from the Joint Economic Committee of the Congress, Melman insisted that "American officials have allowed the fear that foreigners might convert their dollars into gold to become an all-pervasive stifling influence on United States initiative and action on a wide range of domestic and international problems."[14] This was likely due to the encouragement of capital flow out of the United States to places where higher interest rates prevailed, and the outflow resulted in trade deficits and increasing pressure on the gold reserves.

In July 1966, it was Melman who suggested to Salk that a peace organization for the business community was necessary. "I think this may be the proper time, before it is too late, for responsible men of the business community to examine the implications of these propositions. It would seem appropriate that we convene an open meeting of business leaders to explore the meaning of what is happening."[15] Melman's letter to Salk enumerated concerns with respect to Vietnam that would also reflect, if not foreshadow, the concerns of the BEM and others in the business community: Vietnam expenditures are robbing the domestic economy of resources as well as contributing to inflation; the value of the dollar is dropping internationally, and yet the U.S. economy is also ailing in its ability to compete.[16] Only a week after receiving Melman's letter, Salk sent out a dozens of letters to associates around the country trying to interest them in "the convening of a national conference of business leaders from industry, banking, trade, etc., to be held in Washington, D.C., to ponder a number of questions related to [the Vietnam war and military expenditures]."[17]

Around the time that Salk was posting his letters, Mary Cushing Niles, wife of BEM founding member Henry E. Niles (chairman of the Baltimore Life Insurance Company), urged Senator Joseph Tydings of Maryland to speak out against escalation in Vietnam. The senator confided that he was constantly being pressured on the war by professionals of every stripe but never by businessmen. When she told Henry about the conversation, her husband responded with an open letter campaign to the White House that culminated on December 28, 1966, with 83 signatures.[18] The cover letter to President Lyndon Johnson read:

> I believe that you sincerely wish to bring the war in Vietnam to a conclusion. It is known that you are under pressures from many persons who would have you go all out for a military solution by using our tremendous military might to crush North Vietnam. I believe that such a step—aside from its moral aspects which I believe deeply concern you and many of us—would be unlikely to win the lasting peace we want. . . .
>
> My purpose in getting the signatures to the Open Letter was not to add to your heavy burdens but to offset pressure from the 'hawks' and to do a little, which I felt I could do, toward building world peace.[19]

Niles also stated: "Many companies—possibly all companies—may lose their assets, customers and prospects if the war in Vietnam keeps intensifying and widening. As Chairman of the Board of the Baltimore Life Insurance Company, I believe that I have a major responsibility to do what I can to prevent such losses."[20] On May 28, 1967, another full-page ad appeared in the *New York Times*, this one an open letter to President Johnson with 300 signatures. More imploring than the earlier open letter, this one nonetheless urged the president to "stop the bombing, de-escalate military activity in South Vietnam, negotiate with all parties which are now fighting."[21] Given that this letter precedes the Tet Offensive, which had a galvanizing effect on the antiwar position the following year, Johnson should not have been surprised by early 1968 when his own inner circle, responding to many of these same concerns, turned against the war.

The two efforts by Niles and Salk brought the two organizers and their supporters together. A year later, the name of the proposed group was the "National Committee of Business Executives for Peace" (though "for Ending the War" was also recommended). Besides Bud Salk and Henry Niles, the other BEM founders included Harold Willens, a Los Angeles business executive; and William Fischer, president of Fischer Machine Company in Philadelphia. Other executives of various profiles would eventually be active in or supportive of the organization, including Charles Simpson, general manager for Philadelphia Gas Works; and Lee B. Thomas, Jr., president of Vermont American Corporation. Both would sit on the executive board. The first co-chairmen of the organization in 1967 were Niles and Willens. Later, Fischer, Salk, Simpson, Thomas, and Joseph E. McDowell, president of Servomation Corporation in New York, would sit on the executive committee. President Eisenhower's head of the Securities and Exchange Commission, Sinclair Armstrong, and Robert Roosa, former undersecretary of the Treasury, were also among the Washington insiders with BEM membership.

Several of the local affiliates have left behind a documentary record offering insights into the organization's work and its constituents. The St. Louis local was founded by Thomas Hardy, the owner of the Hardy Salt Company, who was later the chairman of the BEM. His committee included dozens of executives from banking, finance, and manufacturing. For an example of the constituents of the BEM, consider this sampling of the active membership of the St. Louis committee:[22]

Marvin L. Madeson, ITT Aetna Finance Co.
Wm. Stix Friedman, Burns, Stix Friedman & Co.
Leo A. Drey, Pioneer Forest
Wilber E. Eckstein, American Commission Paper Co.
Victor H. Gavel, Gaywood Manufacturing Co.
Larry R. Gavel, Gaywood Manufacturing Co.
George T Guernsey, III, Manchester Bank
Harold Hartogensis, George Johnson, Advertising

George Johnson, George Johnson, Advertising
Marvin L. Madeson, IIT Aetna Finance Co.
Lionel Kalish, Jr., Elder Manufacturing Co.
Bernard Kornblum, St. Louis Music Supply Co.
Robert Rudright, Rudright Organization
Richard T. Stith, Fette-Stith Agency
J. A. Zimmerman, Cahokia Flour Company

A similar cross-section of the business community could be found in the organization in Chicago. The national BEM also lined up nearly a dozen military officers and diplomats as sponsors, including Brig. General William Wallace Ford, Brig. General Samuel B. Griffith, Brig. General Robert L. Hughes, Rear Admiral Robert C. Huston, General David M. Shoup, General William B. McKean, and Rear Admiral Arnold E. True. Kennedy confidant John Kenneth Galbraith also was active in the group and gave several lectures on its behalf.[23] A group called Corporate Executives Committee for Peace that eventually merged with the BEM to become the New York branch of the organization had seven Revlon executives on its steering committee. At a June 1970 event for that organization, the speakers included John Kerry, the future senator and secretary of State; a Twentieth Century Fox executive, Hal Davis; as well as Attorney General Ramsey Clark; Democratic Senator Alan Cranston of California; and Harold Willens of the BEM.[24]

The primary figures in the BEM were also often active on several fronts, and antiwar activism served as an extension of their other activities. Salk's congressional testimony suggested that it was a matter of self-interest for the business community, but some background on the men suggests that a deeper commitment also existed. For example, Salk was active on civil rights issues long before he became active on the war. As president of the forty-second largest mortgage firm in the United States, Salk criticized real estate redlining and housing restrictions and underwrote hundreds of social justice causes. Like many of the business executives in the 1960s who were involved in the BEM, he was also a veteran of the Second World War. Salk propelled himself into the public eye with statements in the press, both locally in Chicago, and later nationally, about racist real estate contracts and housing codes. He attacked both as anticapitalist. Salk was aware of the history in the South of black mutual aid societies developing insurance companies and the long history of business apartheid that accompanied segregation.[25] Salk's colleague, Henry Niles, held religious convictions as a

Quaker that compelled his antiwar activities. Niles had connections to the New Left and radical activism through his daughter Alice's marriage to Staughton Lynd, the radical historian whose firing from several universities over his political activities spawned some of the many outcries of the period.[26] Niles would later criticize Nixon, the Quaker president, by telling a House subcommittee that "We feel that we are getting from the military diminishing security at escalating cost. . . . Heavy military spending, started under past administrations but continuing high throughout the Nixon administration has been and now is the major cause of inflation. The production of military hardware, although it generates payrolls, makes no additions to the supply of consumer goods and services available."[27] The activities of Thomas Hardy's family also suggest the ways in which personal commitments play out on the political stage. His wife, Jane, was active in the League of Women Voters and would be an outspoken advocate for the empowerment of the United Nations' International Criminal Court. The Los Angeles chapter of the BEM was headed by A. R. Appleby, who regularly attended stockholder meetings and asked discomfiting questions about the company's ties to Southeast Asian military operations. Harold Willens, president of the Los Angeles–based Factory Equipment Supply Company, eventually devoted himself to full-time activism first with the BEM and later with the nuclear freeze movement. Like Erwin Salk, he had served in the Pacific during the Second World War. The left-wing magazine the *Nation* now sponsors a Nation Institute that endows an award in Willens's honor, the Harold Willens Peace Fellowship.

It was Willens who was instrumental in pulling the founding meeting together in September 1967 at the Statler-Hilton in Washington, D.C., which featured a keynote address from Marriner Eccles, the Utah banker whom President Roosevelt had once appointed chairman of the Federal Reserve Board. Eccles had also been involved that year in forming with former John Kennedy advisors John Kenneth Galbraith and Arthur Schlesinger the group Negotiations Now, which intended to sway policy away from the singular pursuit of military victory.[28] Marriner Eccles's address at the founding is instructive of the BEM's core principles and what worried the Johnson and then Nixon administrations. He began with a rejection of the Cold War consensus and the belief in a monolithic expansionist communism that was directly at odds with the war's conservative supporters.[29] While communism had been advancing, the Soviet Union's control over it had been waning, he argued. "We see every rebellion as the result of a deep plot out of Moscow or

Peking, when it usually is the result of crushing poverty, hunger and intolerable living conditions." In a frank statement of moral equivalency, Eccles wondered what the United States would do if Russia were daily bombing an American ally. "It is inconceivable that we would limit ourselves to providing only military equipment, as they are doing." At the core of the argument was a material concern: "This war is directly causing a substantial increase in the deficiency in our international balance of payments, which is already serious." He then lamented the neglect of the initiatives of Johnson's Great Society. In a bracketed reference at the end of his address, Eccles credits the British historian Arnold Toynbee and the radical historian Howard Zinn (who went on to write *A People's History of the United States*) "for the assistance I received from reading their excellent articles."[30] The parenthetical acknowledgment underscores Niles's earlier admission that the business community was in a sense responding to the antiwar movement already under way and taking that political struggle to the corridors of power in ways that the New Left could not. Unlike the New Left, where the dialogue was predominantly in the streets and on campus, the BEM was bringing that dialogue to Congress and two successive presidents, albeit with a variation on that antiwar message.

It would not be until January that the group finally opened its Washington office under the direction of Robert Maslow, who was formerly employed by the Arms Control and Disarmament Agency. The D.C. office's activities were devoted almost solely to lobbying but also included a two-month speaking tour by Don Luce, the former head of International Voluntary Services in Vietnam. In contrast to other antiwar organizations, the BEM was able to regularly land high-profile meetings with government officials. According to Harold Willens, the initial press coverage of the group was entirely by his own efforts: "That fantastic coverage BEM got through my lengthy interviews on prime time NBC and CBS news shows was not arranged by anyone else. Only by me. I called and got to the right people and 'sold' them on the merit of our story."[31] The meetings with officials would seem to have resulted through the same type of effort and networking. In March 1969, a delegation met with Senator Tydings and also Charles Schultz, the former director of the budget. That same month a meeting was held with Jonathan Moore, special assistant to the undersecretary of state. And in April, the delegation landed a meeting with Henry Kissinger's special assistant, Dean Moor. Then in June, the group's J. Sinclair Armstrong testified before the Defense Subcommittee of the House Appropriations Committee. According to the organization's files, Henry Niles also "made off-the-record contacts with former very high government officials." In May, the organization hosted an "emergency meeting" that included speeches by Senators John Cooper, William Fulbright, and Ralph Yarborough along with several other representatives. By July, the organization had 2,531 members.[32] By the next year, these members included Robert T. Bernstein, president, and Bennett Cerf, chairman of the board, of Random House; Roger Sonnabend, chairman of the board of Sonesta International Hotels; George Weissman, president of Philip Morris; Max Palevsky, chairman of Xerox; and Lawrence Phillips, president of Phillips–Van Heusen Corporation. Membership would top out at 11,000 by the end of 1970, and this growing network alarmed President Nixon, who added the organization to his "Enemies List."[33]

The group became very active, especially its speakers bureau. It actively undertook lobbying activities, coordinated meetings with other groups, funded political campaigns, held luncheons and fund raisers, published a newsletter, underwrote visible public relations campaigns, issued press releases that frequently made it into print, and bought radio spots. Organizing occurred in more than a dozen cities: Chicago, New York, Detroit, Cleveland, Los Angeles, Kansas City, Portland, Oregon; Boston, San Francisco, St. Louis, Baltimore, Seattle, Louisville, and eventually in Milwaukee, Atlanta, and Minneapolis–St. Paul, with chapters also in Indiana, Iowa, Maine, New Mexico, Ohio, Nebraska, and Tennessee.[34]

By 1968, the goals of the BEM became more focused to emphasize the group's nonpartisanship and followed to the letter the 1967 *New York Times* full-page ad with the additional demands to "negotiate with all parties, including the National Liberation Front" and "Support the general principles of the Geneva agreements of 1954."[35] Henry Niles contextualized these goals in the starkest business terms:

> Each individual and each business should do its part toward building a secure and peaceful world. The life insurance business has a particularly strong interest in and obligation toward world security for the following reasons: 1) Even a small war could affect our mortality experience from losses due to direct casualties (which are covered by practically all life insurance contracts now in force) and losses due to the effect of atomic fallout. 2) Huge military expenditures may lead to inflation which will decrease the value of dollars in which we pay our policyholders or their beneficiaries. Too much inflation

would be ruinous to our business. 3) A war which involved action against this country would probably cause great losses in our investment portfolios.[36]

The BEM's activists pushed this line at its various events and through letter writing campaigns, petitions, and congressional lobbying, and in their newspaper and radio ads. In 1970, the BEM also helped finance the Citizens Commission of Inquiry into atrocities in Vietnam. Early that year, the BEM had finally been able to reach out to a separate group of Wall Street activists and forge an alliance with the Corporate Executive Committee for Peace, 350 businessmen who had also made inroads in official Washington.[37]

Despite the wealth of its membership, BEM suffered financial and internecine setbacks. The group experienced infighting, as the Los Angeles chapter's leader pushed for a Daniel Ellsberg support fund, which he played up in the media and gave the impression of the backing of the national organization, whose members forced his resignation. The St. Louis office under Hardy's leadership set up a separate Ellsberg Defense Fund that was distinguished from the BEM and managed to raise several thousand dollars. A Pentagon Papers Defense Fund was also planned in St. Louis.[38] Even though formal membership was rising, a lack of funds necessitated closing the BEM's Washington office. The office was reopened in 1971. The St. Louis and Chicago offices, for which there is good accounting data, both reveal very modest campaigns. St. Louis was only spending close to $1,000–2,000 per month and bringing in barely enough to support its expenditures. A great many of BEM's initial supporters were also not keeping up with their dues, even though they remained on the membership lists and continued receiving the group's monthly newsletter as free riders. In late 1970, Henry Niles wrote to the National Council members that "it was obvious that we have been under-staffed and under-financed for many months, especially during the months of the political campaign when potential contributors were giving heavily to candidates of their choice." A national meeting just held in San Francisco was attended below the quorum of 50 percent of the members.[39]

Still, business executives had access to resources that brought peace advocacy to the establishment. A series of full-page ads in the *Washington Post* and *New York Times* provoking questions about the conflict was difficult to ignore. "How to Make a Killing in the Market," read one header; "That Effete Corps of Impudent Snobs Is About to Do It Again," read another. Creative summaries of the group's official position followed below the banners. The group also co-sponsored with New National Priorities what was called "Operation Housecleaning."[40] In two election cycles, the BEM targeted a group of hawks in Congress, defeating three in each election. The 1970 campaign derived from *Progressive* magazine's "Nixon's Silent House of Hawks," prepared by Garrison Nelson. By the group's own admission, the 1970 effort was poorly coordinated, but the Washington, D.C., office of the BEM expressed satisfaction with its victories that year. In the second cycle, the group endorsed George McGovern and pledged $50,000 to defeat the "deadly dozen" hawks in Congress. "The Deadly Dozen are not necessarily the most pro-war Congressmen. To be selected each must have a definitely pro-war voting record and each must be facing an opponent who is anti-war and who, we believe, is strong enough to make the incumbent vulnerable."[41] The 1972 effort was more concerted but with the same results—three victories—so that over the course of two election cycles, the group had defeated six of its fifteen political targets.[42] Among the congressmen the group backed were Pete McCloskey (California), Eugene Gallegos (New Mexico), and Roger Boas (California). The BEM expenses for 1972 came to $30,660 in direct expenditures to candidates.[43]

The 1970 campaign also brought the executives a new political challenge that mustered the organization's resources in a political battle that has had long-lasting repercussions. As a result of its deep pockets, the group commissioned a series of sixty-second radio spots and attempted to purchase time to air them. A Washington, D.C., station, WTOP, refused to air the messages, at which point the BEM filed a "Fairness Doctrine" complaint with the Federal Communications Commission. The outcome on August 5, 1970, ruled that the radio station could legitimately refuse to sell one-minute segments of its "commercial" spot-announcement time, even though WTOP had previously sold spot announcements to political candidates during election campaigns, because, the commission maintained, BEM's concerns necessitated "more in-depth analysis than can be provided in a 10, 20, 30, or 60 second announcement."[44]

The organization also utilized political theater to make its point. John H. Whitaker, who chaired the Kansas City branch of the organization and owned a local cable company, hatched a plan to meet with executives at the Honeywell Corporation at their headquarters in Minneapolis. Whitaker wrote to Honeywell board chairman James Binger in February 1972, with the observation that Honeywell had begun to realize an increase in its computer business while it had decreases of 24 percent in its defense branch. Whitaker was concerned, "Since the Pentagon frequently asserts that it is attacking only 'military targets' in Vietnam I found it important to know the definition of a military target as stated in the Air Force manual [citing US Air Force ROTC manual of May 1961]." However, he discovered that:

> [M]ost of the victims of anti-personnel bombs are not killed rather they are maimed. . . . Products made by your company are destroying in a massive, indiscriminate, and impersonal way the entire social fabric of part of the world. In 1965, the Catholic Church declared in the Document of Vatican II: "Any act of war aimed indiscriminately at the destruction of entire cities or of extensive areas along with their population is a crime against God and man himself. It merits unequivocal and unhesitating condemnation." (Pastoral Constitution on the Church in the Modern World, n. 80.) I am sure you and your company do not bear this responsibility lightly. . . . As the executive responsible for computer system development and related hardware purchases, I would not consider Honeywell computers until the manufacture and distribution of this inhumane weaponry is ceased. I am going to encourage your Users Group to adopt a similar position by making them aware of the diversity of your interests.[45]

This letter earned him an interview at Binger's Minneapolis office. Whitaker brought with him several other people: Dick Fernandez, Richard Falk, and Fred Branfman. Fernandez was involved in Clergy and Laymen Concerned about Vietnam (CALCAV), which had in 1970 been involved in the planning of the Winter Soldier Investigation. Falk was a Princeton University professor of international relations who was already well known at that time. His recent work is perhaps also relevant—beginning in 2005, he chaired the Board of the Nuclear Age Peace Foundation, a direction that the BEM would take in the 1980s, when Bud Salk attempted to reactivate the organization. Branfman would not necessarily have been known by Binger at the time but is best known now as an antiwar activist who lived in Laos and was responsible for exposing the secret air war there.[46] The resulting press reports of the meeting were devastating for Honeywell. Whitaker claimed in correspondence to Binger after the press treatment that it had not been his intention to invite the one-sided response the meeting attained, though it is difficult to imagine how such a campaign and invited press attention could not have gone otherwise. Binger and Honeywell were driven to damage control, which resulted in a convoluted press release that, rather than point out that Whitaker and his colleagues had been mistaken about Honeywell's present defense production (which apparently they had been), instead offered a terse and flat justification for its military production capacity:

> We cannot agree with this reasoning. So long as a military or defense establishment of some sort is needed, and most Americans agree that one is needed, the ultimate decision as to types and quantities of weapons to be available and used must be the responsibility of the Department of Defense, monitored by the national administration and Congress as representatives of all the people.
>
> It is essential for the survival of our democracy that corporations carry out public policies declared by elected representatives of the people. . . .
>
> Honeywell has been on record for a number of years as wanting the war ended as quickly as possible. Honeywell people share the same human feelings and respect for life that our critics claim as their justification.
>
> Another idea expressed that we feel needs comment is that the war is somehow good for Honeywell's business. From any standpoint we would prefer to conduct business in a world of peace. War is wasteful. It uses tax dollars that could be better utilized to strengthen the economy and meet the needs of our society.
>
> It is apparent that the current wave of protest has as its principal emotional appeal the idea that certain weapons are more horrible than others and that those who make them are war criminals.
>
> There are no nice weapons. It is one of the tragedies of humanity that weapons exist at all, but the stern lesson of history is that those who cherish freedom must be prepared to fight for freedom.
>
> Anti-personnel weapons of the type most frequently criticized have the same purpose as hand grenades, conventional bombs or bullets. They were not developed for use against civilian population as has been charged. . . .
>
> We flatly reject the charge that manufacturing these weapons makes Honeywell people war criminals. This is a slanderous charge that is utterly devoid of merit.[47]

If Whitaker was not a pacifist, one might get the impression by his actions that he was.

While the motivations among the members may have varied, and the group's campaigns were equally diverse, the end results of the group's efforts are best understood in the context of business as usual, which echoed the Paine, Webber assessment and others discussed so far. Two months after the founding of the BEM, Bud Salk's November 9 speech in Chicago was introduced into the Congressional Record by Representative Robert W. Kastenmeier, a Wisconsin Democrat. As he had on the previous occasion before the chamber, Salk began from the claim that "the massive spending for the Vietnam war has been the most significant and unsettling economic factor in determining the priorities of the Federal Budget, and has been the central force in the destabilization and distortion of the American economy. . . . Allocations of American resources for the design, manufacture and the operation of armaments have risen 60 percent in just over two years, and have brought the military budget to a level where it represents the largest single sector of the American economy."[48] From Salk's standpoint as a mortgage banker, this meant that "aside from the virtual depletion of great society programs," the capital market was bearing the brunt of the financing of the war, resulting in a "capital shortage of severe proportions and the highest interest rates since the aftermath of World War I." As he proceeded to explain, the net result was private competition with the government for investment funds, so that in 1966 there was a "12 percent decline in physical volume of construction, even though the needs for virtually every kind of residential, commercial, industrial and public construction increased rapidly." Investors were finding entirely too many opportunities in the bond market to want to invest elsewhere. For Salk, priorities were inverted: "reliable estimates have pointed up that it would only take somewhere between $90 and $120 billion to eradicate all slums and provide decent housing in their place." Invoking Kennedy's and later Martin Luther King, Jr.'s, line on inevitable revolutions, Salk closed by saying: "By ignoring the national priorities at home . . . we plant the very seeds of destruction and revolution that we feel so dedicated to fighting abroad."[49]

These concerns were echoed by Louis B. Lundborg, chairman of the world's largest bank, Bank of America, who testified before the Senate Foreign Relations Committee in April 1970 on "Why Peace Would Be Good for Business." He was not officially affiliated with the BEM, but based on a report by his bank's Economic Department, which reads much like the Paine, Webber analysis, he told the Senate: "[The war in Vietnam] draws off resources that could be put to work towards solving imperative problems facing this nation at home. And despite the protestations of the new left to the contrary, the fact is that an end to the war would be good, not bad, for American business." In his analysis, Lundborg explained that "When we survey the very real needs in our economy in the areas of housing, urban transit, environmental pollution, etc., it is clearly evident that we do not need to create war-related demand for resources in order to maintain full employment." He offered figures: prior to the U.S. commitment to Vietnam, defense spending averaged $50 billion per year. Assuming this would have remained the case, the increase of $118 billion per year was slightly above the annual $112 billion in spending for residential construction. He also insisted that even if the conflict in Vietnam had been profitable for the country, he "would not support our role in the war."[50] War spending had been inflationary since 1965, he concluded, when expenditures for the conflict began to amplify the effects of near full employment.

Besides the board room of Bank of America, other executives also expressed concern. The director of IBM, Thomas J. Watson, Jr., stated that "If we continue, I believe we will soon reach a point where much of the damage will be irreparable." And New York's governor Nelson Rockefeller would call for a hasty conclusion to the conflict in order to avoid "greater disasters in the future."[51] This came at the very moment that the Senate Foreign Relations Committee rescinded the Gulf of Tonkin Resolution by an 81–10 margin and declared that Nixon was in violation of the Constitution.[52]

In short, aside from the growth of the military-industrial complex, a cross-section of the American business community opposed to the war had concerns about inflation, about the neglect of the War on Poverty in order to fund the war, and about Nixon's plan for a 10 percent increase in the income tax. They were not alone in their concerns: President Nixon and economists in his inner circle also observed the effects of the Vietnam War inflation on the trade deficit, as well as other related factors, according to a report by the Commission on International Trade and Investment Policy.[53] Throughout the 1960s, U.S. companies were moving funds abroad to avoid taxation, and depositors were moving funds overseas to find higher rates of return, because the Federal Reserve had imposed a ceiling on interest rates for depositors. There were other moves abroad, like gambling on exchange rates and financing takeovers, that drained the United States of currency. As the Bretton

Woods system required dollars be backed by gold, foreign countries started demanding American gold reserves as the dollar began to lose its value. By 1971, the United States had depleted one-third of its gold reserves, so Nixon decided to stop selling it. The American government in its ongoing expenses for the war was, therefore, also driving inflationary pressures in the bond market, which had ripple effects throughout the economy.[54]

The January 1968 Paine Webber Jackson & Curtis analysis discussed at the outset of this chapter bemoaned that "the escalation of the Vietnam conflict to its present level has created an enormous increase in defense demand" and that "this has been superimposed upon demand from both the private and public sectors of the economy, which—already—had stretched the nation's production facilities to the point where there was virtually no remaining reserve of economic resources." The report went on to suggest that "Funds needed for the war in Vietnam could be rechanneled to the war on poverty. Education, highways, housing—all would come in for higher government appropriations as a result of the end of the war in Vietnam. . . . A substantial reduction in total government spending seems doubtful." It then noted that the United States had developed a sizable balance-of-trade deficit against Britain that was equal to the "dollar flow from our commitment to Vietnam." An end to the war, then, would reduce this deficit and put the country in a better position to achieve a balance of payments.[55] From a later vantage point, it seems clear that the Vietnam War was not the sole cause of the economic problems beginning to confront the United States: these business leaders were in fact observing the decline of the Bretton Woods system. But at the time, the war seemed to be the primary culprit. Indeed, the death knell for the War on Poverty and the budget priorities for 1968 marked a decisive shift in government interest in a healthy demand side of the economy. The New Deal that laid the social foundation for the men of the BEM set as priorities social commitments that were evident in Johnson's War on Poverty but quite absent from the agenda to fight in Vietnam. The use of public funds to stimulate the economy and to assist the impoverished was accepted by these activists, and the inability both to fund the war and to fund social programs was not lost on them. Sargent Shriver, the Kennedy son-in-law who directed the Peace Corps and the War on Poverty, was told that his Community Action Program was to be defunded in order to increase the defense budget.[56]

The efforts of the BEM may even have played a role that was undoubtedly critical in the eventual withdrawal. A recent history of the Tet Offensive suggests that the business community's negative reaction to that event convinced Secretary of Defense (and Wall Street attorney) Clark Clifford of the need for an exit strategy.[57] In March 1968, President Johnson blamed Clifford for what he saw as poisoning his strategic discussion in his National Security team. Johnson's "Wise Men" had turned against the war by early 1968 because of the pervasive belief, according to Clifford, that "Vietnam was weakening us at home and in the rest of the world. And they were right."[58] Clifford's biographer suggests that this conclusion resulted from Clifford's intimate awareness of "what members of the business and legal establishment were thinking."[59] "These guys who have been with us and who have sustained us so far as we are sustained are no longer with us," as Clifford put it. "[M]ajor elements of the national constituency—the business community, the press, the churches, the professional groups, college presidents, students, and most of the intellectual community—have turned against this war."[60] Clifford, like many of these men, also reconsidered his moderate hawkish position after the Tet Offensive. Yet business pressure alone hardly brought Clifford around, as he would privately confide later to Henry Niles: "We have become the barbarians of the world. . . . I would put no limit at all on what Nixon would do."[61]

It is even possible that BEM's organizing fostered business organization later in the 1970s. Given his contacts in the American business community, it seems reasonable to associate Clark Clifford's connections with his appointment to the board of Business Roundtable in 1978 as a sector of American business began to recognize a need for coordinated lobbying.[62] Representative Paul McCloskey (R-California) told Erwin Salk years later that "Many times I have mentioned in a speech that it was really the business community that finally brought the tragedy of Vietnam to an end."[63] Henry Niles could report to the BEM membership in mid-1968 that "Responsible sources in Washington tell us that the growing opposition of the business community has been a vital factor in whatever progress toward peace there has been since the beginning of the year." It is also noteworthy that dissident intellectual Noam Chomsky reasoned at that time that only a shift in elite opinion would bring the war to a close, on the assumption that elite opinion shapes policy to begin with.[64] Moreover, George McGovern claimed to Henry Niles in 1972 that the "Business Executives Move for Vietnam Peace has played a vital role in the search for an end to our national folly in Vietnam. Perhaps the most important contribution has been the breadth you have brought to the anti-war effort."[65]

Momentum against the war among the businessmen had been building for some time, as Yale political scientists Bruce Russett and Elizabeth Hanson found when they published *Interest and Ideology* in 1975. They wanted to gauge the interests of American businessmen on U.S. foreign policy and a number of domestic issues. Utilizing an earlier study of American elites (in the media, organized labor, and business) conducted at Columbia University, Russett and Hanson asked the same questions again of a group of business vice presidents at Fortune 500 firms and another group of ranking officers at the five war colleges. The Yale sample consisted of more than 1,000 businessmen, almost all over the age of 40, and nearly half in their fifties. Nearly three-quarters of these men were veterans of the Second World War. Among the findings were that 61.5 percent of businessmen believed "trade, technical assistance, [and] economic interdependence" were the most important approach to world peace. This reply garnered six times more responses than any other answer. More than 57 percent of businessmen believed that the threat of communism abroad had decreased over the previous decade, and about the same percentage believed (though some of them with qualifications) that the United States had contributed to the escalation of the Cold War "by overreacting to Soviet moves or military developments." The business community was also divided over the cause of poverty being "due to cultural and psychological problems of the poor," with nearly 47 percent in disagreement and just over 53 percent in agreement. More than 52 percent also believed that it had been incorrect to commit ground troops to Vietnam, with an overwhelming 77.1 percent agreeing with the claim that the Vietnam War had been bad for the economy. And nearly 90 percent believed that the war had negative consequences for "American social and political institutions."[66] Coming in 1975, the sentiments could very well have represented hindsight, but given the arguments of the membership of the BEM nearly a decade before, certainly some of those surveyed had come to these conclusions much earlier.

In the final analysis then, what finally threatened the Cold War endeavor of Vietnam was business-as-usual but not necessarily the business of war. Congress responded, McCloskey and others suggest, not to democracy being in the streets but to businessmen concerned about the American economy. The business executives were latecomers to the antiwar movement, though the BEM's founders both had associations and activities peculiar to them that defined their corner of the movement.[67] The emergence of a business opposition to the conflict brought further pressure to bear on the leaders of the United States' aggression abroad. The antiwar segment of the business community saw in the Vietnam War a misallocation of state resources: the cost of borrowing to pay for the war was driving up interests rates for American businesses, infrastructure was being built abroad while neglected at home, and government support for American business was going to those sectors that supported the military rather than to industries that would produce profits and long-term growth. In short, the Vietnam War was bad for American business. That this outlook and its prescription came at a moment when larger structural forces in the global economy shocked the industrialized world and were setting the stage for a postwar readjustment during the 1970s could not have been foreseen.[68] These American businessmen also recognized that war was not necessarily good for the health of the state. Indeed, the work of the Business Executives Move for Vietnam Peace illustrates quite literally that the historical balance sheet of the Vietnam War's costs only ran further into the red.

Chapter 11

Entangled: Civil Rights in Corporate America Since 1964

Pamela Walker Laird

In 2014, more than twelve hundred firms vied for DiversityInc's "Top 50 Companies for Diversity" awards, highlighting the esteem "diversity" had attained in corporate America, fifty years after passage of the 1964 Civil Rights Act. The rigorous award application and review process grades companies based on criteria such as workforce and recruitment statistics, mechanisms for "Equitable Talent Development," evidence of "Leadership Commitment," and "Supplier Diversity."[1] In stark contrast to such institutionalized efforts to diversify corporate workforces and leadership, for decades after 1964, business leaders' responses to obligations to end workplace discrimination mixed uncertainty, tokenism, and resistance. Whether employers wished to fulfill or circumvent the law, they searched widely for clarifications and mechanisms to help them. They turned to state agencies, business publications and associations, and community leaders. Employers responded to those influences in widely disparate ways. Sometimes they resisted integration openly and sometimes covertly. At other times businesspeople led genuine progress beyond tokenism, and sometimes they merely complied with the law and public opinion. For instance, soon after the Equal Employment Opportunity Commission (EEOC) geared up in 1965, one businessman, intent on compliance, rather crudely charged his managers: "You had better call the Urban League or some colored preachers and tell them to send you some colored. We don't want any-body to think we are discriminating."[2]

How can we reach back across the half century separating these snap-shots to understand the history of corporate integration? Not all gloom then or all light now, workplace practices and expectations have changed pro-foundly but not along a readily tracked trajectory; nor are the historical factors influencing those changes easily traced. Analysts' reasonable desires to unravel the web of civil rights history in corporations have often resulted in straightforward but limited narratives. Such approaches follow what Adam Fairclough has called historians' "fondness for neat chains of cause and effect" regarding civil rights in general, missing the history's complexi-ties.[3] Instead, I propose a systemic approach for examining the interactive, iterative processes that continue to evolve and shape the workplace. Rather than "neat chains," I imagine an intricate web of causal threads acting on and reacting to one another.

The threads of civil rights history include activism, cultural and social changes, laws, and enforcement in a web that grew more tangled as those factors interacted in and among institutions. For instance, as legal historian Robert Gordon has argued, "law and society are inextricably mixed," and "accounting for major social change" requires "understanding the constitu-tive role of law in social relationships."[4] Likewise, Gerald N. Rosenberg rea-soned that laws and their enforcement are products of cultural and political contexts. They can both signal reformist trends and encourage changes in their jurisdictions, but they cannot do either independently of political and cultural conditions.[5] Business practices, too, are both products and produc-ers of cultural and political changes. Understanding these complex interac-tions requires moving past debates about prime movers to appreciate the multiple and deep turbulences that energized or, often, dampened reform. A systemic approach appreciates the fullness of the complex web of civil rights history and does not begin by untangling that web's threads. Instead, it considers the tensions and synergies among social and cultural forces, law enforcement, and business practices, and it does not presume that any single factor outweighed any other.[6]

In his 2000 historiographical review, Charles Eagles called for "the exercise of greater historical imagination" in studying civil rights history. Civil rights historians have, he noted, "generally taken an asymmetrical approach," tend-ing "to emphasize one side of the struggle, the movement side." Their "implicit disagreement[s]" have included periodization and "different emphases" on the roles and effects of institutional and individual actors. Other disagreements have "stressed the efficacy of different strategies and tactics." Similarly, Fairclough pointed to dozens of instances in which civil rights scholars used the same evidence to make opposite arguments about blame or credit, depending on their perspectives and proclivities. He, too, critiqued "purely local" studies that "can lead to insularity and incoherence" if they neglect "state, regional, and national context [that] intersected in complex ways."[7]

Because business historians' perspectives encompass what happens in firms and the broad contexts for those actions, we are well situated to exercise Eagles's "greater historical imagination." Moreover, we routinely look to business and popular presses and trade organizations, where business leaders and their advisors left traces of their concerns and actions. These traces also reveal shifts in discourse and culture that yield a complex picture of the interactions of activism, law, corporate leadership, and cultural evolution. All these variables contributed to civil rights history in corporate workplaces—none sufficient alone, but each necessary to the outcome, if in different proportions at different stages. Neither consensus nor a smooth trajectory of progress or resistance to civil rights law and enforcement emerges. Instead, the history reveals business leaders struggling to understand and respond to changing legal and cultural environments according to their various lights.

Corporations and Integration

By the 1960s, large American corporations had developed tools to integrate outsiders through decades of building elaborate personnel systems to manage the recruiting, hiring, training, promotion, and firing of hundreds of employees.[8] Professional gatekeepers aimed to seek out and train qualified employees and then promote the worthy. Whether called human relations, personnel, or, now, human resources (HR) departments, these units oversaw practices that business leaders hoped were meritocratic. Their hopes invariably exceeded the realities, but the diffusion of so-called rationalized personnel processes blinded executives and managers alike to their flaws. These employment practices substantially improved corporate opportunities for white ethnic males in the first two decades after the Second World War, but they did not scratch the surface of discrimination against men of color and all women.[9]

Beliefs that their firms were meritocratic satisfied intense ideological longings among business leaders, as they and their political and professional organizations embraced the Cold War stance that American capitalism and democracy were efficient, productive, and virtuous. As an influential social science study of business leaders explained in 1955, the "American credo" featured the principle "that the best man should get the job." Phrases like the "worth of the individual," "free competition," and "equality of opportunity" vigorously expressed "values and principles basic to the traditional political and economic faith of most Americans," especially businessmen.[10] Yet, businessmen's beliefs about who had merit reflected deep prejudices that typically excluded women and African American men from ostensibly meritocratic competitions. Businessmen applied their stereotypes in all sincerity to explain why people who did not resemble them had no "potential."[11] Thus, despite their illusions of meritocracy, business leaders found themselves thrust into the civil rights maelstrom of the 1960s as targets of activism and changing legal standards. Flagrant workplace discrimination motivated civil rights advocates who, in the streets and in legislative halls, raised awareness of how constraining opportunity contradicted declared national values. Under the pressures of urban riots and political forces from all directions, business leaders struggled to maintain control of their workplaces, cultural authority, and profits, as threats, changing norms, and new expectations reverberated around them.

Struggling with Integration

Until the 1960s, the only significant legal sanctions against discrimination came from local, state, and federal Fair Employment Practices Committees (FEPC) that targeted government agencies and firms seeking or holding government contracts. Advocates argued at every level of government that tax dollars should not go to firms violating "American principles" of equal opportunity. On June 25, 1941, for instance, President Franklin Roosevelt issued his momentous Executive Order 8802 and established the federal FEPC. That FEPC's limited successes through the war years, although curtailed thereafter, pointed to the potential for progress through employment regulation.[12]

Because of firms' experiences with FEPC pressures and executive orders, reinforced by internal efforts to build meritocracies, by the mid-1960s, most U.S. corporations had formal structures and practices for bringing in recruits, and many had experience complying with antidiscrimination regulations.[13] That is not to say, however, that most corporations embraced integration or that corporate decisionmakers acted alike. Some business leaders accepted integration as the "right thing to do," in keeping with Cold War American values, while others were prepared to tolerate integration to reduce unions' power and the strength of the seniority system. For example, the National Association of Manufacturers (NAM), well known for its generally conservative activism on employers' behalf, officially supported racial and gender fair employment as early as 1941. Motivated by anti-union right-to-work principles, meritocratic ideals, and aversion to government regulations, the mid-century NAM consistently supported voluntary nondiscriminatory practices. According to a NAM senior vice president speaking to a largely African American audience in 1954, the nation and every individual in it benefited from universal "freedom of opportunity" that matched abilities with jobs. Through the 1950s, the NAM urged member firms to abide by state fair employment regulations, in part to avoid provoking national regulations.[14]

Still, many business leaders continued to resist changing their firms' ways, often denying wrongdoing until new pressures emerged. Thus, even as forces inside and outside business escalated into the 1960s to urge civil rights progress, prospects for reform appeared bleak. Business leaders' resistance included aggressive pressures during framing of the 1964 Civil Rights Act. Northern and Southern corporations lobbied intensively to ensure that the Act's EEOC "would not have either decision-making power or enforcement power," according to Michael Gottesman, a labor lawyer actively involved in the negotiations. The resulting legislation was deliberately unclear about what violated it, and that made assessment and enforcement frustratingly difficult.[15]

Although business and political leaders thought they could keep negotiations between themselves as elites, actors from other strands in the civil rights web thought otherwise. Civil rights leaders, too, were caught off guard when urban race riots from 1963 through 1968 added urgency to policy deliberations. Among other actions, President Lyndon Johnson established the National Alliance of Businessmen in 1968 explicitly as a response to civil unrest. He instructed members to recruit, train, and retain workers from the "hardcore" unemployed. As the Alliance's first report explained, "Businessmen were suddenly asked to start hiring persons they wouldn't have let past the plant gate a few years ago."[16] Riots in more than 160 cities raised public fears and accelerated the process by which many businessmen accepted responsibility for their failures to integrate. Rochester, New York, for instance, suffered millions of dollars in damage from 1964 riots that unnerved leaders at Xerox and Eastman Kodak Company, embarrassing them nationally and locally as the area's primary employers. Activists had long sought cooperation from the firms with little success. After the riots, civil rights advocates were able to negotiate support for improved employment conditions and business development for African Americans.[17]

Cultural biases wove another thread through the civil rights web. Stereotypes about who belonged in what positions and how they should behave bolstered corporate employers' resistance to grievances from marginalized employees. For instance, self-described "corporate feminist" Lois Kathryn Herr opens *Women, Power, and AT&T: Winning Rights in the Workplace* with her surprise that Bell Labs managers in the 1960s objected to women's wearing pantsuits. A short tunic worn as a miniskirted dress was fine, but wearing the slacks that came with it violated rules in a workplace where science and rationality were supposed to reign. More serious gendered policies at AT&T affected salaries, benefits, and opportunities.[18] Even more egregious were the cultural expectations that once hardwired flight attendants' apparel, ages, sizes, marital status, and attractiveness into their job requirements. Kathleen M. Barry's *Femininity in Flight* details airlines' determination to maintain the rules that ensured women were, as one executive put it, "young, attractive, and unencumbered." Already mobilized and active through their unions, uniformed flight attendants were literally first in line when the EEOC started receiving complaints in 1965. Both these and later petitioners learned, however, as Barry explains, "how much more than a formal change in law it took to fight the entrenched patterns of sex discrimination in American workplaces."[19] Nonetheless, airline executives' traditional expectations for flight attendants became unacceptable legally and culturally in less than a decade. In the web of civil rights history, cultural change and legal change worked symbiotically. Civil rights laws reflected and reinforced changes already occurring in the cultures in which corporate managers and their employees lived.

Enforcement as Education

Commissioners, employers, unions, and all levels of employees wrestled with Title VII of the 1964 Civil Rights Act, which prohibited workplace discrimination, as historians have described well.[20] Yet, if this law had been the only force at work, employment integration would have made little progress. Initially the law's definition of antidiscrimination compliance and its enforcement mechanisms were unclear. Because of the EEOC's initial limitations, uncertainty and impotence dominated its first decade. With no enforcement powers of its own before the Equal Employment Opportunity Act of 1972 took effect, the EEOC could not sue, nor could it unilaterally challenge the practices of government agencies or government contractors. This under-funded and underpowered "toothless tiger," as civil rights advocates often called it, investigated thousands of complaints and provided legal assistance to complainants, including amicus curiae briefs and strategic guidance. Not surprisingly, workplace integration proceeded slowly. Retrospective assess-ments of the first five years typically gave the EEOC and its founding legisla-tion credit for no more than "shaping employment discrimination law" and educating "the public."[21]

Nonetheless, given the synergetic nature of interactions among policy, culture, and business practices, this education process was no small achieve-ment. The EEOC's educational efforts inspired activism and protests that fueled civil rights reform and compliance. As Laura Beth Nielson explained regarding workplace harassment, the "law shapes what remedies [people] be-lieve are possible and plausible." That is, awareness of the possibilities for redress "affects not only how people think about invoking the law or the gen-eral utility of law but also how people interpret events in their everyday lives."[22] Just as reports of the Emancipation Proclamation had spread like wildfire through America's enslaved population, the 1964 Civil Rights Act kindled actions among people—black and white, female and male—who needed no law to convince them of the merits of civil rights. They just needed to believe the law could and would help them. As Martin Luther King, Jr., had said about the impact of *Brown v. Board of Education* in bringing "hope to millions of disinherited Negroes who had formerly dared only to dream of freedom," the 1964 Civil Rights Act, subsequent revisions, and court deci-sions provided hope. And hope inspired action.[23]

Thus, laws can inspire activism as much as they can spring from activ-ism. Betty Friedan, a founder of the National Organization for Women in 1966, later affirmed that Title VII "ignited the organization of the women's movement" even though they came to realize that Title VII was "never meant to be enforced" on behalf of women.[24] Sex had entered the list of Title VII protected categories late in congressional proceedings, and the EEOC only took on this form of discrimination after considerable pressure from women to do so. Much later, high-profile sexual harassment cases, such as Anita Hill's in 1991, prompted EEOC complaints and, often, follow-up litigation.[25]

All the while, to use a phrase from the era, the activity and public debate raised people's consciousness. African American workers in Southern paper and textile companies exemplified the effects of the changing legal environment on civil rights activism, as historian Timothy J. Minchin has shown. After endless frustrations before 1964, Title VII provided new "means to challenge segregation." Thus, "in the textile industry black workers mobilized after 1964 to make the mandate of the act a reality." And they did so with "confidence and determination" through class action lawsuits, as did workers in other industries. Forced to testify under oath, managers admitted their failures to act in good faith to match their public statements about enforcing Title VII.[26] Powerful threads in the web of integration's history grew from people's new sense of justification and eagerness to pursue legal avenues that legislation and the federal courts made possible. Reformist activism and legal reforms also compelled those who objected to make explicit their opposition to equal opportunity and human rights as they defended their "way of life." This backlash, too, formed an important part of the civil rights web, raising awareness and action on every side of the issues.

Such law-inspired activism began slowly, and civil rights historian Hugh Davis Graham has contrasted "the high public visibility of the courts' school desegregation cases, [with] the judicial evolution of equal employment law [that] remained obscure" until 1971. That year, the U.S. Supreme Court's unanimous decision in *Griggs v. Duke Power Co.* "burst like a bombshell," in Graham's words. The Court accepted arguments, buttressed by EEOC briefs and a new set of guidelines, to judge employers based on the "disparate impact" of employment practices on candidates rather than plaintiffs' having to prove employers' intent to discriminate. This change mattered because proving intent to harm is vastly more difficult than demonstrating harm from employment practices that, for instance, filter out candidates using criteria irrelevant to job performance. This momentous decision overrode congressional compromises in the 1964 legislation and vastly improved plaintiffs' chances.[27] The business press snapped to attention, alerting its constituencies that *Griggs* required that employment tests "measure the person for the job and not the person in the abstract," as Chief Justice Warren Burger wrote. *Industrial Management*, for example, asked its readers "Have you looked into the employment and promotional tests being used in your company?" The *American Business Law Journal* warned that the decision "comprehensively affects all business hiring." It also worried that this decision and ensuing EEOC actions would set business and government "at loggerheads," making unlikely "any mutual cooperation between business and government . . . on this issue." Its punch line: "*Caveat* Employer." *Industrial Relations* explained that this and other recent decisions had made "the burden for the [employer] defendant . . . very heavy."[28]

Any corporate leaders still slumbering after *Griggs*, awoke in January 1973 with the widely publicized, multimillion dollar watershed consent decree that the EEOC signed with AT&T, then the world's largest private employer. By 1970, AT&T's female and African American male employees had filed more complaints with the EEOC than had the employees of any other firm. The EEOC sought and gained the support of the Federal Communications Commission, which held decisive regulatory powers over the firm and required equal employment opportunity practices. Because the Federal Communications Commission's role in persuading AT&T to settle was not widely known, however, the giant company seemed to have fallen victim to the EEOC.[29] It seemed reasonable to assume, therefore, that any other firm could succumb.

Until this settlement, many corporate executives had, like those at AT&T, engaged in integration efforts ranging from cosmetic to well intended, but few had invested seriously in Title VII compliance. Later in 1973, the EEOC filed a successful complaint against General Electric, which, despite that company's grand rhetoric about race and sex integration, was severely noncompliant on the ground. Compliance was becoming something to take seriously. As the *Harvard Business Review* explained in 1974, "At first EEO was perceived as a social betterment program. But now the penalties imposed . . . are seen as posing a severe financial threat."[30]

Challenging Exclusionary Discrimination in Corporations

By the early 1970s, corporate managers clearly had fallen into the gap between their patriotic notions of equal opportunity, their public pronouncements about civil rights, and their failures to examine their own firms' actions. Few had invested adequate leadership and resources in changes that could protect them from legal action after the 1971 *Griggs* decision. A 1973 Conference Board guidebook on civil rights compliance noted the surprise of Northern business leaders when they learned they were discriminating according to federal standards. When one such executive discovered the law "meant us," and not just Southern employers, he also admitted that high-profile cases against major firms had convinced him it was not just the "other guy" who was guilty of violating both meritocracy and the law.[31] Thus, in the first of three reports to its members on equal opportunity, the Conference Board quoted a firm's general counsel threatening indifferent middle managers: "If *you* do not expect to comply with all the nondiscrimination laws, consider this to be fair warning. You will be fired." The Conference Board reported as typical one executive's sudden realization that noncompliance was widespread. He responded with alarm to well-publicized enforcement in an unnerving "number of court cases involving prominent national companies."[32] Those shocks drew business leaders' attention to compliance guidelines and generated urgency to tackle the task. Nationwide, corporate spokespersons almost always expressed surprise and dismay as they claimed good intentions but admitted to inadequate efforts.

It is, of course, impossible to generalize across thousands of business leaders and their range of attitudes. Differences across corporations and within them, as well as across time and location, confound all efforts to generalize about whether "business" opposed or supported integration. While some business leaders held to regressive views, most acknowledged the need to adapt to the changing legal and cultural environment. One executive in 1966, for instance, bemoaned that "it looks like times are changing. . . . It looks like I'm going to have to hire some Negroes and learn how to manage them."[33] Other executives and personnel managers were already engaged to varying degrees in equal opportunity efforts and welcomed the legal backing. Most found themselves caught between eloquent statements and inadequate commitment to action. For instance, in 1968, AT&T president Ben S. Gilmer had written in *Business Horizons* that "business has to lead" in solving "urban problems," because it had the jobs necessary to do it. Gilmer expressed his commitment to work with other business leaders in President Johnson's National Alliance of Businessmen to hire the "hardcore" unemployed. The company's modern personnel "training facilities," Gilmer explained, "are adaptable for training the underskilled and unemployed." He declared, "Effective action cannot wait."[34] Yet only when the EEOC brought governmental action against Gilmer's firm and other high-profile violators did the full potential of existing corporate personnel systems turn to recruiting, hiring, and training women and underrepresented minorities.

Historian Jennifer Delton and sociologist Frank Dobbin have effectively argued that some people in corporations, especially human resource professionals, had worked for decades to increase objectivity in personnel procedures and, sometimes, thereby to reduce racial discrimination. Dobbin credited the "pressures for change" as having come "from within industry" rather than as responses to external pressures, such as laws, race riots, and women's politically motivated consumer choices. Although Dobbin acknowledged that presidential executive orders and civil rights laws compelled compliance, in taking his "weak state" position, he, like some businessmen then, argued that government policy merely set requirements in motion, with no influence thereafter.[35] Certainly, industry had to learn how to integrate on its own, but that is the point: it had to do it under the new standards as embodied in new laws, enforced by the EEOC and the courts, and buttressed by changing public opinion. Moreover, decades of lawsuits and hundreds of thousands of EEOC complaints indicate that many firms required—and still require—more than friendly nudges. The business press made clear that public embarrassment and multimillion-dollar lawsuits mattered. As the *Personnel & Guidance Journal* exclaimed in 1976, *Griggs* had, five years before, "set off a near panic among some personnel officers."[36] Corporate leaders always argued for their preference for "voluntarism," but their firms' actions and their own distress at enforcement realities in the 1970s belie any claims that they would have made the necessary investments if left to their own devices. Again, the point is not that business leaders presented a united front against civil rights regulation, but rather that they proceeded along myriad paths away from segregation, always keeping a watchful eye on legal liabilities.

Thus, business leaders increasingly accepted the legal burden of integration. The Conference Board in 1973 indicated that between 1968 and 1972, companies first experienced "virtually no impact" from nondiscrimination regulations, then realized that they were not in compliance, and then moved "just as rapidly as possible—and hope we don't get hit by too many class-action lawsuits in the meantime," as one executive put it. During that "meantime," in August 1973, the EEOC used its new reach to sue Xerox and two other firms, and the next month it charged four major firms and several unions with job discrimination in what the *New York Times* called "the most extensive concerted action of its eight-year history." The EEOC also made clear it would soon charge additional companies in its newly aggressive campaign to achieve out-of-court settlements similar to that with AT&T.[37]

Business leaders noticed. For example, a Continental Can supervisor testified later in 1973 that management "had a lot of conversations about the general subject" of civil rights litigation.[38] In November 1975, *Business Week* reviewed the changing status of women in business. Of "five developments" that explained the modest but accelerating progress, they called the AT&T settlement "the single strongest influence on corporate employment practices regarding women." The second factor was the U.S. Labor Department's 1972 order mandating that government contractors hire and promote women. Factor three referred to the 22,110 EEOC complaints women filed during the first half of 1973, almost seven times the number of complaints filed in all of 1970 and double the number filed in 1972; AT&T's settlement had clearly inspired the 1973 flood. Factor four recognized the broader cultural context for all other factors, namely "Radical changes in social attitudes." The final factor simply summed up: "Companies responded to all of these events." Recognizing the relevance of firm size, *Business Week* concluded that, because "the EEOC seldom squanders its limited funds on small companies," change in large corporations held the most hope for women.[39] The same web of interacting forces held sway for the conditions of minority populations in corporations.

Almost four years later, in 1979, *Business Week* advised on "Coping with employee lawsuits." It quoted a senior vice president for personnel who warned, "We have an employee population that is more aware of its rights than it has ever been before." A company's best protection against discrimination or other complaints, he continued, is to be "committed to personnel development," by which "the likelihood of lawsuits decreases tremendously." Dozens of interviews with business leaders indicated that corporate "staff officers are imposing on their companies new policies to stave off such litigation—or at least to put the company in a better position to defend itself if suits do come." The vice president quoted above advised, "Training managers to deal properly with employees and to treat them as human beings is the best preventive medicine." *Business Week* linked enforcement to changing corporate practices by concluding that "companies with long-established personnel policies are taking steps to make sure that they are followed."[40] Moreover, companies increasingly recognized they should do so for practical and cultural reasons.

Harassment has always manifested the worst possible attitudes toward employees outside a workplace norm. What legal scholar Catharine MacKinnon explained about sexual harassment in 1979 also applies to racial harassment, namely, that harassment makes up "one dynamic which reinforces and expresses women's traditional and inferior role in the labor force." Only in the late 1970s did these long-tolerated weapons for defending insiders' domains against outsiders become subject to law. In 1980, *Per-*

sonnel Administrator warned that "activities that were once viewed as 'harmless'" were fueling successful high-profile claims against employers and individual supervisors under Title VII. In 1986, the Supreme Court ruled unanimously in *Meritor Savings Bank v. Vinson*, its first sexual harassment decision, that both quid pro quo and hostile environment harassments violated Title VII. Such behaviors provided complainants, prosecutors, state agencies, and the courts with clearly actionable cases. The Supreme Court held up, albeit in a limited potency, workers' right to presume their employers were obligated to maintain a nonhostile social environment.[41] The Supreme Court set a high standard of proof for employer responsibility (awareness and implicit ratification of employee actions), but it did not dismiss the possibility of liability.

Only after harassment became highly visible as a species of actionable misdeeds did HR managers and top executives get ahead of the enforcement curve to protect their firms from legal challenges. As *Personnel Administrator* put it in 1980, "it is no longer amusing to be slapped with a lawsuit and lose."[42] *Personnel Journal* cited a 1987 Bureau of National Affairs survey in which 77 percent of responding firms with sexual harassment policies had instituted them to meet EEOC requirements. Whereas 2 percent indicated their policies were designed to "aid employees," 62 percent sought protection from "legal liability." Accepting the 2 percent response as genuine, that sixty-point spread speaks volumes about the importance of legal recourse in fueling HR managers' mandate for reform.[43] "Hostile environment" became an actionable workplace condition, and only then did the evolution of workplace cultures accelerate. As *Personnel Administrator* explained, the cultures were "passing" that had long accepted "sexually tinged" jokes as everyday fare.[44] In sum, workplace and public values regarding harassment evolved reciprocally with required behavioral changes. Mutually reinforcing progress in a web of cultural, social, and legal expectations has thus reduced, if not eliminated, harassment's long-tolerated capacity to humiliate and insult.

Backlash and Momentum

Political backlash against state-based civil rights implementation grew through the 1970s.[45] A 1977 *New York Times*/CBS News poll showed that most Americans still strongly condemned "any job discrimination" based on race or sex and supported laws to prevent it. Yet most respondents objected to "any plan to give these groups a special advantage in hiring to make up for past discrimination." That is, they objected to affirmative actions by which state authorities required employers to offer opportunities to disadvantaged people.[46] As the nation's deregulatory trend accelerated, civil rights enforcement presented a vulnerable target, and "reverse discrimination" became a battle cry. The 1978 landmark Supreme Court decision in *Regents of the University of California v. Bakke* was only the most visible of state and federal court cases that limited affirmative action for addressing the ongoing effects of previous discrimination. Thus, only five years after the EEOC/AT&T settlement, law-based pressures for workplace desegregation—especially for affirmative action—had begun losing legal and popular support. Business leaders and their advocates increasingly claimed they had acted responsibly and that reasonable and adequate measures were in place to prevent discriminatory exclusion.[47]

Nonetheless, as federal enforcement retreated in the 1980s, corporations confounded expectations, hewing instead to the tangled nature of civil rights history. In 1982, Ronald Reagan appointed Clarence Thomas as EEOC chair. Within two years, Thomas proclaimed that reviewing the EEOC's guidelines was "the No. 1 item on my agenda." He sought to reduce "rigidity" in enforcement, reduce employers' costs, and reduce the use of statistics in assessing disparities, what Chief Justice Burger had called the measure of "disparate impact."[48] By 1989, the Reagan Supreme Court had handed down five decisions that reduced federal support for workplace affirmative action and for set-aside programs to award government contracts to underrepresented groups. The *New York Times* warned that "employers might feel free to abandon affirmative action plans."[49] Yet *Business Week* discovered that companies were "nearly unanimous in saying that their day-to-day personnel practices won't change. . . . The court has not changed one comma of the standards in place for private-sector affirmative action programs."[50] The next year, *Employment Relations Today* affirmed that "employers wishing to continue to act affirmatively should take heart," for the Court had not erected "insurmountable barriers" as long as employers avoided reverse discrimination.[51]

How could the business and political climate of the 1980s, which glorified "shareholder value" and resisted regulations, not only continue but accelerate corporate practices that promoted affirmative action? In short, corporations, like universities, had discovered the benefits of what they had come to call "diversity." They had initially moved toward a diverse workforce to reduce threats of lawsuits and complaints to government agencies as well as to minimize negative public opinion. The Conference Board, for instance, warned members at the start of the decade that continuing "to express or act upon *their earlier* [discriminatory] *views*" would prove "costly . . . in terms of poor public relations, backpay awards, or the loss of government contracts" as well as class action suits. Those pressures had fostered reforms, and Kenneth A. Randall, the Conference Board's president, worried that removing government regulations altogether would slow corporate advances in equal opportunity. He observed, though, that "the change process has become so intertwined within the normal operating procedures of major organizations that it is probably irreversible."[52] Instituting practices that could make them "court-proof," as the title of a 1974 *Harvard Business Review* article had put it, had built momentum into corporate integration, and equal opportunity's standing actually grew during the 1980s. Many managers came to accept that previously excluded people *could* be capable employees. Attrition also helped when younger managers stepped into decision-making positions.[53] By the time the federal government reduced its demands for compliance, equal employment opportunity systems and values were in place, if not entirely in force. In addition to making their firms "court-proof," corporate managers had to protect their firms' public reputations from damage due to violating new cultural norms.

Preexisting HR trends in business schools and personnel journals, mainstream cultural attitudes toward equal opportunity, and the force of law combined to generate a new workplace ethos for positions below upper-management levels. A sense grew among business leaders that "fair employment is good business."[54] The Conference Board's 1980 report on "nondiscrimination in employment" explained that during the 1970s, many firms came to appreciate that "overlooking huge pools of talented, willing and productive people" had wasted "valuable human resources."[55] Nonetheless, appreciation of how integration might advance businesses' goals did not become mainstream until later in the 1980s, when HR investments in integration moved beyond public relations and half-hearted compliance-oriented efforts.

Then, in the late 1980s, integration morphed into a business tool. Analysts, such as the conservative Hudson Institute in 1987, increasingly warned business leaders they would soon have to assimilate women and other outsiders, not because of legal compliance but because of demographic changes that necessitated workforce diversity.[56] A few years later, the *Harvard Business Review* published a paradigm-changing article, "From Affirmative

Action to Affirming Diversity." R. Roosevelt Thomas, Jr., argued that affirmative action was no longer useful. Moreover, it did not appeal to the nation's pretensions as the land of equal opportunity and meritocracy, he declared. Affirmative action had served the nation well as "an artificial, transitional intervention" to introduce outsiders to corporate America, but business leaders needed to "develop our capacity to accept, incorporate, and empower the diverse human talents of the most diverse nation on earth." The nation and its firms could only succeed in the global economy if they developed everyone's potential.[57]

This gospel of diversity spread rapidly throughout business literature and business schools. Its advocates promised benefits, including expanded clientele bases, wider and more varied markets, energized innovation, and improved relationships with varied communities.[58] Firms' leaders increasingly saw a diverse workforce "as a competitive issue," according to National Black MBA Association president Barbara L. Thomas in 2005.[59] Thus, despite diminished legal pressures, corporate discourse absorbed a version of civil rights in the name of diversity as a positive value—mainstream, if not universal. For instance, in a 1996 response to a *Harvard Business Review* article urging "a new paradigm for managing diversity," T. J. Rodgers, founder, president, and CEO of California's Cypress Semiconductor, wrote that "we cherish our diversity." He objected strongly, however, to what he called "a religious belief" in deliberate mechanisms motivated by law or good intentions to achieve workforce diversity. Instead, it was "obvious: businesses that are well run will automatically achieve the appropriate level *of* and method *for* achieving diversity; and, furthermore, they will create a healthy form of diversity." The *"self-interest of the company,"* Rodgers concluded, "not . . . some supposedly just and proper program" should guide decisions. After all, "free-market capitalism is the positive moral force that causes companies to make the right decisions about diversity, not vice versa."[60] Clearly this corporate leader saw himself as an agent of civil rights progress, but not as someone who merely submitted to do-gooders or state enforcers. Nonetheless, he had adopted a language by 1996 that would have been alien before enforced compliance had impinged on corporate behaviors.

Conclusion: Limits of the Law

America's Cold War provided the political and cultural contexts for expanding citizens' civil rights in the name of principles that reformers tied to claims of superiority over communism. When the Cold War ended, however, some believed the United States no longer needed to improve upon or defend its moral standing. Accordingly, the federal executive branch and courts reduced their support for civil rights advances. Nonetheless, in most corporate workplaces by the 1980s, practices and presumptions about integration that had once required legal enforcement had become sufficiently embedded to continue, although under a new name—diversity. The twenty-first century business press is awash with advice about achieving this aim, often coupled with cautions about avoiding reverse discrimination charges. For instance, in 2007, *Metropolitan Corporate Counsel*, which publishes legal and regulatory guidance for corporations, offered "practical tips on how to increase your organization's focus on diversity without engaging in blatant reverse discrimination in violation of Title VII." It noted the eagerness of firms to "increase diversity" and the irony that Title VII "imposes obstacles to creating opportunities" for the very groups it was originally "designed" to benefit.[61] "Diversity" has become the back door for advancing integration; it was not the front door through which civil rights advocates had intended to march.

Successes since 1964 in reducing "push," or exclusionary, discrimination have been significant.[62] As corporate leaders proclaimed allegiance to "American" principles of equal opportunity, they also reminded managers and employees that integration was the law and that violators—firms and individuals—faced costly consequences. During turbulent years filled with Cold War rhetoric and civil rights activism, tangled interactions of cultural, social, and legal factors generated new standards for behavior, including presumptions of workplace civility. Prejudices are not subject to the law, but acting on prejudices is. A legal scholar who had served on the early EEOC explained in 1972 that "Discrimination is activity, not a state of mind."[63] Writing from ground level in 1979, *Personnel Journal* advised personnel managers "that attitudes will change to conform with behaviors and not the reverse."[64]

Legal and cultural pressures reduced push discrimination substantially, functioning in mutually reinforcing synergies inside and outside corporations. By the time the political pendulum swung away from aggressively promoting integration through compliance, a form of integration—"diversity"—had become part of mainstream business policies, if not universally or effectively implemented. Yet there remains an essential role for legal pressures, and EEOC complaints averaged more than 97,000 annually during 2009–13.[65]

Managers in large organizations cannot escape the antiharassment training that protects their employers. Likewise, employees involved with hiring must undergo "diversity training," lest their employers be subject to grievances. The threat of legal action against push discrimination constantly looms over corporate managers.

In contrast, "pull" discrimination—the failure to draw outsiders into opportunities—remains outside the reach of U.S. law.[66] Without powers to compel affirmative action, the state can only encourage mechanisms that might spread opportunities to "outsiders," such as the mentoring and networking programs that characterize diversity-related efforts. Yet no one can force people to participate sincerely in them. Thus, a half century of civil rights enforcement has had very different consequences for push and pull discrimination. In 2014, women constituted 45 percent of the workforce in S&P 500 companies and 61.9 percent of mid- and senior-level management occupations. Reducing exclusionary practices has made this possible. Yet in 2014, women held only 19.2 percent of these firms' board seats and 4.6 percent of CEO positions.[67] Social factors still determine access to the tops of corporate ladders, and these will only respond to cultural evolution, not legal action.

This analysis provides one window into the intricate tangle of causes and effects within the web of civil rights history—past and present. We best examine that history, not by untangling its many threads, but by tracking the interactions of the threads as parts of the whole. The results, to be sure, will yield narratives no less complicated and contested than lived experiences.

Notes

Introduction

1. Jerry Z. Muller, "Capitalism and Inequality: What the Right and the Left Get Wrong," *Foreign Affairs* 92 (March–April 2013): 1–21. For assistance, inspiration, and advice in the preparation of this essay, I am grateful to my coeditor, Kim-Phillips Fein, who prepared the first draft, commented on multiple revisions, and provided invaluable counsel via email and telephone. For help with specific issues, thank to Elizabeth Blackmar, William R. Childs, Peter Conti-Brown, Walter A. Friedman, Louis Hyman, Nancy R. John, Kenneth Lipartito, Robert Lockhart, Noam Maggor, Elizabeth Tandy Shermer, Jason Scott Smith, and Mark R. Wilson.

2. Hagley Library collections that are of special relevance to the history of business and politics in the twentieth-century United States include the organizational records of the National Association of Manufacturers and the U.S. Chamber of Commerce and the personal papers of J. Howard Pew and Philip Reed.

3. In addition to the books and articles surveyed below, several recent collections explore the relationship between business and politics in the American past. These include Steve Fraser and Gary Gerstle, *Ruling America: A History of Wealth and Power in a Democracy* (Cambridge, Mass.: Harvard University Press, 2005); Richard R. John, ed., *Ruling Passions: Political Economy in Nineteenth-Century America* (University Park: Pennsylvania State University Press, 2006); Kim Phillips-Fein and Julian Zelizer, ed., *What's Good for Business: Business and Politics Since World War II* (New York: Oxford University Press, 2012); Michael Zakim and Gary Kornblith, ed., *Capitalism Takes Command: The Social Transformation of Nineteenth-Century America* (Chicago: University of Chicago Press, 2012). The present collection differs from these volumes in three respects: first, it takes the entire twentieth century as a unit of analysis—as distinct from the full sweep of American history, the nineteenth century, or the post–Second World War era; second, it brings into a single dialogue the relevant literature in political history, business history, political science, and historical sociology; and, third, it highlights, when appropriate (and as is noted in the text), commonalities between our author's conclusions and the burgeoning literature in the history of capitalism.

4. Charles A. Beard, *An Economic Interpretation of the Constitution of the United States* (New York: MacMillan, 1913); Richard R. John, "Turner, Beard, Chandler: Progressive Historians," *Business History Review* 82 (Summer 2008): 229–31.

5. Matthew Josephson, *The Robber Barons: The Great American Capitalists, 1861–1901* (New York: Harcourt, 1934). Of the many factual errors in Josephson's *Robber Barons*, perhaps the one

that had persisted the longest in popular accounts of post–Civil War America is his mistaken claim that the "robber baron" metaphor originated during the 1880s in the folklore of Kansas populists. In fact, the robber-baron critique had been invented in the previous decades by wealthy and well-respected East Coast merchants and would be popularized beginning in the 1870s by New York City journalists troubled by the wealth and power of the business leaders who controlled the nation's railroads and telegraphs. Richard R. John, "Robber Barons Redux: Antimonopoly Reconsidered," *Enterprise and Society* 13 (March 2012): 1–38, esp. 3–5.

6. Arthur M. Schlesinger, Jr., *The Politics of Upheaval, 1935–36*, rev. ed. (Boston: Houghton Mifflin, 1988 [1960]).

7. Lee Benson, *Merchants, Farmers, and Railroads: Railroad Regulation and New York Politics, 1850–1887* (Cambridge, Mass.: Harvard University Press, 1955); Robert H. Wiebe, *Businessmen and Reform: A Study of the Progressive Movement* (Cambridge, Mass.: Harvard University Press, 1962); Gabriel Kolko, *The Triumph of Conservatism, A Reinterpretation of American History: 1900–1916* (New York: Free Press, 1963); Ellis Hawley, *The New Deal and the Problem of Monopoly: A Study in Economic Ambivalence* (Princeton, N.J.: Princeton University Press, 1966); James Weinstein, *The Corporate Ideal in the Liberal State, 1900–1918* (Boston: Beacon, 1968); James Livingston, *Origins of the Federal Reserve System: Money, Class, and Corporate Capitalism, 1890–1913* (Ithaca, N.Y.: Cornell University Press, 1986); Martin Sklar, *The Corporate Reconstruction of Capitalism, 1890–1916: The Market, the Law and Politics* (New York: Cambridge University Press, 1988). The insights of these historians paralleled the arguments advanced by Marxian economists and sociologists who saw the postwar political economy as a distinct stage of economic development in which capital and the state would be much more closely intertwined than they had been in the past. See, for example, Paul Baran and Paul Sweezy, *Monopoly Capital: An Essay on the American Economic and Social Order* (New York: Monthly Review Press, 1966); G. William Domhoff, *Class and Power in the New Deal: Corporate Moderates, Southern Democrats and the Labor-Liberal Coalition* (Palo Alto, Calif.: Stanford University Press, 2011). Additional monographs that fit comfortably in the corporate liberal tradition include Robert M. Collins, *The Business Response to Keynes, 1929–1964* (New York: Columbia University Press, 1981); William Leach, *Land of Desire: Merchants, Power, and the Rise of a New American Culture* (New York: Vintage, 1993), esp. ch. 12; and Elizabeth Blackmar, "Exercising Power: The New York Chamber of Commerce and the Community of Interest," in *Picturing Power: Portraiture and Its Uses in the New York Chamber of Commerce*, ed. Karl Kusserow (New York: Columbia University Press, 2014), 189–234.

8. The literature on the relationship of business, labor, and politics is voluminous. For the period before the Second World War, see Sidney Fine, *"Without Blare of Trumpets": Walter Drew, the National Erector Association, and the Open Shop Movement, 1903–1957* (Ann Arbor: Michigan University Press, 1995); Jeffrey Haydu, *Citizen Employers: Business Communities and Labor in Cincinnati and San Francisco, 1870–1916* (Ithaca, N.Y.: ILR Press, 2008); Chad Pearson, *Reform or Repression: Organizing America's Anti-Union Movement* (Philadelphia: University of Pennsylvania Press, 2015). For the postwar years, see Howell John Harris, *The Right to Manage: Industrial Relations Policies of American Business in the 1940s* (Madison: University of Wisconsin Press, 1982); Elizabeth Fones-Wolf, *Selling Free Enterprise: The Business Assault on Labor and Liberalism, 1945–1960* (Urbana and Champaign: University of Illinois Press, 1995); Sanford M. Jacoby, *Modern Manors: Welfare Capitalism Since the New Deal* (Princeton, N.J.: Princeton University Press, 1997); Nelson Lichtenstein, *State of the Union: A Century of American Labor* (Princeton, N.J.: Princeton University Press, 2003); Kim Phillips-Fein, *Invisible Hands: The Mak-*

ing of the Conservative Movement from the New Deal to Reagan (New York: W. W. Norton, 2009). The political assault on collective bargaining that has intensified since the 1970s has led some labor historians to characterize the New Deal labor "order" as a short-lived interregnum between two "Gilded Ages." Although this stage model highlights key trends in labor relations, it is not especially useful for charactering the relationships between business and politics in other realms. Jefferson Cowie and Nick Salvatore, "The Long Exception: Rethinking the Place of the New Deal in American History," *ILWCH* 74 (Fall 2008): 1–30.

9. Colin Gordon, *New Deals: Business, Labor and Politics, 1920–1935* (Cambridge: Cambridge University Press, 1994); Thomas Ferguson, *The Golden Rule: The Investment Theory of Party Competition and the Logic of Money-Driven Political Systems* (Chicago: University of Chicago Press, 1995).

10. David Vogel, *Fluctuating Fortunes: The Political Power of Business in America* (New York: Basic Books, 1989); David Vogel, *Kindred Strangers: The Uneasy Relationship between Politics and Business in America* (Princeton, N.J.: Princeton University Press, 1996); Kim McQuaid, *Uneasy Partners: Big Business in American Politics, 1945–1980* (Baltimore: Johns Hopkins University Press, 1994).

11. Cyrus Veeser, *A World Safe for Capitalism: Dollar Diplomacy and America's Rise to Global Power* (New York: Columbia University Press, 2007); J. Lawrence Broz, *The International Origins of the Federal Reserve System* (Ithaca, N.Y.: Cornell University Press, 2009); Michael E. Latham, *The Right Kind of Revolution: Modernization, Development, and U.S. Foreign Policy from the Cold War to the Present* (Ithaca, N.Y.: Cornell University Press, 2011); Daniel Immerwahr, *Thinking Small: The United States and the Lure of Community Development* (Cambridge, Mass: Harvard University Press, 2015); Bartow J. Elmore, *Citizen Coke: The Making of Coca-Cola Capitalism* (New York: W. W. Norton & Co., 2015).

12. Wendy L. Wall, *Inventing the "American Way": The Politics of Consensus from the New Deal to the Civil Rights Movement* (New York: Oxford University Press, 2008).

13. Stephen Mihm, *Nation of Counterfeiters* (Cambridge, Mass.: Harvard University Press, 2007); Julia Ott, *When Wall Street Met Main Street: The Quest for an Investors' Democracy* (Cambridge, Mass.: Harvard University Press, 2011).

14. David Farber, *Sloan Rules: Alfred P. Sloan and the Triumph of General Motors* (Chicago: Universitsy of Chicago Press, 2005); Phillips-Fein, *Invisible Hands*, chs. 1–2.

15. Jennifer Klein, *For All These Rights; Business, Labor and the Shaping of America's Public-Private Welfare State* (Princeton, N.J.: Princeton University Press, 2006).

16. Thomas Sugrue, *Origins of the Urban Crisis: Race and Inequality in Postwar Detroit* (Princeton, N.J.: Princeton University Press, 1997); Jefferson Cowie, *Capital Moves: RCA's Seventy-Year Quest for Cheap Labor* (New York: New Press, 2001); Tami Friedman, "Exploiting the North-South Differential: Corporate Power, Southern Politics and the Decline of Organized Labor After World War II," *Journal of American History* 95 (September 2008): 323–48.

17. Elizabeth Tandy Shermer, *Sunbelt Capitalism: Phoenix and the Transformation of American Politics* (Philadelphia: University of Pennsylvania Press, 2013).

18. Walter A. Friedman, *Fortune Tellers: The Story of America's First Economic Forecasters* (Princeton, N. J.: Princeton University Press, 2013).

19. Benjamin C. Waterhouse, *Lobbying America: The Politics of Business from Nixon to NAFTA* (Princeton, N.J.: Princeton University Press, 2013).

20. Meg Jacobs, "The Politics of Environmental Regulation: Business-Government Relations in the 1970s and Beyond," in Phillips-Fein and Zelizer, *What's Good for Business*, 212–32;

Jacobs, *Panic at the Pump: The Energy Crisis and the Transformation of American Politics in the 1970s* (New York: Hill & Wang, 2016).

21. Archie B. Carroll, Kenneth J. Lipartito, James E. Post, and Patricia H. Werhane, *Corporate Responsibility: The American Experience* (Cambridge: Cambridge University Press, 2012).

22. Bethany Moreton, *To Serve God and Wal-Mart: The Making of Christian Free Enterprise* (Cambridge, Mass.: Harvard University Press, 2009).

23. Greta Krippner, *Capitalizing on Crisis: The Political Origins of the Rise of Finance* (Cambridge, Mass.: Harvard University Press, 2010); Judith Stein, *Pivotal Decade: How the United States Traded Factories for Finance in the Seventies* (New Haven, Conn.: Yale University Press, 2011).

24. Louis Hyman, *Debtor Nation: The History of America in Red Ink* (Princeton, N.J.: Princeton University Press, 2011); Louis Hyman, *Borrow: The American Way of Debt* (New York: Random House, 2012).

25. The large and growing literature in policy history is highly relevant to political history, business history, and the history of capitalism. For a useful introduction to this literature, which draws heavily on APD, as well as an overview of some key debates, see Julian E. Zelizer, *Governing America: The Revival of Political History* (Princeton, N.J.: Princeton University Press, 2012). For a review of APD literature by political scientists on topics in American political history between the founding of the republic and the Second World War, see Richard R. John, "American Political Development and Political History," in *Oxford Handbook of American Political Development*, ed. Richard Valelly, Suzanne Mettler, and Robert Lieberman (New York: Oxford University Press, 2016), 185–206.

26. Louis Galambos, *American Business History* (Washington, D.C.: American Historical Association, 1967), 2.

27. Among the prominent first-generation business historians to oppose the New Deal were N. S. B. Gras and Robert Albion. Galambos, *American Business History*, 4; Clifton Hood, "In Retrospect: Robert G. Albion's 'The Rise of New York Port, 1815–1860,'" *Reviews in American History* 27 (June 1999): 171–79.

28. Mary A. Yeager, "Mavericks and Mavens of Business History: Miriam Beard and Henrietta Larson," *Enterprise and Society* 2 (December 2001): 687–768.

29. Earl Latham, ed., *John D. Rockefeller: Robber Baron or Industrial Statesman?* (Boston: D. C. Heath, 1949).

30. Thomas K. McCraw, "The Intellectual Odyssey of Alfred D. Chandler, Jr.," in *The Essential Alfred Chandler*, ed. Thomas K. McCraw (Boston: Harvard Business School Press, 1988), 1–21; for Chandler's relationship with the Du Pont family, see p. 16.

31. Alfred D. Chandler, Jr., "Business History: A Personal Experience," *Business and Economic History* 7 (1978): 1–8.

32. Alfred D. Chandler, Jr., "Industrial Revolutions and Institutional Arrangements," *Bulletin of the American Academy of Arts and Sciences* 33 (May 1980): 33–50.

33. McCraw, "Intellectual Odyssey," 4–5.

34. Thomas K. McCraw, *American Business, 1920–2000: How It Worked*, 1st ed. (Wheeling, Ill.: Harlan Davidson, 2000), front cover; Thomas K. McCraw, *American Business Since 1920: How It Worked*, 2nd ed. (Wheeling, Ill.: Harlan Davidson, 2009), front cover. For an introduction to the history of U.S. military procurement during the Second World War that critically engages with key Chandlerian themes, see Mark R. Wilson, *Destructive Creation: American Business and the Winning of World War II* (Philadelphia: University of Pennsylvania Press, 2016).

35. Alfred D. Chandler, Jr., "Government Versus Business: An American Phenomenon" [1979], in McCraw, *Essential Alfred Chandler*, 425.

36. Alfred D. Chandler, Jr., *The Visible Hand: The Managerial Revolution in American Business* (Cambridge, Mass.: Belknap Press of Harvard University Press, 1977). For a critique and an appreciation of Chandler's magnum opus and the literature it spawned, see Richard R. John, "Elaborations, Revisions, Dissents: Alfred D. Chandler, Jr.'s., The *Visible Hand* after Twenty Years," *Business History Review* 71 (Summer 1997): 151–200; for an update, see Steven Usselman, "Still Visible: Alfred D. Chandler's *The Visible Hand*," *Technology and Culture* 47 (July 2006): 584–96. The Chandlerian internalist agenda—with its tight focus on modes of administrative coordination—remains an inspiration for many business historians. For a synthesis of the internalist literature, with a platform of citations, see Naomi R. Lamoreaux, Daniel M. G. Raff, and Peter Temin, "Beyond Markets and Hierarchies: Toward a New Synthesis of American Business History," *American Historical Review* 108 (April 2003): 404–33.

37. For an elaboration by a close colleague of Chandler's distinctive analysis of the relationship of business and politics, see Thomas K. McCraw, "The Public and Private Spheres in Historical Perspective," in *Public-Private Partnership: New Opportunities and Meeting Social Needs*, ed. Harvey Brooks, Lance Liebman, and Corinne S. Schelling (Cambridge, Mass.: American Academy of the Arts and Sciences, 1984), 31–60.

38. The Chandlerian "adversarial relationship" thesis is related to, yet distinct from, the now-discredited assumption of many historians and political scientists active in the 1970s and 1980s that the United States in the pre–New Deal era had a "weak" or "laissez-faire" state of "courts and parties" that was dominated by venal party bosses and a pro-business judiciary that had been captured by the business elite. Few of the many historians who have challenged this hoary shibboleth have paid much attention to the "adversarial relationship" thesis. For an exception, see William J. Novak, "Law and the Social Control of American Capitalism," *Emory Law Review* 60 (2010): 377–405, esp. 384–85. Novak provides a judicious overview of persistent myths about the nineteenth-century political economy, which he supplements with a brief and admiring discussion of the utility of the Chandlerian "adversarial relationship" thesis in explaining Progressive-era business regulation. For an introduction to the burgeoning literature on political economy in the early republic, see Richard R. John, "Why Institutions Matter," *Common-place* 9 (October 2008), http://www.common-place-archives.org/vol-09/no-01/john/. For a recent history of the American state that contends that it been simultaneously "strong" and "weak" since the moment of its founding, see Gary Gerstle, *Liberty and Coercion: The Paradox of American Government from the Founding to the Present* (Princeton, N.J.: Princeton Universitsy Press, 2015).

39. Louis Galambos, "The Emerging Organizational Synthesis in Modern American History," *Business History Review* 44 (Autumn 1970): 279–90; Louis Galambos, "Technology, Political Economy, and Professionalization: Central Themes of the Organizational Synthesis," *Business History Review* 57 (Winter 1983): 471–93; Louis Galambos, "Recasting the Organizational Synthesis: Structure and Process in the Twentieth and Twenty-First Centuries," *Business History Review* 79 (Spring 2005): 1–38.

40. William H. Becker, *The Dynamics of Business-Government Relations: Industry and Exports, 1893–1921* (Chicago: University of Chicago Press, 1982); Richard H. K. Vietor, *Energy Policy in America Since 1945: A Study of Business-Government Relations* (Cambridge: Cambridge University Press, 1984); Thomas K. McCraw, *Prophets of Regulation: Charles Frances Adams, Louis D. Brandeis, James M. Landis, Alfred E. Kahn* (Cambridge, Mass.: Belknap Press of Harvard University Press, 1984); William R. Childs, *Trucking and the Public Interest: The Emergence*

of Federal Regulation, 1914–1940 (Knoxville: University of Tennessee Press, 1985); Steven W. Usselman, *Regulating Railroad Innovation: Business, Technology, and the State, 1840–1920* (Cambridge: Cambridge University Press, 2002).

41. Jennifer Delton, *Racial Integration and Corporate America, 1940–1990* (Cambridge: Cambridge University Press, 2009).

42. Neil Fligstein, *The Transformation of Corporate Control* (Cambridge, Mass: Harvard University Press, 1990); William G. Roy, *Socializing Capital: The Rise of the Large Industrial Corporation in* America (Princeton, N.J.: Princeton University Press, 1997); William Lazonick, *Business Organization and the Myth of the Market Economy* (Cambridge: Cambridge University Press, 1993); Richard Bensel, *The Political Economy of American Industrialization, 1877–1900* (Cambridge: Cambridge University Press, 1998).

43. Colleen A. Dunlavy, *Politics and Industrialization: Early Railroads in Prussia and the United States* (Princeton, N.J.: Princeton University Press, 1994).

44. Richard White, *Railroaded: The Transcontinentals and the Making of Modern America* (New York: W. W. Norton & Co., 2012); Richard R. John, *Network Nation: Inventing American Telecommunications* (Cambridge, Mass.: Belknap Press of Harvard University Press, 2010). See also Joshua D. Wolff, *Western Union and the Creation of the American Corporate Order, 1845–1893* (New York: Cambridge University Press, 2013).

45. Gerald Berk, *Louis D. Brandeis and the Making of Regulated Competition* (Cambridge: Cambridge University Press, 2012); Shane Hamilton, *Trucking Country: The Road to America's Wal-Mart Economy* (Princeton, N.J.: Princeton University Press, 2008).

46. The history of the rise of China as a low-cost exporter remains to be written. On the decline of the New England cotton textile industry, see David Koistinen, *Confronting Decline: The Political Economy of Deindustrialization in Twentieth-Century New England* (Gainesville: University Press of Florida, 2013).

47. John, "Robber Barons Redux." The innovativeness of industrial districts, small and midsized manufacturers, and batch production has been explored with subtlety and sophistication by Philip Scranton. Though Scranton downplayed the often-critical role of tariff legislation in protecting the markets of the firms he chronicled, his history of specialty production, which he contrasted with mass production, raises enduring questions about the relationship of business, innovation, and politics. Philip Scranton, *Endless Novelty: Specialty Production and American Industrialization, 1865–1925* (Princeton, N.J.: Princeton University Press, 1997).

48. Although the history of capitalism is still young, its practitioners have been quick to sketch its character and significance. For two useful introductions to the literature, see Sven Beckert, "History of American Capitalism," in *American History Now*, ed. Eric Foner and Lisa McGirr (Philadelphia: Temple University Press, 2011); and "Interchange: The History of Capitalism," *Journal of American History* 101 (September 2014): 503–36.

49. Louis Hyman, "Why Write the History of Capitalism?" *Symposium Magazine*, July 2013, http://www.symposium-magazine.com/why-write-the-history-of-capitalism-louis-hyman/.

50. This rallying cry can be found on the website for Louis Hyman's "History of Capitalism Initiative" at Cornell University's School of Industrial and Labor Relations, accessed April 13, 2016, http://hoc.ilr.cornell.edu/faculty.

51. Hyman, "Why Write the History of Capitalism?"

52. Kenneth Lipartito, "Reassembling the Economic: New Departures in Historical Materialism," *American Historical Review* 121 (February 2016): 101–39; Karl Polanyi, *The Great Transformation: The Political and Economic Origins of Our Time* (New York: Farrar & Rinehard, 1944). For a

brief overview of Polanyi's project, with a focus on its relationship to the more general sociological problem of "embeddedness," see Greta R. Krippner and Anthony S. Alvarez, "Embeddedness and the Intellectual Project of Economic Sociology," *Annual Review of Sociology* 33 (2007): 219–40. For a thoughtful collection of original essays that explore some of the intellectual issues that historians of capitalism are engaging, see Nelson Lichtenstein, ed., *American Capitalism: Social Thought and Political Economy in the Twentieth Century* (Philadelphia: University of Pennsylvania Press, 2006). For an exemplary monograph on the rise of market fundamentalism, see Angus Burgin, *The Great Persuasion: Reinventing Free Markets Since the Depression* (Cambridge, Mass.: Harvard University Press, 2012). For a lucid appreciation of a rival tradition, see Howard Brick, *Transcending Capitalism: Visions of a New Society in Modern American Thought* (Ithaca, N.Y.: Cornell University Press. 2006).

53. Fraser and Gerstle, *Ruling America,* 26. The disinclination of post–Second World War historians to emphasize social class sets them apart from the progressives, for whom it remained a critical analytical category.

54. Ibid., 4. For a similar conclusion that is more directly indebted to the literature of business history, see Philip Scranton and Patrick Fridenson, *Reimagining Business History* (Baltimore: Johns Hopkins University Press, 2013).

55. The literature on the relationship of business and politics in the Progressive era and the 1920s is voluminous. For relevant citations, see Thomas K. McCraw, "The Progressive Legacy," in Lewis L. Gould, ed., *The Progressive Era* (Syracuse, N.Y.: Syracuse University Press, 1974), 35–54; Martin J. Sklar, *The United States as a Developing Country: Studies in U.S. History in the Progressive Era and the 1920s* (Cambridge: Cambridge University Press, 1992); Daniel T. Rodgers, *Atlantic Crossings: Social Politics in a Progressive Age* (Cambridge, Mass.: Harvard University Press, 1998); Novak, "Law and the Social Control of American Capitalism." For case studies, see Olivier Zunz, *Making America Corporate, 1870–1920* (Chicago: University of Chicago Press, 1990); Andrea Tone, *The Business of Benevolence: Industrial Paternalism in Progressive America* (Ithaca, N.Y.: Cornell University Press, 1997); Roland Marchand, *Creating the Corporate Soul: The Rise of Public Relations and Corporate Imagery in American Big Business* (Berkeley: University of California Press, 1998); John, *Network Nation,* chs. 8–11; Gerald Berk, *Louis D. Brandeis and the Making of Regulated Competition* (Cambridge: Cambridge University Press, 2012).

The rejection of laissez-faire by American business leaders is a major theme of historical writing on the mindset of nineteenth-century business leaders. Unfortunately, this fact is sometimes overlooked by historians unfamiliar with the late nineteenth century who reiterate the mistaken—and self-serving—boast of New Deal liberals that the economic order that the Democratic party established in the 1930s decisively overthrew an ancien regime mesmerized by laissez-faire dogma. The actual historical record is quite different. To the extent that the late nineteenth century can be characterized as a "gilded age"—a contested claim—the values that business leaders espoused in this period had remarkably little in common with the dogmatic market fundamentalism common today. Nineteenth-century business leaders defended competition (as business leaders have throughout history), yet few endorsed radical laissez-faire, and, in the opinion of a leading historian of the subject, and with the notable exception of Andrew Carnegie—an outlier in almost every conceivable respect—few even read Herbert Spencer or could be fairly characterized as Social Darwinists. Irvin G. Wyllie, "Social Darwinism and the Businessman," *Proceedings of the American Philosophical Society* 103 (1959): 629–35. The literature on the mindset of nineteenth-century business leaders is surprisingly thin. For notable exceptions, see

Irvin G. Wyllie, *The Self-Made Man in America: The Myth of Rags to Riches* (New Brunswick, N.J.: Rutgers University Press, 1954); Edward Chase Kirkland, *Dream and Thought in the Business Community, 1860–1900* (Ithaca, N.Y.: Cornell University Press, 1956); Roy Rosenzweig and Elizabeth Blackmar, *The Park and the People: A History of Central Park* (Ithaca, N.Y.: Cornell University Press, 1992); Pamela Walker Laird, *Advertising Progress: American Business and the Rise of Consumer Marketing* (Baltimore: Johns Hopkins University Press, 1998); Sven Beckert, *Monied Metropolis: New York City and the Consolidation of the American Bourgeoisie, 1850–1896* (Cambridge: Cambridge University Press, 2001); Scott A. Sandage, *Born Losers: A History of Failure in America* (Cambridge, Mass.: Harvard University Press, 2005); Pamela Walker Laird, *Pull: Networking and Success Since Benjamin Franklin* (Cambridge, Mass.: Harvard University Press, 2006); Noam Maggor, "Politics of Property: Urban Democracy in the Age of Capital, Boston 1865–1900" (Ph.D. diss., Harvard University, 2010).

56. The consensus of our contributors regarding the relationship between business and politics in twentieth-century America is broadly similar to the conclusion that Thomas K. McCraw reached in a clear and penetrating comparative institutionalist overview of the entire sweep of "American Capitalism." In this essay, McCraw laid out four "broad categories" of government intervention in capitalist economies: (1) laissez-faire, with minimum intervention; (2) frequent uncoordinated intervention in a mostly free market; (3) systematic state guidance of private decisionmaking; and (4) thorough state management and decisionmaking for the whole economy. The "record" of American history, McCraw concluded, hovered around the second category; our authors concur. Laissez-faire has never been the American norm, and neither has systematic state guidance, nor thorough state management and decisionmaking. Thomas K. McCraw, "American Capitalism," in *Creating Modern Capitalism: How Entrepreneurs, Companies, and Countries Triumphed in Three Industrial Revolutions*, ed. Thomas K. McCraw (Cambridge, Mass.: Harvard University Press, 1997), 316–17.

57. For more on public investments and deficit spending in the New Deal, see Thomas K. McCraw, "The New Deal and the Mixed Economy," in *Fifty Years Later: The New Deal Evaluated*, ed. Harvard Sitkoff (New York: Alfred A. Knopf, 1985), 37–67; Jason Scott Smith, *Building New Deal Liberalism: The Political Economy of Public Works, 1933–1956* (Cambridge: Cambridge University Press, 2009). For an overview of the New Deal's balance sheet, with a focus on its prodigious long-term contribution to economic growth, see Jason Scott Smith, *A Concise History of the New Deal* (Cambridge: Cambridge University Press, 2014). For an eye-opening quantitative analysis of the positive economic legacy of the 1930s, a decade not often regarded as a crucible of innovation, see Alexander J. Field, *A Great Leap Forward: 1930s Depression and U.S. Economic Growth* (New Haven, Conn.: Yale University Press, 2011).

58. K. Austin Kerr, *Organized for Prohibition: A New History of the Anti-Saloon League* (New Haven, Conn.: Yale University Press, 1985); Lisa McGirr, *The War on Alcohol: Prohibition and the Rise of the American State* (New York: W. W. Norton & Co., 2016).

59. Louis Hyman, "Short-Sighted," 13; manuscript in author's possession.

Chapter 1. Trade Associations, State Building, and the Sherman Act

This essay benefited from the generous feedback and discussion from Richard John, Kimberly Phillips-Fein, Tony Freyer, Benjamin Waterhouse, Brent Cebul, Daniel Amsterdam, Roger Horowitz, Shaun Nichols, Logan E. Sawyer, the participants at the 2013 Hagley conference, and the two anonymous readers for the Press.

1. In March 1913, the Department of Labor formed its own administrative bureau separate from Commerce. On the Department of Commerce, see Ellis W. Hawley, "Herbert Hoover, the Commerce Secretariat, and the Vision of an 'Associative State,' 1921–1928," *Journal of American History* 61 (June 1974): 116–40. On the FTC, see Gerald Berk, *Louis D. Brandeis and the Making of Regulated Competition, 1900–1932* (Cambridge: Cambridge University Press, 2009). See also Laura Phillips Sawyer, *American Fair Trade: Proprietary Capitalism, Networks, and the "New Competition": 1890–1940* (Cambridge: Cambridge University Press, forthcoming).

2. On the adversarial relationship, see Thomas K. McCraw, "Business and Government: The Origins of the Adversary Relationship," *California Management Review* 36 (Winter 1984): 33–52, 38; Robert Wiebe, *Businessmen and Reform: A Study of the Progressive Movement* (Cambridge, Mass.: Harvard University Press, 1962), 220. On the Chamber's influence on antiregulation politics in the post–Second World War era, see Benjamin Waterhouse, *Lobbying America: The Politics of Business from Nixon to NAFTA* (Princeton, N.J.: Princeton University Press, 2014).

3. Sherman Antitrust Act, 26 Stat. 209 (1890).

4. See note 19.

5. Legal and business historians have dismissed early administrative reforms as resulting in very little regulatory change and have portrayed antitrust law as settled by 1911. See Martin Sklar, *The Corporate Reconstruction of American Capitalism, 1890–1916: The Market, the Law, and Politics* (Cambridge: Cambridge University Press, 1988): 106; Thomas K. McCraw, *Prophets of Regulation: Charles Francis Adams, Louis D. Brandeis, James M. Landis, Alfred E. Kahn* (Cambridge, Mass.: Harvard University Press, 1984). However, USCC documents demonstrate a continued sense of uncertainty and persistent discussion of antitrust reforms that lasted through the New Deal. See Berk, *Brandeis*, 111. Berk argues that the FTC, rather than ending the debate on competition policy, fostered continued debate.

6. See Richard R. John, *Network Nation: Inventing American Telecommunications* (Cambridge, Mass.: Harvard University Press, 2010), 122–24, 350–51, 370. John demonstrates that telephone and telegraph corporations developed public relations campaigns to thwart public demands for government ownership of telecommunication utilities. In contrast, the industries that dominated the USCC in the early twentieth century were largely from the "ordinary trades" rather than utilities.

7. On the public-interest literature on public-private governance, see David Moss and Michael Fein, "Radio Regulation Revisited: Coase, the FCC, and the Public Interest," *Journal of Policy History* 15, no. 4 (2003): 389–416.

8. Wiebe, *Businessmen and Reform*, 33–41.

9. A. H. Baldwin (Department of Commerce) to G. Grosvenor Dawe (Southern Commercial Congress), Chamber of Commerce of the United States Records, Accession No. 1960, Box 1 (February 20, 1912) Hagley Museum and Library. (Hereafter Chamber Records.)

10. Richard Hume Werking, "Bureaucrats, Businessmen, and Foreign Trade: The Origins of the United States Chamber of Commerce," *Business History Review* 52 (Autumn 1978): 321–41, 322. In this prescient article, Werking argued that government bureaucrats not only administer but also create regulatory policy, thereby participating in "bureaucratic entrepreneurism" (322). There has not been a systematic study performed on the early years of the USCC; however, Gerald Berk emphasizes the role of the USCC and National Association of Cost Accountants in supporting trade association information-sharing practices in the 1920s. Berk, *Brandeis*, 184. Werking emphasized export promotion, not domestic trade rules.

11. Chamber Records, Box 1 (February 12, 1912), 4–5.

12. "Notes for the Conference of February 12, 1912," ibid., 2.

13. Open letter released to President Taft, April 1912, Chamber Records, Box 1 (February 12, 1912), leaflet.

14. Ibid.

15. Meeting minutes, Chamber Records, Box 1 (April 22–23, 1912), 5–6.

16. Charles Nagel, Chamber Records, Box 1 (April 1912), 34–38.

17. Ibid., 34.

18. *US v. Trans-Missouri Freight Association*, 166 U.S. 290 (1897), 323; *US v. Joint Traffic Association*, 171 U.S. 505 (1898). *Addyston Pipe and Steel Co. v. US*, 175 U.S. 211 (1899), extended the literalist interpretation to manufacturers.

19. *Standard Oil Co. of New Jersey v. U.S.*, 221 U.S. 1 (1911); *U.S. v. American Tobacco Company*, 221 U.S. 106 (1911).

20. Owen Fiss, *Troubled Beginnings of the Modern State, 1888–1910* (New York: Macmillan, 1993); Tony Freyer, *Regulating Big Business: Antitrust in Great Britain and America, 1880–1990* (Cambridge: Cambridge University Press, 1992), 25, 33.

21. McCraw, *Prophets of Regulation*. "Brandeis offered regulatory solutions grounded on a set of economic assumptions that were fundamentally wrong" (84). It should be noted that, in 2006, the Supreme Court overturned its previous ruling striking down resale price maintenance contracts, which allow manufacturers to set retail prices on brand name goods.

22. Louis D. Brandeis, "The Democracy of Business," Chamber Records, Box 1 (February 12, 1912), 168–72, 168.

23. Ibid., 169–170. See also Berk, *Brandeis*, 21, 77–78.

24. See Hearings before the Committee on Interstate and Foreign Commerce, House of Representatives, 63rd Cong., 2nd sess., January 9, 1914; Louis D. Brandeis, "Cutthroat Prices—The Competition that Kills," *Harper's Weekly* (November 15, 1913): 67.

25. Charles Richard Van Hise, "Co-operation in Industry," an address to the National Lumber Manufacturers Association, in *Problems in Lumber Distribution* (Chicago: National Lumber Manufacturers Association, 1916): 1–15, 6–7.

26. Van Hise repeated the conventional theory that the Court's attack on loose combinations encouraged corporate consolidation and later holding companies. Prof. Charles Van Hise, "Concentration of Industry in the United States," Chamber Records, Box 7 (February 12, 1914), 111–21, 116–17.

27. Van Hise, "Co-operation in Industry," 13. Van Hise was also a member of a joint committee of the USCC and the American Federation of Labor, which he urged the lumbermen's association to work alongside.

28. Charles Van Hise, *Concentration and Control: A Solution of the Trust Problem in the United States* (New York: Macmillan, 1912). See "Van Hise on the Trusts: Nation Must Control Without Bridling Industrial Genius," *New York Times*, October 14, 1912, p. 14; McCraw, *Prophets of Regulation*, 128, 139.

29. Raymond Moley, *After Seven Years*, 4th ed. (New York: Harper Bros., 1939), 184, 24. Van Hise's text served as a precursor to Rexford Tugwell, *Industrial Discipline and the Governmental Arts* (New York: Columbia University Press, 1933).

30. *Federal Trade Commission v. Gratz*, 253 U.S. 427 (1920).

31. See note 56. The Court did relax the per se prohibition on resale price maintenance contracts, *U.S. v. Colgate & Co.*, 250 U.S. 300 (1919).

32. McCraw, *Prophets of Regulation*, 144–45; Anne Mayhew, "How American Economists Came to Love the Sherman Act," *History of Political Economy* 30 supplement (1990): 179–201.

33. "Report of the Federal Trade Commission on Resale Price Maintenance" (Washington, D.C.: Government Printing Office, 1945), 41–44. R. H. Macy led opposition to the fair trade bills, along with R. H. Macy & Co., represented by Edmond A. Wise (attorney) and Percy S. Straus (vice president); National Retail Dry Goods Association, represented by Lew Hahn (managing director); O'Neill & Co. (Baltimore, Md.), represented by R. C. Hudson; National Grange, represented by A. M. Loom; and Frank C. McKinney, Homemakers' Association (N.J.).

34. Appendix III: "Statement of Law Annexed to Minority Report," Chamber Records, Box 7 (February 10, 1916), 240–88, 255.

35. Ibid., 256. The report states, "the situation changed . . . [when] the people themselves believed combinations, and particularly combinations regulating prices, [were] against public policy."

36. Berk, *Brandeis*, 121–30. Hurley sent out the FTC publication, Federal Trade Commission, *Fundamentals of the Cost System* (Washington, D.C.: Government Printing Office, 1916).

37. Federal Trade Commission, *Annual Report of the Federal Trade Commission* (Washington, D.C.: Government Printing Office, 1916), 15.

38. Robert D. Cuff, *The War Industries Board: Business-Government Relations During World War I* (Baltimore: The Johns Hopkins University Press, 1973). Cuff argues that "the WIB and its administrative program were a bundle of paradoxes" (148–49).

39. Hawley, "Hoover, the Commerce Secretariat," 117.

40. Herbert Hoover, Chamber Records, Box 8 (September 19, 1917), 129. Veblen served on the Food Administration with Hoover before joining Mitchell at the New School for Social Research. Malcolm Rutherford, "Understanding Institutional Economics: 1918–1929," *Journal of the History of Economic Thought* 22, no. 3 (2000): 277–308, 282.

41. George Peek, "Government Organization in Relation to War," Chamber Records, Box 8 (April 9, 1918), 94–121, 97.

42. Ibid., 98.

43. Resolution: "Price Fixing and Cost Accounting," ibid., 151.

44. George Peek, Chamber Records, Box 8 (April 9, 1918), 227. Peek, who represented the WIB, read the letter from Baruch to the Chamber assembly.

45. Resolution: "Industrial Cooperation," Chamber Records, Box 8 (April 9, 1918), 230. This language was repeated in the formal resolution that passed the Chamber. See also Chamber Records, Box 1 (December 3–6, 1918), 5.

46. Resolution: "Trade Marks and Copyright," Chamber Records, Box 8 (April 9, 1918), 257.

47. Walton H. Hamilton, "The Institutional Approach to Economic Theory," *American Economic Review* 9 (March 1919): 309–18; William J. Barber, *From New Era to New Deal: Herbert Hoover, the Economists, and American Economic Policy, 1921–1933* (Cambridge: Cambridge University Press, 1985), 2–4; Arthur E. Swanson, "The Harvard Bureau of Business Research," *Journal of Political Economy* 22 (November 1914): 896–900. See also Kyle Bruce, "Activist Management: Henry S. Dennison's Institutional Economics," *Journal of Economic Issues* 40 (December 2006): 1113–36.

48. "Guesswork Blamed for Business Slump," *New York Times*, October 6, 1921, p. 3.

49. "Would Spur Public Works to Aid Idle," *Washington Post*, September 28, 1921, p. 5; "To Meet Needs of Unemployed," *Los Angeles Times*, September 30, 1921, p. 6. See also "Engineers Endorse Hoover Work Plan," *New York Times*, September 11, 1921, p. 30. Between 1921 and 1928, state and local government provided approximately 90 percent of public spending outlays, which

the federal government supported by exempting state and municipal bonds from income taxes. Barber, *New Era to New Deal*, 20–21.

50. "Country's Business Continues to Increase," *Wall Street Journal*, December 8, 1921, p. 2.

51. Barber, *New Era to New Deal*, 8. Hoover's Advisory Committee on Statistics included Mitchell, "Edwin R. A. Seligman ([Professor of Economics] Columbia University), Allyn A. Young ([Professor of Economics] Harvard), Walter F. Willcox ([Professor of Economics and Statistics] Cornell), Carroll W. Doten ([Professor of Economics] Massachusetts Institute of Technology), Edwin F. Gay (then president of the *New York Evening Post*, who had formerly served as the first dean of the Harvard Business School), and William S. Rossiter (formerly the head of the U.S. Census Bureau)."

52. Jeff Biddle, "Social Science and the Making of Social Policy: Wesley Mitchell's Vision," in *The Economic Mind in America: Essays in the History of American Economics*, ed. Malcolm Rutherford (New York: Routledge, 1998), 43–79, 59.

53. "Cement Men Face Trial as a Trust," *New York Times*, April 5, 1922, p. 13.

54. "The Lockwood Housing Investigation in New York City," *Domestic Engineering and the Journal of Mechanical Contracting* 94 (February 1921): 364–65. Samuel Untermeyer's prosecution focused on Robert P. Brindell, leader of the Building Trade Employers' Association, despite Untermeyer's admission that the mortgage finance industry had more to do with the housing shortage in New York City.

55. M. Browning Carrott, "The Supreme Court and American Trade Associations, 1921–1925," *Business History Review* 44 (Autumn 1970): 320–38, 329.

56. *U.S. v. American Column and Lumber Co.*, 263 Fed. 147, at 156. *American Column and Lumber Co. v. U.S., Records and Briefs of the United States Supreme Court*, 257 U.S. 377, contains information on the type of data exchanged by members of the association. "Court Dissolves Cement Combine," *New York Times*, October 24, 1923, p. 21. *U.S. v. American Linseed Oil Co.*, 262 U.S. 371 (1923), similarly struck down information sharing through the Armstrong Bureau of Related Industries in Chicago.

57. *American Column and Lumber Co. v. U.S.*, 257 U.S. 377, at 412.

58. National Industrial Conference Board, *Trade Associations: Their Economic and Legal Status* (Washington, D.C.: Government Printing Office, 1929), 16; Milton N. Nelson, "The Effect of Open Price Association Activities on Competition and Prices," *American Economic Review* 13 (June 1923): 258–75.

59. Milton N. Nelson, *Open Price Associations* (Urbana: University of Illinois Studies in the Social Sciences, 1923), 10; Carrott, "American Trade Associations," 322.

60. Louis Galambos, *Competition and Cooperation: The Emergence of a National Trade Association* (Baltimore, Md.: The Johns Hopkins University Press, 1966): 79.

61. Hoover, Chamber Records, Box 11 (May 7, 1924), 169–80, 173.

62. "Report of the Committee on Trade Associations," Chamber Records, Box 11, Referendum 41 (February 1923), 1.

63. Col. George T. Buckingham (of the Defrees, Buckingham & Eaton Company of Chicago), "The Opportunities and Responsibilities of Trade Associations," Chamber Records, Box 11, (May 7, 1924), 214–25, 219.

64. Ibid., 220.

65. Ibid., emphasis added.

66. Ibid., 224.

67. Ibid., 225.

68. Ellis W. Hawley, "Herbert Hoover and the Sherman Act, 1921–1933: An Early Phase of a Continuing Issue," *Iowa Law Review* 74 (1988–1989): 1067–1104, 1082–83.

69. "Court Upholds Trade Alliance," *Los Angeles Times*, June 2, 1925, p. 11. (Quoting Justice Harlan Fiske Stone majority opinion for the Court.)

70. *Cement Manufacturers' Association v. United States*, 268 U.S. 588 (1925), 602.

71. Id., 598.

72. Id., 606.

73. Id., 583.

74. Id., 582–83.

75. Id., 583.

76. Humphrey, Chamber Records, Box 11 (May 19, 1925), 58–65. The Chamber passed a resolution in support of these changes to the FTC (ibid., 177). See also Robert F. Himmelberg, *The Origins of the National Recovery Administration: Business, Government, and the Trade Association Issue, 1921–1933*, 2nd ed. (New York: Fordham University Press, 1993), 49.

77. Thomas Blaisdell, *The Federal Trade Commission: An Experiment in the Control of Business* (New York: Columbia University Press, 1932), 44.

78. *Public Regulation of Competitive Practices*, revised ed. (Washington, D.C.: National Conference Board, 1929). This publication of the National Conference Board categorized the complaints received and issued by the FTC. See Richard Tedlow, "From Competitor to Consumer: The Changing Focus of Federal Regulation of Advertising, 1914–1938," *Business History Review* 55 (Spring 1981): 35–58.

79. Hoover, Chamber Records, Box 11 (May 10, 1926), 191–207, 195.

80. Ibid., 196.

81. Himmelberg, *Origins*, 62.

82. Hawley, "Hoover and the Sherman Act," 1084. See also Himmelberg, *Origins*, 48–51, 54–67; Federal Trade Commission, *Annual Report* (Washington, D.C.: Government Printing Office, 1926), 5, 47–48; Federal Trade Commission, *Trade Practice Conferences* (Washington, D.C.: Government Printing Office, 1929), v–vii.

83. For example, the U.S. Supreme Court held that the Court and not the FTC would determine what constituted "unfair competition" in *Federal Trade Commission v. Gratz*. The Court circumscribed the *Maple Flooring* decision in *US v. Trenton Potteries* 273 U.S. 392 (1927), reiterating that any explicit price-fixing contract was illegal per se.

84. See Alan Brinkley, *The End of Reform: New Deal Liberalism in Recession and War* (New York: Knopf, 1995).

Chapter 2. Toward a Civic Welfare State

1. Daniel T. Rodgers, *Atlantic Crossings: Social Politics in a Progressive Age* (Cambridge, Mass.: Belknap Press of Harvard University Press, 1998), 7.

2. See especially Theda Skocpol, *Protecting Soldiers and Mothers: The Political Origins of Social Policy in the United States* (Cambridge, Mass.: Belknap Press of Harvard University Press, 1992); Margaret Weir and Theda Skocpol, "State Structures and the Possibilities for 'Keynesian' Responses to the Great Depression in Sweden, Britain, and the United States," in *Bringing the State Back In*, ed. Peter Evans, Dietrich Rueschemeyer, and Theda Skocpol (New York: Cambridge University Press, 1985); Jacob S. Hacker and Paul Pierson, "Business Power and Social Policy: Employers and the Formation of the American Welfare State," *Politics and Society* 30 (June 2002) 277–325.

3. See, for example, Lizabeth Cohen, *Making a New Deal: Industrial Workers in Chicago* (New York: Cambridge University Press, 1990), ch. 4; Andrea Tone, *The Business of Benevolence: Industrial Paternalism in Progressive America* (Ithaca, N.Y.: Cornell University Press, 1997); Sanford M. Jacoby, *Modern Manors: Welfare Capitalism Since the New Deal* (Princeton, N.J.: Princeton University Press, 1997), ch. 1; Colin Gordon, *New Deals: Business, Labor and Politics in America, 1920–1935* (New York: Cambridge University Press, 1992).

4. For example, see Edward Berkowitz and Kim McQuaid, *Creating the Welfare State: The Political Economy of Twentieth-Century Reform*, 2nd ed. (New York: Praeger, 1988), 115–26; Sanford M. Jacoby, "Employers and the Welfare State: The Role of Marion B. Folsom," *Journal of American History* 80 (September 1993), 527–44; Gordon, *New Deals.*

5. U.S. Bureau of the Census, *Statistics of Cities Having a Population over 30,000: 1904* (Washington, D.C.: Government Printing Office, 1906); U.S. Bureau of the Census, *Financial Statistics of Cities Having a Population over 30,000*, 20 vols. (Washington, D.C.: Government Printing Office, 1913–34). I measure against a prewar baseline because municipal spending plummeted during the war. These figures and those in the next paragraph include only the money that public officials spent to provide actual services and to run everyday operations, not the costs that governments paid to finance their debts, which grew rapidly across urban America in the 1920s.

For additional discussion of this data, see Daniel Amsterdam, *Roaring Metropolis: Businessmen's Campaign for a Civic Welfare State* (Philadelphia: University of Pennsylvania Press, 2016).

6. Los Angeles's budget grew nearly 300 percent between 1916 and 1929 adjusted for inflation, all of this growth following the war. New York's nearly doubled. Philadelphia's rose by 75 percent, and Chicago's by 85 percent. Out of the twenty-one cities with populations of more than 300,000 in 1920, sixteen experienced a higher rate of growth in government spending per capita adjusted for inflation between 1916 and 1928 than between 1904 and 1916. Increased social spending drove a significant portion of this growth. Overall, in the nation's largest cities—those with populations over 300,000—spending per person on schooling rose 73 percent adjusted for inflation; on recreational programs spending grew 72 percent; on libraries, 47 percent; on hospitals, 44 percent; on sewer systems, 30 percent; and on other facets of public health, 45 percent.

On Prohibition and government growth in the 1920s, see James A. Morone, *Hellfire Nation: The Politics of Sin in American History* (New Haven, Conn.: Yale University Press, 2003); Lisa McGirr, *The War on Alcohol: Prohibition and the Rise of the American State* (New York: W. W. Norton & Co., 2015). On experiments with federal economic planning during the decade, see, for example, Ellis W. Hawley, "Herbert Hoover, The Commerce Secretariat, and the Vision of an 'Associative State,' 1921–1928," *Journal of American History* 61 (June 1974): 116–40. Despite the contributions of Hawley, Morone, and others, portraits of the 1920s as an antigovernment moment have persisted. For instance, see Lynn Dumenil, *The Modern Temper: American Culture and Society in the 1920s* (New York: Hill and Wang, 1995). Lizabeth Cohen's influential study of business and labor in the interwar period likewise reinforces this view of the decade, among other reasons, because it pays scant attention to Chicago's rapidly expanding public sector in the 1920s aside from discussing public assistance to the poor—a minor facet of municipal spending in the early twentieth century. Cohen, *Making a New Deal.*

7. Robert Wiebe, *Businessmen and Reform: A Study of the Progressive Movement* (Cambridge, Mass.: Harvard University Press, 1962), 158. Wiebe's examination of business interests' political attitudes during the early twentieth century is more wide ranging than many explorations of the topic but pays only passing attention to businessmen's political activism on the local stage.

8. Gosta Esping-Anderson, *The Three Worlds of Welfare Capitalism* (Princeton, N.J.: Princeton University Press, 1990), ch. 1.

9. On workmen's compensation, see James Weinstein, *The Corporate Ideal in the Liberal State* (Boston: Beacon Press, 1968), ch. 2; Skocpol, *Protecting Soldiers and Mothers*, 285–98. Scholars have debated the precise extent of employers' support of workmen's compensation. See, for example, David Moss, *Socializing Security: Progressive-Era Economists and the Origins of American Social Policy* (Cambridge, Mass.: Harvard University Press, 1996), 129–31. On business support for old-age pensions in the late 1920s, see Jill Quadagno, *The Transformation of Old Age Security: Class and Politics in the American Welfare State* (Chicago: University of Chicago Press, 1988); Christopher Cyphers, *The National Civic Federation and the Making of a New Liberalism, 1900–1915* (Westport, Conn.: Praeger, 2002), Conclusion. On businessmen and unemployment relief in the early 1920s, see Daniel Amsterdam, "Before the Roar: U.S. Unemployment Relief after World War I and the Long History of a Paternalist Welfare Policy," *Journal of American History* 101 (March 2015): 1123–43. For an overview and an astute assessment of the extensive literature on how and to what degree corporate executives influenced the Social Security Act of 1935, see Hacker and Pierson, "Business Power and Social Policy." Quoted 299. For a recent work that revisits many of these arguments, see G. William Domhoff and Michael J. Webber, *Class and Power in the New Deal: Corporate Moderates, Southern Democrats, and the Liberal-Labor Coalition* (Palo Alto, Calif.: Stanford University Press, 2001), which attempts to move beyond focusing exclusively on a small number of corporate actors in directly shaping the Social Security Act of 1935 toward an examination of the research that wealthy benefactors helped fund and that, in turn, may have helped inform the act's provisions.

10. David Brody, *Workers in Industrial America: Essays on the Twentieth Century Struggle* (New York: Oxford University Press, 1980), 59–60; National Industrial Conference Board, *Industrial Relations Programs in Small Plants* (New York: National Relations Conference Board, 1929), 13, 16; Berkowitz and McQuaid, *Creating the Welfare State*, 54–56; Jacoby, *Modern Manors*, 20, 24, 26–31; Michael B. Katz, *In the Shadow of the Poorhouse: A Social History of Welfare in America* (New York: Basic Books, 1996), 196.

11. Donald Finlay Davis, *Conspicuous Production: Automobile Elites in Detroit, 1899–1933* (Philadelphia: Temple University Press, 1988) chs. 1, 4. On Detroit's economy during the period, see especially Olivier Zunz, *The Changing Face of Inequality: Urbanization, Industrialization and Immigrants in Detroit, 1880–1920* (Chicago: University of Chicago Press, 1982).

12. Davis, *Conspicuous Production*, 61–63, 125–37. Davis depicts James Couzens (discussed below) as similarly alienated from the city's corporate elite. I have not found this to be the case when it comes to many facets of social politics. See, for example, Davis, *Conspicuous Production*, 11–12, 132–35, 137–43.

13. Melvin Holli, ed., *Detroit* (New York: Viewpoints, 1976), 120; Davis, *Conspicuous Production*, 101–3.

14. Daniel M. Bluestone, "Detroit's City Beautiful and the Problem of Commerce," *Journal of the Society of Architectural Historians* 47 (September 1988): 245–62, quoted 257–58; "How the Board Helped Secure the New Library," *Detroiter*, March 19, 1921, p. 9; Frank B. Woodford, *Parnassus on Main Street: A History of the Detroit Public Library* (Detroit: Wayne State University Press, 1965), chs. 11, 13; Jeffry Abt, *A Museum on the Verge: A Socioeconomic History of the Detroit Institute of Arts, 1882–2000* (Detroit: Wayne State University Press, 2001), ch. 2.

15. "The Child—An Unfinished Product," *Detroiter*, November 1913, pp. 11, 21 (quoted); "Splendid Recreation System Is Assured," *Detroiter*, May 3, 1915, p. 1.

16. On Detroit's charter reform campaign, see especially Raymond R. Fragnoli, *The Transformation of Reform, Progressivism in Detroit—and After, 1912-1933* (New York: Garland, 1982). For a useful discussion of business interests' varying attitudes toward Prohibition and an overview of the pertinent literature, see Ranjit S. Dighe, "The U.S. Business Press and Prohibition," *Social History of Alcohol and Drugs* 22 (Spring 2008): 228–42.

17. Fragnoli, *Transformation of Reform*, ch. 4; Abt, *Museum on the Verge*, ch. 2; Jeffrey Mirel, *The Rise and Fall of an Urban School System: Detroit, 1907-1981*, 2nd ed. (Ann Arbor: University of Michigan Press, 1999), ch. 1.

18. Mirel, *Rise and Fall of an Urban School System*, 53. For the endorsements of the Detroit Citizens League during the 1920s, see its official publication, *The Civic Searchlight*.

19. On the upheaval that followed the First World War, see, for instance, Nell Irvin Painter, *Standing at Armageddon: The United States, 1877-1919* (New York: W. W. Norton & Co., 1987).

20. "Labor Is Cure for City Ills," *Detroit Free Press*, October 17, 1919, clipping, scrapbook 3, MS Detroit Citizens League (henceforth DCL), Burton Historical Collection (henceforth BHC), Detroit Public Library (henceforth DPL), includes quotes; Davis, *Conspicuous Production*, 103.

21. "City Administration Essays Solving Many Problems in 1920," *Detroiter*, January 3, 1920, p. 3.

22. "Couzens Asks Rent Sermon," *Detroit News*, August 21, 1920, clipping, scrapbook 4, DCL, BHC, DPL.

23. "Detroit Has Made Splendid Beginning on Program of Parks and Playgrounds," *Detroiter*, August 13, 1919, p. 4; Woodford, *Parnassus on Main Street*, 225. On the school budget, see *Seventy-Eighth Annual Report of the Superintendent of Schools* (Detroit: Board of Education, City of Detroit, 1921), 7, 14.

24. "Schools," *Detroiter*, September 10, 1923, p. 12.

25. "City Bond Limit Passed by 37 Million," *Detroit Free Press*, March 19, 1923, clipping, scrapbook 6, DCL, BHC, DPL; "City at Crisis, Mayor Urges Rigid Economy," May 26, 1923, clipping, scrapbook 6, DCL, BHC, DPL. On the KKK in Detroit and the 1924 election, see Kevin Boyle, *Arc of Justice: A Saga of Race, Civil Rights and Murder in the Jazz Age* (New York: Henry Holt, 2004); Kenneth T. Jackson, *The Ku Klux Klan in the City, 1915-1930* (New York: Oxford University Press), ch. 9.

26. John W. Smith, "Business Men Will Probe City's Finances," *Detroiter*, January 5, 1925, p. 7; "An Open Letter to Richard P. Joy," *Detroiter*, January 12, 1925, p. 1 (first quote); "Committee on City Loan Funds," *Civic Searchlight*, January 1925, p. 3; *Detroit Labor News*, August 19, 1927 (second quote).

27. "444 Millions Asked for City," *Detroit News*, May 22, 1925, clipping, scrapbook 8; DCL, BHC, DPL.

28. Abt, *Museum on the Verge*, ch. 3; Davis, *Conspicuous Production*, 170–74; *Detroit Labor News*, October 21, 1927.

29. "We Have Faith in Atlanta," *Journal of Labor*, October 9, 1925.

30. "Senate Declined to Accept Report," *Atlanta Constitution*, August 15, 1918, p. 4; "$1,000,000 Bond Election Called," *Atlanta Constitution*, January 24, 1919, p. 1.

31. "'Greater Atlanta' by a Million Dollars in Bonds," *Atlanta Constitution*, February 19, 1908, p. 6.

32. "The City Bond Issue," *Atlanta Constitution*, August 12, 1908, p. 6. See also "Reports Favor Big Bond Issue of $1,500,000," *Atlanta Constitution*, March 28, 1908, p. 1.

33. Thomas Mashburn Deaton, "Atlanta During the Progressive Era" (Ph.D. diss., University of Georgia, 1969), 346–47.

34. "Inaugural Speech Made by President F. J. Paxon," *Atlanta Constitution*, December 17, 1909, p. 2; Franklin M. Garrett, *Atlanta and Environs: A Chronicle of Its People and Events*, Vol. II, (Athens: University of Georgia Press, 1954), 375–77.

35. "Build for Future of Atlanta, Say Business Men Indorsing Movement for Bond Issue," *Atlanta Constitution*, November 30, 1912, p. 1; "Preachers to Aid Grady Bond Issue," *Atlanta Constitution*, April 30, 1914, p. 4; "Favor Bond Issue to Furnish Work for Unemployed," *Atlanta Constitution*, January 28, 1915, p. 1; "Georgia Cities Will Help in Fight to Change the Bond Election Laws," *Atlanta Constitution*, February 13, 1917, p. 6.

36. For an in-depth discussion of these dynamics, along with pertinent citations, see Amsterdam, *Roaring Metropolis*, ch. 4.

37. "Civic Engineers and Realty Men Favor Zone Plan," *Atlanta Constitution*, February 17, 1922, p. 1.

38. Howard L. Preston, *Automobile Age Atlanta: The Making of a Southern Metropolis: 1900–1935* (Athens: University of Georgia Press, 1979), 149, 157; "Atlanta Planning Board Will Meet for Organiation [*sic*]," *Atlanta Constitution*, October 25, 1920, p. 4; Garrett, *Atlanta and Environs*, Vol. II, 771, 777; Michael Perman, *Struggle for Mastery: Disfranchisement in the South, 1898–1908* (Chapel Hill: University of North Carolina Press, 2001), 289–93; Ronald Bayor, *Race and the Shaping of Twentieth-Century Atlanta* (Chapel Hill: University of North Carolina Press, 1996), 54–55.

39. On the depression and municipal finances in Detroit and Atlanta, see, for example, *Frank Murphy: The Detroit Years* (Ann Arbor: University of Michigan Press, 1975); Erik H. Monkonnen, *The Local State: Public Money and American Cities* (Palo Alto, Calif.: Stanford University Press, 1995); Mark I. Gelfand, *A Nation of Cities: The Federal Government and Urban America, 1933–1965* (New York: Oxford University Press, 1975); Roger Biles, *The South and the New Deal* (Lexington: University of Kentucky Press, 1994); Douglas Lee Fleming, "Atlanta, the Depression and the New Deal" (Ph.D. diss., Emory University, 1984).

Chapter 3. The "Monopoly" Hearings, Their Critics, and the Limits of Patent Reform in the New Deal

1. Franklin D. Roosevelt, "Message from the President of the United States Transmitting Recommendations Relative to the Strengthening and Enforcement of Antitrust Laws," April 29, 1938, in *Investigation of Concentration of Economic Power: Hearings before the Temporary National Economic Committee*, 31 vols. (Washington, D.C.: Government Printing Office, 1939–1941), Part 1, Exhibit 1, 185–91, quoted 185, 189. Hereafter, I refer to the published testimony and exhibits as *TNEC*.

2. *Final Report and Recommendations of the Temporary National Economic Committee* (Washington, D.C.: Government Printing Office, 1941), 696, 729.

3. B. Zorina Khan, *The Democratization of Invention: Patents and Copyrights in American Economic Development, 1790–1920* (Cambridge: Cambridge University Press, 2005). Khan and other scholars also acknowledge that it was initially difficult for antebellum inventors to profit economically from their patents because of rampant infringement and lax enforcement. See Steven Lubar, "The Transformation of Antebellum Patent Law," *Technology and Culture* 32 (October 1991): 932–59.

4. Petra Moser, "Patents and Innovation: Evidence from Economic History," *Journal of Economic Perspectives* 27 (Winter 2013): 23–44; Tom Nicholas, "Are Patents Creative or Destructive?" *Antitrust Law Journal* 79, no. 2 (2014): 405–21; James Bessen and Michael J. Meurer, *Patent Failure: How Judges, Bureaucrats, and Lawyers Put Innovators at Risk* (Princeton, N.J.: Princeton University Press, 2008).

5. On the emergence of industrial research and corporate patenting, see David Hounshell, "The Evolution of Industrial Research in the United States," in *Engines of Innovation: U.S. Industrial Research at the End of an Era*, ed. Richard S. Rosenbloom and William J. Spencer (Boston: Harvard Business School Press, 1996); David Noble, *America by Design: Science, Technology, and the Rise of Corporate Capitalism* (New York: Knopf, 1977); and Catherine L. Fisk, *Working Knowledge: Employee Innovation and the Rise of Corporate Intellectual Property, 1800–1930* (Chapel Hill: University of North Carolina Press, 2009).

6. Christopher Beauchamp, *Invented by Law: Alexander Graham Bell and the Patent That Changed America* (Cambridge, Mass.: Harvard University Press, 2015); Harold Passer, *The Electrical Manufacturers, 1875–1900: A Study in Competition, Entrepreneurship, Technical Change, and Economic Growth* (Cambridge, Mass.: Harvard University Press, 1953).

7. Edwin J. Prindle and L. W. Moffet, quoted in Noble, *America by Design*, 89 (first quote), 85 (second quote).

8. Ellis W. Hawley, *The New Deal and the Problem of Monopoly* (Princeton, N.J.: Princeton University Press, 1966); Tony Freyer, *Regulating Big Business: Antitrust in Great Britain and America, 1880–1990* (Cambridge: Cambridge University Press, 1992); Tony Freyer, *Antitrust and Global Capitalism, 1930–2004* (Cambridge: Cambridge University Press, 2006); Wyatt Wells, *Antitrust and the Formation of the Postwar World* (New York: Columbia University Press, 2002).

9. An exception is Larry Owens, who focuses on the "frontier" rhetoric of the hearings; see Owens, "Patents, the 'Frontiers' of American Invention, and the Monopoly Committee of 1939: Anatomy of a Discourse," *Technology and Culture* 32 (October 1991): 1076–93.

10. On NAM's early history, see its pamphlets, *The Public Be Served: NAM, What It Is, What It Has Done, What It Believes, How It Operates* (New York: NAM, 1949); and NAM President Wallace F. Bennett, *The Very Human History of "NAM"* (New York: Newcomen Society of America, 1949). Scholarly studies include Albion G. Taylor, *Labor Policies of the National Association of Manufacturers* (Urbana: University of Illinois, 1928); Albert K. Steigerwalt, *The National Association of Manufacturers, 1895–1914: A Study in Business Leadership* (Ann Arbor: University of Michigan, 1964); Alfred S. Cleveland, "Some Political Aspects of Organized Industry" (Ph.D. diss., Harvard University, 1947); John N. Stalker, "The National Association of Manufacturers: A Study in Ideology" (Ph.D. diss., University of Wisconsin, 1951); and Jennifer Delton's essay in this volume (Chapter 9).

11. Hawley, *The New Deal and the Problem of Monopoly*, 7–146, quoted 14.

12. Ibid., 383–419. David Lynch, *Concentration of Economic Power* (New York: Columbia University Press, 1946), 8–25.

13. Franklin D. Roosevelt, "Message to Congress on Stimulating Recovery," April 14, 1938, in John T. Woolley and Gerhard Peters, eds., *The American Presidency Project*, accessed January 9, 2015, http://www.presidency.ucsb.edu/ws/?pid=15626; Roosevelt, "Message Relative to the Strengthening and Enforcement of Antitrust Laws."

14. Laurence Stern, "Outline of a New Economic Order," *Magazine of Wall Street* 62 (September 24, 1938): 670–72, as quoted in Lynch, *Concentration of Economic Power*, 54.

15. On the institutionalists, see Malcolm Rutherford, *The Institutionalist Movement in American Economics, 1918–1947: Science and Social Control* (Cambridge: Cambridge University Press, 2011) and essays by Laura Phillips Sawyer (Chapter 1) and Richard R. John and Jason Scott Smith (Chapter 5) in this volume. On the Berle memorandum, see Lynch, *Concentration of Economic Power*, 55–57. Finally, see Walton Hamilton, *Patents and Free Enterprise*, TNEC Monograph 31 (Washington, D.C.: Government Printing Office, 1941).

16. Joseph C. O'Mahoney, *Preliminary Report of Temporary National Economic Committee*, 76th Cong., 1st sess., 1939, S. Doc. 95, 5–22.

17. On Arnold, see Corwin D. Edwards, "Thurman Arnold and the Antitrust Laws," *Political Science Quarterly* 58 (September 1943): 338–55; Gene M. Gressley, "Thurman Arnold, Antitrust, and the New Deal," *Business History Review* 38 (Summer 1964): 214–31; Wilson Miscamble, "Thurman Arnold Goes to Washington: A Look at Antitrust Policy in the Later New Deal," *Business History Review* 56 (Spring 1982): 1–15; and Alan Brinkley, "The Antimonopoly Ideal and the Liberal State: The Case of Thurman Arnold," *Journal of American History* 80 (September 1993): 557–79.

18. *TNEC*, Part 2, 256, 665.

19. William Greenleaf, *Monopoly on Wheels: Henry Ford and the Selden Automobile Patent.* (Detroit: Wayne State University Press, 2011). Individual patentees also extorted the railroad industry; see Steven W. Usselman and Richard R. John, "Patent Politics: Intellectual Property, the Railroad Industry, and the Problem of Monopoly," *Journal of Policy History* 18, no. 1 (2006): 96–125.

20. *TNEC*, Part 2, 256–328.

21. For a helpful summary, see George E. Folk, *Patents and Industrial Progress: A Summary, Analysis, and Evaluation of the Record on Patents of the Temporary National Economic Committee*, 2nd ed. (New York: Harper & Brothers, 1942), 28. For Farley's quotation, see *TNEC*, Part 2, 262–63.

22. This evidence had been uncovered via subpoenas in a pending case that Arnold's Antitrust Division was preparing against firms in the glassware industry. Hartford-Empire was eventually convicted of antitrust violations. See "Hartford-Empire v. United States: Integration of the Anti-Trust and Patent Laws," *Columbia Law Review* 45 (July 1945): 601–25.

23. See *TNEC*, Part 2, 377–667, as well as Exhibits 112–62, 303, and 431 in the Appendix, 737–834. For the percentages, see p. 383 and "Major Inter-Company Relations in the Glass Container Industry," Exhibit 113, *TNEC* Part 2, 762. For helpful summaries, see Folk, *Patents and Industrial Progress*, 29–61; and Lynch, *Concentration of Economic Power*, 162–64, 227–31, 273–79.

24. "Hartford-Empire Company—Annual Receipts from Royalties and License Fees," Exhibit 115, *TNEC*, Part 2, 764.

25. Hartford-Empire delayed the issuance of the Steimer "gob-feed" patent for about twenty years. See *TNEC*, Part 2, 438–41; also Exhibit 199, *TNEC*, Part 3, 1134; also Lynch, *Concentration of Economic Power*, 230.

26. *TNEC*, Part 2, 624–37.

27. See *TNEC*, Part 2, 400–426; also "Memorandum as to Hartford-Fairmont and Hartford-Empire History and Policy," March 26, 1928, Exhibit 124, *TNEC*, Part 2, 768–71.

28. "Memorandum on Policy of Hartford-Empire Company," February 18, 1930, Exhibit 125, *TNEC* Part 2, 771–80. Also see *TNEC*, Part 2, 386–96, 449–52; and Lynch, *Concentration of Economic Power*, 162–63.

29. *TNEC*, Part 2, 455–56.

30. *TNEC*, Part 3, 838–67, 1043–44, quoted 859; also see Exhibits 179–205, pp. 1123–37.

31. *TNEC*, Part 3, 853–54, 860–61; Exhibits 198–99, pp. 1133–34.

32. *TNEC*, Part 3, 854–55, 861–62; Exhibit 193, p. 1130; Exhibits 200–201, pp. 1134–35.

33. *TNEC*, Part 3, 855–57, 860; Exhibit 202, p. 1136.

34. *TNEC*, Part 3, 862.

35. *TNEC*, Part 3, 838–43, quoted 842; Exhibits 163–78, pp. 1107–22.

36. *TNEC*, Part 3, 863.

37. "Map Wide Inquiry on Patent System," *New York Times*, August 7, 1938, p. 18.

38. *Final Report and Recommendations*, 36–37.

39. "Map Wide Inquiry on Patent System."

40. For Farnsworth's testimony, see *TNEC*, Part 3, 981–1006. For Coe's example of the small-scale engine inventor, see Conway Coe to Joseph O'Mahoney, March 7, 1941, reprinted in *TNEC*, Part 31-A, 18475–78.

41. On the "pioneering" rhetoric, see Owens, "Patents, the 'Frontiers' of American Invention, and the Monopoly Committee of 1939." For Jewett's quotation, see *TNEC*, Part 3, 977.

42. *Final Report and Recommendations*, 36.

43. For NAM member firms, see minutes of the NAM Patent Committee, November 16, 1938, and December 7, 1939, in the chronological "NAM Committee Minutes," folders from 1938–39, Box 150, National Association of Manufacturers Records, Hagley Museum and Library, Wilmington, Delaware, (hereafter NAM Records).

44. John Scoville and Noel Sargent, *Fact and Fancy in the TNEC Monographs* (New York: National Association of Manufacturers, 1942).

45. I've found no evidence that NAM's lobbying influenced Coe's TNEC testimony or recommendations; rather, the Coe-NAM relationship apparently developed after the hearings. On the town hall meetings, see "Minutes of the Modern Pioneers Executive Committee," July 18, 1939, Folder: "NAM Committee Minutes 1939, July–October;" on NAM's Patent Office tour, see"Report of the Meeting of the Patent Procedure Subcommittee with Conway P. Coe, United States Commissioner of Patents," Folder: "NAM Committee Minutes 1939, April–June;" all in Box 150, NAM Records.

46. For the NAM's positions, see "Minutes of Patent Legislation Subcommittee of the Patents and Trademarks Committee," March 16, 1939, Folder: "NAM Committee Minutes 1939, January–April," Box 150, NAM Records; also Robert Lund's address before NAM's 44th Congress of American Industry, December 7, 1939, reprinted as *Patents and Free Enterprise* (New York: NAM, 1940).

47. NAM member testifying before the TNEC patent hearings included George Baekeland (Bakelite Corporation), William Coolidge (General Electric), F. Goodwin Smith (Hartford-Empire), Milton Tibbetts (Packard Motor Car Co.), and Clarence C. Carlton (Motor Wheel Corporation). On witness preparations, see minutes of the "Special Research Subcommittee Meeting to Consider the Patent Hearings," October 31, 1938, Folder: "NAM Committee Minutes 1938, July–November," Box 150, NAM Records.

48. See Folk, *Patents and Industrial Progress*. Pamphlets include *How to Analyze the Patent Situation in Your Company* (New York: NAM, 1939); *Limitations of the Right to License Patents* (New York: NAM, 1939?); *You and Patents* (New York: NAM, 1939?); *Inventive America* (New York: NAM, 1941); *Patents and Invention* (New York: NAM, 1942); and George E. Folk, *A Review of Proposals for Revision of the United States Patent System* (New York: NAM, 1946).

49. "Minutes of the Meeting of N.A.M. Committee on Patents and Trademarks," April 26, 1938, Folder: "NAM Committee Minutes 1939, January–April," Box 150, NAM Records.

50. See NAM, "Telling America the Truth About Our Patent System," March 1940, Folder: "Modern Pioneers Folder #2," Box 195, NAM Records. The NICB-AEC report was to be completed in April 1940; however, I have been unable to locate a copy in the NAM Records. The quote is from the AEC's Fairfield E. Raymond,"Minutes of Meeting of NAM Committee on Patents and Research," April 12, 1940, Folder: "NAM Committee Minutes 1940, April," Box 151, NAM Records.

51. Richard Tedlow, "The National Association of Manufacturers and Public Relations During the New Deal," *Business History Review* 50 (Spring 1976): 25–45.

52. "Telling America the Truth About Our Patent System," under "I. The Modern Pioneer Program."

53. "Minutes of Meeting of the National Modern Pioneers Executive Committee," July 18, 1939, Folder: "NAM Committee Minutes 1939, July–October," Box 150, NAM Records. Also, see "Entries for NAM Awards to Inventors Close December 1," press release, November 28, 1939, Folder: "Modern Pioneers Folder #1," Box 195, NAM Records. Finally, see "Nomination for Modern Pioneer on the American Frontier of Industry," an entry blank, 1939, Folder: "Modern Pioneers Folder #2," Box 195, NAM Records.

54. Historian Frederick Jackson Turner believed that the struggle to overcome the American frontier inspired the nation's exceptional and democratic qualities; see *The Frontier in American History* (New York: Henry Holt and Co., 1920).

55. "Entries for NAM Awards to Inventors Close December 1."

56. Ibid.

57. For the award winners, see the banquet program, "National Modern Pioneers Banquet," February 27, 1940, Folder: "Modern Pioneers Folder #2," Box 195, NAM Records.

58. NAM, "Telling America the Truth About Our Patent System," also "Summary of the 13 Regional Modern Pioneers Banquets," 1940, Folder: "Modern Pioneers Folder #1," Box 195, NAM Records.

59. Robert L. Lund, "Patents Make Jobs," NBC radio address, February 26, 1940, printed in *Our Modern Pioneers and the American Patent System: A Series of Addresses Given at the National Modern Pioneers Banquet* (New York: National Association of Manufacturers, 1940), 23–29, quoted 26, 29.

60. For all the speeches, see *Our Modern Pioneers and the American Patent System*.

61. See NAM, "Telling America the Truth;" also "Summary of the 13 Regional Modern Pioneers Banquets."

62. *Final Report and Recommendations*, 36–37, 357–59; Lynch, *Concentration of Economic Power*, 359, 376.

63. F. L. O. Wadsworth, "The Guild's Relation to Patent Practise," presented at a meeting of the Inventors' Guild, November 1910 and subsequently reprinted in 1913 as Wadsworth, "Preliminary Report to the Inventors' Guild—I," *Scientific American Supplement* 1940 (March 8, 1913): 146–47; Wadsworth, "Preliminary Report to the Inventors' Guild—II," *Scientific American Supplement* 1941 (March 15, 1913): 166; and Wadsworth, "Preliminary Report to the Inventors' Guild—III," *Scientific American Supplement* 1942 (March 22, 1913): 178–79.

64. "Inventors to Back Patent Reforms," *New York Times*, December 13, 1910, p. 11.

65. Eric S. Hintz, "The Post-Heroic Generation: American Independent Inventors, 1900–1950," (Ph.D. diss., University of Pennsylvania, 2010), especially ch. 2: "The Professional Lives of American Independent Inventors."

66. Alan Brinkley, *The End of Reform: New Deal Liberalism in Recession and War* (New York: Knopf, 1995), 106–36.

67. Freyer, *Antitrust and Global Capitalism*, 32–59; Wells, *Antitrust and the Formation of the Postwar World*, 27–136. On the AT&T consent decree, see Gerald W. Brock, *The Second Information Revolution* (Cambridge, Mass.: Harvard University Press, 2003), 116–20.

68. In 1982, Congress established the Court of Appeals for the Federal Circuit in Washington, D.C., with nationwide appellate jurisdiction over all patent cases. See U.S. Courts, "Court Jurisdiction," accessed July 28, 2014, http://www.cafc.uscourts.gov/the-court/court-jurisdiction .html. On implementation of the twenty-year rule, see M. Henry Heines, *Patent Empowerment for Small Corporations* (Westport, Conn.: Quorum, 2001), 64.

69. Smith-Leahy America Invents Act of 2011, Pub. L. No. 112-29, 125 Stat. 284 (2011). For the NAM's endorsement, see NAM's Dorothy Coleman to members of the House of Representatives, June 20, 2011, accessed January 17 2015, http://www.nam.org/Issues/Intellectual-Property/NAM -Letter-to-Support-H_R_-1249—the-America-Invents-Act/. For the impact on independent inventors, see Steve Lohr," Inventor Challenges a Sweeping Revision in Patent Law," *New York Times*, August 27, 2012, p. B1.

Chapter 4. Farewell to Progressivism

1. Claude A. Swanson to FDR, March 31, 1937, Folder: Navy Department 1933–40, Box 7, President's Secretary's File, Franklin D. Roosevelt Presidential Library and Museum, available in digital format at http://www.fdrlibrary.marist.edu (accessed December 2013; referred to hereafter as PSF-FDR); Robert Gannon, *Hellions of the Deep: The Development of American Torpedoes in World War II* (University Park: Pennsylvania State University Press, 1996), 28–34; Thomas Wildenberg and Norman Polmar, *Ship Killer: A History of the American Torpedo* (Annapolis, Md.: Naval Institute Press, 2010), 33–57. On Bliss, the Navy, and torpedoes before the First World War, see Katherine C. Epstein, *Torpedo: Inventing the Military-Industrial Complex in the United States and Great Britain* (Cambridge, Mass.: Harvard University Press, 2014).

2. W. R. Furlong memo on "Expansion of Torpedo Production," January 5, 1938, Folder: Navy January–February 1938, Box 58, PSF-FDR; W. H. P. Brandy undated 1941 memo on torpedoes, Folder: Navy July–December 1940, Box 59, PSF-FDR.

3. Michael Reich, "Does the U.S. Economy Require Military Spending?" *American Economic Review* (March 1972): 299.

4. John Kenneth Galbraith, *The New Industrial State* (Boston: Houghton Mifflin, 1967); Seymour Melman, *Pentagon Capitalism: The Political Economy of War* (New York: McGraw Hill, 1970); Robert L. Heilbroner, "The State Within a State: An Essay on Pentagon Capitalism," in *Arms, Industry, and America*, ed. Kenneth S. Davis (New York: H. W. Wilson, 1971), 142–44.

5. Naomi Lamoreaux, Daniel M. G. Raff, and Peter Temin,"Beyond Markets and Hierarchies: Toward a New Synthesis of American Business History," *American Historical Review* 108, no. 2 (2003): 404–33.

6. One of these generated several major articles but was never published as a whole book: Barton Jannen Bernstein, "The Truman Administration and the Politics of Inflation" (Ph.D. diss., Harvard University, 1964). For the others, I cite the published book versions: Susan H. Armitage, *The Politics of Decontrol of Industry: Britain and the United States* (London: Weidenfeld and Nicholson, 1969); Paul A. C. Koistinen, *The Hammer and the Sword: Labor, the Military, and Industrial Mobilization, 1920–1945* (New York: Arno Press, 1979); Robert D. Cuff, *The War Industries Board: Business-Government Relations during World War I* (Baltimore: Johns Hopkins University Press, 1973); Melvin I. Urofksy, *Big Steel and the Wilson Administration: A Study in Government-Business Relations* (Columbus: Ohio State University Press, 1969); Benjamin Frank-

lin Cooling, *Gray Steel and Blue Water Navy: The Formative Years of America's Military-Industrial Complex, 1881–1917* (Hamden, Conn.: Archon, 1979).

7. On Mills's early concerns, see Kevin Mattson, *Intellectuals in Action: The Origins of the New Left and Radical Liberalism, 1945–1970* (University Park: Pennsylvania State University Press, 2002), 43–96.

8. Joseph D. Phillips, "Economic Effects of the Cold War," in *Corporations and the Cold War*, ed. David Horowitz (New York: Monthly Review Press, 1969), 190; John Kenneth Galbraith, *How to Control the Military* (New York: Doubleday, 1969); Melman, *Pentagon Capitalism*; Charles C. Moskos, Jr., "The Concept of the Military-Industrial Complex: Radical Critique or Liberal Bogey?" *Social Problems* 21, (April 1974): 498–512; James Ledbetter, *Unwarranted Influence: Dwight D. Eisenhower and the Military-Industrial Complex* (New Haven, Conn.: Yale University Press, 2011), 147–51.

9. Among them was Eisenhower himself. See Alex Roland, "The Military-Industrial Complex: Lobby and Trope," in *The Long War: A New History of U.S. National Security Policy Since World War II*, ed. Andrew J. Bacevich (New York: Columbia University Press, 2007), 336–38; Ledbetter, *Unwarranted Influence*, 106–31; Dolores E. Janiewski, "Eisenhower's Paradoxical Relationship with the 'Military-Industrial Complex,'" *Presidential Studies Quarterly* 41 (December 2011): 667–92.

10. For an insider's critique, see William Proxmire, *Report from Wasteland: America's Military-Industrial Complex* (New York: Praeger, 1970). For a more recent account from a libertarian-minded economic historian, see Robert Higgs, *Depression, War, and Cold War: Studies in Political Economy* (Oakland, Calif.: Independent Institute, 2006), 176–85.

11. Stanley Lieberson, "An Empirical Study of Military-Industrial Linkages," *American Journal of Sociology* 76, no. 4 (1971): 562–84; Roland, "Military-Industrial Complex," 344–46; Ledbetter, *Unwarranted Influence*, 188; Benjamin Franklin Cooling, "The Military-Industrial Complex," in *A Companion to American Military History*, ed. James C. Bradford (Malden, Mass.: Wiley-Blackwell, 2010), 2: 966–89.

12. A few examples, out of a large body of important works, include Merritt Roe Smith, *Harpers Ferry Armory and the New Technology: The Challenge of Change* (Ithaca, N.Y.: Cornell University Press, 1977); David A. Hounshell, *From the American System to Mass Production, 1800–1932: The Development of Manufacturing Technology in the United States* (Baltimore: Johns Hopkins University Press, 1984); David F. Noble, *Forces of Production: A Social History of Industrial Automation* (New York: Knopf, 1984); Stuart W. Leslie, *The Cold War and American Science: The Military-Industrial-Academic Complex at Stanford and MIT* (New York: Columbia University Press, 1993); Martin J. Collins, *Cold War Laboratory: RAND, the Air Force, and the American State, 1945–1950* (Washington, D.C.: Smithsonian Institution Press, 2002); Christophe Lécuyer, *Making Silicon Valley: Innovation and the Growth of High Tech* (Cambridge, Mass.: MIT Press, 2007); Jeffrey A. Engel, *Cold War at 30,000 Feet: The Anglo-American Fight for Aviation Supremacy* (Cambridge, Mass.: Harvard University Press, 2007); Jonathan Reed Winkler, *Nexus: Strategic Communications and American Security in World War I* (Cambridge, Mass.: Harvard University Press, 2008); Philip Scranton, "Mastering Failure: Technological and Organisational Challenges in British and American Military Jet Propulsion, 1943–57," *Business History* 53 (July 2011): 479–504; Epstein, *Torpedo*.

13. For two intriguing works on successful Cold War weapons programs, which suggest the absurdity of leaving military actors out of our stories, see Harvey M. Sapolsky, *The Polaris System Development: Bureaucratic and Programmatic Success in Government* (Cambridge, Mass.:

Harvard University Press, 1972); and Glenn E. Bugos, *Engineering the F-4 Phantom II: Parts into Systems* (Annapolis, Md.: Naval Institute Press, 1996).

14. For one recent study that is well crafted and provocative but contains remarkably little evidence from the records of the key contractor and the key military procurement agency in the story, see Robert M. Neer, *Napalm: An American Biography* (Cambridge, Mass.: Harvard University Press, 2013).

15. Samuel P. Huntington, *The Soldier and the State: The Theory and Politics of Civil-Military Relations* (Cambridge, Mass.: Harvard University Press, 1981).

16. Terrence James Gough, "The Battle of Washington: Soldiers and Businessmen in World War I" (Ph.D. diss., University of Virginia, 1997); Mark R. Wilson, *Destructive Creation: American Business and the Winning of World War II* (Philadelphia: University of Pennsylvania Press, 2016).

17. Irving Brinton Holley, Jr., *Buying Aircraft: Matériel Procurement for the Army Air Forces* (Washington, D.C.: Office of the Chief of Military History, 1964); Elliott V. Converse III, *Rearming for the Cold War, 1945–1960* (Washington, D.C.: Historical Office of the Secretary of Defense, 2012); Walter S. Poole, *Adapting to Flexible Response, 1960–1968* (Washington, D.C.: Historical Office of the Office of the Secretary of Defense, 2013). There are many other important works by military establishment insiders. See, for example, Jacques S. Gansler, *The Defense Industry* (Cambridge, Mass.: MIT Press, 1980), and his subsequent works, as well as the work of Gary E. Weir, including his *Forged in War: The Naval-Industrial Complex and American Submarine Construction, 1940–1961* (Washington, D.C.: Naval Historical Center, 1993).

18. Daniel Carpenter and David A. Moss, eds., *Preventing Regulatory Capture: Special Interest Influence and How to Limit It* (New York: Cambridge University Press, 2014); Benjamin C. Waterhouse, *Lobbying America: The Business of Politics from Nixon to NAFTA* (Princeton, N.J.: Princeton University Press, 2014); Eduardo Federico Canedo, "The Rise of the Deregulation Movement in Modern America, 1957–1980" (Ph.D. diss., Columbia University, 2008).

19. For example, Kenneth R. Mayer, *The Political Economy of Defense Contracting* (New Haven, Conn.: Yale University Press, 1991); Rebecca U. Thorpe, *The American Warfare State: The Domestic Politics of Military Spending* (Chicago: University of Chicago Press, 2014); Eugene Gholz, "The Curtiss-Wright Corporation and Cold War-Era Defense Procurement: A Challenge to Military-Industrial Complex Theory," *Journal of Cold War Studies* 2 (Winter 2000): 35–75. For a historically informed, policy-oriented primer with up-to-date citations, see Harvey M. Sapolsky, Eugene Gholz, and Caitlin Talmadge, *US Defense Politics: The Origins of Security Policy*, 2nd ed. (London and New York: Routledge, 2014).

20. Jeffrey A. Engel, ed., *Local Consequences of the Global Cold War* (Palo Alto, Calif.: Stanford University Press, 2008); Gretchen Heefner, *The Missile Next Door: The Minuteman in the American Heartland* (Cambridge, Mass: Harvard University Press, 2012); Kari Frederickson, *Cold War Dixie: Militarization and Modernization in the American South* (Athens: University of Georgia Press, 2013); Kate Brown, *Plutopia: Nuclear Families, Atomic Cities, and the Great Soviet and American Plutonium Disasters* (New York: Oxford University Press, 2013). Related earlier studies include Roger W. Lotchin, *Fortress California, 1910–1961: From Warfare to Welfare* (New York: Oxford University Press, 1992).

21. Stephen G. Brooks, *Producing Security: Multinational Corporations, Globalization, and the Changing Calculus of Conflict* (Princeton, N.J.: Princeton Unviersity Press, 2005); Tara M. Lavallee, "Globalizing the Iron Triangle: The Changing Face of the United States Defense Indus-

try" (Ph.D. diss., University of Connecticut, 2005); Daniel Wirls, *Irrational Security: The Politics of Defense from Reagan to Obama* (Baltimore: Johns Hopkins University Press, 2010).

22. John A. Alic, "Managing U.S. Defense Acquisition," *Enterprise & Society* 14 (March 2013): 1–36; Thomas C. Lassman, "Reforming Weapons System Acquisition in the Department of Defense: The Case of the U.S. Army's Advanced Attack Helicopter," *Journal of Policy History* 25 (April 2013): 173–206.

23. Dan Briody, *The Iron Triangle: Inside the Secret World of the Carlisle Group* (New York: John Wiley & Sons, 2003); William D. Hartung, *Prophets of War: Lockheed Martin and the Making of the Military-Industrial Complex* (New York: Nation Books, 2011); Andrew Feinstein, *The Shadow World: Inside the Global Arms Trade*, revised ed. (New York: Picador, 2012); David N. Gibbs, "The Military-Industrial Complex in a Globalized Context," in *Corporate Power and Globalization in U.S. Foreign Policy*, ed. Ronald W. Cox (London and New York: Routledge, 2012), 95–113; Steven Rosefielde and Daniel Quinn Mills, *Democracy and Its Elected Enemies: American Political Capture and Economic Decline* (New York: Cambridge University Press, 2013), 116–25.

24. Paul A. C. Koistinen, *State of War: The Political Economy of American Warfare, 1945–2011* (Lawrence: University Press of Kansas, 2012), 4, 237–43.

25. Cooling, "Military-Industrial Complex," 968–74; Epstein, *Torpedo*, 229; see also Kurt Hackemer, *The U.S. Navy and the Origins of the Military-Industrial Complex, 1847–1883* (Annapolis, Md.: Naval Institute Press, 2001).

26. Epstein, *Torpedo*, 229.

27. This has long been familiar to readers of Gary Weir's outstanding work on submarine construction. See Gary E. Weir, *Building American Submarines, 1914–1940* (Washington, D.C.: Naval Historical Center, 1991); Weir, *Forged In War*. For more recent pieces that call our attention to the public-private balance of warship construction in the first half of the twentieth century, see Mark R. Wilson, "Spinning Mars: Democracy in Britain and the United States and the Economic Lessons of War," in *In War's Wake: International Conflict and the Fate of Liberal Democracy*, ed. Elizabeth Kier and Ron Krebs (New York: Cambridge University Press, 2010), 162–85; Rodney K. Watterson, *32 in '44: Building the Portsmouth Submarine Fleet in World War II* (Annapolis, Md.: Naval Institute Press, 2011); Thomas Heinrich, "'We Can Build Anything at Navy Yards': Warship Construction in Government Yards and the Political Economy of American Naval Shipbuilding, 1928–1945," *International Journal of Maritime History* 24 (December 2012): 155–80.

28. For a review of the literature on the industrial mobilization for the Great War, see Mark R. Wilson, "Economic Mobilization," in *A Companion to Woodrow Wilson*, ed. Ross Kennedy (New York: John Wiley's Sons, 2013), 289–307. For valuable accounts of the interwar era that suggest that major American military contractors were rather tightly regulated, not dominated, by the military and Congress, see Jacob A. Vander Meulen, *The Politics of Aircraft: Building an American Military Industry* (Lawrence: University Press of Kansas, 1991); David A. Mindell, *Between Human and Machine: Feedback, Control, and Computing Before Cybernetics* (Baltimore: Johns Hopkins University Press, 2002), 43–102.

29. Wilson, *Destructive Creation*.

30. The lack of any in-house warship construction after the mid-1960s seems all the more remarkable, given that standing federal law, reiterated in 1965, required presidents to sign special orders if they departed from the legal standard of awarding half of all warship orders to the

Navy's in-house yards. See Laird memo to Nixon, "Proposed Construction in a Private Shipyard of Two Nuclear-Powered Attack Submarines," January 30, 1969, Folder: Shipyards (U.S. Shipyard Capabilities) 1969, Box A91, Melvin Laird Papers, Ford Presidential Library, Ann Arbor, Mich.

31. Neil Fligstein and Doug McAdam, *A Theory of Fields* (New York: Oxford University Press, 2012).

32. Wilson, *Destructive Creation*, chapter 6; Jennifer Mittelstadt, *The Rise of the Military Welfare State* (Cambridge, Mass: Harvard University Press, 2015), 29, 197.

33. For McNamara's own claims about his pursuit of "effectiveness and efficiency," see Robert S. McNamara, *The Essence of Security: Reflections in Office* (New York: Harper & Row, 1968).

34. Among the best of these now numerous studies remain P. W. Singer, *Corporate Warriors: The Rise of the Privatized Military Industry* (Ithaca, N.Y.: Cornell University Press, 2003); Deborah D. Avant, *The Market for Force: The Consequences of Privatizing Security* (New York: Cambridge University Press, 2005).

35. Mittelstadt, *Rise of the Military Welfare State.*

36. Evidently, two-thirds of warships authorized in 1866–83 were built by the U.S. Navy Yards. Bruce G. Brunton, "Institutional Origins of the Military-Industrial Complex," *Journal of Economic Issues* 22 (June 1988): 602. See also Mark R. Wilson, *The Business of Civil War: Military Mobilization and the State, 1861–1865* (Baltimore: Johns Hopkins University Press, 2006); Hackemer, *U.S. Navy and the Origins of the Military-Industrial Complex.*

37. Aaron L. Friedberg, *In the Shadow of the Garrison State: America's Antistatism and Its Cold War Grand Strategy* (Princeton, N.J.: Princeton University Press, 2000).

38. Michael Sherry, "Feature Review: A Hidden-Hand Garrison State?" *Diplomatic History* 27 (January 2003): 163–66, quoted 165. On Sherry vs. Friedberg, see also Roland, "Military-Industrial Complex," 352–55. For one political scientist's book-length response to Friedberg that proceeds along lines similar to those suggested by Sherry, see Linda Weiss, *America Inc? Innovation and Enterprise in the National Security State* (Ithaca, N.Y.: Cornell University Press, 2014).

39. Thomas L. McNaugher, *New Weapons, Old Politics: America's Military Procurement Muddle* (Washington, D.C.: Brookings Institution, 1989); Harvey M. Sapolsky and Eugene Gholz, "Private Arsenals: America's Post-Cold War Burden," in *Arming the Future: A Defense Industry for the 21st Century*, ed. Ann R. Markusen and Sean S. Costigan (New York: Council on Foreign Relations Press, 1999), 191–206; Daniel Wirls, *Buildup: The Politics of Defense in the Reagan Era* (Ithaca, N.Y.: Cornell University Press, 1992); Wirls, *Irrational Security.*

40. For one recent work that succeeds in showing how libertarian economic thinking contributed to military reforms, see Beth Bailey, *America's Army: Making the All-Volunteer Force* (Cambridge, Mass.: Harvard University Press, 2009).

41. Don J. DeYoung, "The Silence of the Labs," *Defense Horizons* 21 (January 2003): 1–8; Don J. DeYoung, "Breaking the Yardstick: The Dangers of Market-Based Governance," *Defense Horizons* 67 (May 2009): 1–8.

42. Ann R. Markusen, "The Case Against Privatizing National Security," *Governance: An International Journal of Policy, Administration, and Institutions* 16 (October 2003): 471–501.

43. I do not think that this idea has been well developed by scholars, but there is some suggestive work, including Jennifer S. Light, *From Warfare to Welfare: Defense Intellectuals and Ur-*

ban Problems in Cold War America (Baltimore: Johns Hopkins University Press, 2003); Mittelstadt, *Rise of the Military Welfare State.*

Chapter 5. Beyond the New Deal

1. Beth Bailey, "Obligation," *Reviews in American History* 42 (June 2014): 385. For suggestions and advice, we are grateful to William C. Childs, Walter A. Friedman, Nancy R. John, Rowena Olegario, Kim Phillips-Fein, and Mark R. Wilson.

2. Eric Foner and Lisa McGirr, eds., *American History Now* (Philadelphia: Temple University Press, 2011).

3. Sven Beckert, "History of American Capitalism," in *American History Now*, ed. Foner and McGirr (Philadelphia: Temple University Press, 2011), 314–35. For some brief yet insightful autobiographical ruminations about how and why the history of capitalism emerged when it did, why its practitioners emphasize certain themes rather than others, and what they hoped to accomplish, see Louis Hyman, "Why Write the History of Capitalism?" *Symposium Magazine*, July 8, 2013, http://www.symposium-magazine.com/why-write-the-history-of-capitalism-louis -hyman/.

4. Beckert, "History of American Capitalism," 321.

5. Thomas K. McCraw, *Prophets of Regulation: Charles Francis Adams, Louis D. Brandeis, James M. Landis, Alfred E. Kahn* (Cambridge, Mass.: Harvard University Press, 1984).

6. Thomas K. McCraw, *Prophet of Innovation: Joseph Schumpeter and Creative Destruction* (Cambridge, Mass.: Belknap Press of Harvard University Press, 2007); Thomas K. McCraw, *Founders and Finance: How Hamilton, Gallatin, and Other Immigrants Forged a New Economy* (Cambridge, Mass.: Belknap Press of Harvard University Press, 2012).

7. Richard R. John, "Prophet of Perspective: Thomas K. McCraw," *Business History Review* 88 (Spring 2015): 129–53.

8. Thomas K. McCraw, "Introduction," in Joseph A. Schumpeter, *Capitalism, Socialism, and Democracy* (New York: Harper Perennial, 2008 [1942]), ix.

9. Sven Beckert, "History of American Capitalism," in Foner and McGirr, *American History Now*, 319. In addition to the scholarship Beckert cites, see also the essays brought together in Kim Phillips-Fein and Julian A. Zelizer, eds., *What's Good for Business: Business and Politics Since World War II* (New York: Oxford University Press, 2012). For a longer view, see the September 2008 *Enterprise and Society* roundtable on political economy, which includes essays by Robin L. Einhorn, Richard R. John, and Jason Scott Smith: "Bringing the State Back In," *Enterprise and Society* 9 (September 2008): 487–534. For the nineteenth century, see Richard R. John, ed., *Ruling Passions: Political Economy in Nineteenth Century America* (University Park: Penn State University Press, 2006); and Michael Zakim and Gary Kornblith, eds., *Capitalism Takes Command: The Social Transformation of Nineteenth-Century America* (Chicago: University of Chicago Press, 2011).

10. Schumpeter, *Capitalism, Socialism, and Democracy*, 83–84.

11. Thomas K. McCraw, "What Economists Have Thought About Competition, and What Difference It Makes," *Proceedings of the Massachusetts Historical Society* 101 (1989): 43, quoting Schumpeter, *Capitalism, Socialism, and Democracy*, 84.

12. Thomas K. McCraw, *American Business Since 1920: How It Worked*, 2nd ed. (Wheeling, Ill.: Harlan Davidson, 2009), 58. For more on McCraw's positive assessment of the New Deal, see Thomas K. McCraw, "The New Deal and the Mixed Economy," in Harvard Sitkoff, ed., *Fifty Years Later: The New Deal Evaluated* (New York: Alfred A. Knopf, 1985), 37–67; and Thomas K.

McCraw, review of Alan Brinkley, *The End of Reform: New Deal Liberalism in Recession and War* in *Journal of American History* 82 (December 1995): 1170–71.

13. For an elaboration on some of these themes, see Jason Scott Smith, *A Concise History of the New Deal* (Cambridge: Cambridge University Press, 2014).

14. Timothy Shenk, "Apostles of Growth," *Nation*, November 14, 2014, http://www.thenation .com/article/apostles-growth/.

15. The "five layers" heuristic, a coinage of the Dutch economist Henrik Wilm Lambers, was originally intended to describe Schumpeter's historical method; it could equally well describe McCraw's. Thomas K. McCraw, "The Creative Destroyer: Schumpeter's Capitalism, Socialism, and Democracy," EH.net, accessed April 16, 2016, https://eh.net/book_reviews/capitalism -socialism-and-democracy/. The five-layer heuristic can be used as a diagnostic device to clarify distinctions between different ways of writing about the relationship of business and politics. Historians of capitalism often neglect three of the layers—namely, the firm, institutions, and leadership—while, prior to the publication of *Founders and Finance,* McCraw devoted relatively little attention to a sixth layer—namely, social class—to which historians of capitalists are highly attentive, given their commitment to writing history from the "bottom up"—all the way to the top. The class-based social movements that historians of capitalism are most intent on exploring, it is perhaps worth underscoring, are elite-led (rather than mass-backed), in keeping with their assumption that, at least in the recent past, the *few* have typically played a far more consequential role than the *many.*

16. Thomas K. McCraw, "The Progressive Legacy," in *The Progressive Era,* ed. Lewis L. Gould (Syracuse, N.Y.: Syracuse University Press, 1974), 200.

17. Susman is quoted in Peter Novick, *That Noble Dream: The "Objectivity Question" and the American Historical Profession* (New York: Cambridge University Press, 1988), 346.

18. Ibid., 420.

19. Thomas K. McCraw, review of Martin J. Sklar, *The Corporate Reconstruction of American Capitalism, 1890–1916: The Market, the Law, and Politics,* in *American Journal of Legal History* 33 (October 1989): 373–75.

20. Thomas K. McCraw, "Ideas, Policies, and Outcomes in Business History," *Business and Economic History* 19 (1990): 7.

21. Ibid.

22. Thomas Kincaid McCraw, "TVA and the Power Fight, 1933–1939" (Ph.D. diss., University of Wisconsin, Madison, 1970), final page (unpaginated).

23. McCraw, "Ideas, Policies, and Outcomes," 8.

24. Thomas K. McCraw, *Morgan vs. Lilienthal: The Feud Within the TVA* (Chicago: Loyola University Press, 1970), 107.

25. Thomas K. McCraw, *TVA and the Power Fight, 1933–1939* (Philadelphia: J. B. Lippincott, 1971), vii.

26. Ibid., 7.

27. Ibid., 9.

28. McCraw, "Ideas, Policies, and Outcomes," 8.

29. Thomas K. McCraw, "Regulation in America: A Review Article," *Business History Review* 49 (Summer 1975): 160.

30. Ibid., 170–71.

31. Ibid., quoting Kolko, 165.

32. Ibid., 171.

33. Ibid., 174–75.

34. Thomas K. McCraw, "Regulation, Chicago Style," *Reviews in American History* 4 (June 1976): 303. Although McCraw remained throughout his career a vigorous critic of the Chicago School, he was willing to concede that the law-and-society scholars could provide interesting perspectives on topics that historians might otherwise neglect. To drive this point home, McCraw liked to quote a statement attributed to the Keynesian economist Paul Samuelson: "Just because Milton Friedman says something doesn't necessarily mean that it's not true."

35. The issues that McCraw highlighted in his 1975 essay have spawned a large literature that built on his critique of "public interest" and "capture" approaches to economic regulation. For a recent update, with relevant citations, see William J. Novak, "A Revisionist History of Regulatory Capture," in *Preventing Regulatory Capture: Special Interest Influence and How to Limit It*, ed. Daniel Carpenter and David A. Moss (Cambridge, Mass.: Cambridge University Press, 2014), 25–48.

36. McCraw, "Regulation in America," 181.

37. This meeting was the third in a series of annual conferences that would jumpstart "policy history" as a subfield. Julian A. Zelizer, "Clio's Lost Tribe: Public Policy History Since 1978," *Journal of Policy History* 12, no. 3 (2000): 375; John, "Prophet of Perspective."

38. Thomas K. McCraw, "Rethinking the Trust Question," in Thomas K. McCraw, ed., *Regulation in Perspective: Historical Essays* (Cambridge: Harvard University Press, 1981), 1–55.

39. Ibid., 20.

40. Ibid., 36.

41. Ibid., 54.

42. Ibid, 54–55.

43. Gerald Berk, *Alternative Tracks: The Constitution of American Industrial Order, 1854–1917* (Baltimore: Johns Hopkins University Press, 1994); Gerald Berk, *Louis D. Brandeis and the Making of Regulated Competition, 1900–1932* (New York: Cambridge University Press, 2009).

44. Richard Hofstadter, *The Age of Reform: From Bryan to FDR* (New York: Vintage, 1955), ch. 6.

45. McCraw, "Ideas, Politics, and Outcomes," 8.

46. Thomas K. McCraw, "With Consent of the Governed: SEC's Formative Years," *Journal of Policy Analysis and Management* 1 (Spring 1982): 363.

47. Charles Schultze, *The Public Use of Private Interest* (Washington, D.C.: Brookings Institution, 1977), quoted in McCraw, "Consent of the Governed," 348.

48. McCraw, "Consent of the Governed," 350.

49. Thomas K. McCraw, review of Donald A. Ritchie, *James M. Landis: Dean of the Regulators,* in *Business History Review* 54 (Autumn 1980): 397–99.

50. McCraw, *Prophets of Regulation.*

51. McCraw, "Ideas, Policies, and Outcomes," 8.

52. Ibid., 9.

53. McCraw, *Prophets of Regulation,* 304.

54. Ibid., 305.

55. Ibid., 305, emphasis in original.

56. Barry D. Karl, review of Thomas K. McCraw, *Prophets of Regulation,* in *Business History Review* 59 (Spring 1985): 117.

57. Gavin Wright, "Regulation in History: The Human Touch," *Reviews in American History* 14 (June 1986): 164. For a broader perspective on the intellectual revival of the market, see

Daniel T. Rodgers, *Age of Fracture* (Cambridge, Mass.: Harvard University Press, 2011), esp. ch. 2, "The Rediscovery of the Market."

58. Wright, "Regulation in History," 167; Naomi R. Lamoreaux, *The Great Merger Movement in American Business, 1895–1904* (New York: Cambridge University Press, 1988).

59. Wright, "Regulation in History," 168, citing McCraw, *Prophets of Regulation*, 340–41, n. 124.

60. Wright, "Regulation in History," 168.

61. McCraw, "Ideas, Policies, and Outcomes," 9.

62. Gras as quoted in McCraw, "Teaching History Courses to Harvard MBA Students: Building Enrollment from 21 to 1,300," *Business and Economic History* 28 (Winter 1999): 154. See also Thomas K. McCraw, Nancy F. Koehn, and H. V. Nelles, "Business History," in *The Intellectual Venture Capitalist: John H. McArthur and the Work of the Harvard Business School, 1980–1995*, ed. Thomas K. McCraw and Jeffrey L. Cruikshank (Boston: Harvard Business School Press, 1999), 246–47.

63. McCraw, "Harvard MBA Students," 156, emphasis in original.

64. Thomas K. McCraw, "The Public and Private Spheres in Historical Perspective," in *Public and Private Partnership: New Opportunities for Meeting Social Needs*, ed. Harvey Brooks, Lance Liebman, and Corinne Schelling (Cambridge, Mass.: Ballinger, 1984), ch. 2. For a briefer and more polished version of the essay, see "Business and Government: The Origins of the Adversary Relationship," *California Management Review* 26 (Winter 1984): 33–52.

65. McCraw, "Ideas, Policies, and Outcomes," 3; Thomas K. McCraw, ed., *America versus Japan: A Comparative Study of Business-Government Relations* (Boston: Harvard Business School Press, 1986).

66. Thomas K. McCraw, "American versus Japan: Conclusions and Implications," in McCraw, *America versus Japan*, 373.

67. W. Mark Fruin, review of *America versus Japan*, in *Business History Review* 61 (Autumn 1987): 528. Italics added.

68. Thomas K. McCraw, ed., *Creating Modern Capitalism: How Entrepreneurs, Companies, and Countries Triumphed in Three Industrial Revolutions* (Cambridge, Mass.: Harvard University Press, 1997).

69. Ibid., vi, 2.

70. William P. Kennedy, review of *Creating Modern Capitalism*, in *American Historical Review* 104 (October 1999): 1271; Richard R. John, "Contextualizing the Corporation," *Journal of Policy History* 12, no. 2 (2000): 287–92, esp. 291.

71. Thomas K. McCraw, *American Business Since 1920: How It Worked* (Wheeling, Ill.: Harlan Davidson, 2000). A second edition was published in 2009; a third edition, with McCraw's former student William R. Childs as the second author, is currently in preparation.

72. Thomas K. McCraw, "The Challenge of Alfred D. Chandler, Jr.: Retrospect and Prospect," *Reviews in American History* 15 (March 1987): 165.

73. Thomas K. McCraw, "Schumpeter Ascending," *American Scholar* 60 (Summer 1991): 371–92.

74. Among historians, the debate over the "Schumpeter hypothesis" continues apace. To cite but one example, the ascendency in the 1910s as the nation's dominant network provider of American Telephone and Telegraph (or Bell, as it was popularly known) over its non-Bell or independent rivals, was long attributed by business historians who were sympathetic to, and in some instances funded by, Bell, to the roll-out by Bell's high-tech research and development labo-

ratory of transcontinental telephony, a blockbuster innovation that (or so they assumed) could only have originated in an organization of Bell's huge size. Revisionist historians, in contrast, debunk this bigger-is-better origins story as a public relations ploy concocted by Bell corporate publicists to forestall adversarial federal legislation. Far more consequential as a locus of innovation, in their view, were municipal operating companies—whether Bell or independent. For the case for Bell, see Richard R. John, *Network Nation: Inventing American Telecommunications* (Cambridge, Mass.: Belknap Press of Harvard University Press, 2010). For the case for the independents, see Robert McDougall, *The People's Network: The Political Economy of the Telephone in the Gilded Age* (Philadelphia: University of Pennsylvania Press, 2014).

75. McCraw, "Schumpeter Ascending."

76. *National Competition Policy: Historians' Perspectives on Antitrust and Government-Business Relations in the United States* (Washington, D.C.: Federal Trade Commission, 1981), 185. Galambos was responding to an unidentified participant, who—surprised by Galambos's small-is-beautiful interpretation of *Capitalism, Socialism, and Democracy*—voiced the then-common view that Schumpeter was "more commonly associated with the notion that you have to be very big in order to innovate." Quoted 184.

77. McCraw, *Creating Modern Capitalism*, 6.

78. Thomas K. McCraw, "Schumpeter's Business Cycles as Business History," *Business History Review* 80 (Summer 2006): 231–61.

79. David Felix, "Economics for the Real World," *Review of Politics* 70 (Winter 2008): 136–39.

80. McCraw, *Prophet of Innovation*, 639–40, n. 25, quoted 650, n. 87.

81. With the exception of *Founders and Finance*, in which immigrant entrepreneur Alexander Hamilton took center stage—uncannily anticipating a plot line in the blockbuster Broadway musical, "Hamilton"—McCraw would publish only a single essay on his new project: McCraw, "Immigrant Entrepreneurs in U.S. Financial History, 1775–1914," *Capitalism and Society* 5, no. 1 (2010): 1–47.

82. Among the factors that hastened the decline of political economy as a subfield for academic historians was the determination of certain conservative corporate philanthropists to discourage its study. For a case study of how one philanthropist tried in the late 1950s to shift the intellectual agenda of American historians at Harvard University from political economy to civil society, see Richard R. John, "From Political Economy to Civil Society: Arthur W. Page, Corporate Philanthropy, and the Reframing of the Past in Post-New Deal America," in *Boundaries of the State in U.S. History*, ed. James T. Sparrow, William J. Novak, and Stephen W. Sawyer (Chicago: University of Chicago Press, 2015), 295–324.

83. Angus Burgin, "Interchange: The History of Capitalism," *Journal of American History* 101 (September 2014): 507.

84. Among the social scientists to earn McCraw's unstinting admiration were Adolf A. Berle, Jr., and Gardiner C. Means. Berle, a lawyer, and Means, an economist, were the coauthors of *Modern Corporation and Private Property* (1932), a landmark in institutional economics. It would be hard to name more than one of two other books on the "dynamics of twentieth-century economies" that could surpass *Modern Corporation* in influence, McCraw reflected in 1990. This was because Berle and Means had addressed in it the "very nature of capitalism" by etching in the minds of a "broad body of intellectuals" two powerful ideas—namely, industrial concentration and the separation of ownership and control. Thomas K. McCraw, "Berle and Means," *Reviews in American History* 18 (December 1990): 592.

85. For McCraw's critique of the financial crisis, see Thomas K. McCraw, "Regulate, Baby, Regulate," *New Republic* (March 18, 2009), 16. McCraw's last book, *Founders and Finance,* can be read as an impassioned critique of the short-termism that has today become dogma in many business sectors, including finance, as well as in the training of MBAs. For an assessment of *Founders and Finance* that contends that it subtly departed from the industry-centric essentialism of *Prophets of Regulation,* see John, "Prophet of Perspective."

Chapter 6. "Free Enterprise" or Federal Aid?

1. Judith Stein, *Pivotal Decade: How the United States Traded Factories for Finance in the Seventies* (New Haven, Conn.: Yale University Press, 2010).

2. For postwar economic restructuring, see, for example, Laurence F. Gross, *The Course of Industrial Decline: The Boott Cotton Mills of Lowell, Massachusetts, 1835–1955* (Baltimore: Johns Hopkins University Press, 1993); Thomas Sugrue, *The Origins of the Urban Crisis: Race and Inequality in Postwar Detroit* (Princeton, N.J.: Princeton University Press, 1996); Jefferson Cowie, *Capital Moves: RCA's 70-Year Quest for Cheap Labor* (Ithaca, N.Y.: Cornell University Press, 1999); essays in Jefferson Cowie and Joseph Heathcott, eds., *Beyond the Ruins: The Meanings of Deindustrialization* (Ithaca, N.Y.: ILR Press, 2003); and Thomas Dublin and Walter Licht, *The Face of Decline: The Pennsylvania Anthracite Region in the Twentieth Century* (Ithaca, N.Y.: Cornell University Press, 2005). For economic development strategies, see Howard Gillette, Jr., *Camden After the Fall: Decline and Renewal in a Post-Industrial City* (Philadelphia: University of Pennsylvania Press, 2005); Guian A. McKee, *The Problem of Jobs: Liberalism, Race, and Deindustrialization in Philadelphia* (Chicago: University of Chicago Press, 2008); Gregory S. Wilson, *Communities Left Behind: The Area Redevelopment Administration, 1945–1965* (Knoxville: University of Tennessee Press, 2009); David Koistinen, *Confronting Decline: The Political Economy of Deindustrialization in Twentieth-Century New England* (Gainesville: University Press of Florida, 2013); and Elizabeth Tandy Shermer, *Sunbelt Capitalism: Phoenix and the Transformation of American Politics* (Philadelphia: University of Pennsylvania Press, 2013). For business and the federal state, see Robert M. Collins, *The Business Response to Keynes, 1929–1964* (New York: Columbia University Press, 1981); Kim McQuaid, *Uneasy Partners: Big Business in American Politics, 1945–1990* (Baltimore: Johns Hopkins University Press, 1994); Kim Phillips-Fein, *Invisible Hands: The Making of the Conservative Movement from the New Deal to Reagan* (New York: W. W. Norton, 2009); Dominique A. Tobbell, "Pharmaceutical Politics and Regulatory Reform in Postwar America," in *What's Good for Business: Business and American Politics Since World War II,* ed. Kim Phillips-Fein and Julian E. Zelizer (New York: Oxford University Press, 2012), 123–39; and Mark R. Wilson, "The Advantages of Obscurity: World War II Tax Carryback Provisions and the Normalization of Corporate Welfare," ibid., 16–44.

3. William H. Chafe, *The Unfinished Journey: America Since World War II,* 4th ed. (New York: Oxford University Press, 1999), 112–19; Robert Brenner, "The Political Economy of the Rank-and-File Rebellion," in *Rebel Rank and File: Labor Militancy and Revolt from Below in the Long 1970s,* ed. Aaron Brenner, Robert Brenner, and Cal Winslow (London: Verso, 2010), 47–50; David Brody, "The Uses of Power I: Industrial Battleground," in *Workers in Industrial America: Essays on the 20th Century Struggle* (New York: Oxford University Press, 1981), 191–94, quoted 192.

4. Tami J. Friedman, "'Acute Depression . . . in . . . the Age of Plenty': Capital Migration, Economic Dislocation, and the Missing 'Social Contract' of the 1950s," *Labor: Studies in Working-Class History of the Americas* 8 (Winter 2011): 89–113; Philip F. Maguire to Dear Mr. Secretary, August 26, 1949, Folder: "Steelman's Letter of August 26, 1949," Box 4, John F.

Steelman Files, Harry S. Truman Papers, Harry S. Truman Library, Independence, Mo.; "The Distressed Area: A Growing National Problem," *Economic Outlook* 16 (July–August 1955), 56–57, Folder: "Labor-Unemployment, Task Force on, 1955 (2)," Box 112, Arthur F. Burns Papers, Dwight D. Eisenhower Presidential Library, Abilene, Kans.; A. H. Raskin, "Hard-Core Unemployment a Rising National Problem," *New York Times*, April 6, 1961, pp. 1, 18; Michael Harrington, *The Other America: Poverty in the United States*, reprint ed. (Baltimore: Penguin, 1965), 30–42. In the mid-1950s, the U.S. Department of Labor defined a major labor-market area as having at least one city of 50,000 or more residents, and a smaller area as having a labor force of at least 15,000.

5. *Economic Report of the President*, January 8, 1947, 26, Folder: "Previous Programs Designed to Relieve Unemployment," Box 4, Steelman Files; *Midyear Economic Report of the President*, July 11, 1949, esp. 3 and 12, Folder: "August 1949," Box 1, ibid.; news release, September 27, 1949, Folder: "Steelman's Letter of September 27, 1949," Box 4, ibid.; Collis Stocking to R. J. Saulnier, memo, November 22, 1955, 3, Folder: "Areas, Depressed, Community Assistance (2)," Box 4, Council of Economic Advisors Records, Eisenhower Library.

6. Senate Subcommittee on Labor of the Committee on Labor and Public Welfare, *Area Redevelopment: Hearings, Part 1*, 84th Cong., 2nd sess., January–February 1956, 138 (Eisenhower remarks); Arthur F. Burns talk, October 14, 1955, esp. 22, Folder: "Program for Assistance to Depressed Localities, Talk Delivered at Cabinet Meeting, October 14, 1955," Box 75, Burns Papers. For background on the campaign for area redevelopment legislation, see Sar A. Levitan, *Federal Aid to Depressed Areas: An Evaluation of the Area Redevelopment Administration* (Baltimore: Johns Hopkins Press, 1964); William F. Hartford, *Where Is Our Responsibility? Unions and Economic Change in the New England Textile Industry, 1870–1960* (Amherst: University of Massachusetts Press, 1996), 183–95; and Wilson, *Communities Left Behind*.

7. NAM Board of Directors (hereafter BOD), "Federal Aid to Depressed Areas," June 15, 1956, Folder: "Federal Aid to Depressed Areas, 1956, 1961–1965," Box 103, Series 1, National Association of Manufacturers Records, Accession No. 1411, Hagley Museum and Library, Wilmington, Del. (hereafter NAM Records); "Statement of Robert P. Lee for the Chamber of Commerce of the United States," Subcommittee of Senate Committee on Banking and Currency, *Area Redevelopment: Hearings, Part 1*, 85th Cong., 1st sess., March–May 1957, 632, 633–34; Chamber of Commerce (hereafter COC), *The Promise of Economic Growth: Prospects, Costs, Conditions* (1960), 18–19, Box 88, Series IV, Subseries F, Chamber of Commerce of the United States Records, Accession No. 1960, Hagley Museum and Library (hereafter Chamber Records); COC, *How National Chamber Policy Is Formed*, Folder: "49th Annual Meeting Packet April 30, May 1–3, 1961," Box 34, Series I, Subseries E, Chamber Records.

8. Hartford, *Where Is Our Responsibility?* 183–95; memorandum for Mr. Steelman, April 19, 1950, Folder: "Press Reports—Miscellaneous," Box 7, Steelman Files.

9. "Industry Migration," *Economic Intelligence* (September 1955), 1, Box 72, Series IV, Subseries F, Chamber Records; *Officers, Directors, Committeemen of the Chamber of Commerce of the United States, 1959–1960*, Folder: "48th Annual Meeting Packet May 1–4, 1960," Box 34, Series I, Subseries E, Chamber Records; "Favorable Business Climate," February 10, 1960, Folder: "Positions—Favorable Business Climate," Box 103, Series 1, NAM Records; NAM BOD meeting minutes, Folder: "Board of Directors Minutes," Box 54, Series 1, NAM Records.

10. "The Riddle of Surplus Labor and Defense Contracts," *Labor Relations Letter* (December 1951), 4, Box 72, Series IV, Subseries F, Chamber Records; "New High U.S. Employment Discredits Gloomy Prophets," *Washington Report* (hereafter WR), August 12, 1955, Hagley Museum.

11. "Jobs and Markets," *National Chamber Washington Report* (hereafter *NCWR*), December 4, 1953, Hagley Museum; COC, *A Program for Maintaining Jobs, Markets and Production* (1953), 4, Box 85, Series IV, Subseries F, Chamber Records; F. A. Hayek, *The Road to Serfdom* (London: Routledge & Kegan Paul, 1944), 89–99, esp. 92, 30, 52; Russell Baker, "Eisenhower Backs 'Point 4' Project for Parts of U.S.," *New York Times*, October 25, 1955, pp. 1, 22, Folder: "Areas, Depressed, Community Assistance (2)," Box 4, Council of Economic Advisors Records.

12. Harry A. Bullis presentation in minutes, 37th Annual COC Meeting, May 2–5, 1949, Box 33, Series I, Subseries E, Chamber Records; "Tax Allowances Adopted to Aid Jobless Areas," *NCWR*, November 13, 1953; "New Movie Tells How to Do Business with Air Force," *Chamber of Commerce Newsletter* (hereafter *Newsletter*) (January 1953), 6, Box 74, Series IV, Subseries F, Chamber Records; "Chamber Asks U.S. Aid for Shipbuilding," *WR*, June 25, 1954; COC, *Program for Maintaining Jobs*, 15.

13. "Statement of Donald J. Hardenbrook," Subcommittee of Senate Committee on Banking and Currency, *Area Redevelopment: Hearings, Part 1* (1957), 651–52; remarks of Milton C. Lightner, Subcommittee of Senate Committee on Banking and Currency, *Area Redevelopment Act: Hearings*, 86th Cong., 1st sess., February 1959, 189, 188; NAM BOD meeting minutes, September 18–19, 1958, 6, Folder: "1958," Box 54, Series 1, NAM Records; COC, "Political Party Objectives and National Chamber Policy: A Staff Document" (October 1960), 49, Box 88, Series IV, Subseries F, Chamber Records.

14. Thomas Kennedy to John R. Steelman, October 3, 1949, Folder: "Pennsylvania [1]," Box 3, Steelman Files; United Steel Workers of America Local 1780, "Resolution," March 2, 1950, ibid.; U.S. Department of Labor, Bureau of Employment Security, "Community Programs to Combat Unemployment: A Survey of Regional, State, and Local Activities," November 30, 1949, 22 (Utica), Folder: "Community Programs to Combat Unemployment," Box 10, ibid.; U.S. Department of Labor, news release, October 24, 1949, 1, 4, Folder: "Joint Committee on the Economic Report-Subcommittee on Employment," Box 6, ibid.; Raymond J. Blair, "Textile Workers Have Little Hope of Re-employment After Layoff," *New York Herald Tribune*, April 17, 1950, Folder: "Maryland," Box 2, ibid.; A. H. Raskin, "Many Hard-Core Jobless Feel They Are Unwanted," *New York Times*, April 8, 1961, pp. 1, 22.

15. COC, *For the Greater Good of All* (Washington, D.C., 1955), 6 (affiliate data), Box 86, Series IV, Subseries F, Chamber Records; COC, *Program for Maintaining Jobs*, 1, 10–12.

16. COC, *For the Greater Good of All*, 6 ("grass-roots"); "Hulcy Asks Local Chambers to Pledge Against Requests for Federal Money," *NCWR*, January 18, 1952; Paul G. Pierpaoli, *Truman and Korea: The Political Culture of the Early Cold War* (Columbia: University of Missouri Press, 1999), 133–35, 173–74; "Businessmen Pay 'Economy' Visit to Hill," *NCWR*, June 20, 1952; "Labor Resources Survey Run for Industrial Prospect," *Newsletter* (August 1953), 4, Box 74, Series IV, Subseries F, Chamber Records.

17. "Statement of Donald J. Hardenbrook," 648–50, esp. 648 and 649; Galaxy, Inc., *Economic Effect of Textile Mill Closings: Selected Communities in Middle Atlantic States* (Washington, D.C.: Government Printing Office, 1963), 11–13; U.S. Department of Labor, Bureau of Employment Secretary, *Area Labor Market Trends* (January 1958), 13; ibid. (January 1959), 11; ibid. (January 1961), 19; "Report of Lewis C. Kleinhans . . . on Proposed Position on 'Favorable Business Climate,'" February 10–12, 1960, 2, Folder: "Positions—Favorable Business Climate," Box 103, Series 1, NAM Records.

18. U.S. Department of Commerce, news release, August 31, 1949, Folder: "Commerce—Secretary Sawyers Reports on Field Trips," Box 5, Steelman Files; Byron Mitchell to J. Otis Garber, memo, September 20, 1949, 7–8 (Southwest), Folder: "Budget Bureau-Miscellaneous,"

ibid.; O. M. Deibler to U.S. Department of Commerce, March 25, 1950, Folder: "Commerce–Labor Committee [1 of 2]," Box 13, ibid.; William Davlin to H. B. McCoy and James Kelley, memo, February 2, 1950, 2, Folder: "Illinois," Box 2, ibid.; letter from John A. Toomey, January 23, 1950, Folder: "Massachusetts," Box 3, ibid.; William M. Boyle, Jr., to David Kauffman, March 26, 1951, Folder: "Maryland, Cumberland," Box 2, ibid.

19. Ralph B. Wilkinson to Thomas J. Lane, March 27, 1950, Folder: "Massachusetts," Box 3, Steelman Files.

20. "Federal Aid Opposition Still Rising," *NCWR*, March 14, 1952; "225 Local Chambers Promise Full Support in Economy Campaign," *NCWR*, February 22, 1952; "Daytonians Have a Habit of Paying Their Own Way," *NCWR*, November 28, 1952; "Federal Drought Aid Is Rejected as Banks Agree to Private Loans," *NCWR*, August 22, 1952; "Federal Aid Declined by Arkansas Citizens," *WR*, February 26, 1954.

21. John R. Steelman to Charles C. Fichtner, August 12, 1949, Folder: "August 1949," Box 1, Steelman Files; Frank T. McCue to H. B. McCoy, memo, July 30, 1949, 4, Folder: "Steelman's Letter of August 9, 1949," Box 4, ibid.; "Report on the Operations of the Federal Procurement Information Center," December 12, 1949, attached to form letter, H. B. McCoy, December 16, 1949, Folder: "Commerce—Commerce Factual and Firm Reports, Procurement Information Centers," Box 5, ibid.; Jack K. Busby, *Attacking the Distressed Areas Problem* (Allentown: Pennsylvania Power & Light, 1961), Box 223, Series 16, NAM Records.

22. "Biddeford-Sanford, Maine, Sample Survey—Unemployment and Production," September 1949, Folder: "Biddeford–Sanford–York County–Commerce Reports–Fact Finding," Box 11, Steelman Files; "Lawrence, Massachusetts—Sample Survey—Unemployment and Production," September 1949, Folder: "Lawrence–Commerce–Fact Finding and Firm," ibid.; "Joining of Local Chambers Ordered by Stamford Firm," *WR*, March 19, 1954.

23. "Fact-Finding Survey of the New Bedford (Mass.) Labor Market Area," [August 1949?], 2, 3, Folder: "New Bedford–Commerce Reports–Fact Finding," Box 11, Steelman Files; "Statement of Karl M. Kempf," Labor Subcommittee of Senate Labor and Public Welfare Committee, *Area Redevelopment: Hearings, Part 1* (1956), 140–43, esp. 142; "Statement of William F. Wright, Jr.," Labor Subcommittee of Senate Labor and Public Welfare Committee, *Area Redevelopment: Hearings, Part 2*, 84th Cong., 2nd sess., February–April 1956, 852–56; untitled meeting notes [New England Council], [Spring 1956], quoted 14 (Wright), Folder: "Areas, Depressed, Community Assistance (3)," Box 4, Council of Economic Advisors Records.

24. "Fact-Finding Survey of the New Bedford (Mass.) Labor Market Area," 2–3; Philip F. Maguire, "Memorandum to Mr. Steelman," February 28, 1950 (Meehan quotation), Folder: "Massachusetts," Box 3, Steelman Files; "Greater Lawrence Committee for Industrial Development Organizes," *Lawrence Evening Tribune*, April 26, 1950, 19, ibid.; David Kauffman to Harry S. Truman, March 13, 1951, 1–8, esp. 7, Folder: "Maryland, Cumberland," Box 2, ibid.; Kauffman, "Statement . . . Concerning a Suggested Federal Program of Participation of Aid to 'E' Areas" [March 1951?], ibid.; Victor Roterus to John Houston, March 29, 1951, ibid.

25. Untitled [New England Council] meeting notes, 15, 16; "Statement of Robert P. Lee," 632. For Danielson, see Subcommittee of the Senate Committee on Banking and Currency, *Area Redevelopment: Hearings, Part 1* (1957), 653, table. For Burlington and Connecticut's major areas, see U.S. Department of Labor, Bureau of Employment Security, *Area Manpower Guidebook* (Washington, D.C.: Government Printing Office, 1957), 36, 38, 40, 42, 44, 46, 308.

26. Untitled [New England Council] meeting notes, 13, 16, 14 (Wright quotation on waiting period); "Statement of William F. Wright, Jr.," esp. 852, 853; "Statement of Hon. Kevin F. Coleman,

Mayor of Woonsocket, R.I.," Labor Subcommittee of Senate Committee on Labor and Public Welfare, *Area Redevelopment: Hearings, Part 1* (1956), 220; "Statement of Karl M. Kempf," 139.

27. The Greater Lawrence chamber and the Greater Lawrence Citizens Committee provided information to the President's Commission on Foreign Economic Policy, indicating that the group established by the mayor in 1950 "produced no results" but was reorganized by a new mayor in January 1952, with positive results. *Staff Papers Presented to the Commission on Foreign Economic Policy* (Washington, D.C.: Government Printing Office, 1954), 415. Hartford, *Where Is Our Responsibility?* 190–92, esp. 191; Kurtz M. Hanson to Hon. Paul H. Douglas, Subcommittee of Senate Committee on Banking and Currency, *Area Redevelopment: Hearings, Part 1* (1957), esp. 185; "Hanson Recounts Story of Greater Lawrence Recovery," *Evening Tribune,* April 3, 1957, ibid., 185–90, esp. 186 and 189; "Policy Statement by the NPA Committee on Depressed Areas," ibid., esp. 509. For unemployment rates, see ibid., 652, table; and William H. Miernyk, "The Problem of Depressed Areas," *Monthly Labor Review* 80 (March 1957), 303, table.

28. "Fact-Finding Survey of the Port Huron (Mich.) Labor Market Area," September 1949, Folder: "Port Huron–Fact Finding–Commerce," Box 12, Steelman Files; "Fact Finding Survey of the Worcester (Mass.) Labor Market Area," [Fall 1949?], 3, Folder: "Worcester–Commerce Reports–Fact Finding," ibid.; "Fact-Finding Survey of the Lowell (Mass.) Labor Market Area" (October 1949), Folder: "Lowell–Commerce–Fact-Finding and Firm," Box 11, ibid.; "Fact-Finding Survey of Waterbury, Connecticut Labor Market Area," August 1949, 2, Folder: "Waterbury–Commerce Reports–Fact Finding," ibid.

29. Thomas G. Paterson, "The Quest for Peace and Prosperity: International Trade, Communism, and the Marshall Plan," in *Politics and Policies of the Truman Administration,* ed. Barton J. Bernstein (Chicago: Quadrangle, 1970), 78–112; Dwight D. Eisenhower, "Special Message to the Congress on Foreign Economic Policy," March 30, 1954, *American Presidency Project,* accessed April 18, 2016, www.presidency.ucsb.edu/ws/?pid=10195; "Fact-Finding Survey of the Bristol (Conn.) Labor Market Area," August 1949, Folder: "Bristol–Commerce Reports–Fact Finding," Box 11, Steelman Files; A. Henry Thurston and E. K. Slaughter to H. B. McCoy, memo, July 30, 1949, Folder: "Providence–Commerce Reports–Fact Finding," Box 12, ibid.; "Fact-Finding Survey of the Danielson (Conn.) Labor Market Area," 2, August 1949, Folder: "Danielson–Commerce Reports–Fact Finding," Box 11, ibid.; chamber of commerce, Amsterdam, New York, petition, attached to Herbert H. Lehman to Hon. Harry F. Byrd, March 12, 1955, Senate Committee on Finance, *Trade Agreements Extension: Hearings, Part 4,* 84th Cong., 1st sess., March 1955, 2218–19; "1961 NAM Policy Committees, Approved by the Board September 15, 1960," Appendix A, 4, Folder: "Directors Minutes 1960, 100-Q," Box 54, Series 1, NAM Records; "Trade Views of Chamber Are Outlined," *NCWR,* October 30, 1953, 1, 2. Similar tensions concerning trade and tariff policy emerged in the labor movement; see Dana Frank, *Buy American: The Untold Story of Economic Nationalism* (Boston: Beacon Press, 1999), 102–28.

30. Charles E. Egan, "Chamber Rejects GATT Unit Entry," *New York Times,* June 23, 1956, p. 38; COC BOD meeting minutes, June 15–16, 1956, Appendix 1, 7 (Ohio Chamber resolution), Box 3, Series I, Subseries B, Chamber Records; COC BOD meeting minutes, January 31–February 1, 1958, Appendix 2, 9, ibid.

31. "G.E. Chooses New Location," *Newsletter,* June 1956, 6, Box 74, Series IV, Subseries F, Chamber Records; "Statement of William F. Wright, Jr.," 854.

32. Levitan, *Federal Aid to Depressed Areas,* 26–27, 56–57, 79–80, 106–7, 66, table 3-1 (data on eligible areas); Wilson, *Communities Left Behind,* 44–47, 66–71, 106, 111–15, 145 (data on final out-

comes); James L. Sundquist, *Politics and Policy: The Eisenhower, Kennedy, and Johnson Years* (Washington, D.C.: Brookings Institution, 1968), 105–10.

33. Wilson, *Communities Left Behind*, 62–63, 146–53, esp. 62.

Chapter 7. "They Were the Moving Spirits"

1. *Southern Secretary*, December 1937, Box 2, Rome, Georgia, Chamber of Commerce Papers, Sarah Hightower Special Collections, Rome-Floyd County Library, Rome, Georgia (hereafter RCCP).

2. Most investigations of Southern economic development emphasize the perspectives of state and national political elites rather than local actors. See especially Bruce J. Schulman, *From Cotton Belt to Sun Belt: Federal Policy, Economic Development, and the Transformation of the South 1938–1980* (Durham, N.C.: Duke University Press, 1994); and James C. Cobb, *The Selling of the South: The Southern Crusade for Industrial Development, 1936–1950* (Urbana-Champaign: University of Illinois Press, 1993).

3. Jason Scott Smith argues that New Deal public works should be considered nascent economic development programs. Jason Scott Smith, *Building New Deal Liberalism: The Political Economy of Public Works, 1933–1956* (New York: Cambridge University Press, 2006). When considering business and the New Deal, historians have largely focused on national elites and business lobbying associations' anti–New Deal mobilization. See especially Kim Phillips-Fein, *Invisible Hands: The Making of the Conservative Movement from the New Deal to Reagan* (New York: W. W. Norton, 2009).

4. For a discussion of the conceptual problems involved with the New Deal order polarities, see Matthew D. Lassiter, "Political History Beyond the Red-Blue Divide," *Journal of American History* 98 (December 2011): 760–764. On the drawbacks of scholars' tendency to assess American state building and political development from the Weberian perspective, see especially William J. Novak, "The Myth of the 'Weak' American State," *American Historical Review* 113, (June 2008): 752–72, esp. 752–763.

5. Brian Balogh, *The Associational State: American Governance in the Twentieth Century* (Philadelphia: University of Pennsylvania Press, 2015), esp. ch. 5.

6. Thomas Sugrue, "'All Politics is Local': The Persistence of Localism in Twentieth-Century America," in *The Democratic Experiment*, ed. Meg Jacobs, William Novak, and Julian Zelizer (Princeton, N.J.: Princeton University Press, 2003). On "infrastructural" power versus despotic power, see Michael Mann, "The Autonomous Power of the State: Its Origins, Mechanisms and Results," *European Journal of Sociology* 25 (November 1984), 185–213.

7. Jon C. Teaford, *The Unheralded Triumph: City Government in America, 1870–1900* (Baltimore: Johns Hopkins University Press, 1984).

8. Smith, *Building New Deal Liberalism*, 105.

9. On the emergence of local chambers' sense of civic stewardship, see Alison Isenberg, *Downtown America: A History of the Place and the People Who Made It* (Chicago: University of Chicago Press, 2004), 35–37.

10. Franklin D. Roosevelt, "Second Fireside Chat," May 7, 1933, in John T. Woolley and Gerhard Peters, eds., *The American Presidency Project*, http://www.presidency.ucsb.edu/ws/?pid=14636.

11. On the reciprocal growth of voluntary associations and government, see Theda Skocpol, Marshall Ganz, and Ziad Munson, "A Nation of Organizers: The Institutional Origins of Civic

Voluntarism in the United States," *American Political Science Review* 94 (September 2000): 527–46.

12. Victor R. Fuchs, "The Growing Importance of the Service Industries," *Journal of Business* 38 (October 1965): 344.

13. In 1929, the U.S. Chamber of Commerce reported 1,587 dues-paying local chambers. Many more business-oriented associations—Lions, Kiwanis, Rotary, and non-dues-paying chambers—focused on community development. Robert M. Collins, *The Business Response to Keynes, 1929–1964* (New York: Columbia University Press, 1982), 23; Robert Putnam, *Bowling Alone: The Collapse and Revival of American Community* (New York: Simon and Schuster, 2000), 48–64; Suzanne Mettler, *Soldiers to Citizens: The GI Bill and the Making of the Greatest Generation* (New York: Oxford University Press, 2005), 123–35.

14. Charles E. Merriam, *Public and Private Government* (New Haven, Ct.: Yale University Press, 1944), 57.

15. Alan Brinkley, *The End of Reform: New Deal Liberalism in Recession and War* (New York: Vintage, 1995); Lizabeth Cohen, *A Consumer's Republic: The Politics of Mass Consumption in Postwar America* (New York: Vintage, 2003); S. M. Amadae, *Rationalizing Democratic Capitalism: The Cold War Origins of Rational Choice Liberalism* (Chicago: University of Chicago Press, 2003). On locally enforced racial boundaries to New Deal liberalism, see Ira Katznelson, *When Affirmative Action Was White* (New York: W.W. Norton, 2005).

16. See, for instance, Peter Eisinger, *The Rise of the Entrepreneurial State: State and Local Economic Development Policy in the United States* (Madison: University of Wisconsin Press, 1989).

17. On the United States and centralized industrial policy, see Otis Graham, *Losing Time: The Industrial Policy Debate* (Cambridge, Mass.: Harvard University Press, 1994).

18. Seymour Harris, *Saving American Capitalism: A Liberal Economic Program* (New York: Alfred A. Knopf, 1948), 501.

19. Alvin H. Hansen, "Economic Progress and Declining Population Growth," *American Economic Review* 29 (March 1939): 10; Alvin H. Hansen, *Economic Policy and Full Employment* (New York: McGraw-Hill, 1947), 182.

20. Harris, *Saving American Capitalism*, 147–50.

21. Merle Fainsod, "Government and Business in a Mixed Economy," in Harris, ed., *Saving American Capitalism*, 178, 182.

22. Alvin E. Hansen, "Planning Full Employment," *Nation*, October 21, 1944, p. 492. Hansen was then developing his proposal for what became Urban Renewal, which would return blighted land to the private sector for new "productive" uses.

23. On the New Deal and Southern poverty, see David Carlton and Peter Coclanis, *Confronting Southern Poverty in the Great Depression* (Boston: Bedford-St. Martin's, 1996). See also Schulman, *From Cotton Belt to Sun Belt*, Introduction and ch. 1.

24. On the Research Triangle Park, see Michael Luger and Harvey Goldstein, *Technology in the Garden* (Chapel Hill: University of North Carolina Press, 1991). On South Carolina, see Kari Frederickson, *Cold War Dixie: Militarization and Modernization in the American South* (Athens: University of Georgia Press, 2013). On Atlanta, see Margaret O'Mara, *Cities of Knowledge: Cold War Science and the Search for the Next Silicon Valley* (Princeton, N.J.: Princeton University Press, 2005), ch. 5.

25. This chapter does not explore these aspects of local boosters' politics. See, for instance, Elizabeth Tandy Shermer, *Sunbelt Capitalism: Phoenix and the Transformation of American Politics* (Philadelphia: University of Pennsylvania Press, 2013).

26. Michael S. Holmes, *The New Deal in Georgia: An Administrative History* (Westport, Conn.: Greenwood Press, 1974), 333.

27. Quoted in Smith, *Building New Deal Liberalism,* 210.

28. Gregory Wilson, *Communities Left Behind: The Area Redevelopment Administration, 1945–1965* (Knoxville: University of Tennessee Press, 2009), 34–47.

29. Untitled clipping, *Gadsden Times,* November 9, 1941, Box 1, RCCP.

30. Minutes of Meeting with Representatives from Rome, Dalton, and Cartersville, January 19, 1945, Box 2, RCCP; Minutes of Meeting of Representatives of Northwest Georgia Counties, February 16, 1945, ibid.; and Robert F. Nelson, "Report Dealing with the Potentialities of Northwest Georgia from the Standpoint of the Tourist Trade," undated, ibid.

31. Nelson, "Potentialities of Northwest Georgia," undated, Box 2, RCCP.

32. Meeting of Representatives of Northwest Georgia Counties, February 16, 1945.

33. "Rome Leaders Awaiting Area Tourist Meet," *Rome News Tribune* (hereafter *RNT*), August 24, 1955, p. 1.

34. Schulman, *From Cotton Belt to Sun Belt,* 129.

35. "Governor Arnall Points the Way to Greater Progress in Georgia," *Georgia Progress,* September 15, 1944, Binder 1, Economic Development, Georgia Power Corporate Archives, Atlanta, Georgia (hereafter GPCA).

36. "Industry Panel Program Goes Forward at Meetings in 200 Georgia Towns," *Georgia Progress,* January 1, 1945, Binder 1, Economic Development, GPCA.

37. Richard S. Combes and William J. Todd, "From Henry Grady to the Georgia Research Alliance: A Case Study of Science-Based Development in Georgia," undated, 8, Binder 1, Economic Development, GPCA.

38. Richard Snyder Combes, "Origins of Industrial Extension: A Historical Case Study in Georgia" (M.A. thesis, Georgia Institute of Technology, 1992), p. 42, Folder: EES-Industrial Extension Division, GTA Subject File, Georgia Institute of Technology Archives, Atlanta, Georgia.

39. On Northern states' reluctance to fund similar organizations, see David Kostinen, "Public Policies for Countering Deindustrializing in Postwar Massachusetts," *Journal of Policy History* 18, no. 3 (2006): 340. By the late 1950s, most New England states began creating state development bodies to counter deindustrialization.

40. On the CEA, see Robert Collins, *More: The Politics of Economic Growth in Postwar America* (New York: Oxford University Press, 2002), 35–36.

41. Margaret O'Mara, *Cities of Knowledge: Cold War Science and the Search for the Next Silicon Valley* (Princeton, N.J.: Princeton University Press, 2005), 202.

42. Combes, "Origins of Industrial Extension," 63.

43. *25 Years of Progress: Coosa Valley Area Planning and Development Commission, 1958–1983,* July 21, 1983, 2, in author's possession.

44. Ibid.

45. "Area Planning Group Maps Broad Program," *RNT,* June 24, 1959, p. 1.

46. *25 Years of Progress,* 2.

47. Carl Feiss, "The Foundations of Federal Planning Assistance: A Personal Account of the 701 Program," *Journal of the American Planning Association* 51, no. 12 (1985): 175–84.

48. Howard, "Home Rule in Georgia: An Analysis of State and Local Power," *Georgia Law Review* 9, no. 757 (1975).

49. "25 Years of Progress," 3.

50. "Area Planners Set Budget, Sign New Tech Contract," *RNT,* July 19, 1963, p. 3.

51. Michael Bradshaw, *The Appalachian Regional Commission: Twenty-Five Years of Government Policy* (Lexington, Ky.: University of Kentucky Press, 1992), 27.

52. On the political construction of Cold War Americanism, see Wendy L. Wall, *Inventing the "American Way": The Politics of Consensus from the New Deal to the Civil Rights Movement* (New York: Oxford University Press, 2008), esp. 189–93.

53. "Coosa Planners to Hold Annual Session Thursday," *RNT*, July 17, 1960, p. 1.

54. On the discourse of "community" flattening of distinctions between groups and marginalized interests, see, for instance, Iris Marion Young, "The Ideal of Community and the Politics of Difference," in *Feminism and Community*, ed. Penny A. Weiss and Marilyn F. Friedman (Philadelphia: Temple University Press, 1995).

55. CVAPDC Newsletter, May 1969, Rome-Floyd County Library Heritage Room Archives (hereafter RFCL).

56. CVAPDC Newsletter, February 1969, RFCL.

57. CVAPDC Newsletter, November 1969, RFCL.

58. *RNT*, July 17, 1960.

59. "25 Years of Progress," 4.

60. "Rome Chosen as Site for Area Engineering Branch," *RNT*, July 21, 1960, p. 1.

61. Rome-Floyd County Chamber of Commerce News-Letter, September 1963, Hargrett Special Collections Library, University of Georgia, Athens.

62. Combes, "Origins of Industrial Extension," 47.

63. Northwest Georgia Branch to CVAPDC, January 14, 1963, RFCL.

64. Rome-Floyd County Chamber of Commerce News-Letter, July 1962, Hargrett Special Collections Library, University of Georgia, Athens.

65. Howard A. Schretter, "The Area Planning and Development Commission: Its Relationship with Local Planning Programs," Institute of Community and Area Development, University of Georgia, Athens, Georgia, October 18, 1963, Folder: Speeches, Draft of Speeches, Notes [2], Box 5, Jimmy Carter Papers, Pre-Presidential, 1962–76, Jimmy Carter Presidential Library, Atlanta, Georgia (hereafter, JCL).

66. "West Central Georgia Area Planning and Development Commission: Area Planning and Development Commissions in Georgia," undated, Folder: Speeches, Draft of Speeches, Notes [2], Box 5, Jimmy Carter Papers, Pre-Presidential, 1962–76, JCL.

67. Burton Sparer, "Area Planning and Development Commissions in Georgia Today," February 1975, Prepared by the Legislative Research Division of the Institute of Government, University of Georgia, 7, in author's possession.

68. "25 Years of Progress," 3.

69. Collins, *More*, 43.

70. Ibid., 40–68.

71. See, for example, "Federal Expenditure Policy for Economic Growth and Stability: Papers Submitted by Panelists Appearing Before the Subcommittee on Fiscal Policy," Joint Economic Committee, November 5, 1957 (Washington, D.C.: Government Printing Office, 1957).

72. Wilson, *Communities Left Behind*, 51–52.

73. Bradshaw, *The Appalachian Regional Commission*, 28.

74. Glen Edward Taul, "Poverty, Development, and Government in Appalachia: Origins of the Appalachian Regional Commission," Ph.D. diss., University of Kentucky, 2001.

75. On the Coosa Commission as a model for federal policymakers, see ARC, *The Appalachian Experiment, 1965–1970* (ARC, 1972), 90; Bradshaw, *The Appalachian Regional Commission,* 26–28.

76. ARC, *The Appalachian Experiment,* 9.

77. Wilson, *Communities Left Behind,* 88–89.

78. Bradshaw, *The Appalachian Regional Commission,* 29; "An Inventory of Selected Federal Projects and Programs in Appalachia," November 1962, Department of Commerce, Office of Planning and Research, Area Redevelopment Administration, July 31, 1961–October 2, 1962, General File, 1954–1964, Series 1, White House Staff Files of Lee C. White, Presidential Papers of John F. Kennedy, digital ID: JFKWHSFLCW-001-011 (hereafter LCWP).

79. "Texans Resent U.S. Listing as Depressed Area," August 1, 1961, news clipping, Area Redevelopment Administration, July 31, 1961–October 2, 1962, LCWP.

80. Wilson, *Communities Left Behind,* 52.

81. John F. Kennedy to John E. Horne, February 27, 1962, Area Redevelopment Administration, July 31, 1961–October 2, 1962, LCWP.

82. William L. Batt, recorded interview by Larry J. Hackman, May 10, 1967, 164, John F. Kennedy Library Oral History Program.

83. Ibid., 191. On the administration's belief that a new South was in the offing, see Daniel Galvin, *Presidential Party Building: Dwight D. Eisenhower to George W. Bush* (Princeton, N.J.: Princeton University Press, 2009), 174–75. On similar developments in Roosevelt's view of federal aid, party building, and Southern economic development, see Schulman, *From Cotton Belt to Sun Belt,* 46–62.

84. "Coosa Area Planners Praised by Roosevelt," *RNT,* October 4, 1964, p. 3.

85. On the Coosa Commission as a model for policymakers, see ARC, *The Appalachian Experiment,* 90; Bradshaw, *The Appalachian Regional Commission,* 26–28.

86. Bradshaw, *The Appalachian Regional Commission,* 26–28.

87. ARC, *Annual Report of the Appalachian Regional Commission* (Washington, D.C.: ARC, 1965), 4.

88. President's Appalachian Regional Commission, Report of the Subcommittee on Highways of the Transportation Committee, October 25, 1963, Area Redevelopment Administration, 1963: October 25–November 19 and undated, LCWP.

89. Joe W. Fleming, II, Oral History Interview, February 19, 1969, p. 13, Lyndon Johnson Oral History Project, Miller Center, accessed July 2014, http://web2.millercenter.org/lbj/oralhistory /fleming_joe_1969_0219.pdf.

90. William L. Batt, recorded interview by Larry J. Hackman, May 10, 1967, 191, John F. Kennedy Library Oral History Program.

91. Ibid., 198.

92. Ibid., 177.

93. CVAPDC Annual Report, June 30, 1966, 15–16, RFCL.

94. CVAPDC Annual Report, 1971, RFCL.

95. CVAPDC Newsletter, August 1970, RFCL.

96. CVAPDC Newsletter, November 1969; CVAPDC Newsletter, August 1969, RFCL.

97. CVAPDC Newsletter, June 1969, RFCL.

98. Charles Prejean, "Georgia and Local Government Modernization: The Georgia Area Planning and Development Commissions," 31, Folder 1447, Box 226, Record Group 3.1, Rockefel-

ler Brothers Fund Papers, Rockefeller Archive Center, Tarrytown, N.Y. My thanks to Alec Hickmott for sharing this report.

99. "Coosa Valley Planners Win Worldwide Fame," *RNT*, July 15, 1966, p. 3.

100. Undated Clipping, *Atlanta Constitution*, June 1966, Planning Commission, RFCL.

101. Sparer, "Area Planning," 11–12.

102. James Tobin, "Hansen and Public Policy," *Quarterly Journal of Economics* 90 (February 1976): 34.

Chapter 8. A Fraught Partnership

1. Tony Judt, "America, My New-Found-Land," *New York Review of Books*, May 27, 2010, accessed May 7, 2016, http://www.nybooks.com/articles/archives/2010/may/27/america-my-new-found-land/?pagination=false.

2. Elizabeth Tandy Shermer, *Sunbelt Capitalism: Phoenix and the Transformation of American Politics* (Philadelphia: University of Pennsylvania Press, 2014), 39–92.

3. Ibid.

4. Ibid., 93–224.

5. Ibid., 184–224, quoted 202.

6. Christopher P. Loss, *Between Citizens and the State: The Politics of American Higher Education in the 20th Century* (Princeton, N.J.: Princeton University Press, 2013), 53–90; Ronald Story, "The New Deal and Higher Education," in *The New Deal and the Triumph of Liberalism*, ed. Sidney M. Milkus and Jerome M. Mileur (Amherst: University of Massachusetts Press, 2002), 272–96; Paula Fass, "Without Design: Education Policy in the New Deal," 91 *American Journal of Education* (November 1982): 36–64.

7. Loss, *Between Citizens and the State*; Glenn Altschuler and Stuart Blumin, *The GI Bill: The New Deal for Veterans* (Oxford: Oxford University Press, 2009); Hugh Davis Graham, *Uncertain Triumph: Federal Education Policy in the Kennedy and Johnson Years* (Chapel Hill: University of North Carolina Press, 1984).

8. Dean Smith, *Grady Gammage: ASU's Man of Vision* (Tempe: Arizona State University, 1989), 1–108.

9. Ibid., 1–108.

10. Ibid., 51–108, quoted 86, 91.

11. Ibid., quoted 104; Ernest J. Hopkins and Alfred Thomas, Jr., *The Arizona State University Story* (Phoenix: Southwest Publishing, 1960), 245–94, quoted 256.

12. Shermer, *Sunbelt Capitalism*, 200–218, quoted 207.

13. Ibid., 55–61, 207–8.

14. Ibid., 200–218, quoted 208–9.

15. Ibid., 200–218.

16. Ibid, quoted 210.

17. Ibid, 200–218, quoted 211.

18. Ibid., 200–218

19. Ibid., quoted 204, 211.

20. Ibid., 200–218.

21. Warren Ashby, *Frank Porter Graham: A Southern Liberal* (J. F. Blair, 1980); Luther H. Hodges, *Businessman in the Statehouse: Six Years as Governor of North Carolina* (Chapel Hill: University of North Carolina Press, 1962), esp. 196–97.

22. Shermer, *Sunbelt Capitalism*, 212–14.

23. Ibid., 213.

24. Hodges, *Businessman in the Statehouse*, 6–19, 156–225, esp. 187, 189–90.

25. Ibid., quoted 198.

26. Ibid., 156–225, esp. 156, 177, 203, 204; Shermer, *Sunbelt Capitalism*, 184–224; Margaret Pugh O'Mara, *Cities of Knowledge: Cold War Science and the Search for the Next Silicon Valley* (Princeton, N.J.: Princeton University Press, 2005), 216–17.

27. Shermer, *Sunbelt Capitalism*, 184–224, 277–78.

28. Paddy Riley, "Clark Kerr: From the Industrial to the Knowledge Economy," in *American Capitalism: Social Thought and Political Economy in the Twentieth Century*, ed. Nelson Lichtenstein (Philadelphia: University of Pennsylvania Press, 2006), 71–87; Clark Kerr, "The Multiversity: Are Its Several Souls Worth Saving?" *Harper's*, November 1963, pp. 37–42, quoted 37–38, 41.

29. Shermer, *Sunbelt Capitalism*, quoted 277–78.

30. Minutes of the Meeting of the Education Committee, January 11, 1943, Folder 4, Box 30, San Diego Chamber of Commerce Records, Special Collections and University Archives, San Diego State University, San Diego, Calif. (hereafter referred to as SD); Minutes of the Meeting of the Education Committee, November 19, 1947, 3, Folder 5, Box 30, ibid.; Minutes of the Meeting of the Education Committee with the State College and Public Schools Advisory Group, April 15, 1948, Folder 5, Box 30, ibid.; Minutes of the Meeting of the Education Committee, September 6, 1949, 3, Folder 5, Box 30, ibid.; Panel Meeting of the Five Members of the Education Committee with Teacher Statements of San Diego State College, November 19, 1951, Folder 5, Box 30, ibid.; Minutes of the Meeting of the Education Committee, November 21, 1952, September 21, 1953, September 20, 1954, September 18, 1954, Folder 5, Box 30, ibid.; Education Committee Program of Work, February 20, 1956, Folder 8, Box 32, ibid.; Minutes of the Meeting of the Education Committee, April 8, 1960, Folder 7, Box 29, ibid.

31. Harry Foster to O. W. Todd, Jr., December 22, 1950, Folder 3, Box 26, SD; University of California Committee [Roster]; January 26, 1956, Folder 14, Box 92, SD; Organizational Structure of the Sub-Committee of the Chamber of Commerce Education Committee, [1956], ibid.; Minutes of the University of California Committee Meeting, August 17, 1956, Folder 1, Box 92, SD; Notes on the University of California meeting, March 22, 1956, ibid.; Arnold Klaus to T. C. Holy, April 3, 1956, ibid.; R. H. Biron to T. C. Holy and Hubert H. Semans, February 21, 1956, Folder 12, Box 92, SD; "University of California, La Jolla Campus Expansion: History of Events to the Present," July 12, 1957, 1, quoted 9, Folder 1, Box 92, SD.

32. Kenneth Lamott, "La Jolla's New University, Olympus on a Mesa," *Harper's*, August 1966, pp. 82–88; Nancy Scott Andersen, *An Improbable Venture: A History of the University of California, San Diego* (La Jolla: University of California, San Diego Press, 1993), quoted 37, 73.

33. Sheridan Hegland, "Regents OK U.C. Branch in San Diego," *Independent*, August 26, 1956, p. 1, Folder 11, Box 92, SD; Henry Love, "Scripps Institution Expansion Approved," *San Diego Union*, August 25, 1956, p. 1, ibid.

34. Quoted in Andersen, *An Improbable Venture*, 92–95; John Galbraith, Untitled Speech, September 22, 1965, 1–2, Folder 8, Box 29, SD.

35. Seth Rosenfeld, *Subversives: The FBI's War on Student Radicals and Reagan's Rise to Power* (New York: Farrar, Straus, and Giroux, 2012); Gerard J. DeGroot, "Ronald Reagan and Student Unrest in California, 1966–1970," *Pacific Historical Review* 65, no. 1 (1996): 107–29; Bill to Lucille, June 28, 1967, Folder 1, Box 34, San Diego Chamber of Commerce Records, San Diego State University Special Collections (San Diego, Calif.); Clark Kerr, *The Gold and the Blue: A Personal Memoir of the University of California, 1949–1967*, vol. 2 (Berkeley: University of

California Press, 2004); Robert P. Sutton, "Tuition or Not Tuition—That Is The Question," July 31, 1967, typescript, quoted p. 1, Folder 1, Box 34, SD.

36. John Galbraith, "Higher Education as an Economic Force in San Diego," January 27, 1967, quoted p. 1, Folder 2, Box 34, SD; Synopsis of the Minutes of the San Diego Chamber of Commerce Board of Directors, March 8, 1967, Folder 10, Box 30, SD; Minutes of the Meeting of the Educational Committee, September 11, 1967, quoted p. 1, Folder 10, Box 30, SD; "Preserving the Master Plan," unattributed clipping, Folder 10, Box 30, SD.

37. Christopher Newfield, *Unmaking the Public University: The Forty-Year Assault on the Middle Class* (Cambridge: Harvard University Press, 2011).

38. Andersen, *An Improbable Venture*, 92–95; Michael Hiltznik, "Napolitano Throws Cold Water on the Online Education Craze," *Los Angeles Times*, March 26, 2014, accessed May 7, 2016, http://www.latimes.com/business/hiltzik/la-fi-mh-uc-prexy-napolitano-20140326-story .html.

39. Hodges, *Businessman in the Statehouse*, 65–78; James C. Cobb, *Selling of the South: The Southern Crusade for Industrial Development, 1936–90* (Urbana: University of Illinois Press, 1993), 171–76; Correspondence and speeches in regard to Medicare/Medicaid: Folder 2051, Luther Hartwell Hodges Papers, Southern Historical Collection, Louis Round Wilson Special Collections Library, University of North Carolina–Chapel Hill; Folders 305, 821, and 1599, Research Triangle Park Papers and Folder 1706, UNC Board of Trustees Papers, Wilson Library, University of North Carolina–Chapel Hill; Press Release, "$100 Million," December 3, 2014, https://pharmacy .unc.edu/news/schoolnews/100-million-eshelman-gift-to-fund-innovation-center-is-largest-ever -to-a-pharmacy-school.

40. Shermer, *Sunbelt Capitalism*, 250–255, 336–40; Andrew Ross, *Bird on Fire: Lessons from the World's Least Sustainable City* (Oxford: Oxford University Press, 2011), 174–84, 239–50.

41. "Starbucks Offers Full Tuition," June 15, 2014, https://news.starbucks.com/news/starbucks -offers-full-tuition-reimbursement-for-employees-to-complete-a-bac; Alan Pike, "Critics Warn Starbucks Employees to Read the Fine Print of New Tuition Plan," *Think Progress*, June 17, 2014, http://thinkprogress.org/education/2014/06/17/3449906/starbucks-tuition-plan-fine-print/; Ned Resnikoff, "Starbucks Free Tuition Plan Comes at a Cost," June 16, 2014, http://www.msnbc.com /msnbc/starbucks-offers-employees-free-tuition-arizona-state-university-online; Carol Straum-sheim, "The Starbucks-ASU Contract," *Inside Higher Ed*, June 23, 2014, https://www.insidehighered .com/news/2014/06/23/contract-reveals-arizona-state-u-starbucks-partnership-details.

Chapter 9. The Triumph of Social Responsibility in the National Association of Manufacturers in the 1950s

1. The idea of corporate liberalism was originally developed in the work of historians Martin Sklar, James Weinstein, and Gabriel Kolko, although credit for the term is usually given to Sklar, "Woodrow Wilson and the Political-Economy of Modern United States Liberalism," *Studies on the Left* 1 (Fall 1960), reprinted in Martin J. Sklar, *The United States as a Developing Country: Studies in U.S. History in the Progressive Era and the 1920s* (Cambridge: Cambridge University Press, 1992), pp. 102–42. See Martin Sklar, *The Corporate Reconstruction of Capitalism, 1890–1916* (Cambridge: Cambridge University Press, 1988); Gabriel Kolko, *The Triumph of Conservatism* (New York: Free Press, 1963); James Weinstein, *The Corporate Ideal in the Liberal State, 1900–1918* (Boston: Beacon, 1968); and Ellis Hawley, "The Study and Discovery of a Corporate Liberalism," *Business History Review* 52 (Autumn 1978), 309–20. My definition of "corporate liberalism" hews closely to that in Sklar's *Corporate Reconstruction*.

2. Quotes from Sklar, *Corporate Reconstruction*, 428–29; Hartz castigates Wilson's Lockean-ism in *The Liberal Tradition in America* (New York: Harcourt, Brace and Company, 1955).

3. Sklar, *Corporate Reconstruction*, 435.

4. See especially Alan Brinkley, *The End of Reform: New Deal Liberalism in Recession and War* (New York: Knopf, 1995).

5. Sklar, *The United States as a Developing Country*, 214; this is very much in accord with the description of the U.S. political economy in Godfrey Hodgson, *America in Our Time* (New York: Random House, 1976).

6. The editors of *Fortune* in collaboration with Russell W. Davenport, *U.S.A.—The Permanent Revolution* (New York: Prentice Hall, 1951), 79.

7. Quoted in ibid., 80.

8. See Howard Bowen, *The Social Responsibility of the Businessman* (New York: Harper & Brothers, 1953), esp. p. 6; James Worthy, "Social Responsibility of Business," in *Social Responsibility of Business: Two Points of View*, by James Worthy and Theodore Levitt (Chicago: Industrial Relations Center, 1959); Kenneth Goodpaster, ed., *Corporate Responsibility: The American Experience* (New York: Cambridge University Press, 2012), esp. chs. 4 and 6. On the more liberal management and political stances of U.S. corporations in the mid-twentieth century, see Kim McQuaid, *Uneasy Partners: Big Business in American Politics, 1945–1990* (Baltimore: Johns Hopkins University Press, 1994); Stephen B. Adams, *Mr. Kaiser Goes to Washington: The Rise of a Government Entrepreneur* (Chapel Hill: University of North Carolina Press, 2009); Robert Collins, *The Business Response to Keynes, 1929–1964* (New York: Columbia University Press, 1981); Thomas Watson, Jr., with Peter Petre, *Father Son & Co.: My Life at IBM and Beyond* (New York: Bantam Books, 1990).

9. Worthy, "Social Responsibility of Business," 4.

10. The best description of the group-based ideas of mid-century social science is in Daniel T. Rodgers, *Age of Fracture* (Cambridge: Cambridge University Press, 2011), 4–5. On the promises of Human Relations as a management technique, see Stuart Chase, *The Proper Study of Mankind: An Inquiry into the Science of Human Relations*, revised ed. (New York: Harper and Row, 1956); William Foote Whyte, "Human Relations Theory—A Progress Report," *Harvard Business Review* 34 (September–October 1956): 125–32. For a more critical perspective, see Sanford Jacoby, *Modern Manors: Welfare Capitalism Since the New Deal* (Princeton, N.J.: Princeton University Press, 1997); Daniel Bell, "Adjusting Men to Machines," *Commentary* 3 (January 1947): 79–88; Howell John Harris, *The Right to Manage: Industrial Relations Policies of American Business in the 1940s* (Madison: University of Wisconsin Press, 1982).

11. Peter Drucker, *The New Society* (New York: Harper, 1962), 44.

12. Editors of *Fortune* and Davenport, *U.S.A.—The Permanent Revolution*, 89–108.

13. The Business Advisory Council was a bastion of corporate liberalism and was widely regarded as an alternative to the NAM. See McQuaid, *Uneasy Partners*, esp. 19–25.

14. Dwight D. Eisenhower, *Mandate for Change 1953–1956* (Garden City, N.Y.: Doubleday & Company, 1963), 129; McQuaid, *Uneasy Partners*, 74–75.

15. On this group, see Kim Phillips-Fein, *Invisible Hands: The Making of the Conservative Movement from the New Deal to Reagan* (New York: W. W. Norton, 2009), which likewise characterizes its members as having a minority viewpoint at this time.

16. The best description of the liberal consensus is still Hodgson, *America in Our Time*, ch. 4

17. See, for instance, Gary Gerstle, "Race and the Myth of the Liberal Consensus," *Journal of American History* 82 (September 1995): 579–86; Thomas Sugrue, *The Origins of the Urban Crisis:*

Race and Inequality in Postwar Detroit (Princeton, N.J.: Princeton University Press, 1997); Jerry Podair, *The Strike That Changed New York* (New Haven, Conn.: Yale University Press, 2002).

18. Jefferson Cowie, *Capital Moves: RCA's Seventy Year Quest for Cheap Labor* (New York: New Press, 2001). General Electric's leadership represented a corporate liberal ethos, especially in their "stakeholders" model of social responsibility, but they also hired the combative, anti-union Lemuel Boulware as their Industrial Relations head.

19. Lisa McGirr, *Suburban Warriors: The Origins of the New American Right* (Princeton, N.J.: Princeton Univesity Press, 2002); Phillips-Fein, *Invisible Hands.*

20. "Renovation in the NAM," *Fortune* (July 1948): 72–75, 165–69, quoted 72. There is no book-length treatment of the NAM, but the following articles together provide an overview: Philip H. Burch, Jr., "The NAM as an Interest Group," *Politics and Society* 4, no. 1 (1973): 97–130; Jonathan Soffer, "The National Association of Manufacturers and the Militarization of American Conservatism," *Business History Review* 75 (Winter 2001): 775–805; Andrew Workman, "Manufacturing Power: The Organizational Revival of the National Association of Manufacturers, 1941–45," *Business History Review* 72 (Summer 1998): 279–317.

21. Neither Grede Foundries nor Hyster was a publicly traded corporation at this time, so it is difficult to ascertain size. Kimberly-Clark had 13,000 employees in 1955, and J. I. Case was a major, publicly traded corporation with more than 10,000 employees when Grede directed it. See Craig Miner, *Grede of Milwaukee* (Wichita, Kans.: Watermark Press, 1989). For information on Cola Parker, see the obituary in *Chicago Tribune*, June 28, 1962, http://archives.chicagotribune.com/1962/06/28/page/204/article/cola-parker-industrialist-banker-dies; on Swigert, see the obituary in *New York Times*, December 8, 1986, http://www.nytimes.com/1986/12/08/obituaries/ernest-g-swigert-dies-at-94-led-group-of-manufacturers.html.

22. The conservatives on the Executive Committee complained about and tried to hamstring staff departments with which they disagreed. See correspondence in Box 24, Folder 1 in the William J. Grede Papers, 1909–1979, at the Wisconsin State Historical Society, Madison, Wisconsin (henceforth WJGP). See also the Minutes of Executive Committee Meetings, Series 13, Box 250, in National Association of Manufacturers records (Accession 1411), Hagley Museum and Library, Wilmington, Delaware (henceforth NAM Records).

23. Philip Cortney to H. W. Prentiss, November 6, 1953, Box 4, Folder 6, WJGP.

24. Robert Gaylord to William Grede, September 10, 1956, Box 24, Folder 1, WJGP.

25. Quote from William Grede to Clark C. Thompson, September 14, 1953, Box 25, Folder 6, WJPP. Thompson was from the National Industrial Conference Board and was surveying employers about their views on public relations. Grede's complaint was the very basis of corporate liberal arguments about "social responsibility," as indicated by James Worthy: "The big company in particular has developed into a quasi-public institution, and as such has social and economic responsibilities beyond those of small companies." Worthy, "Social Responsibility of Business," 5.

26. Miner, *Grede of Milwaukee*, 94; Leonard Read, "On That Day Began Lies," originally published in 1949, reprinted at http://www.thefreemanonline.org, accessed April 24, 2016.

27. It was not just the Right that made this criticism of groups and pluralism. William H. Whyte, Jr.'s *The Organization Man* argued that the social ethos of the workplace, engineered by industrial relations experts, led to conformity and what would later be called "groupthink." Theodore Lowi's *The End of Liberalism* critiqued pluralism's hollow content and obsession with group reconciliation. The Right's concern about conformity and individualism was later echoed by the counterculture. See Theodore Lowi, *The End of Liberalism: Ideology, Policy and the Crisis of Public Authority* (New York: W. W. Norton, 1969); William H. Whyte, Jr., *The Organization*

Man (Garden City, N.Y.: Doubleday-Anchor, 1957); Thomas Frank, *The Conquest of Cool* (Chicago: University of Chicago Press, 1998).

28. Described in Miner, *Grede of Milwaukee*, 217–24; See also the minutes of the Board of Directors Meeting, September 14, 15, 16, 1960, Series 13, Box 242, Vol. 52, NAM Records.

29. David M. Reeves to Member, January 2, 1961, Box 24, Folder 3, WJGP.

30. H. L. Derby to Grede, November 27, 1961; and Grede to Ernie Swigert, July 26, 1962, both Box 24, Folder 3, WJGP.

31. Soffer, "Militarization of American Conservatism."

32. See Alfred Cleveland, "NAM: Spokesman for Industry?" *Harvard Business Review* (May 1948): 353–71. You can see some of these complaints in correspondence in "Albert Cleveland" files, Series 12, Box 192, NAM Records.

33. Soffer, "Militarization of American Conservatism," 787; "N.A.M. Elects Permanent Head Under Plan for Reorganization," *New York Times*, September 20, 1962, p. 45.

34. Worthy, "Social Responsibility of Business," 16.

35. See Kevin Mattson, *When America Was Great: The Fighting Faith of Postwar Liberalism* (New York: Routledge, 2004), chs. 4–5.

36. "Minority Program," n.d., Series 7, Box 135, NAM Records.

37. See Soffer, "Militarization of American Conservatism," 788, Theodore Leavitt, "The Johnson Treatment," *Harvard Business Review* (January–February 1967): 114–28; Series 7, Boxes 136 and 143, "Human Relations" and "Employee Relations" folders, NAM Records.

38. Soffer, "Militarization of American Conservatism," 786–88; see also "The Surging Tide of Change," an Address by J. Stanford Smith, December 1, 1964, Series 7, Box 135, NAM Records.

39. Foster Hailey, "New Head of N.A.M. Foresees Economic Gains," *New York Times*, December 5, 1962, p. 29.

40. "N.A.M. Pledges Aid to Johnson," *New York Times*, December 5, 1963, p. 27.

41. On the NAM's support for implementing Title VII, see Jennifer Delton, *Racial Integration in Corporate America* (New York: Cambridge University Press, 2009), ch. 7.

42. W. P. Gullander to Grede, March 18, 1964, Box 24, Folder 3, WJGP.

43. Dillard Munford to Grede, July 2, 1965; and W. B. McMillan to Gullander, December 7, 1965, both in Box 24, Folder 1, WJGP.

44. Gullander to Grede, May 19, 1965, Box 24, Folder 3 in WJGP. These were old arguments. See Osborn Elliott, *Men at the Top* (New York: Harper & Brothers, 1959), 209; "Renovation in the NAM," cited above.

45. Gullander to Grede, January 18, 1967, Box 24, Folder 3; Gullander to W. B. McMillan, December 8, 1965, Box 24, Folder 1, WJGP.

46. Gullander to Grede, January 18, 1967, Box 24, Folder 3; Gullander to W. B. McMillan, December 8, 1965, Box 24, Folder 1, WJGP.

47. Grede to Gullander, December 20, 1965, Box 24, Folder 3, WJGP.

48. Grede to Gullander, May 26, 1965, Box 24, Folder 3, WJGP.

49. Grede to Gullander, June 21, 1967, in response to Gullander's defense of the NAM's cooperation with Sargent Shriver and the North Carolina Manpower Development Corporation, June 16, 1967, both in Box 24, Folder 4, WJGP.

50. Assistant counsel to Mr. M. E. DeNeui, March 10, 1970, Box 64, Series 5, Folder: Philadelphia Plan, NAM Records. On the OFCC's infamous "Order No. 4," see Hugh Davis Graham, *The Civil Rights Era: Origins and Development of National Policy, 1960-1972* (Oxford: Oxford University Press, 1990) and Delton, *Racial Integration in Corporate America*, 211–24.

51. Delton, *Racial Integration in Corporate America*, chs. 7–8.

52. It is hard to read Sklar's ideas about the U.S.'s "mixed economy" and not hear Grede's arguments. Both essentially believed that corporate liberalism had bought socialism to the United States. See especially Sklar, "The Corporate Reconstruction of American Capitalism: A Note on the Capitalism-Socialism Mix in the United States," in Sklar, *The United States as a Developing Country*. On Sklar's belief that corporate liberalism was akin to socialism, see also John Judis, "Martin Sklar and the Search for a Usable Past, *New Republic*, June 17, 2014, https://newrepublic.com/article/118187/martin-j-sklar-and-search-usable-past.

53. Kim Phillips-Fein, "Right On," *Nation*, September 28, 2009, pp. 25–32, quoted 30.

54. Ibid., 30.

Chapter 10. "What Would Peace in Vietnam Mean for You as an Investor?"

1. The delegation also met with Michigan Republican representative Gerald Ford, Illinois Democratic representative Sidney Yates, and Illinois Republican representative Donald Rumsfeld. Betty Flynn, "Dovish Execs Fail to Sway Dirksen," *Chicago Daily News*, May 22, 1968, Folder 14, Box 2, Erwin Salk Multicultural Collection, University of Illinois at Chicago Special Collections, Chicago, Illinois (henceforth SMC).

2. Byron C. Hulsey, *Everett Dirksen and His Presidents: How a Senate Giant Shaped American Politics* (Lawrence: University Press of Kansas, 2000), 223.

3. For the context of these businessmen's activities, see, for instance, Howard Brick, *The Age of Contradiction: American Thought and Culture in the 1960s* (New York: Twayne Publishers, 1998), 1–5, 44–65.

4. I say men *and* women, given that one identifiable female executive shows up at a meeting (Lillian Kanterman of Kay Distributing Co.) in one of the three archival collections available. List of officers, Folder: Detroit Chapter, 1967–68, Box 58, Series D, Business Executives Move, Swarthmore College Peace Collection, Swarthmore, Pennsylvania (henceforth SCPC). There are other references though not by name, in for example, "An Open Letter to the President of the United States [from the Drapery and allied Home Furnishings Industries]," November 14, 1969, in *Home Furnishings Daily*, Folder: New York Chapter, 1967–69, Series D, Box 58, SCPC. Some of women also served on the staff of local groups.

5. Gerard J. DeGroot, *The Sixties Unplugged: A Kaleidoscopic History of a Disorderly Decade* (Cambridge, Mass.: Harvard University Press, 2008), 2. Nancy Zarourlis and Gerald Sullivan have argued that the BEM was generally not pacifist but practical, that they opposed the war "not because it was wrong . . . but because it wasn't working." This claim did not necessarily apply to all members of the organization or its supporters. Nancy Zarourlis and Gerald Sullivan, *Who Spoke Up? American Protest Against the War in Vietnam, 1963–1975* (Garden City, N.Y.: Doubleday and Company, 1984), 153.

6. For a treatment of the Moratorium, which "drew attention quite deliberately to its relative moderation" in contrast to the more radical Mobilization coalition, see Todd Gitlin, *The Whole World Is Watching: Mass Media in the Making & Unmaking of the New Left* (Los Angeles: University of California Press, 2003), 218–25, quoted 219.

7. The BEM's members were from a different cross-section of business than, for instance, Joseph Coors, who in 1968 was actively trying to shut down the Students for a Democratic Society on the University of Colorado campus. See Kimberly Phillips-Fein, *Invisible Hands: The Making of the Conservative Movement from the New Deal to Reagan* (New York: W. W. Norton, 2009), 169–70. For contrast with other activities of businessmen in this period, see David Vogel,

Fluctuating Fortunes (New York: Basic Books, 1989), 3–15, 192–227; Benjamin C. Waterhouse, *Lobbying America: The Politics of Business from Nixon to NAFTA* (Princeton, N.J.: Princeton University Press, 2013), 6–18; Cathie Jo Martin, "Business and the New Economic Activism: The Growth of Corporate Lobbies in the Sixties," *Polity* 27 (Autumn 1994): 49–76. For a treatment of the National Association of Manufacturers just prior to this period, see Elizabeth Fones-Wolf, *Selling Free Enterprise: The Business Assault on Labor and Liberalism, 1945–1960* (Urbana and Chicago: University of Illinois Press, 1994), 257–84.

8. Paine, Webber, Jackson & Curtis, "Peace in Vietnam?" Research Bulletin 7, January 1968, Folder 1338, Box 155, SMC.

9. Victor J. Hillery, "Dovish Wall Street: Intensification of War in Vietnam Now Causes Big Stock-Price Drops" [copy], *Wall Street Journal*, n.d. [March 6, 1968], Folder: New York Chapter, 1967–69, Box 58, Series D, SCPC.

10. Ibid.

11. Sandra Scanlon, *The Pro-War Movement: Domestic Support for the Vietnam War and the Making of Modern American Conservatism* (Amherst: University of Massachusetts Press, 2013), 35–36.

12. See Melman's obituary by Jennifer Bayot, "Seymour Melman, 86, Dies; Spurred Antiwar Movement," *New York Times*, December 18, 2004, http://www.nytimes.com/2004/12/18 /obituaries/18melman.html?_r=0; Seymour Melman, *Our Depleted Society* (New York: Dell, 1965), quoted viii, 3–4. Melman's concerns also persisted throughout his lifetime, as is evident from this piece on the Iraq War: Seymour Melman, "In the Grip of a Permanent War Economy," *Counterpunch*, March 15–17, 2003, http://www.counterpunch.org/2003/03/15/in-the-grip-of-a -permanent-war-economy/.

13. A Private Memorandum from Seymour Melman, January 7, 1966, Folder 153, Box 1512, SMC.

14. Melman, *Our Depleted Society*, 133–35.

15. Seymour Melman to Erwin Salk, July 18, 1966, Folder 134, Box 86, SMC.

16. Ibid.

17. Salk sent out copies of Melman's 1970 book *Pentagon Capitalism* to members of Congress and still had several dozen copies in his possession at the time of his death in 2000. The author processed Salk's papers when they arrived at the University of Illinois at Chicago (UIC) and was responsible for culling the collection, including the dozens of copies of this book. Salk also cited Melman's work in one of his Senate testimonies. Salk to Edwin P. Neilan, July 27, 1966, Folder 1232, Box 145, SMC. See also Testimony Before the Senate Appropriations Committee, February 2, 1927, Folder 1602, Box 160, SMC.

18. Fact sheet about: BEM—Business Executives Move for Vietnam Peace and New National Priorities, Folder: New York Chapter, 1967–69, Box 58, Series D, SCPC. The original appeal can be found in: Niles to LBJ December 30, 1966 [open letter], Folder: Letters, Box 7, Series C, Swarthmore. The same details are available in *Baltimore Magazine*, "Misc. File: The Niles Crusade," August 1968, 8 in Folder 1341, Box 155, SMC.

19. Open Letter Niles to LBJ, December 30, 1966, Folder: Letters, Series C, Box 7, BEM, SCPC.

20. Ibid.

21. Reprint of ad, *New York Times*, May 28, 1967, Folder 735, Box 86, SMC.

22. This list derives from Membership List, Folder 2, Box 1, Business Executives Move For Vietnam Peace, St. Louis Area Committee Records, 1966–74, State Historical Society of Missouri, St. Louis, Missouri (henceforth SHSM).

23. Baltimore Office 1970–1972, Folder 1244, Box 147, SMC.

24. E. J. Kahn, "Talk of the Town: Concerned Businessmen," *New Yorker* (June 27, 1970): 26–27.

25. Because businessmen inhabited social space as well as business space, it is no surprise that we find among Salk's papers a civil rights pamphlet published by Clairol, *A Voyage of Awareness: A Prelude to Action!: A Guide for Business Executives Covering the History of Blackness in America* (Clairol, 1970), Series IV: Race and Civil Rights Pamphlet Series, Box 195, SMC. On business and civil rights, see also David Farber, "The New American Revolution: The Movement and Business," in *The Sixties: From Memory to History*, ed. David Farber (Chapel Hill: University of North Carolina Press, 1994), 179.

26. In the unprocessed portion of Niles's papers at Swarthmore are a comprehensive set of interviews Lynd conducted in Vietnam. Niles had direct access to such resources, and these were only possible through the antiwar movement.

27. Testimony of Henry Niles, chairman of BEM, submitted to Subcommittee on the Department of Defense of the Appropriations Committee of the House of Representatives, April 26, 1972, Folder 1243 BEM—Baltimore office, 1972, Box 147, SMC. Various statements in his private correspondence suggest that Niles's public positions adhered more to an official BEM position than his personal beliefs, which appear genuinely pacifist.

28. Brick, *Age of Contradiction*, 153.

29. Containment was not an option for the war's supporters, and "rollback" was essential; see Scanlon, *The Pro-War Movement*, 28.

30. Speech of Marriner Eccles, September 27, 1967, Box 148, Folder 1253, SMC.

31. Harold Willens to Salk, October 13, 1967, Folder 1299, Box 152, SMC. Todd Gitlin suggests that the media also had an agenda in elevating certain star personalities during this period. See his *The Whole World Is Watching*, 149.

32. Summary of Activities in First Seven Months of 1969, Folder 1244, Box 147, SMC.

33. The BEM's Harold Willens and Erwin Salk also drew FBI attention for their contact with and travel to China, but Salk was also suspected of ties to American Communist activities as his file reveals. See FBI Report, DOCID-59163133, Harold Willens; and FBI Report, 1193255-2—100-HQ-387835 SER 2216p4, 7, 13; 2362p4, 7, 8; 2636p4, 8; 2860p4, 7; 2956—100-HQ-387835 SER 2636p4, 8-Section 92, Erwin Salk; and FBI Report, 1193255-2—HQ File 1, Erwin Salk.

34. *News Notes*, June 17, 1971, Folder 1298, Box 152, Salk, UIC.

35. To BEM Executive Committee, From Henry Niles and Harold Willens, August 19, 1968, Folder 1341, Box 155, SMC.

36. *Congressional Record*, December 30, 1959, Folder: Letter to Congressman Porter, Box 1, Series A, BEM, SCPC.

37. E. J. Kahn, "Talk of the Town: Concerned Businessmen," *New Yorker*, June 27, 1970, http://www.newyorker.com/search/query?keyword=Davis%200044%20%20Hal#ixzz28Ng5EMnc.

38. Niles to Members of National Council, July 12, 1971, Folder 37, Box 1, SHSM.

39. Niles to National Council Members, November 18, 1970, Folder 1244, Box 147, SMC.

40. Operation Housecleaning Leaflet, Box 147, Folder 1243, SMC.

41. *News Notes*, April 14, 1972, Folder 1298, Box 152, SMC.

42. From Operation Housecleaning leaflet, Box 147, Folder 1243, SMC. The deadly dozen were California representatives Republican William Mailliard and Democrat George Miller; Colorado Democrat Wayne Asinall; Nebraska Republican Charles Thone; New Mexico Republican Manuel Lujan; New York Democrats James J. Delaney and John J. Rooney, and Republican

Henry P. Smith; North Carolina Republican Wilmer David Mizell; Pennsylvania Republican Lawrence G. Williams; Viriginia Republican Joel T. Broyhill; and Republican Alvin E. O'Konski of Wisconsin.

43. Operation Housecleaning—1972, November 30, 1972, Folder 1243, Box 147, SMC. One can contrast this with the $2 million the business conservatives of the Committee for the Survival of a Free Congress attempted to raise in 1974 to defeat the 100 "most liberal, anti-business and pro-welfare congressmen on Capitol Hill." See Phillips-Fein, *Invisible Hands*, 171.

44. Nicholas Johnson and Tracy A. Westen, "A Twentieth-Century Soapbox: The Right to Purchase Radio and Television Time," *Virginia Law Review* 57 (May 1971): 574–634.

45. Whitaker to Binger, February 8, 1972, Folder 105, National Council: Kansas City Chapter, 1971–72, Box 2, BEM, SHSM. The collection at Swarthmore contains Whitaker's entire research file. Parentheses in original.

46. Fred Branfman's Blog, "Automated War—Laos Then, Af-Pak Today?" accessed July 24, 2014, https://fredbranfman.wordpress.com/about.

47. Honeywell Responds to War Production Critics, Press Release, April 18, 1972, Folder 105 National Council: Kansas City chapter, 1971–72, Box 2, BEM, SHSM. Carl Gerstacker, the chairman for Dow Chemical, which was also a visible target, would lament: "We've been hurt by these demonstrations. . . . I wish we'd never heard of napalm." See Farber, "The New American Revolution," quoted 181.

48. Congressional Record, November 27, 1967, A5810–5811, Box 153, Folder 1315, SMC.

49. Charles DeBenedetti and Charles Chatfield, *An American Ordeal: The Antiwar Movement of the Vietnam Era* (New York: Syracuse University, 1990), 253. For a larger context on the interwoven and seemingly contradictory developments of the era, see especially the first chapter of Howard Brick's *Age of Contradiction*, 1–22.

50. "Why Peace Would Be Good for Business?" Box 147, Folder 1244, SMC. This item was entered into the minutes of the Senate Foreign Relations Committee, April 15, 1970.

51. George Katsiaficas, *The Imagination of the New Left: A Global Analysis of 1968* (Boston: South End Press, 1999), 152.

52. Katsiaficas, *Imagination of the New Left*, 153.

53. Alfred E. Eckes, Jr., *Opening America's Market: U.S. Foreign Trade Policy Since 1776* (Chapel Hill: University of North Carolina Press, 1995), 203. See also Waterhouse, *Lobbying America*, 34–35. The U.S. government was also underwriting in Vietnam the very improvements that the BEM wanted to see at home; see Marc Levinson, *The Box: How the Shipping Container Made the World Smaller and the World Economy Bigger* (Princeton, N.J.: Princeton University Press, 2006), 174.

54. For a detailed treatment of this crisis, see Judith Stein, *The Pivotal Decade: How the United States Traded Factories for Finance in the Seventies* (New Haven, Conn.: Yale University Press, 2011), ch. 2.

55. Paine, Webber, Jackson & Curtis, "Peace in Vietnam?" Research Bulletin No. 7, January 1968, Folder 1338, Box 155, Salk, UIC.

56. Michael L. Gillette, *Launching the War on Poverty: An Oral History* (New York: Oxford University Press, 2010), 207.

57. David F. Schmitz, *The Tet Offensive: Politics, War, and Public Opinion* (Oxford: Rowman & Littlefield, 2005), xv. As Schmitz states it: "the Tet Offensive was the decisive moment in the Vietnam War due to its impact on senior officials in the Johnson administration and *elite opinion* that brought about Johnson's dramatic decisions and change in policy." (Emphasis

mine.) Clifford was among the most notable officials. See also Schmitz's concluding comments, 162–67.

58. Clark Clifford, *Counsel to the President: A Memoir* (New York, Random House: 1991), 519.

59. John Acacia, *Clark Clifford: The Wise Man of Washington* (Lexington: University Press of Kentucky, 2009), 279.

60. Ibid. See also Townsend Hoopes, "The Fight for the President's Mind—And the Men Who Won It," *Atlantic Monthly* (October 1969): 11.

61. Niles [personal memorandum], December 27, 1972, Folder: Clark Clifford Luncheon, Box 45, Series D, BEM, SCPC.

62. In the July 1969 issue of *Foreign Affairs* it was possible for Clifford to write: "Nothing we might do could be so beneficial . . . as to begin to withdraw our combat troops. Moreover . . . we cannot realistically expect to achieve anything more through our military force, and the time has come to begin to disengage. That was my final conclusion as I left the Pentagon on January 20, 1969." Clark M. Clifford, "A Viet Nam Reappraisal," *Foreign Affairs* (July 1969): 601–622, http://www. foreignaffairs.com/articles/24081/clark-m-clifford/a-viet-nam-reappraisal. For more on Walker's organizing skills, see Jacob S. Hacker and Paul Pierson, *Winner Take All Politics: How Washington Made the Rich Richer—and Turned Its Back on the Middle Class* (New York: Simon and Schuster, 2010), 125.

63. McCloskey to Salk, September 24, 1981, Box 167, Folder 1491, SMC.

64. Niles to All Members, July 17, 1968, Folder 1341, Box 155, SMC; Noam Chomsky, *At War with Asia* (New York: Pantheon Books, 1970), 4–8, 24–30.

65. George McGovern to Niles April 3, 1970, Folder: Congressional Support Statements, 1970, Box 8, Series C, BEM, SCPC.

66. Bruce M. Russett and Elizabeth C. Hanson, *Interest and Ideology: Foreign Policy Beliefs of American Businessmen* (New York: W. H. Freeman & Co., 1975), 271–80.

67. The BEM officially ceased operation in 1983 and was succeeded by Business Executives for National Security (BENS), headed by Stanley Weiss. Unprocessed materials, Folder: BEM Letter Re: Dissolution of BEM, n.d. [1984], SCPC.

68. This long view derives from Thomas Piketty, *Capital in the Twenty-First Century* (Cambridge, Mass.: Belknap Press of Harvard University Press, 2014), 72–109.

Chapter 11. Entangled

Edward J. Balleisen first suggested that I think about how civil rights law has affected corporate practices; I am very grateful for his initial inspiration and encouragement since. I also appreciate advice and support from Frank N. Laird, Kenneth J. Lipartito, Chad Pearson, Mark H. Rose, Benton Williams, and Jarett Zuboy. Finally, many thanks to Kim Phillips-Fein and Richard R. John for their interest and guidance.

1. DiversityInc.com, accessed December 18, 2014, http://www.diversityinc.com/diversityinc-top-50-survey-faqs/ and http://bestpractices.diversityinc.com/diversityinc-best-practices-guided-tour/.

2. George Schermer, *Employer's Guide to Equal Opportunity* (Washington, D.C.: Potomac Institute, 1966), 23.

3. Adam Fairclough, "Historians and the Civil Rights Movement," *Journal of American Studies* 24 (December 1990): 387–98, quoted 398.

4. Robert Gordon, "Critical Legal Histories," *Stanford Law Review* 36 (January 1984): 57–125, quoted 106–7.

5. Gerald N. Rosenberg, *The Hollow Hope: Can Courts Bring about Social Change?* 2nd ed. (Chicago: University of Chicago Press, 2008).

6. Ludwig von Bertalanffy, "An Outline of General System Theory," *British Journal for the Philosophy of Science* 1 (August 1950): 134–65; Ludwig von Bertalanffy, *General System Theory* (New York: G. Braziller, 1968).

7. Charles W. Eagles, "Toward New Histories of the Civil Rights Era," *Journal of Southern History* 66 (November 2000): 815–48, quoted 815–17, 848; Fairclough, "Historians," 394, 395, 398.

8. William Edward Nelson, *The Legalist Reformation: Law, Politics, and Ideology in New York, 1920–1980* (Chapel Hill: University of North Carolina Press, 2001), 290, 327–28.

9. Jennifer Delton, *Racial Integration in Corporate America, 1940–1990* (New York: Cambridge University Press, 2009), chs. 4–5; Frank Dobbin, *Inventing Equal Opportunity* (Princeton, N.J.: Princeton University Press, 2009), ch. 5.

10. Delton, *Racial Integration*, 42, 59–63; Pamela Walker Laird, *Pull: Networking and Success Since Benjamin Franklin* (Cambridge, Mass.: Harvard University Press, 2006), 94–100. W. Lloyd Warner and James C. Abegglen, *Big Business Leaders in America* (New York: Harper & Brothers, 1955), quoted 224–25. Mary L. Dudziak, "Desegregation as a Cold War Imperative," *Stanford Law Review* 41 (November 1988): 61–120; Thomas Borstelmann, *The Cold War and the Color Line: American Race Relations in the Global Arena* (Cambridge, Mass.: Harvard University Press, 2001), 93–95.

11. Laird, *Pull*, 124–36.

12. Delton, *Racial Integration*, ch. 1; Jennifer Delton, "Before the EEOC: How Management Integrated the Workplace," *Business History Review* 81 (Summer 2007): 269–95; Paul D. Moreno, *From Direct Action to Affirmative Action: Fair Employment Law and Policy in America, 1933–1972* (Baton Rouge: Louisiana State University Press, 1997), 162–77; Anthony S. Chen, *The Fifth Freedom: Jobs, Politics, and Civil Rights in the United States, 1941–1971* (Princeton, N.J.: Princeton University Press, 2009), ch. 2; Nancy MacLean, *Freedom Is Not Enough: The Opening of the American Workplace* (New York and Cambridge, Mass.: Russell Sage Foundation and Harvard University Press, 2006), 22, 79–80.

13. Jack M. Bloom, *Class, Race, and the Civil Rights Movement* (Bloomington: Indiana University Press, 1987), 88, 215.

14. Delton, *Racial Integration*, 61–63, 199–204. Quote from Kenneth R. Miller, "The American Negro in Industry," press release, National Association of Manufacturers, New York, June 5, 1954, 6, NAM Records, Hagley Museum and Library, Wilmington, Delaware.

15. EEOC, *Celebrating the 40th Anniversary of Title VII*, Panel I, "First Principles," June 22, 2004, http://www.eeoc.gov/eeoc/history/40th/panel/40thpanels/panel1/transcript.html; Hugh Davis Graham, *The Civil Rights Era: Origins and Development of National Policy* (New York: Oxford University Press, 1990), 146–51, 248; Chen, *Fifth Freedom*, 179–90.

16. Laird, *Pull*, 214–15, 388, n. 51.

17. Laura Warren Hill, "'Strike the Hammer While the Iron Is Hot': The Black Freedom Struggle in Rochester, NY, 1940–1970" (Ph.D. diss., Binghamton University, 2010), ch. 5; Hill, "FIGHTing for the Soul of Black Capitalism: Struggles for Black Economic Development in Postrebellion Rochester," in *The Business of Black Power: Community Development, Capitalism and Corporate America*, ed. Laura Warren Hill and Julia Rabig (Rochester, N.Y.: University of Rochester Press, 2012), 45–67.

18. Lois Kathryn Herr, *Women, Power, and AT&T: Winning Rights in the Workplace* (Boston: Northeastern University Press, 2003), ch. 1.

19. Kathleen M. Barry, *Femininity in Flight: A History of Flight Attendants* (Durham: University of North Carolina Press, 2007), ch. 6, quoted 145, 146.

20. Paul Burstein, *Discrimination, Jobs, and Politics: The Struggle for Equal Employment Opportunity in the United States Since the New Deal* (Chicago: University of Chicago Press, 1985); Chen, *Fifth Freedom*; Delton, *Racial Integration*; Dobbin, *Inventing Equal Opportunity*; Graham, *Civil Rights Era*; MacLean, *Freedom Is Not Enough*; Moreno, *From Direct Action*, chs. 7–9.

21. EEOC, *The Story of the United States Equal Employment Opportunity Commission: Ensuring the Promise of Opportunity for 35 Years, 1965–2000* (Washington, D.C.: U.S. EEOC, 2000), 5–10, 15–16; EEOC, *Celebrating*; Graham, *Civil Rights Era*, 156–59, 248–51.

22. Laura Beth Nielson, "Situating Legal Consciousness: Experiences and Attitudes of Ordinary Citizens about Law and Street Harassment," *Law and Society Review* 34 (2000): 1055–90, quoted 1087.

23. David J. Garrow, "Hopelessly Hollow History: Revisionist Devaluing of *Brown v. Board of Education*," *Virginia Law Review* 80 (February 1994): 151–60, King quoted 155.

24. Barry, *Femininity in Flight*, ch. 6, Friedan quoted 153.

25. Jill Smolowe, "Anita Hill's Legacy," *Time*, October 19, 1992, www.time.com; Julie Berebitsky, *Sex and the Office: A History of Gender, Power, and Desire* (New Haven, Conn.: Yale University Press, 2012), 4.

26. Timothy J. Minchin, *The Color of Work: The Struggle for Civil Rights in the Southern Paper Industry, 1945–1980* (Chapel Hill: University of North Carolina Press, 2001), 208–13; Timothy J. Minchin, "Black Activism, the 1964 Civil Rights Act, and the Racial Integration of the Southern Textile Industry," *Journal of Southern History* 65 (November 1999): 809–44, quoted 813–14, 828.

27. Graham, *Civil Rights Era*, 383, 386–89.

28. John E. Burns, "Job Related Tests Only" (editorial), *Industrial Management* 13 (October 1971): 1; Theodore Chase, "*Griggs v. Duke Power Company*: Equal Employment Opportunity Activity," *American Business Law Journal* 10 (Spring 1972): 73–80, quoted 77, 79, 81; William B. Gould, "Racial Discrimination, the Courts, and Construction," *Industrial Relations* 11 (October 1972): 380–93, quoted 387.

29. Benton Williams, "AT&T and the Private-Sector Origins of Private-Sector Affirmative Action," *Journal of Policy History* 20, no. 4 (2008): 543–68.

30. Antonia Handler Chayes, "Make Your Equal Opportunity Program Court-Proof," *Harvard Business Review* 52 (September–October 1974): 81–89, quoted 81.

31. Ruth G. Shaeffer, *Nondiscrimination in Employment: Changing Perspectives, 1963–1972* (New York: Conference Board, 1973), 3, 7–8.

32. Ibid.

33. "What It's Like to Be a Negro in Management," *Business Management* 29 (April 1966): 60–64, 69–77, quoted 60.

34. Ben S. Gilmer, "Business Involvement in Urban Problems: A Look at One Company's Search for Solutions," *Business Horizons* 11 (June 1968): 15–22, quoted 16, 19, 20, 21, 22.

35. Delton, *Racial Integration*, 194–95, 204–8, 211, 223–24; Dobbin, *Inventing Equal Opportunity*, quoted 82. Those same HR systems often erected barriers before they turned to equalizing opportunity; Laird, *Pull*, ch. 4. MacLean, *Freedom Is Not Enough*, regarding the importance of decades of grassroot "activists for inclusion."

36. Donald J. Willis and Jared H. Becker, "The Assessment Center in the Post-*Griggs* Era," *Personnel & Guidance Journal* 55 (December 1976): 201–5, quoted 202.

37. Shaeffer, *Nondiscrimination in Employment*, 2–3; Marjorie Hunter, "Xerox, 2 Others Sued on Job Bias," *New York Times*, August 30, 1973; Philip Shabecoff, "Job Bias Charged to 4 Companies and Major Unions," *New York Times*, September 18, 1973, p. 1.

38. Quotation in Minchin, *Color of Work*, 232, n. 109.

39. "Up the Ladder, Finally," *Business Week*, 24 November 1975, p. 58.

40. "Coping with employee lawsuits," *Business Week*, 27 August 1979, pp. 66, 68.

41. Catharine A. MacKinnon, *Sexual Harassment of Working Women: A Case of Sex Discrimination* (New Haven: Yale University Press, 1979), 4; Sandra Sawyer and Arthur A. Whatley, "Sexual Harassment: A Form of Sex Discrimination," *Personnel Administrator* 25 (January 1980): 36–38, quoted 36; Martha Chamallas, "Writing About Sexual Harassment: A Guide to the Literature," *UCLA Women's Law Journal* 4, no. 1 (Fall 1993): 37–58.

42. Sawyer and Whatley, "Sexual Harassment," 38.

43. James G. Frierson, "Reduce the Costs of Sexual Harassment," *Personnel Journal* 68 (November 1989): 79–85. Clifford M. Koen, Jr., "Sexual Harassment Claims Stem from a Hostile Work Environment," *Personnel Journal* 69 (August 1990): 88–99.

44. Sawyer and Whatley, "Sexual Harassment," 38.

45. *Story of the United States Equal Employment Opportunity Commission*, 15–29.

46. Robert Reinhold, "Public Found Against Welfare Idea but in Favor of What Programs Do," *New York Times*, August 3, 1977. David E. Rosenbaum, "New Drive to Compensate Blacks for Past Injustice Perplexes Nation," *New York Times*, July 3, 1977.

47. *Regents of the University of California v. Bakke*, 438 U.S. 265 (1978). "The New Bias on Hiring Rules," *Business Week*, May 25, 1981, pp. 123, 127; "Affirmative Action: A Storm Over Self-Policing," *Business Week*, May 21, 1984, p. 136. Jonathan J. Bean, *Big Government and Affirmative Action: The Scandalous History of the Small Business Administration* (Lexington, Ky.: University Press of Kentucky, 2001), 106–7, 131–33.

48. Robert Pear, "Changes Weighed in Federal Rules on Discrimination," *New York Times*, December 3, 1984.

49. Linda Greenhouse, "Job Ruling Makes It Clear: Court Has Shifted Right," *New York Times*, June 7, 1989, p. 16.

50. Paula Dwyer, "The Blow to Affirmative Action May Not Hurt That Much," *Business Week*, July 3, 1989, pp. 61–62.

51. Rebecca A. Thacker, "Affirmative Action after the Supreme Court's 1988–1989 Term: What Employers Need to Know," *Employment Relations Today* 17 (Summer 1990): 139–44, quoted 139.

52. Ruth G. Shaeffer, *Nondiscrimination in Employment—and Beyond* (New York: Conference Board, 1980), v, 1, 17, emphasis added.

53. Chayes, "Make your Equal Opportunity Program Court-Proof"; Frank Dobbin and John R. Sutton, "The Strength of a Weak State: The Rights Revolution and the Rise of Human Resources Management Division," *American Journal of Sociology* 104 (September 1998): 441–76, quoted 442; Delton, *Racial Integration*; Dobbin, *Inventing Equal Opportunity*, 278–79.

54. This is the title of chapter 2 of Delton, *Racial Integration* (p. 42).

55. Shaeffer, *Nondiscrimination in Employment—and Beyond*, 1–2.

56. Rohini Anand and Mary-Frances Winters, "A Retrospective View of Corporate Diversity Training from 1964 to the Present," *Academy of Management Learning and Education* 7 (September 2008): 356–72.

57. R. Roosevelt Thomas, Jr., "From Affirmative Action to Affirming Diversity," *Harvard Business Review* 68 (March–April 1990): 107–17, quoted 108, 117.

58. Anand and Winters, "Retrospective View"; Delton, *Racial Integration*, 280–83. Gloria Moss, ed., *Profiting from Diversity: The Business Advantages and the Obstacles to Achieving Diversity* (Hampshire, England: Palgrave Macmillan, 2010).

59. Dianne Solis, "Going Beyond Diversity," *Dallas Morning News,* May 22, 2005.

60. T. J. Rodgers, Letter to the Editor, *Harvard Business Review* 74 (November–December 1996): 177–78, emphasis in original.

61. Jonathan A. Segal and K. Steven Blake, "Diversity v. Title VII," *Metropolitan Corporate Counsel* 15 (February 2007): 54. For a helpful overview of the history of diversity in corporations and scholarship on the subject, see Richard L. Zweigenhaft and G. William Domhoff, *The New CEOs: Women, African American, Latino, and Asian American Leaders of* Fortune *500 Companies* (Lanham, Md.: Rowman & Littlefield Publishers, 2011), 105–16.

62. Laird, *Pull*, 4–5. Joni Hersch and Jennifer Bennett Shinall, "Fifty Years Later: The Legacy of the Civil Rights Act of 1964," *Journal of Policy Analysis and Management* 34 (Spring 2015): 424–56.

63. Alfred W. Blumrosen, "Civil Rights Conflicts: The Uneasy Search for Peace in Our Time," *Arbitration Journal* 27 (March 1972): 35–46, quoted 37.

64. David A. Brookmire, "Designing and Implementing Your Company's Affirmative Action Program" *Personnel Journal* 58 (April 1979): 232–37, quoted 236.

65. Of the 99,922 individual filings the EEOC received in fiscal year 2010, many claimed multiple forms of discrimination. EEOC "Charge Statistics," accessed July 26, 2011, and December 30, 2014, http://www.eeoc.gov/eeoc/statistics/enforcement/charges.cfm. "EEOC Releases FY 2013 Enforcement and Litigation Data," press release, February 5, 2014, www1.eeoc.gov/eeoc/newsroom/release2-4-14.cfm.

66. Laird, *Pull*, 4–5. In contrast, the European Parliament voted in 2013 to require quotas of women in corporate boardrooms.

67. Catalyst, *Pyramid: Women in S&P 500 Companies* (New York: Catalyst), accessed August 5, 2015, http://catalyst.org/knowledge/women-sp-500-companies.

Contributors

Daniel Amsterdam is an assistant professor in the School of History and Sociology at the Georgia Institute of Technology. He is the author of *Roaring Metropolis: Businessmen's Campaign for a Civic Welfare State* (2016).

Brent Cebul is the Mellon Postdoctoral Research Scholar at the University of Richmond's Digital Scholarship Lab. His current book project, forthcoming from the University of Pennsylvania Press, explores the politics of economic growth, business, and poverty in the United States since the New Deal.

Jennifer Delton is the Douglas Family Chair in American Culture, History, and Literary and Interdisciplinary Studies at Skidmore College. She is the author most recently of *Rethinking the 1950s: How Anticommunism and the Cold War Made America Liberal* (2013) and is currently writing a history of the National Association of Manufacturers.

Tami J. Friedman is an associate professor of history at Brock University. Her article, "Exploiting the North-South Differential: Corporate Power, Southern Politics, and the Decline of Organized Labor After World War II," received the 2009 Organization of American Historians Binkley-Stephenson Award. She is completing a book on the causes and consequences of postwar capital migration in the U.S. carpet industry.

Eric S. Hintz is a historian with the Lemelson Center for the Study of Invention and Innovation at the Smithsonian's National Museum of American History. His current book project explores the changing fortunes of American independent inventors in the first half of the twentieth century.

Richard R. John is a professor of history and communications at Columbia University and a former president of the Business History Conference. He is the author of *Spreading the News: The American Postal System from Franklin to Morse* (1995), which was awarded the Allan Nevins Prize, and *Network Nation: Inventing American Telecommunications* (2010), which received the Gomery Prize.

Pamela Walker Laird is a professor of history at the University of Colorado Denver. Among her publications is *Pull: Networking and Success Since Benjamin Franklin* (2006), which received the Hagley Prize in Business History. She is the recipient of the Harold F. Williamson Prize for her contributions to business history and has served as president of the Business History Conference.

Kim Phillips-Fein is an associate professor at the Gallatin School of Individualized Study of New York University, where she is also associated faculty in the history department. Her publications include *Invisible Hands: The Making of the Conservative Movement from the New Deal to Reagan* (2009). She is currently a distinguished lecturer for the Organization of American Historians and has served on the editorial board of the *Journal of American History*.

Laura Phillips Sawyer is an assistant professor in the Business, Government, and International Economy unit at Harvard Business School. Her articles have appeared in the *Journal of the Gilded Age and Progressive Era* and the *Business History Review*. Her first book, *American Fair Trade: Proprietary Capitalism, Networks, and the "New Competition," 1890–1940*, is forthcoming from Cambridge University Press.

Elizabeth Tandy Shermer is an assistant professor of history at Loyola University Chicago. Her publications include opinion pieces, journal articles, book chapters, edited collections, and *Sunbelt Capitalism: Phoenix and the Transformation of American Politics* (2013). She is currently writing a book on the financial underpinnings of higher education.

Eric R. Smith is an instructor at the Illinois Mathematics and Science Academy. His publications include *American Relief Aid and the Spanish Civil War* (2013).

Jason Scott Smith is a professor of history at the University of New Mexico. His publications include *Building New Deal Liberalism* (2006) and *A Concise History of the New Deal* (2014).

Mark R. Wilson is an associate professor of history at the University of North Carolina, Charlotte. He is the author of *The Business of Civil War* (2006) and *Destructive Creation: American Business and the Winning of World War II* (2016).

Index

Lightning Source UK Ltd.
Milton Keynes UK
UKHW010653260519
343323UK00001B/93/P